Twin Star Exorcists

ONMYOJI

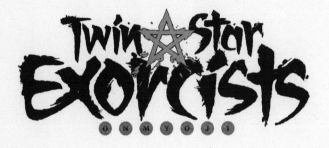

Twin ✦ Star Exorcists

O N M Y O J I

4

STORY & ART
YOSHIAKI SUKENO

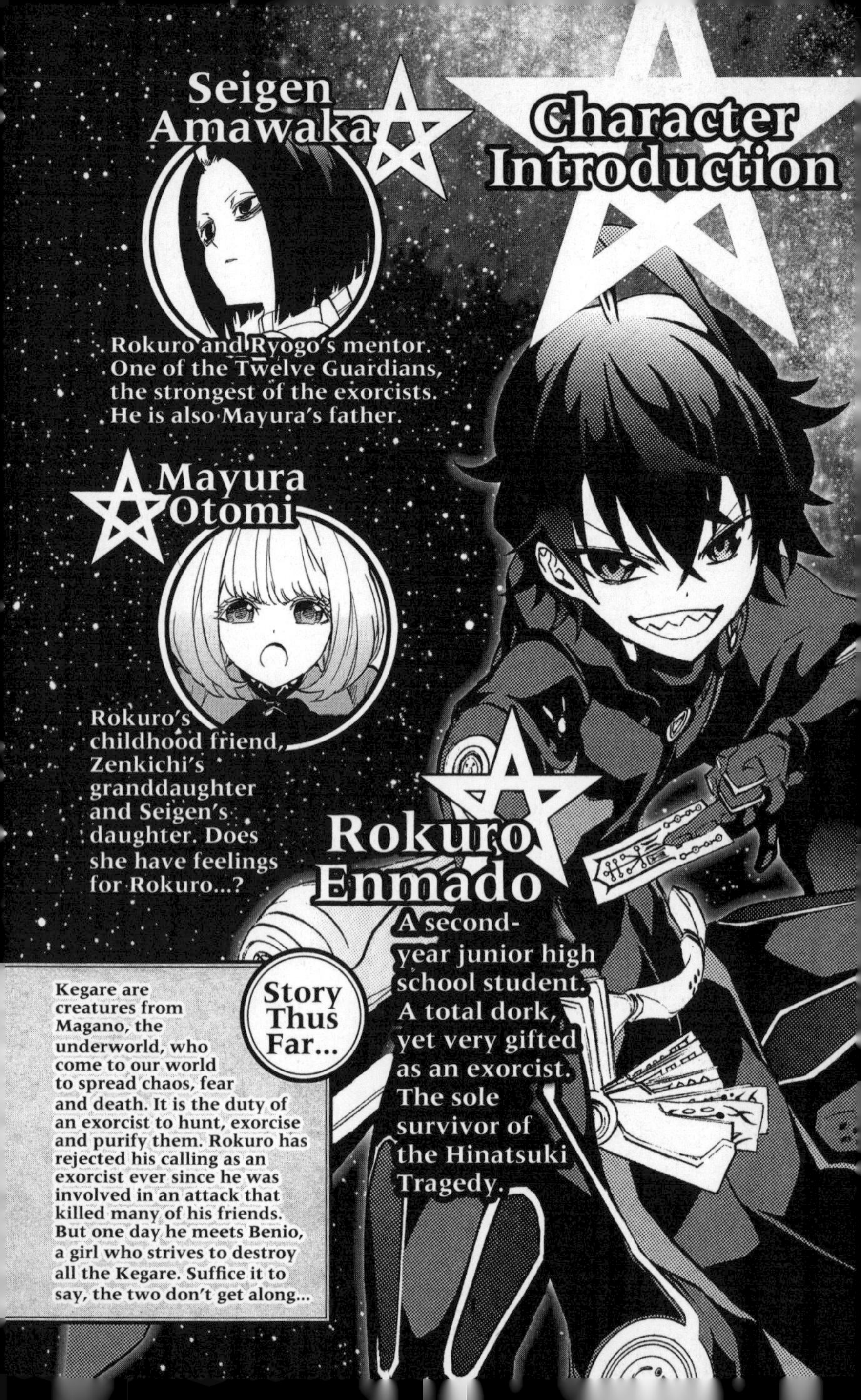
Character Introduction
Seigen Amawaka
Rokuro and Ryogo's mentor. One of the Twelve Guardians, the strongest of the exorcists. He is also Mayura's father.
Mayura Otomi
Rokuro's childhood friend, Zenkichi's granddaughter and Seigen's daughter. Does she have feelings for Rokuro...?
Rokuro Enmado
A second-year junior high school student. A total dork, yet very gifted as an exorcist. The sole survivor of the Hinatsuki Tragedy.
Story Thus Far...
Kegare are creatures from Magano, the underworld, who come to our world to spread chaos, fear and death. It is the duty of an exorcist to hunt, exorcise and purify them. Rokuro has rejected his calling as an exorcist ever since he was involved in an attack that killed many of his friends. But one day he meets Benio, a girl who strives to destroy all the Kegare. Suffice it to say, the two don't get along...

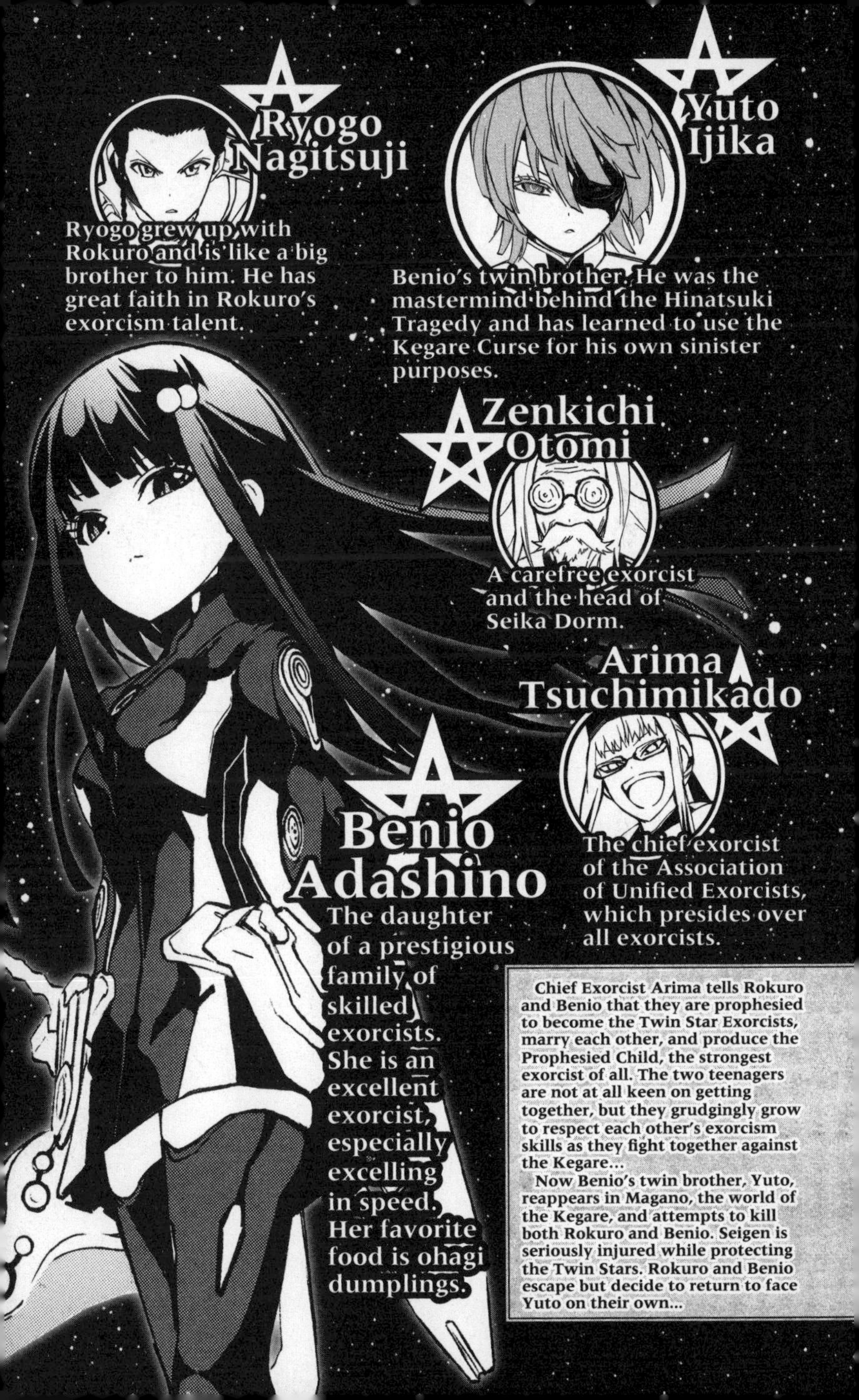
Yuto Ijika
Benio's twin brother. He was the mastermind behind the Hinatsuki Tragedy and has learned to use the Kegare Curse for his own sinister purposes.
Ryogo Nagitsuji
Ryogo grew up with Rokuro and is like a big brother to him. He has great faith in Rokuro's exorcism talent.
Zenkichi Otomi
A carefree exorcist and the head of Seika Dorm.
Arima Tsuchimikado
The chief exorcist of the Association of Unified Exorcists, which presides over all exorcists.
Benio Adashino
The daughter of a prestigious family of skilled exorcists. She is an excellent exorcist, especially excelling in speed. Her favorite food is ohagi dumplings.

Chief Exorcist Arima tells Rokuro and Benio that they are prophesied to become the Twin Star Exorcists, marry each other, and produce the Prophesied Child, the strongest exorcist of all. The two teenagers are not at all keen on getting together, but they grudgingly grow to respect each other's exorcism skills as they fight together against the Kegare...

Now Benio's twin brother, Yuto, reappears in Magano, the world of the Kegare, and attempts to kill both Rokuro and Benio. Seigen is seriously injured while protecting the Twin Stars. Rokuro and Benio escape but decide to return to face Yuto on their own...

Twin ☆ Star Exorcists

ONMYOJI

EXORCISMS

ONMYOJI have worked for the Imperial Court since the Heian era. In addition to exorcising evil spirits, as civil servants they performed a variety of roles, including advising nobles by foretelling the future, creating the calendar, observing the movements of the stars, measuring time…

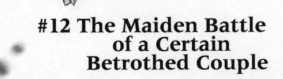

#12 The Maiden Battle of a Certain Betrothed Couple

Twin Star Exorcists

O N M Y O J I

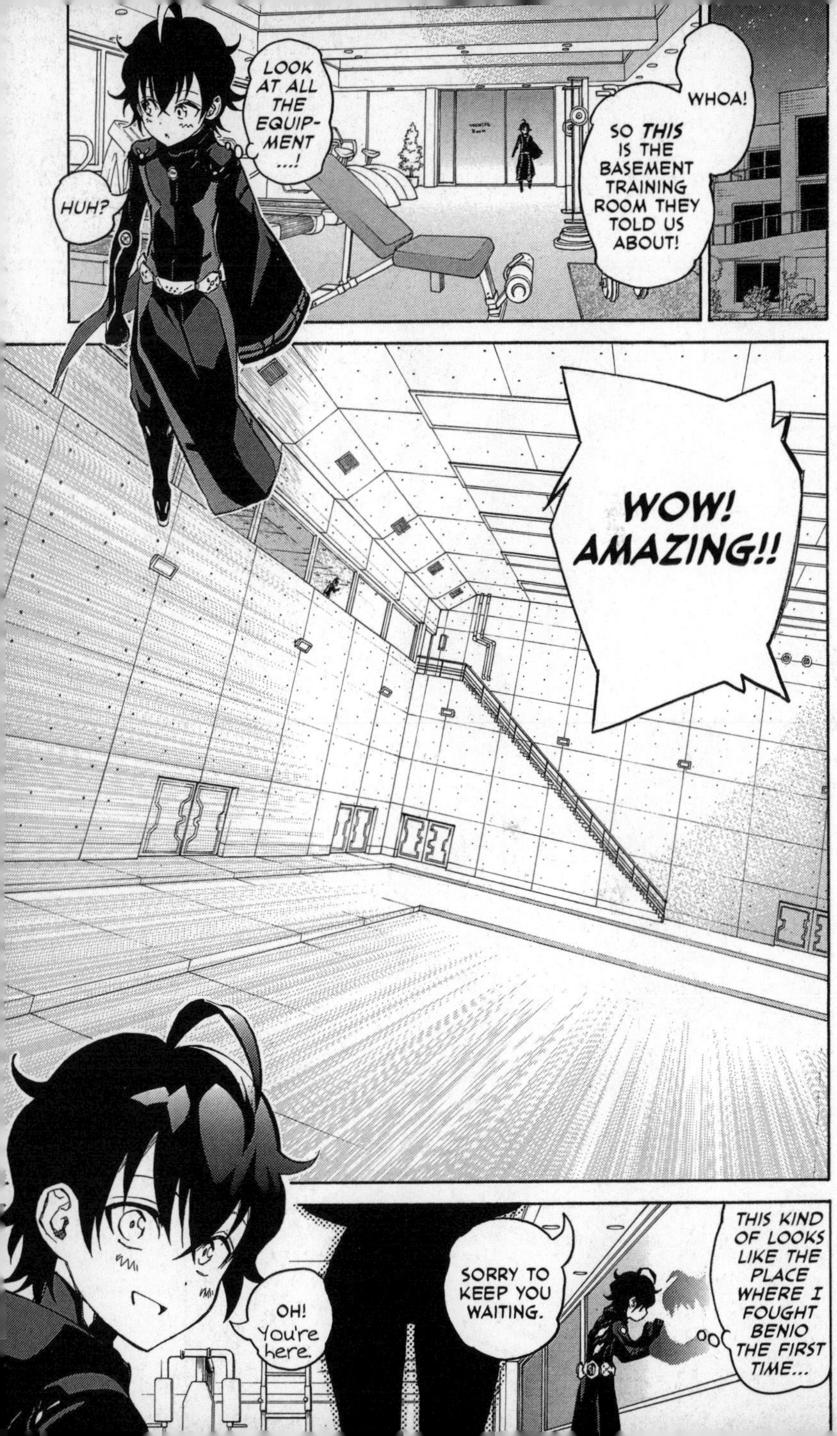
WHOA!
SO THIS IS THE BASEMENT TRAINING ROOM THEY TOLD US ABOUT!
LOOK AT ALL THE EQUIPMENT...!
HUH?
WOW! AMAZING!!
THIS KIND OF LOOKS LIKE THE PLACE WHERE I FOUGHT BENIO THE FIRST TIME...
SORRY TO KEEP YOU WAITING.
OH! You're here.

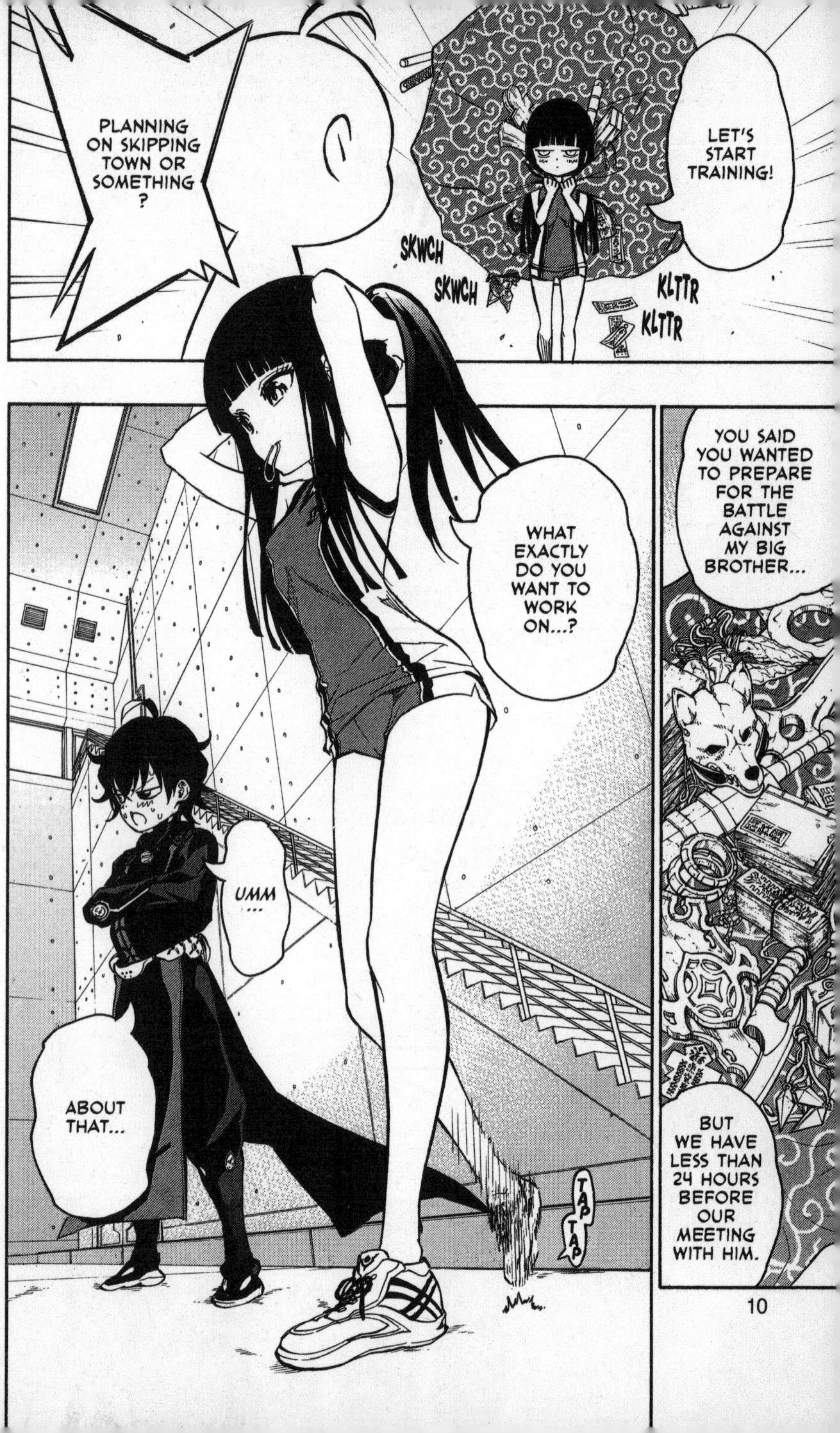
LET'S START TRAINING!
SKWCH SKWCH
KLTTR KLTTR
PLANNING ON SKIPPING TOWN OR SOMETHING?
YOU SAID YOU WANTED TO PREPARE FOR THE BATTLE AGAINST MY BIG BROTHER...
BUT WE HAVE LESS THAN 24 HOURS BEFORE OUR MEETING WITH HIM.
WHAT EXACTLY DO YOU WANT TO WORK ON...?
UMM...
TAP TAP
ABOUT THAT...

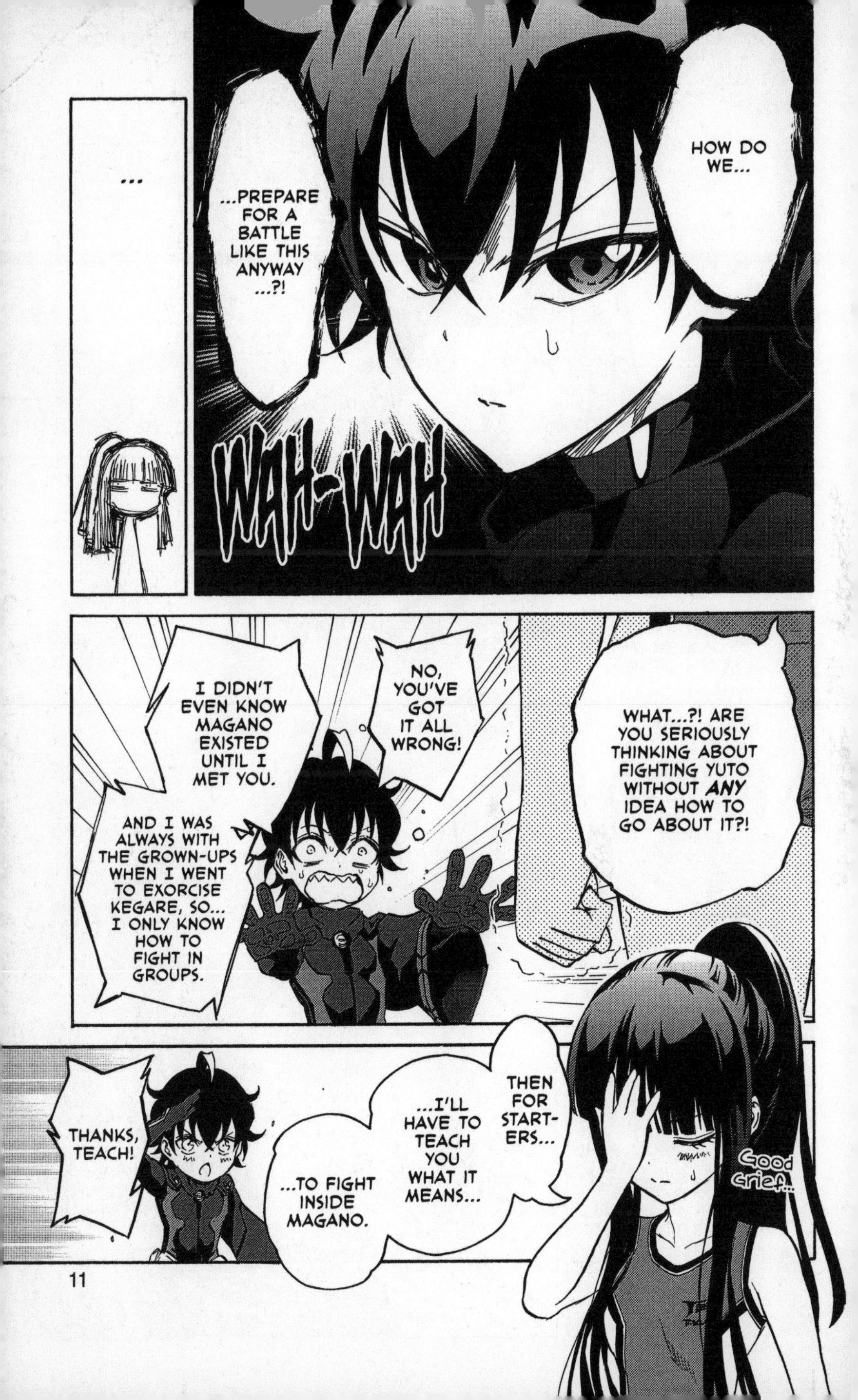
HOW DO WE...
...PREPARE FOR A BATTLE LIKE THIS ANYWAY ...?!
WAH-WAH
...
WHAT...?! ARE YOU SERIOUSLY THINKING ABOUT FIGHTING YUTO WITHOUT ***ANY*** IDEA HOW TO GO ABOUT IT?!
NO, YOU'VE GOT IT ALL WRONG!
I DIDN'T EVEN KNOW MAGANO EXISTED UNTIL I MET YOU.
AND I WAS ALWAYS WITH THE GROWN-UPS WHEN I WENT TO EXORCISE KEGARE, SO... I ONLY KNOW HOW TO FIGHT IN GROUPS.
Good grief...
THEN FOR STARTERS...
...I'LL HAVE TO TEACH YOU WHAT IT MEANS...
...TO FIGHT INSIDE MAGANO.
THANKS, TEACH!

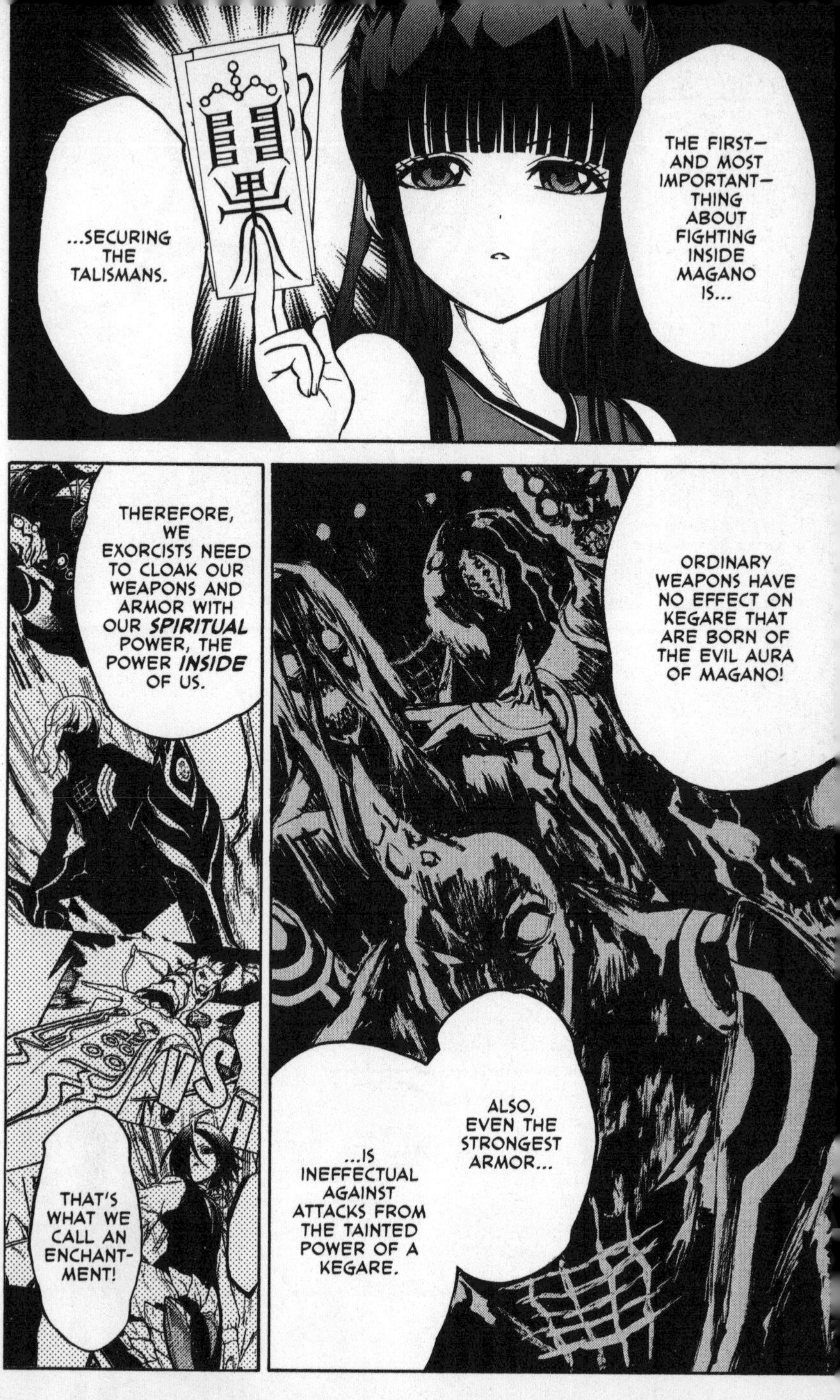
THE FIRST—AND MOST IMPORTANT—THING ABOUT FIGHTING INSIDE MAGANO IS...
...SECURING THE TALISMANS.
ORDINARY WEAPONS HAVE NO EFFECT ON KEGARE THAT ARE BORN OF THE EVIL AURA OF MAGANO!
ALSO, EVEN THE STRONGEST ARMOR...
...IS INEFFECTUAL AGAINST ATTACKS FROM THE TAINTED POWER OF A KEGARE.
THEREFORE, WE EXORCISTS NEED TO CLOAK OUR WEAPONS AND ARMOR WITH OUR SPIRITUAL POWER, THE POWER INSIDE OF US.
THAT'S WHAT WE CALL AN ENCHANTMENT!

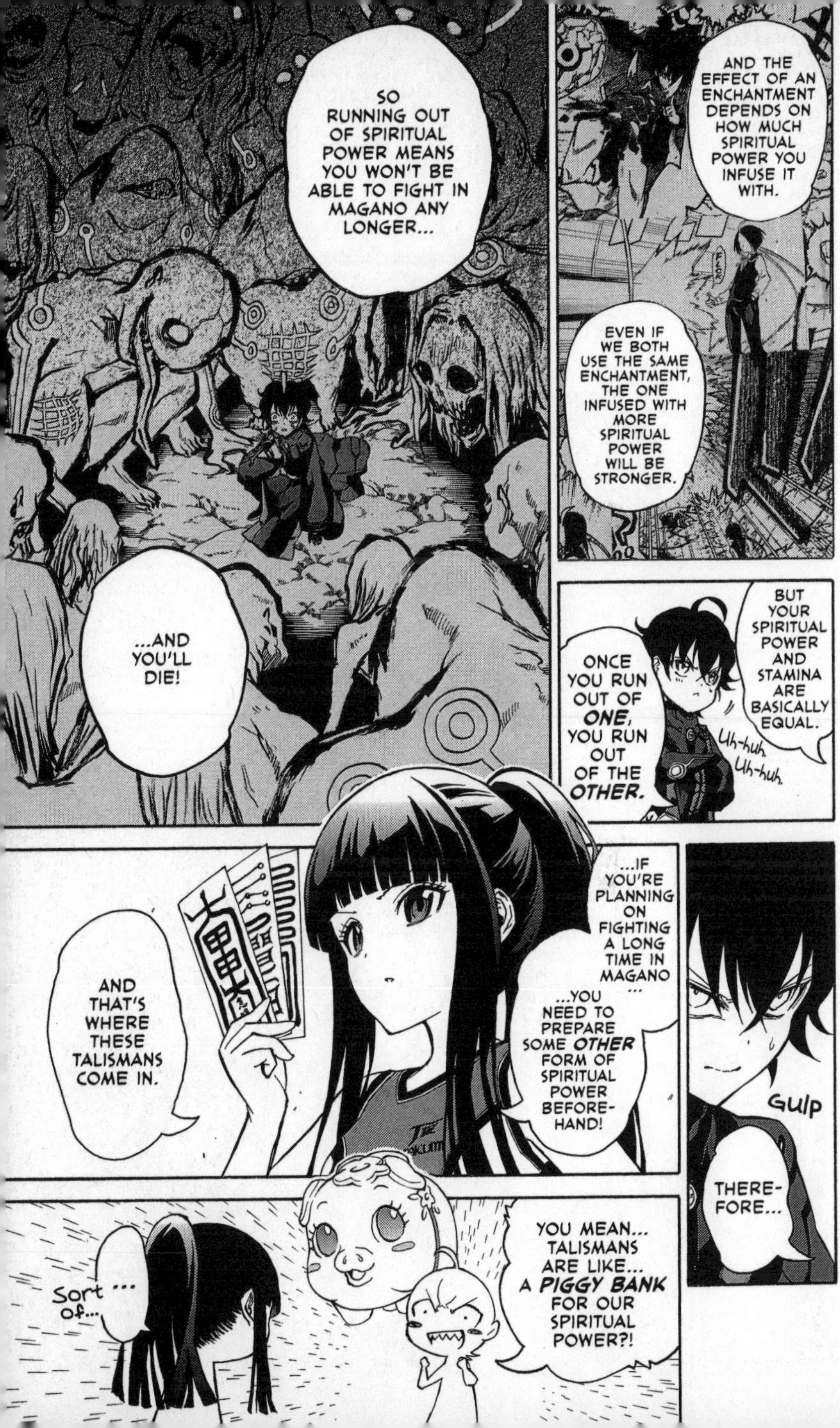
AND THE EFFECT OF AN ENCHANTMENT DEPENDS ON HOW MUCH SPIRITUAL POWER YOU INFUSE IT WITH.
FLICK
EVEN IF WE BOTH USE THE SAME ENCHANTMENT, THE ONE INFUSED WITH MORE SPIRITUAL POWER WILL BE STRONGER.
BUT YOUR SPIRITUAL POWER AND STAMINA ARE BASICALLY EQUAL.
Uh-huh. Uh-huh.
ONCE YOU RUN OUT OF ONE, YOU RUN OUT OF THE OTHER.
SO RUNNING OUT OF SPIRITUAL POWER MEANS YOU WON'T BE ABLE TO FIGHT IN MAGANO ANY LONGER...
...AND YOU'LL DIE!
Gulp
THERE-FORE...
...IF YOU'RE PLANNING ON FIGHTING A LONG TIME IN MAGANO...
...YOU NEED TO PREPARE SOME OTHER FORM OF SPIRITUAL POWER BEFORE-HAND!
AND THAT'S WHERE THESE TALISMANS COME IN.
YOU MEAN... TALISMANS ARE LIKE... A PIGGY BANK FOR OUR SPIRITUAL POWER?!
Sort of...

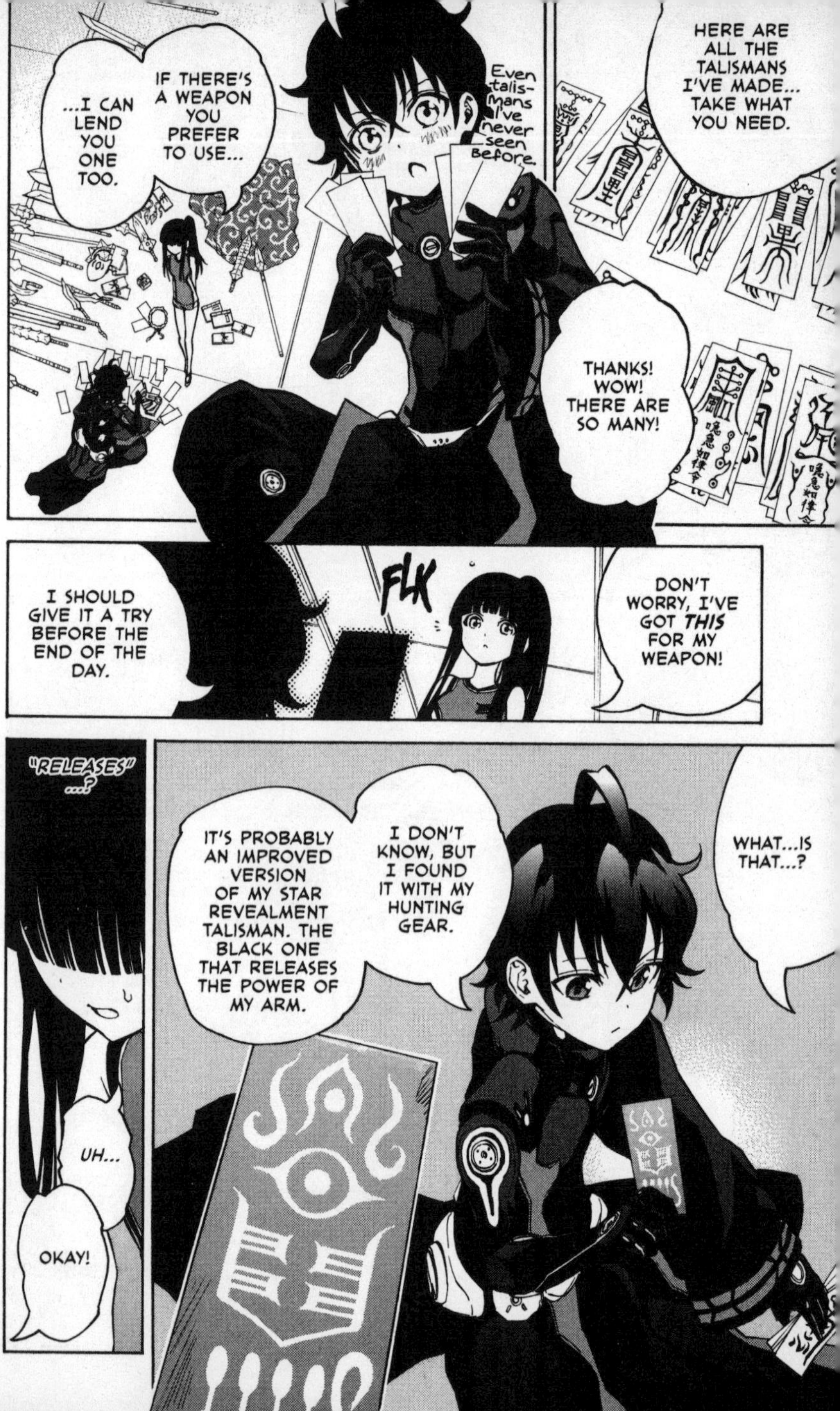
HERE ARE ALL THE TALISMANS I'VE MADE... TAKE WHAT YOU NEED.
THANKS! WOW! THERE ARE SO MANY!
Even talismans I've never seen before.
IF THERE'S A WEAPON YOU PREFER TO USE...
...I CAN LEND YOU ONE TOO.
DON'T WORRY, I'VE GOT *THIS* FOR MY WEAPON!
FLK
I SHOULD GIVE IT A TRY BEFORE THE END OF THE DAY.
WHAT...IS THAT...?
I DON'T KNOW, BUT I FOUND IT WITH MY HUNTING GEAR.
IT'S PROBABLY AN IMPROVED VERSION OF MY STAR REVEALMENT TALISMAN. THE BLACK ONE THAT RELEASES THE POWER OF MY ARM.
"RELEASES" ...?
UH...
OKAY!

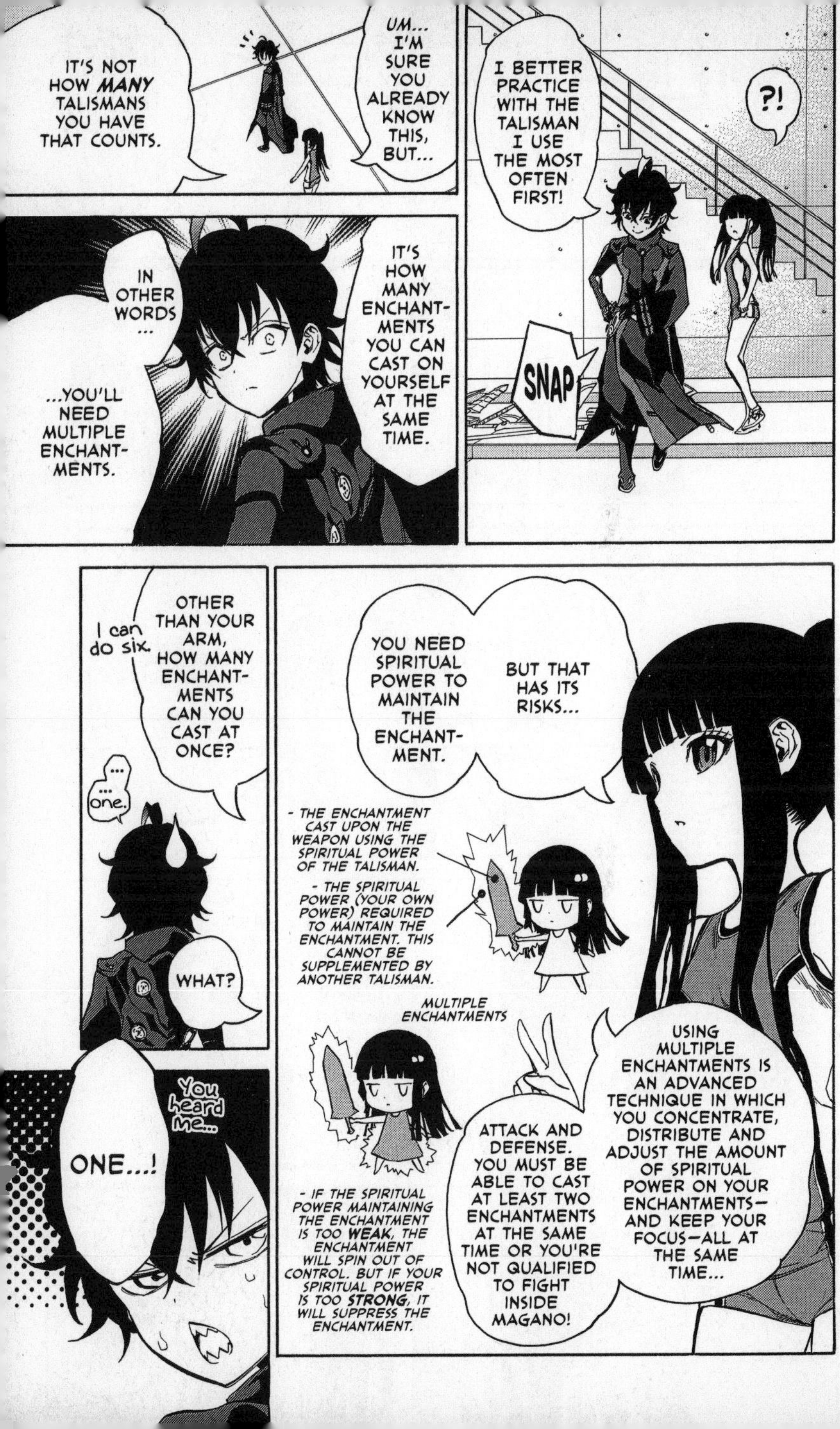
I BETTER PRACTICE WITH THE TALISMAN I USE THE MOST OFTEN FIRST!
SNAP
?!
UM... I'M SURE YOU ALREADY KNOW THIS, BUT...
IT'S NOT HOW MANY TALISMANS YOU HAVE THAT COUNTS.
IT'S HOW MANY ENCHANT-MENTS YOU CAN CAST ON YOURSELF AT THE SAME TIME.
IN OTHER WORDS...
...YOU'LL NEED MULTIPLE ENCHANT-MENTS.
YOU NEED SPIRITUAL POWER TO MAINTAIN THE ENCHANT-MENT.
BUT THAT HAS ITS RISKS...
- THE ENCHANTMENT CAST UPON THE WEAPON USING THE SPIRITUAL POWER OF THE TALISMAN.
- THE SPIRITUAL POWER (YOUR OWN POWER) REQUIRED TO MAINTAIN THE ENCHANTMENT. THIS CANNOT BE SUPPLEMENTED BY ANOTHER TALISMAN.
MULTIPLE ENCHANTMENTS
- IF THE SPIRITUAL POWER MAINTAINING THE ENCHANTMENT IS TOO WEAK, THE ENCHANTMENT WILL SPIN OUT OF CONTROL. BUT IF YOUR SPIRITUAL POWER IS TOO STRONG, IT WILL SUPPRESS THE ENCHANTMENT.
USING MULTIPLE ENCHANTMENTS IS AN ADVANCED TECHNIQUE IN WHICH YOU CONCENTRATE, DISTRIBUTE AND ADJUST THE AMOUNT OF SPIRITUAL POWER ON YOUR ENCHANTMENTS—AND KEEP YOUR FOCUS—ALL AT THE SAME TIME...
ATTACK AND DEFENSE. YOU MUST BE ABLE TO CAST AT LEAST TWO ENCHANTMENTS AT THE SAME TIME OR YOU'RE NOT QUALIFIED TO FIGHT INSIDE MAGANO!
OTHER THAN YOUR ARM, HOW MANY ENCHANT-MENTS CAN YOU CAST AT ONCE?
I can do six.
... ...one.
WHAT?
ONE...!
You heard me...

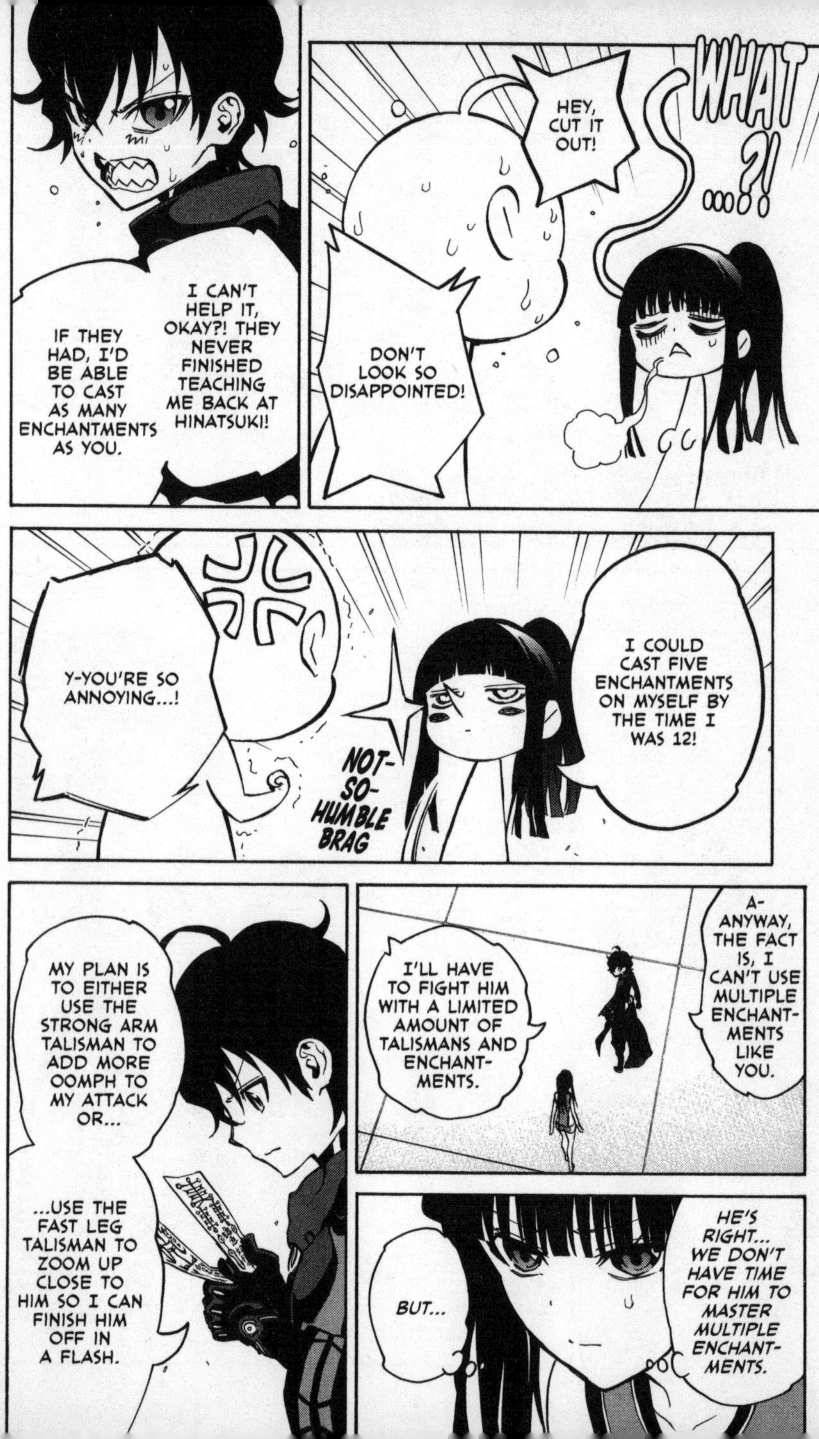
WHAT...?!
HEY, CUT IT OUT!
DON'T LOOK SO DISAPPOINTED!
I CAN'T HELP IT, OKAY?! THEY NEVER FINISHED TEACHING ME BACK AT HINATSUKI!
IF THEY HAD, I'D BE ABLE TO CAST AS MANY ENCHANTMENTS AS YOU.
I COULD CAST FIVE ENCHANTMENTS ON MYSELF BY THE TIME I WAS 12!
NOT-SO-HUMBLE BRAG
Y-YOU'RE SO ANNOYING...!
A-ANYWAY, THE FACT IS, I CAN'T USE MULTIPLE ENCHANT-MENTS LIKE YOU.
I'LL HAVE TO FIGHT HIM WITH A LIMITED AMOUNT OF TALISMANS AND ENCHANT-MENTS.
HE'S RIGHT... WE DON'T HAVE TIME FOR HIM TO MASTER MULTIPLE ENCHANT-MENTS.
BUT...
MY PLAN IS TO EITHER USE THE STRONG ARM TALISMAN TO ADD MORE OOMPH TO MY ATTACK OR...
...USE THE FAST LEG TALISMAN TO ZOOM UP CLOSE TO HIM SO I CAN FINISH HIM OFF IN A FLASH.

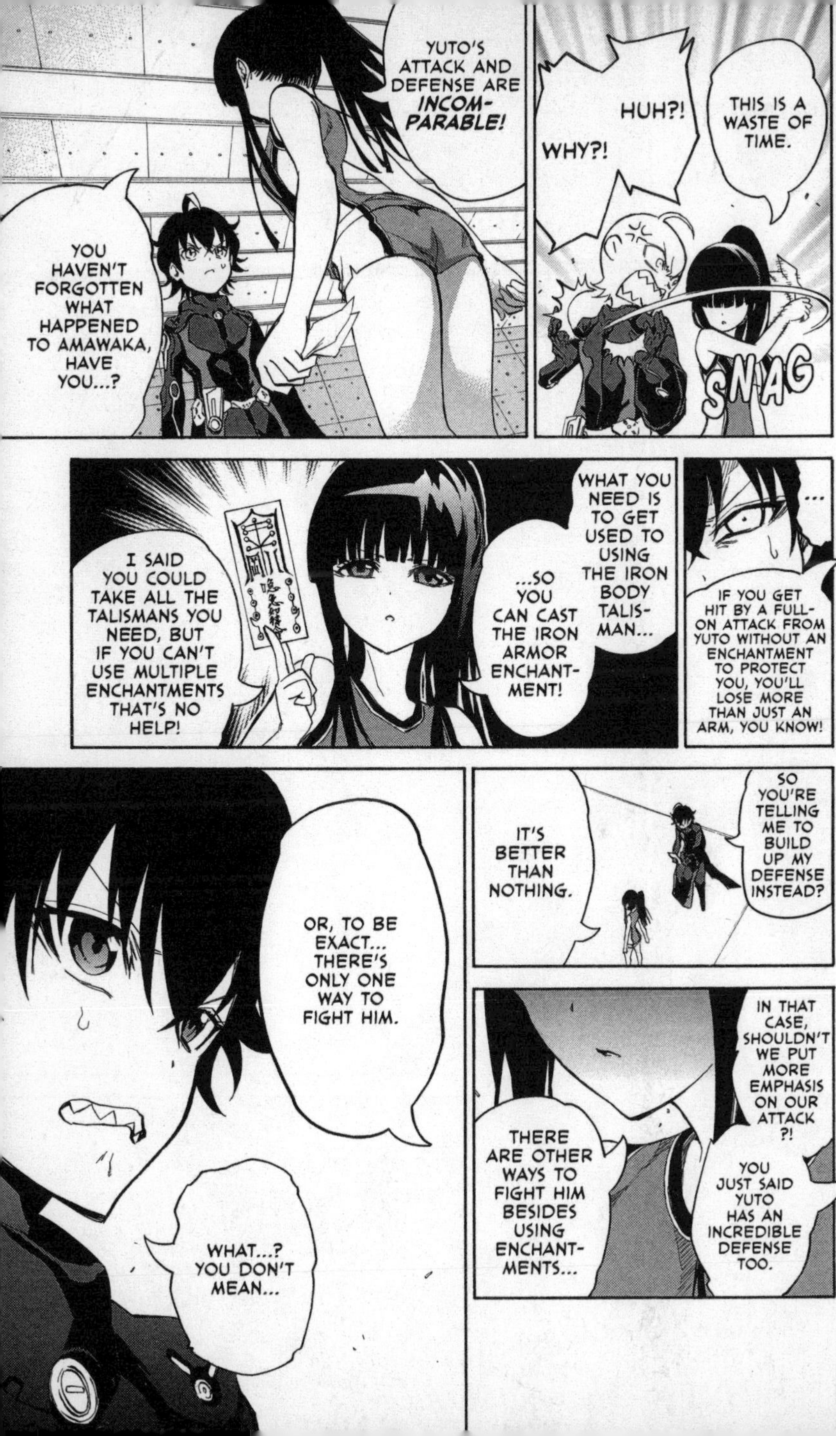
THIS IS A WASTE OF TIME.
HUH?!
WHY?!
SNAG
YUTO'S ATTACK AND DEFENSE ARE INCOMPARABLE!
YOU HAVEN'T FORGOTTEN WHAT HAPPENED TO AMAWAKA, HAVE YOU...?
...
IF YOU GET HIT BY A FULL-ON ATTACK FROM YUTO WITHOUT AN ENCHANTMENT TO PROTECT YOU, YOU'LL LOSE MORE THAN JUST AN ARM, YOU KNOW!
WHAT YOU NEED IS TO GET USED TO USING THE IRON BODY TALISMAN...
...SO YOU CAN CAST THE IRON ARMOR ENCHANTMENT!
I SAID YOU COULD TAKE ALL THE TALISMANS YOU NEED, BUT IF YOU CAN'T USE MULTIPLE ENCHANTMENTS THAT'S NO HELP!
SO YOU'RE TELLING ME TO BUILD UP MY DEFENSE INSTEAD?
IT'S BETTER THAN NOTHING.
IN THAT CASE, SHOULDN'T WE PUT MORE EMPHASIS ON OUR ATTACK?!
YOU JUST SAID YUTO HAS AN INCREDIBLE DEFENSE TOO.
THERE ARE OTHER WAYS TO FIGHT HIM BESIDES USING ENCHANTMENTS...
OR, TO BE EXACT... THERE'S ONLY ONE WAY TO FIGHT HIM.
WHAT...? YOU DON'T MEAN...

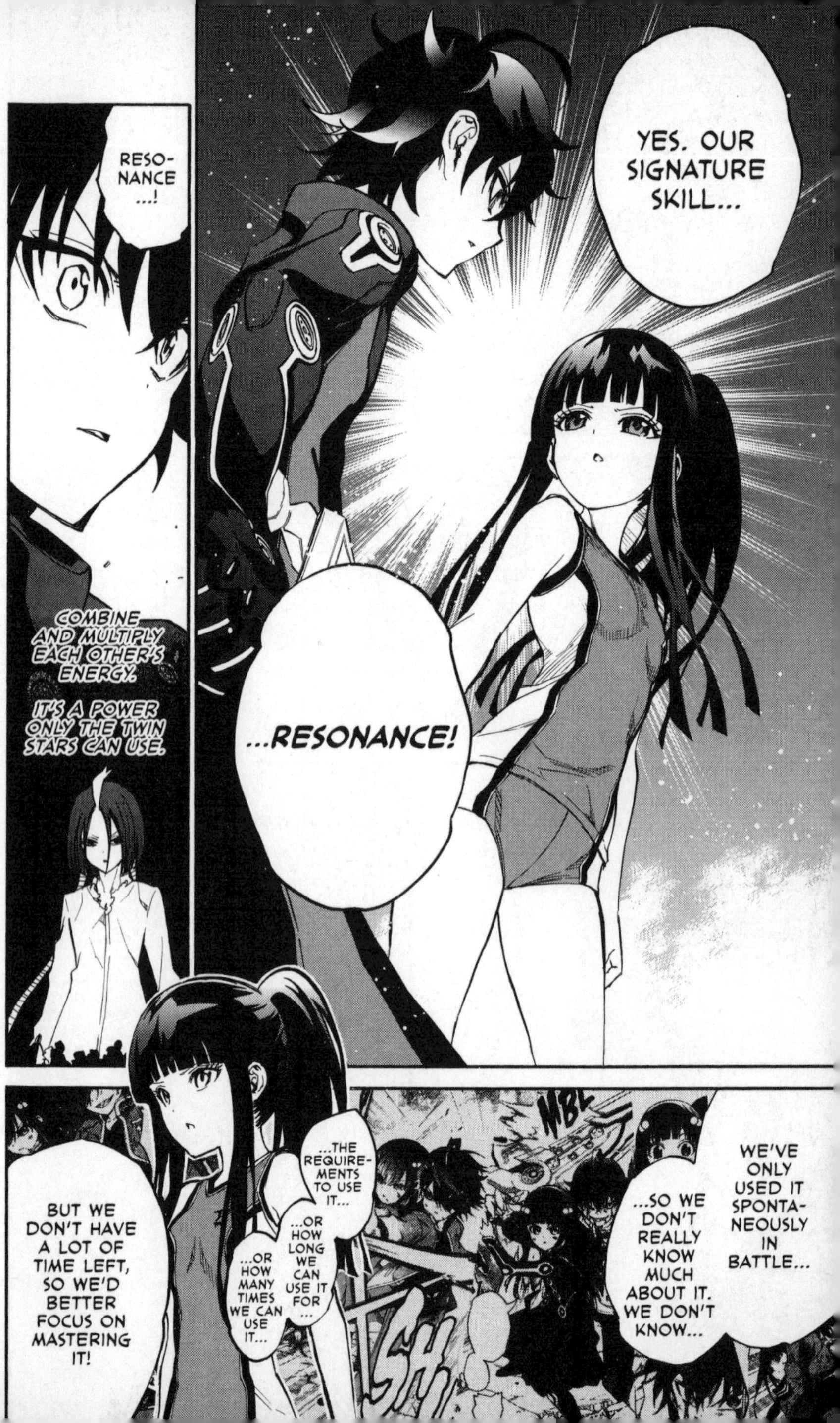

YES. OUR SIGNATURE SKILL...
...RESONANCE!
RESO-NANCE ...!
COMBINE AND MULTIPLY EACH OTHER'S ENERGY.
IT'S A POWER ONLY THE TWIN STARS CAN USE.
WE'VE ONLY USED IT SPONTA-NEOUSLY IN BATTLE...
...SO WE DON'T REALLY KNOW MUCH ABOUT IT. WE DON'T KNOW...
...THE REQUIRE-MENTS TO USE IT...
...OR HOW LONG WE CAN USE IT FOR...
...OR HOW MANY TIMES WE CAN USE IT...
BUT WE DON'T HAVE A LOT OF TIME LEFT, SO WE'D BETTER FOCUS ON MASTERING IT!

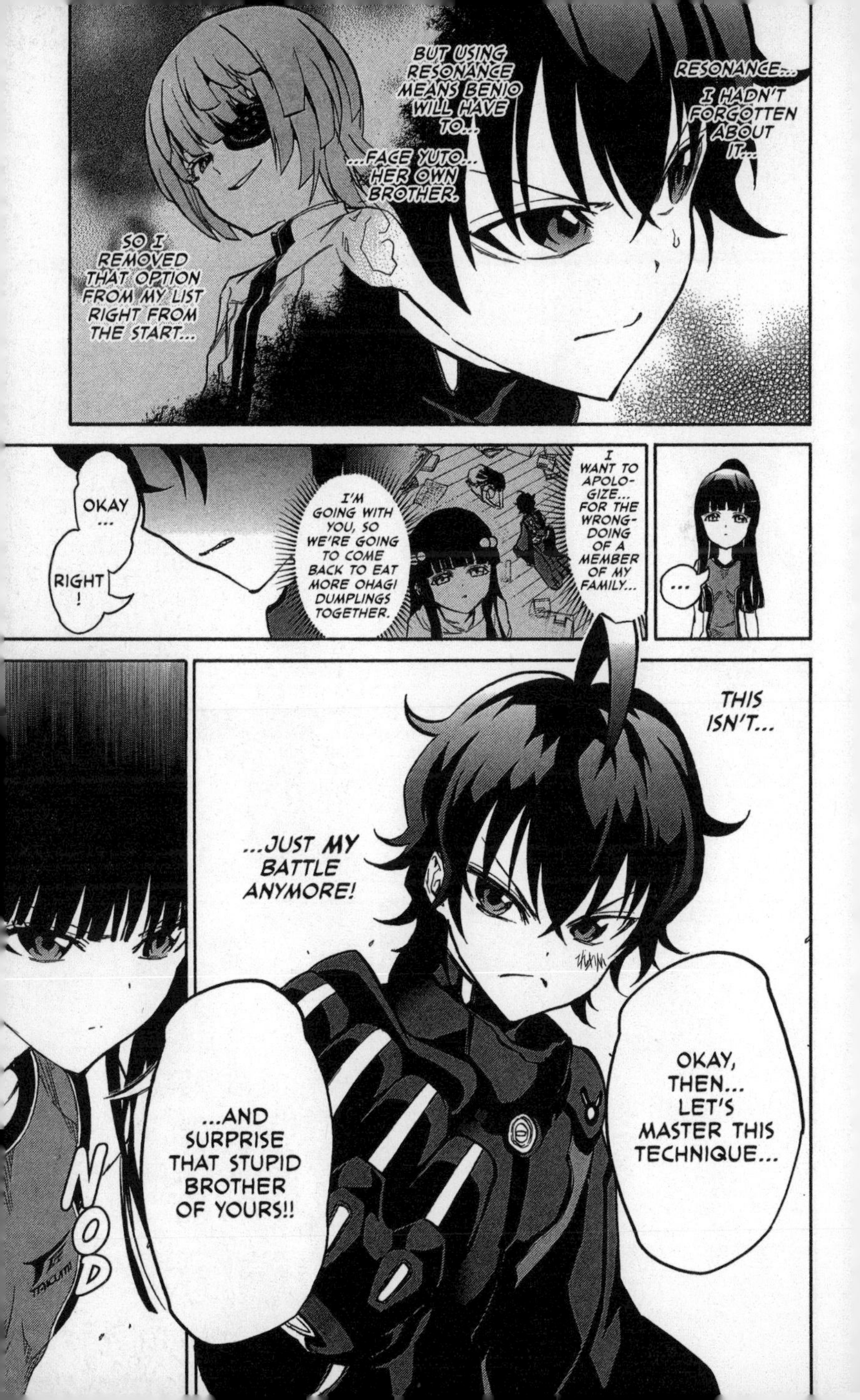
RESONANCE... I HADN'T FORGOTTEN ABOUT IT...
BUT USING RESONANCE MEANS BENIO WILL HAVE TO...
...FACE YUTO... HER OWN BROTHER.
SO I REMOVED THAT OPTION FROM MY LIST RIGHT FROM THE START...
...
I WANT TO APOLOGIZE... FOR THE WRONGDOING OF A MEMBER OF MY FAMILY...
I'M GOING WITH YOU, SO WE'RE GOING TO COME BACK TO EAT MORE OHAGI DUMPLINGS TOGETHER.
OKAY... RIGHT!
THIS ISN'T...
...JUST MY BATTLE ANYMORE!
OKAY, THEN... LET'S MASTER THIS TECHNIQUE...
...AND SURPRISE THAT STUPID BROTHER OF YOURS!!
NOD

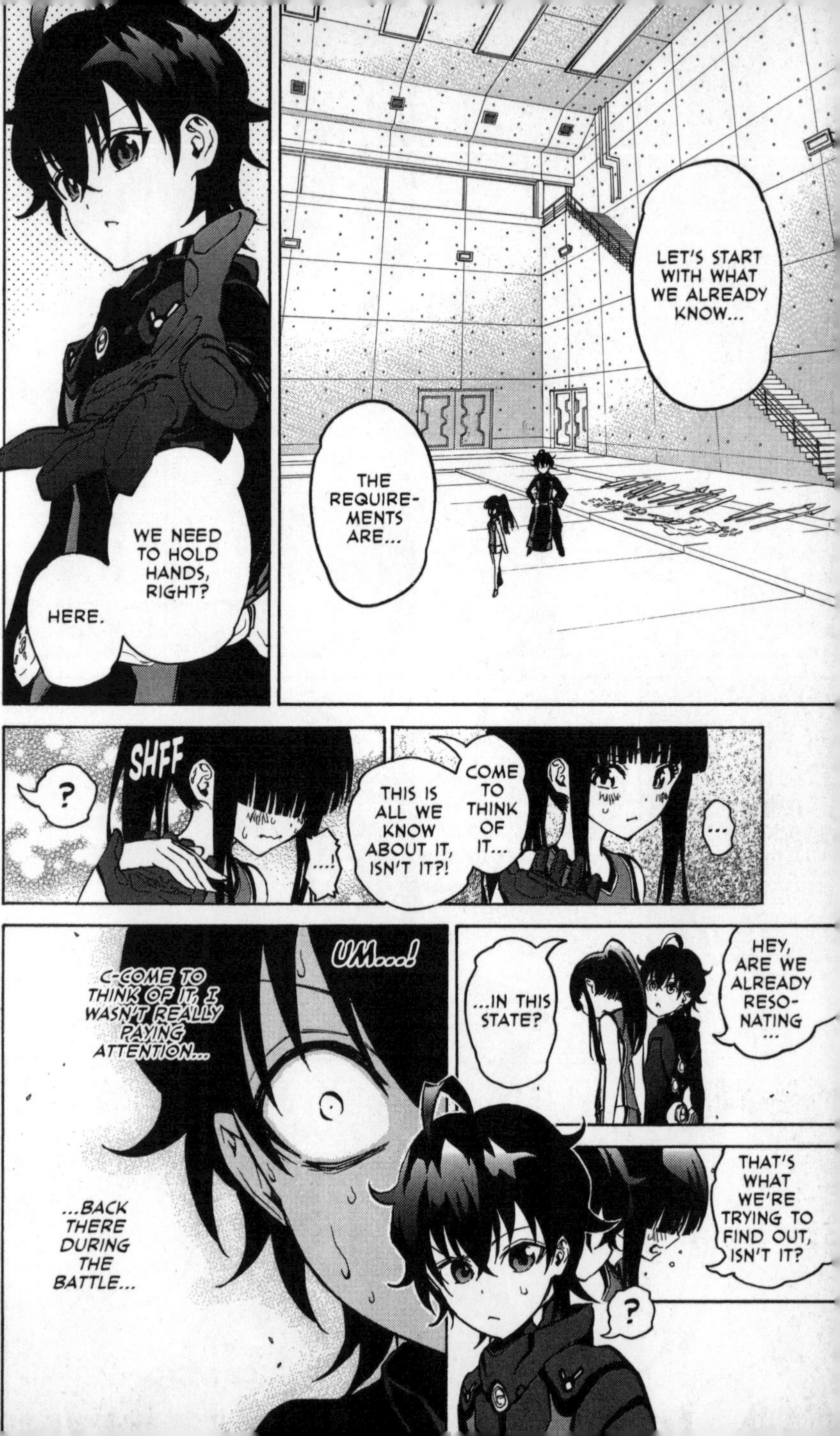
LET'S START WITH WHAT WE ALREADY KNOW...
THE REQUIRE-MENTS ARE...
WE NEED TO HOLD HANDS, RIGHT?
HERE.
...
COME TO THINK OF IT...
THIS IS ALL WE KNOW ABOUT IT, ISN'T IT?!
...!
SHFF
?
HEY, ARE WE ALREADY RESO-NATING ...
...IN THIS STATE?
THAT'S WHAT WE'RE TRYING TO FIND OUT, ISN'T IT?
?
UM...!
C-COME TO THINK OF IT, I WASN'T REALLY PAYING ATTENTION...
...BACK THERE DURING THE BATTLE...

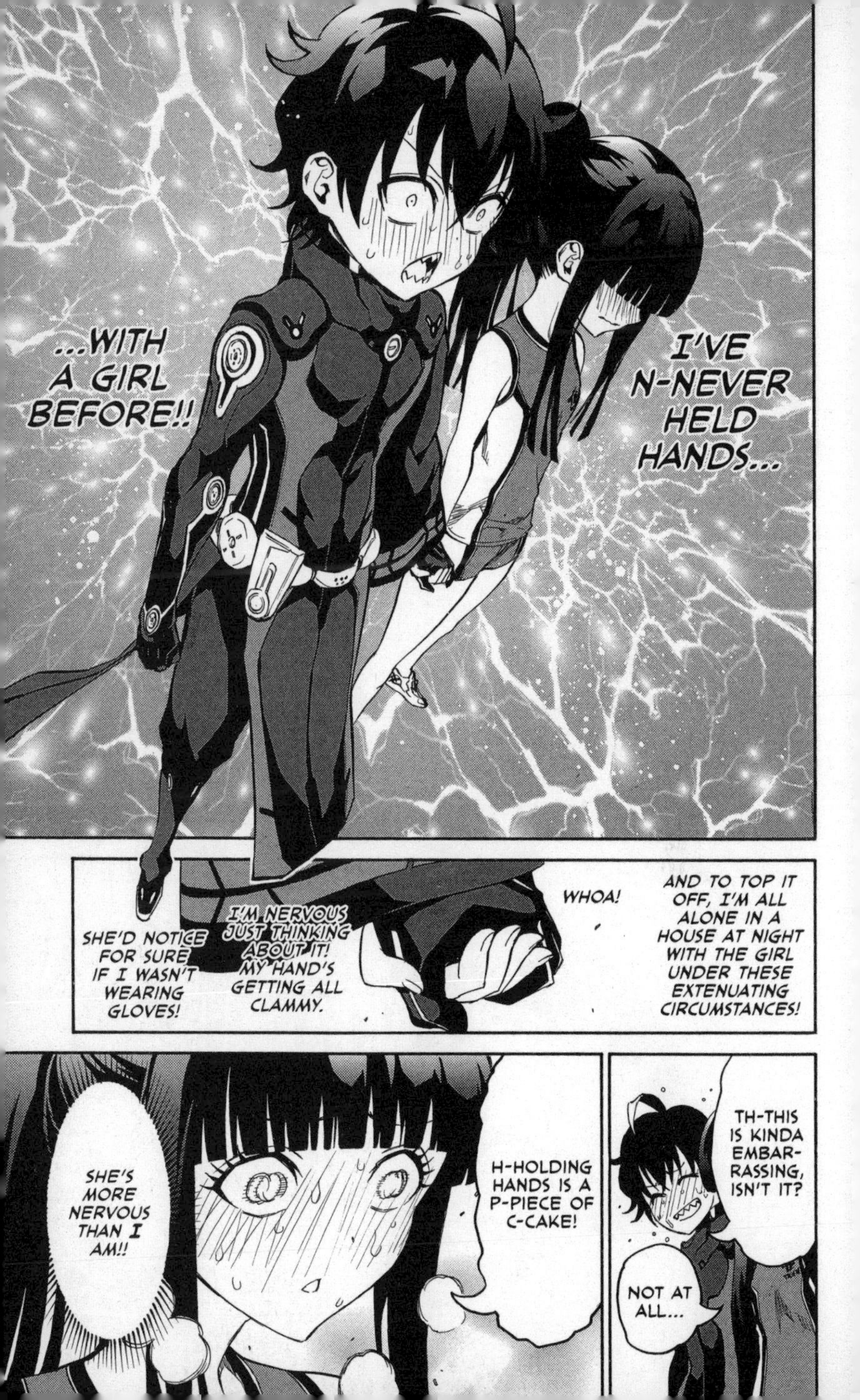
I'VE N-NEVER HELD HANDS...
...WITH A GIRL BEFORE!!
AND TO TOP IT OFF, I'M ALL ALONE IN A HOUSE AT NIGHT WITH THE GIRL UNDER THESE EXTENUATING CIRCUMSTANCES!
WHOA!
I'M NERVOUS JUST THINKING ABOUT IT! MY HAND'S GETTING ALL CLAMMY.
SHE'D NOTICE FOR SURE IF I WASN'T WEARING GLOVES!
TH-THIS IS KINDA EMBARRASSING, ISN'T IT?
NOT AT ALL...
H-HOLDING HANDS IS A P-PIECE OF C-CAKE!
SHE'S MORE NERVOUS THAN I AM!!

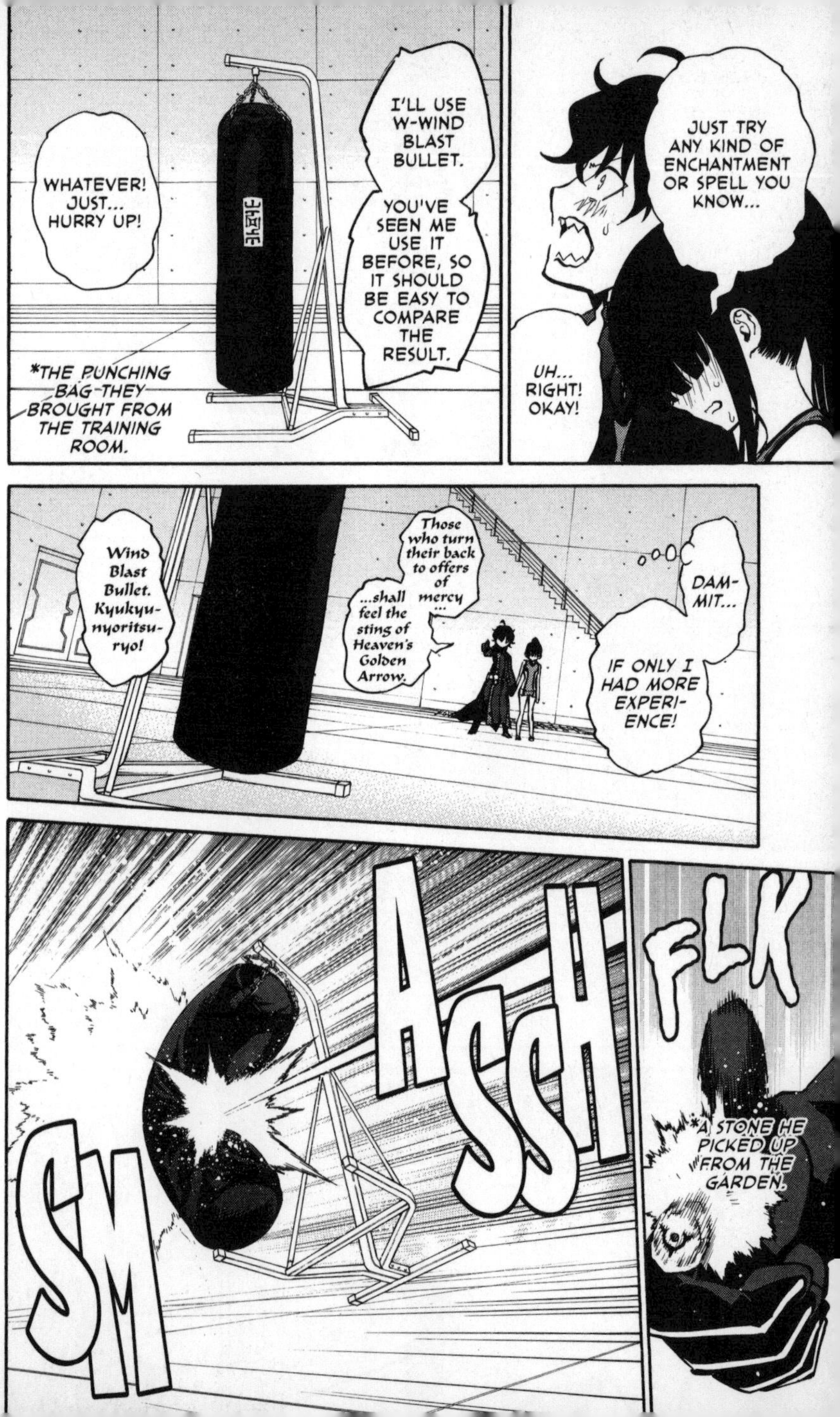

JUST TRY ANY KIND OF ENCHANTMENT OR SPELL YOU KNOW...
UH... RIGHT! OKAY!
I'LL USE W-WIND BLAST BULLET.
YOU'VE SEEN ME USE IT BEFORE, SO IT SHOULD BE EASY TO COMPARE THE RESULT.
WHATEVER! JUST... HURRY UP!
*THE PUNCHING BAG THEY BROUGHT FROM THE TRAINING ROOM.
DAMMIT...
IF ONLY I HAD MORE EXPERIENCE!
Those who turn their back to offers of mercy...
...shall feel the sting of Heaven's Golden Arrow.
Wind Blast Bullet. Kyukyunyoritsuryo!
FLK
*A STONE HE PICKED UP FROM THE GARDEN.
SMASSH

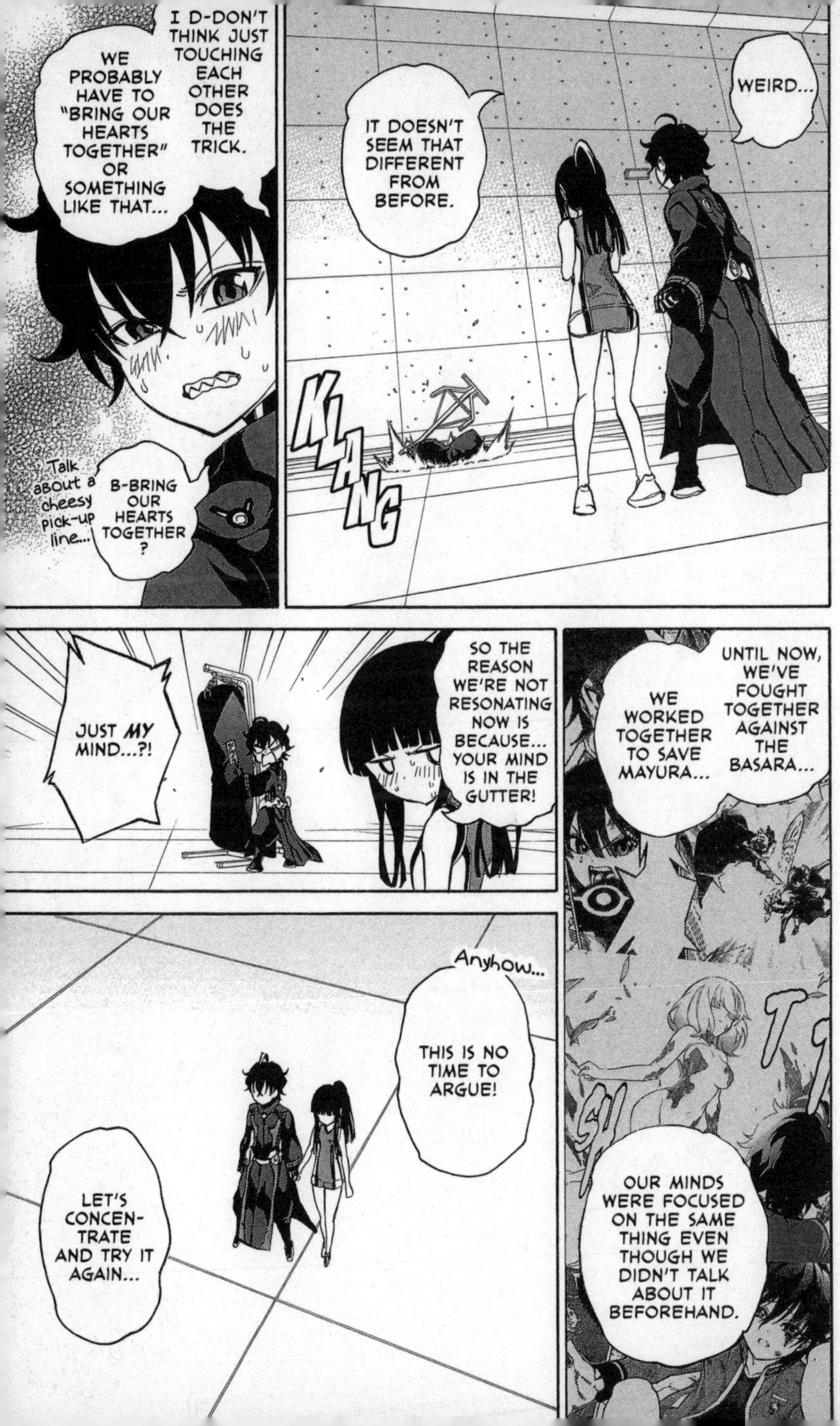
WEIRD...
IT DOESN'T SEEM THAT DIFFERENT FROM BEFORE.
KLANG
I D-DON'T THINK JUST TOUCHING EACH OTHER DOES THE TRICK.
WE PROBABLY HAVE TO "BRING OUR HEARTS TOGETHER" OR SOMETHING LIKE THAT...
B-BRING OUR HEARTS TOGETHER?
Talk about a cheesy pick-up line...
UNTIL NOW, WE'VE FOUGHT TOGETHER AGAINST THE BASARA...
WE WORKED TOGETHER TO SAVE MAYURA...
OUR MINDS WERE FOCUSED ON THE SAME THING EVEN THOUGH WE DIDN'T TALK ABOUT IT BEFOREHAND.
SO THE REASON WE'RE NOT RESONATING NOW IS BECAUSE... YOUR MIND IS IN THE GUTTER!
JUST MY MIND...?!
Anyhow...
THIS IS NO TIME TO ARGUE!
LET'S CONCENTRATE AND TRY IT AGAIN...

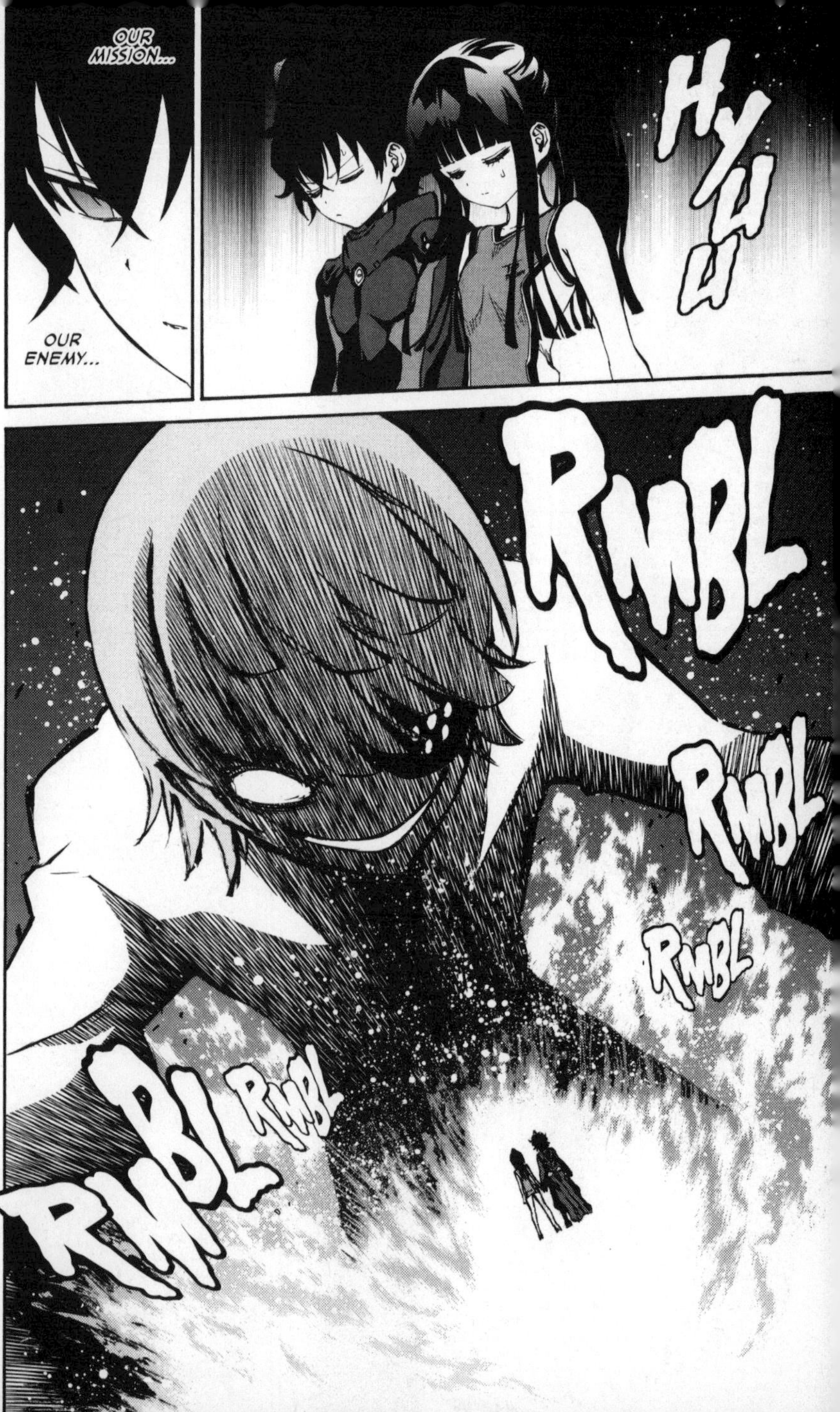
HYUUU
OUR MISSION...
OUR ENEMY...
RMBL
RMBL
RMBL
RMBL
RMBL

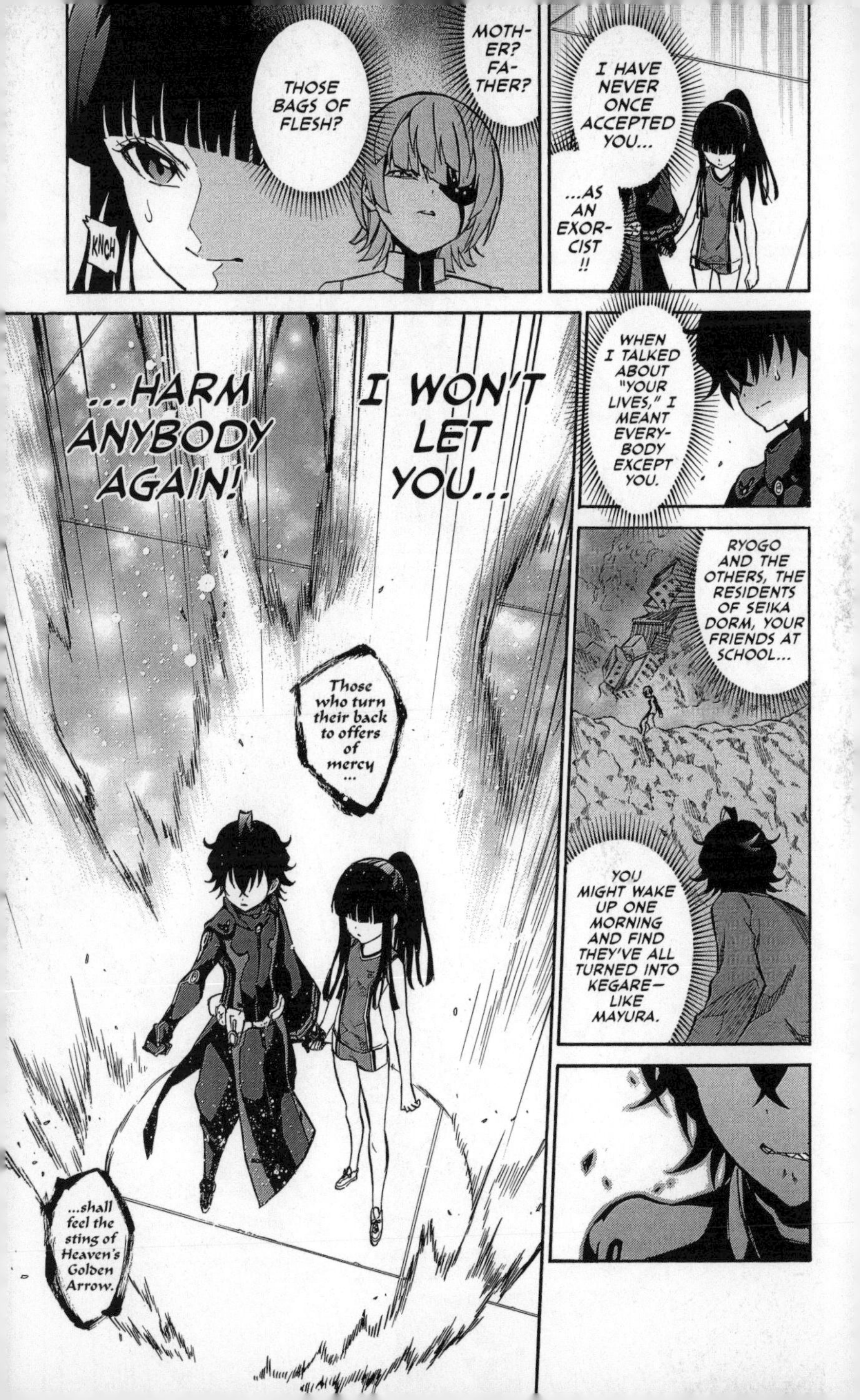
I HAVE NEVER ONCE ACCEPTED YOU...
...AS AN EXORCIST!!
MOTHER? FATHER?
THOSE BAGS OF FLESH?
KNCH
WHEN I TALKED ABOUT "YOUR LIVES," I MEANT EVERYBODY EXCEPT YOU.
RYOGO AND THE OTHERS, THE RESIDENTS OF SEIKA DORM, YOUR FRIENDS AT SCHOOL...
YOU MIGHT WAKE UP ONE MORNING AND FIND THEY'VE ALL TURNED INTO KEGARE—LIKE MAYURA.
I WON'T LET YOU...
...HARM ANYBODY AGAIN!
Those who turn their back to offers of mercy...
...shall feel the sting of Heaven's Golden Arrow.

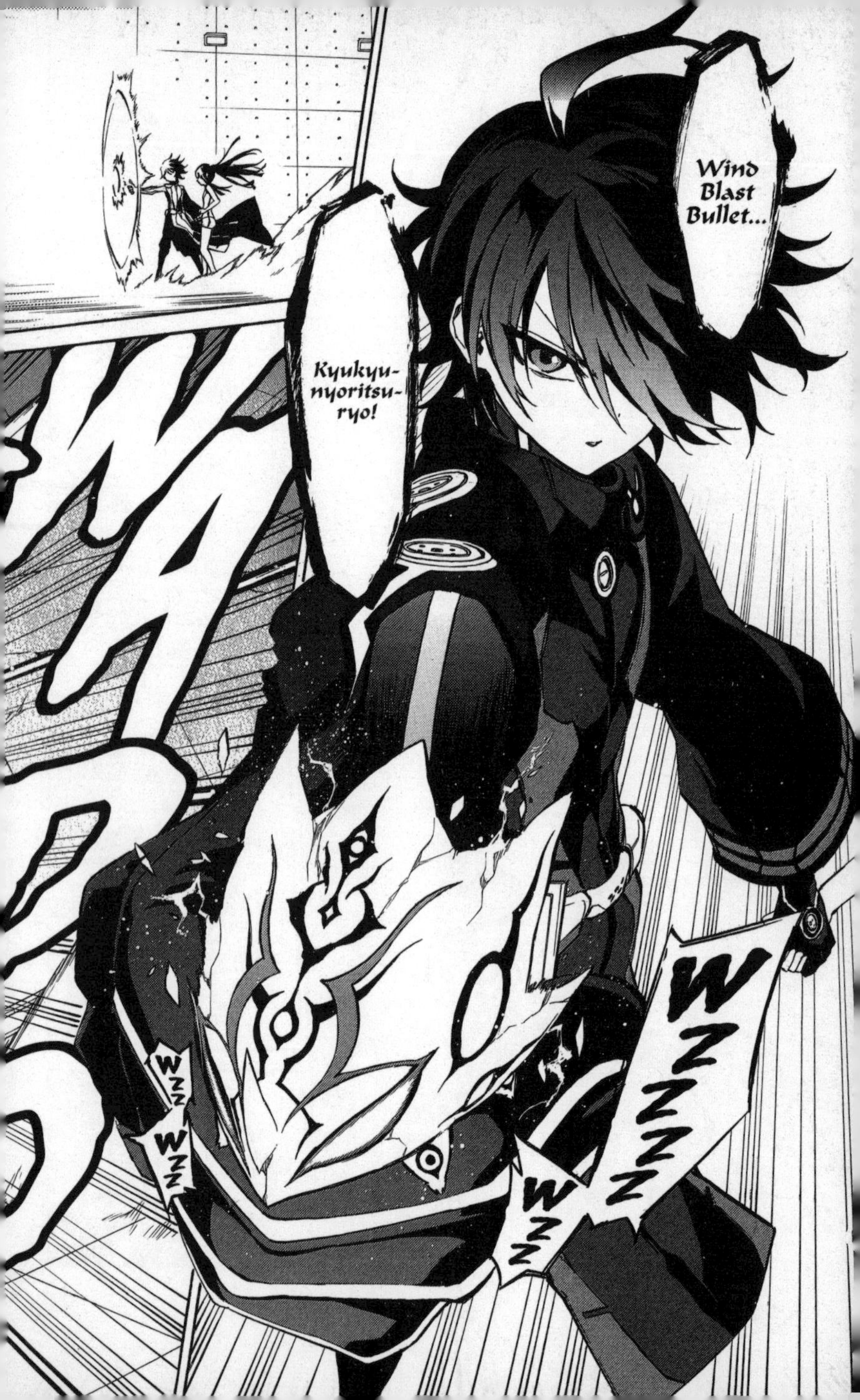
Wind Blast Bullet...
Kyukyu-nyoritsu-ryo!
WZZZZZ
WZZ
WZZ
WZZ

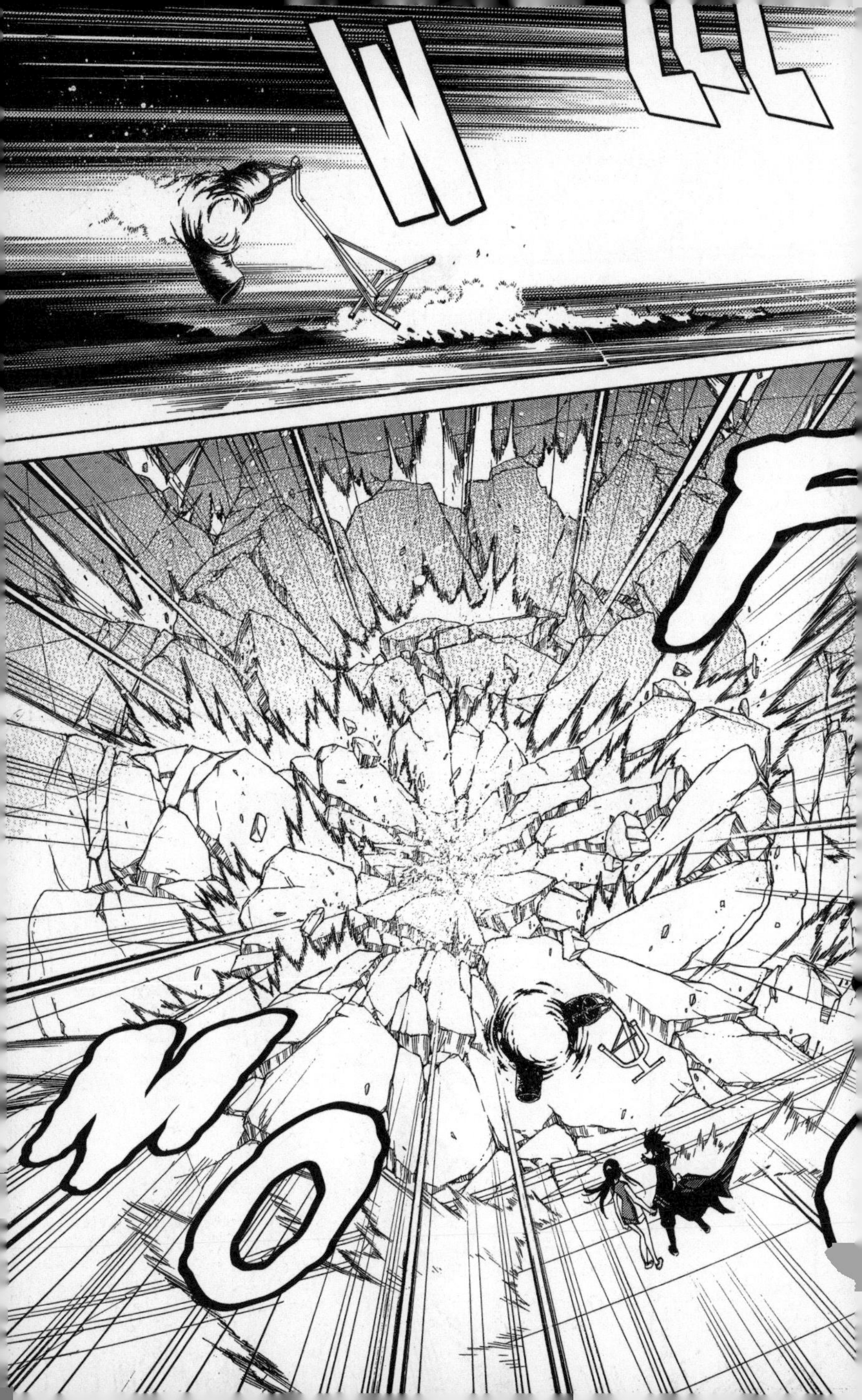

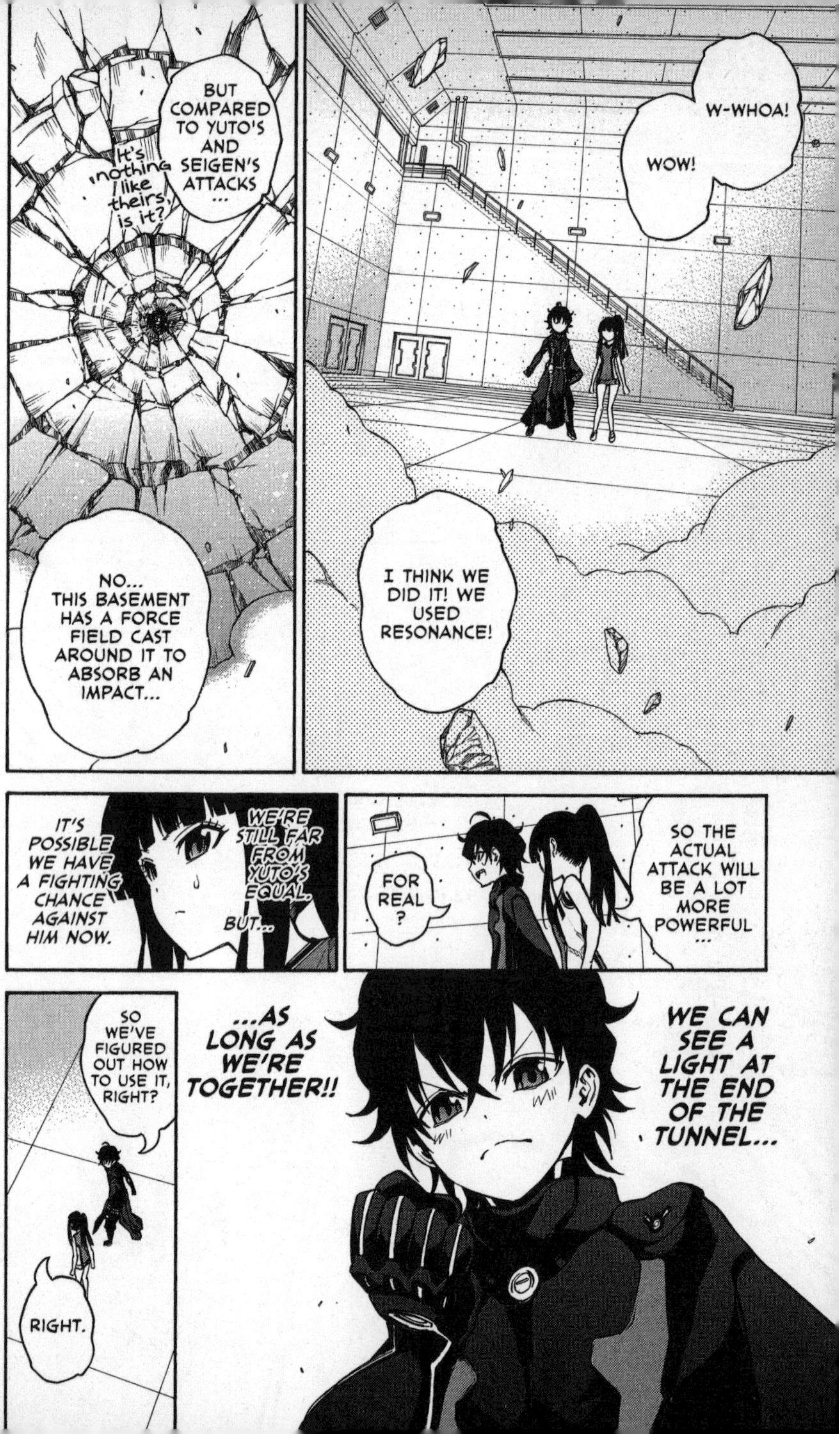
W-WHOA!
WOW!
I THINK WE DID IT! WE USED RESONANCE!
BUT COMPARED TO YUTO'S AND SEIGEN'S ATTACKS...
It's nothing like theirs, is it?
NO... THIS BASEMENT HAS A FORCE FIELD CAST AROUND IT TO ABSORB AN IMPACT...
SO THE ACTUAL ATTACK WILL BE A LOT MORE POWERFUL...
FOR REAL?
WE'RE STILL FAR FROM YUTO'S EQUAL.
BUT...
IT'S POSSIBLE WE HAVE A FIGHTING CHANCE AGAINST HIM NOW.
WE CAN SEE A LIGHT AT THE END OF THE TUNNEL...
...AS LONG AS WE'RE TOGETHER!!
SO WE'VE FIGURED OUT HOW TO USE IT, RIGHT?
RIGHT.

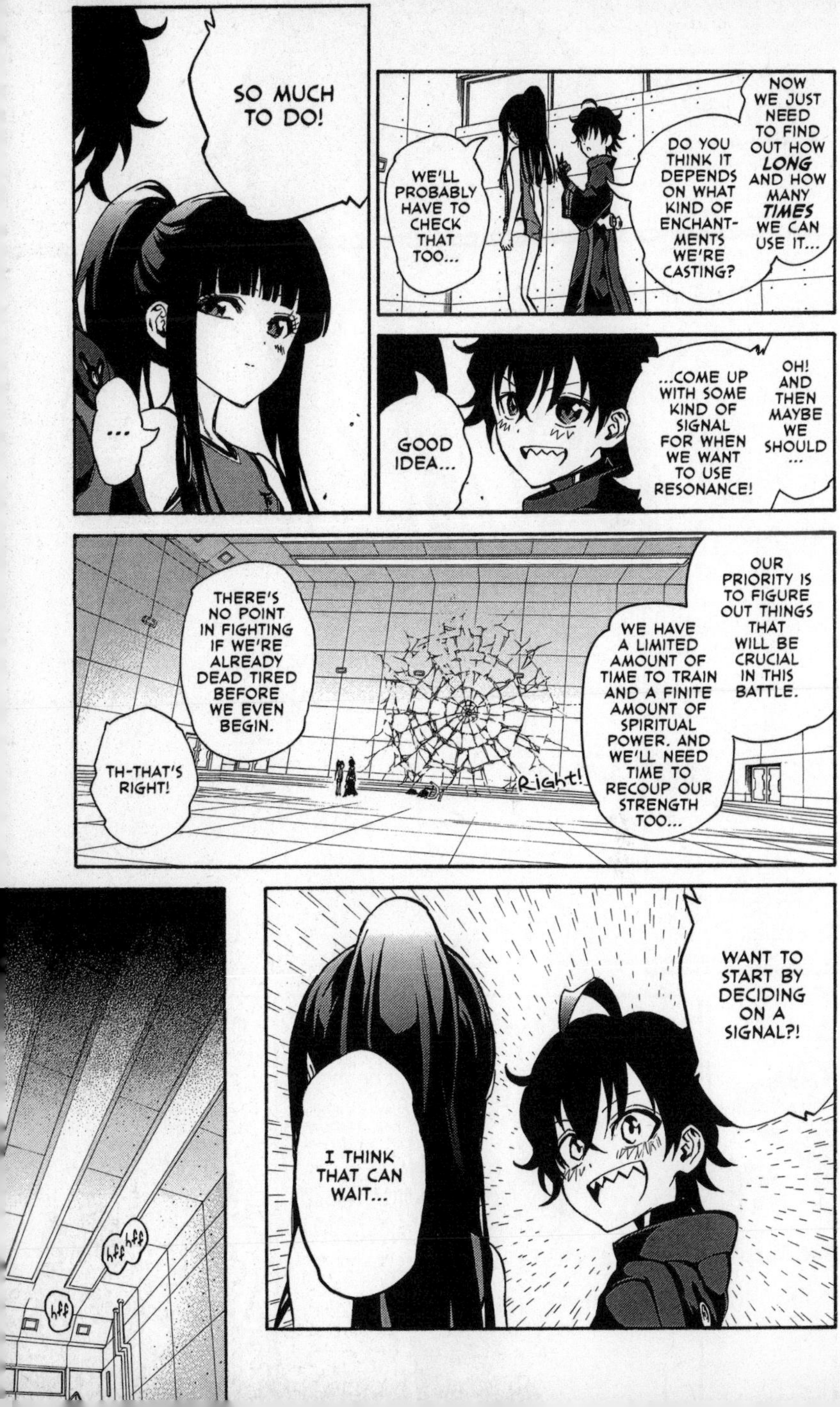
NOW WE JUST NEED TO FIND OUT HOW *LONG* AND HOW MANY *TIMES* WE CAN USE IT...
DO YOU THINK IT DEPENDS ON WHAT KIND OF ENCHANTMENTS WE'RE CASTING?
WE'LL PROBABLY HAVE TO CHECK THAT TOO...
OH! AND THEN MAYBE WE SHOULD ...
...COME UP WITH SOME KIND OF SIGNAL FOR WHEN WE WANT TO USE RESONANCE!
GOOD IDEA...
SO MUCH TO DO!
...
OUR PRIORITY IS TO FIGURE OUT THINGS THAT WILL BE CRUCIAL IN THIS BATTLE.
WE HAVE A LIMITED AMOUNT OF TIME TO TRAIN AND A FINITE AMOUNT OF SPIRITUAL POWER. AND WE'LL NEED TIME TO RECOUP OUR STRENGTH TOO...
Right!
THERE'S NO POINT IN FIGHTING IF WE'RE ALREADY DEAD TIRED BEFORE WE EVEN BEGIN.
TH-THAT'S RIGHT!
WANT TO START BY DECIDING ON A SIGNAL?!
I THINK THAT CAN WAIT...
hff hff
hff

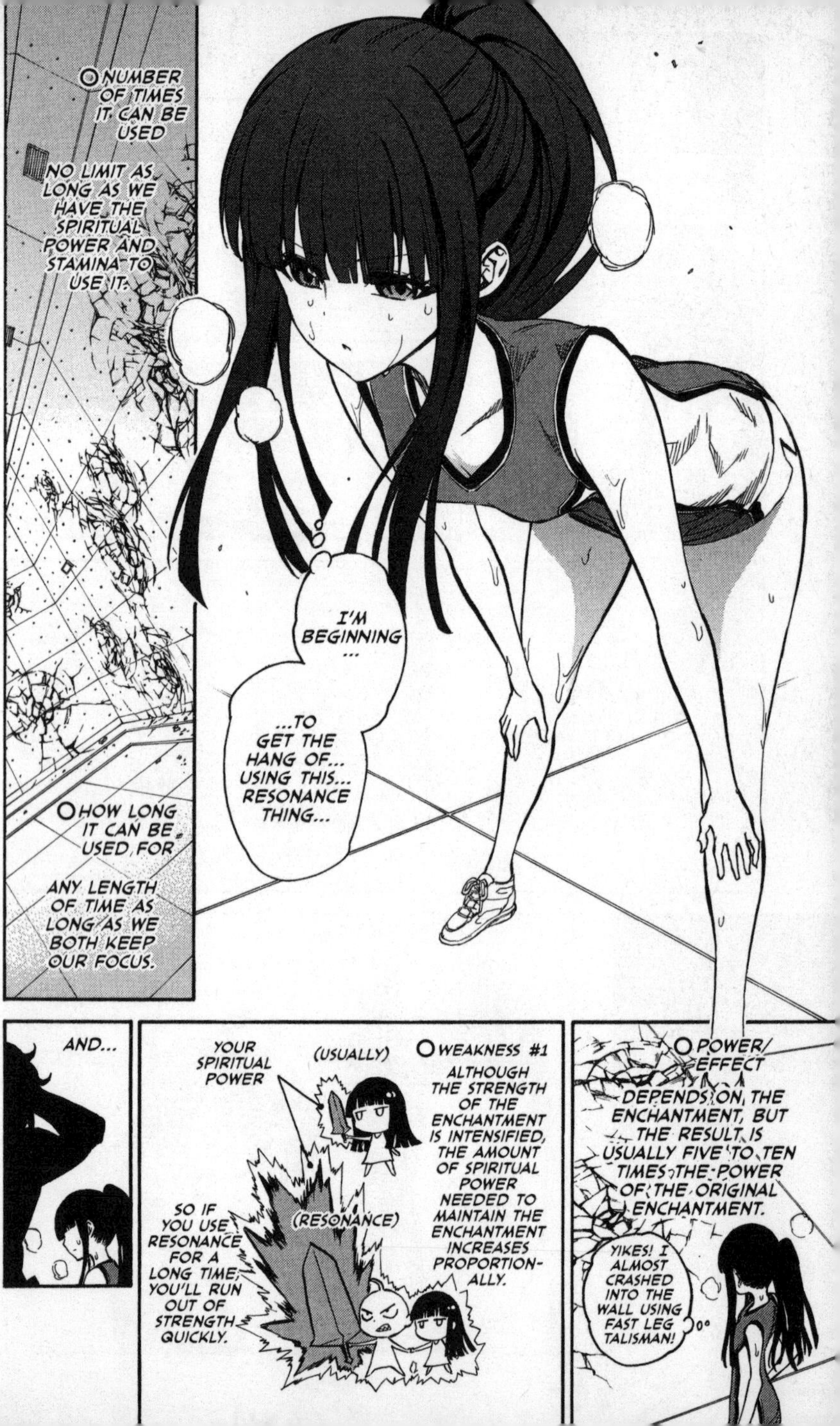

I'M BEGINNING...
...TO GET THE HANG OF... USING THIS... RESONANCE THING...
○NUMBER OF TIMES IT CAN BE USED
NO LIMIT AS LONG AS WE HAVE THE SPIRITUAL POWER AND STAMINA TO USE IT.
○HOW LONG IT CAN BE USED FOR
ANY LENGTH OF TIME AS LONG AS WE BOTH KEEP OUR FOCUS.
○POWER/EFFECT
DEPENDS ON THE ENCHANTMENT, BUT THE RESULT IS USUALLY FIVE TO TEN TIMES THE POWER OF THE ORIGINAL ENCHANTMENT.
YIKES! I ALMOST CRASHED INTO THE WALL USING FAST LEG TALISMAN!
○WEAKNESS #1
ALTHOUGH THE STRENGTH OF THE ENCHANTMENT IS INTENSIFIED, THE AMOUNT OF SPIRITUAL POWER NEEDED TO MAINTAIN THE ENCHANTMENT INCREASES PROPORTIONALLY.
(USUALLY)
YOUR SPIRITUAL POWER
(RESONANCE)
SO IF YOU USE RESONANCE FOR A LONG TIME, YOU'LL RUN OUT OF STRENGTH QUICKLY.
AND...

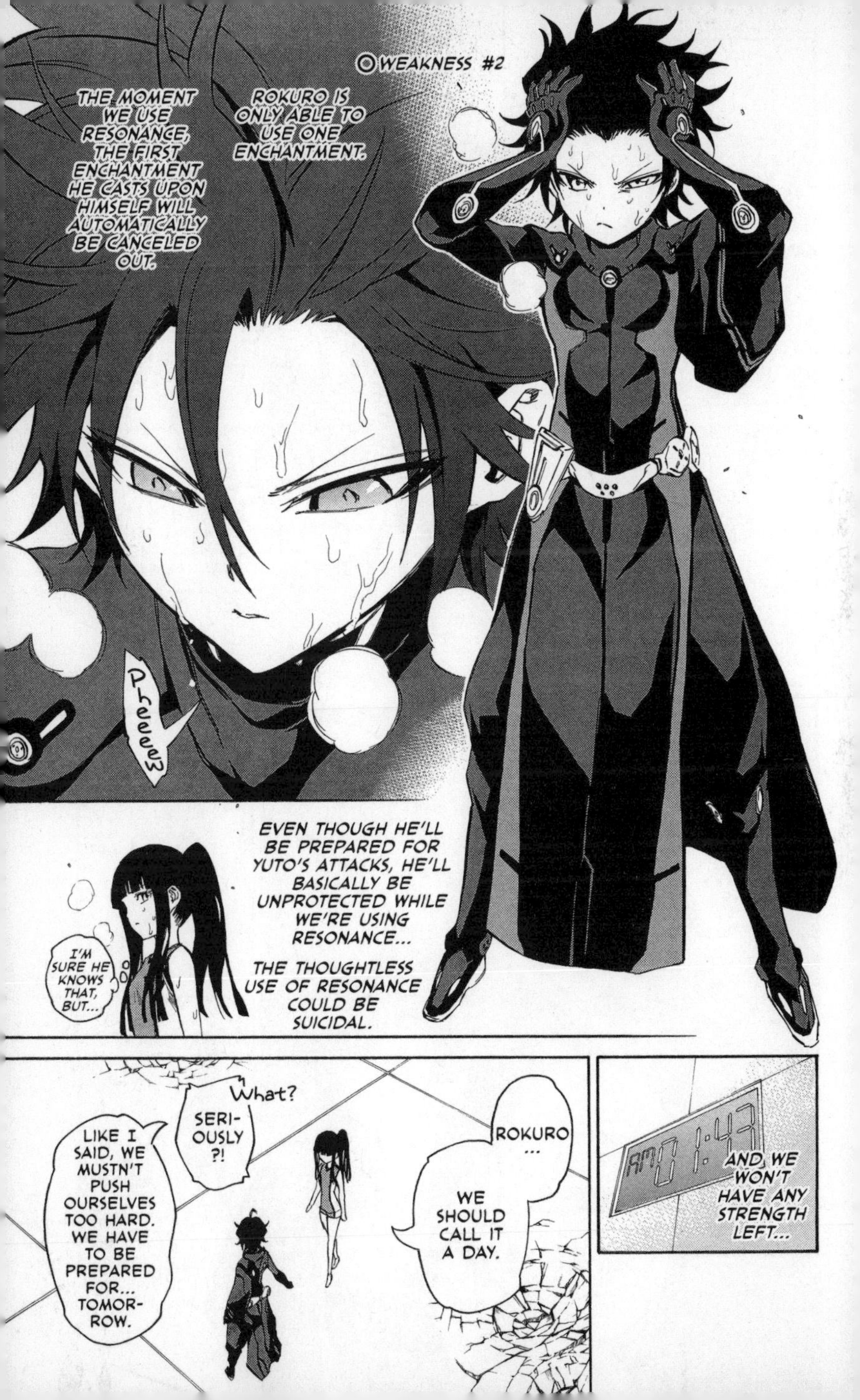
WEAKNESS #2
ROKURO IS ONLY ABLE TO USE ONE ENCHANTMENT.
THE MOMENT WE USE RESONANCE, THE FIRST ENCHANTMENT HE CASTS UPON HIMSELF WILL AUTOMATICALLY BE CANCELED OUT.
Pheeeew
EVEN THOUGH HE'LL BE PREPARED FOR YUTO'S ATTACKS, HE'LL BASICALLY BE UNPROTECTED WHILE WE'RE USING RESONANCE...
THE THOUGHTLESS USE OF RESONANCE COULD BE SUICIDAL.
I'M SURE HE KNOWS THAT, BUT...
AM 01:43
AND, WE WON'T HAVE ANY STRENGTH LEFT...
ROKURO...
WE SHOULD CALL IT A DAY.
What?
SERIOUSLY?!
LIKE I SAID, WE MUSTN'T PUSH OURSELVES TOO HARD. WE HAVE TO BE PREPARED FOR... TOMORROW.

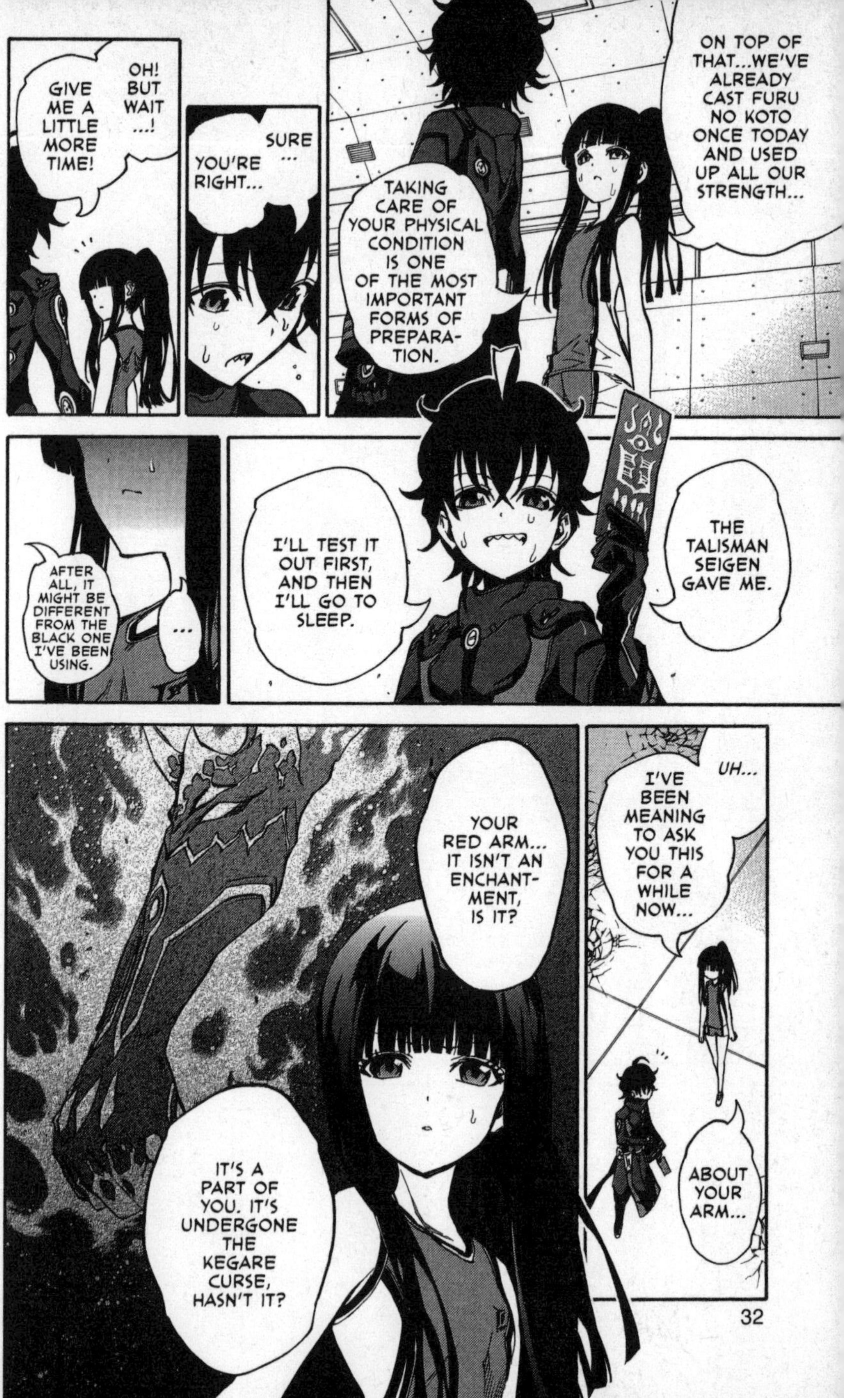
ON TOP OF THAT...WE'VE ALREADY CAST FURU NO KOTO ONCE TODAY AND USED UP ALL OUR STRENGTH...
TAKING CARE OF YOUR PHYSICAL CONDITION IS ONE OF THE MOST IMPORTANT FORMS OF PREPARATION.
SURE...
YOU'RE RIGHT...
OH! BUT WAIT...!
GIVE ME A LITTLE MORE TIME!
THE TALISMAN SEIGEN GAVE ME.
I'LL TEST IT OUT FIRST, AND THEN I'LL GO TO SLEEP.
...
AFTER ALL, IT MIGHT BE DIFFERENT FROM THE BLACK ONE I'VE BEEN USING.
UH...
I'VE BEEN MEANING TO ASK YOU THIS FOR A WHILE NOW...
ABOUT YOUR ARM...
YOUR RED ARM... IT ISN'T AN ENCHANTMENT, IS IT?
IT'S A PART OF YOU. IT'S UNDERGONE THE KEGARE CURSE, HASN'T IT?

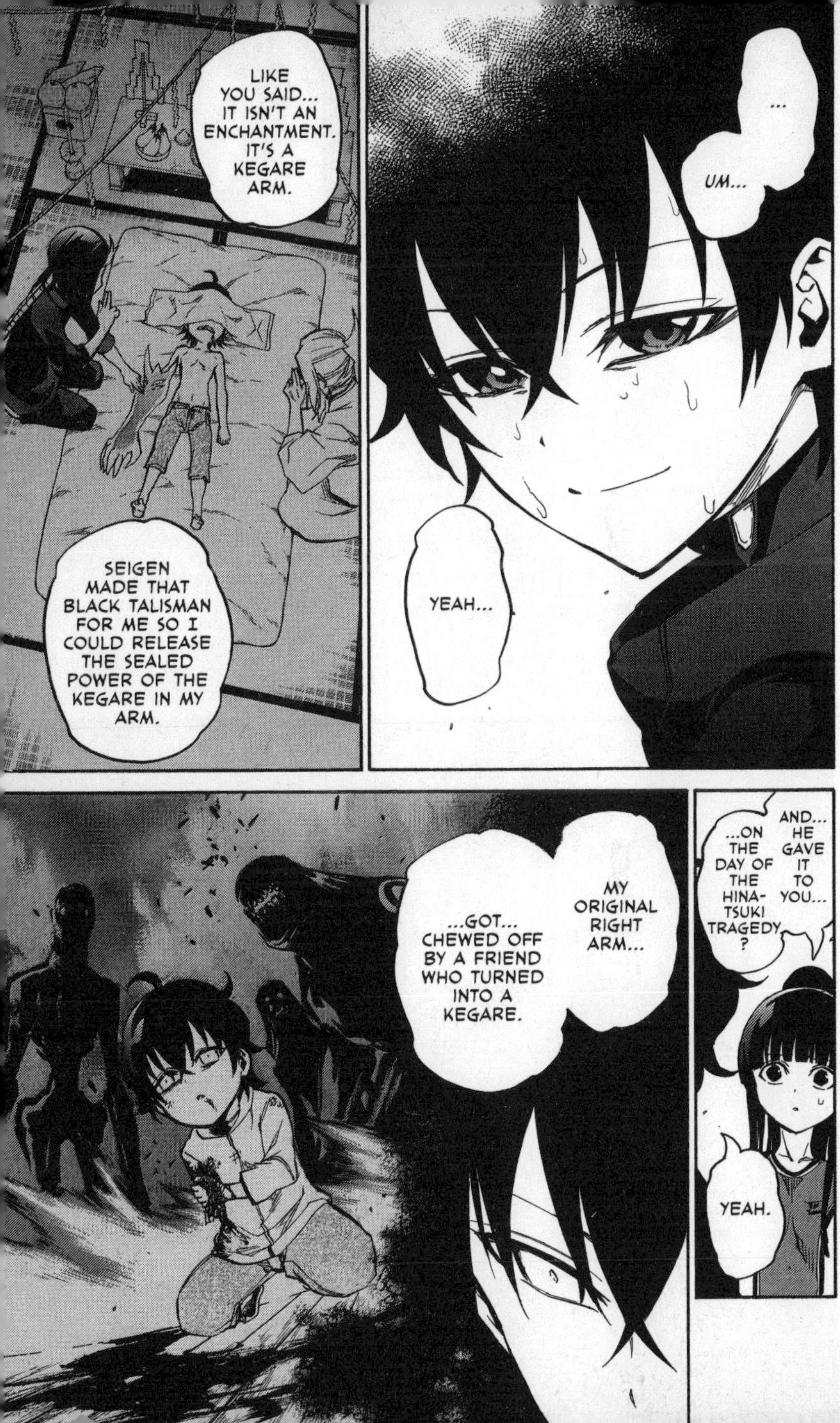
...
UM...
YEAH...
LIKE YOU SAID... IT ISN'T AN ENCHANTMENT. IT'S A KEGARE ARM.
SEIGEN MADE THAT BLACK TALISMAN FOR ME SO I COULD RELEASE THE SEALED POWER OF THE KEGARE IN MY ARM.
AND... HE GAVE IT TO YOU...
...ON THE DAY OF THE HINA-TSUKI TRAGEDY?
YEAH.
MY ORIGINAL RIGHT ARM...
...GOT... CHEWED OFF BY A FRIEND WHO TURNED INTO A KEGARE.

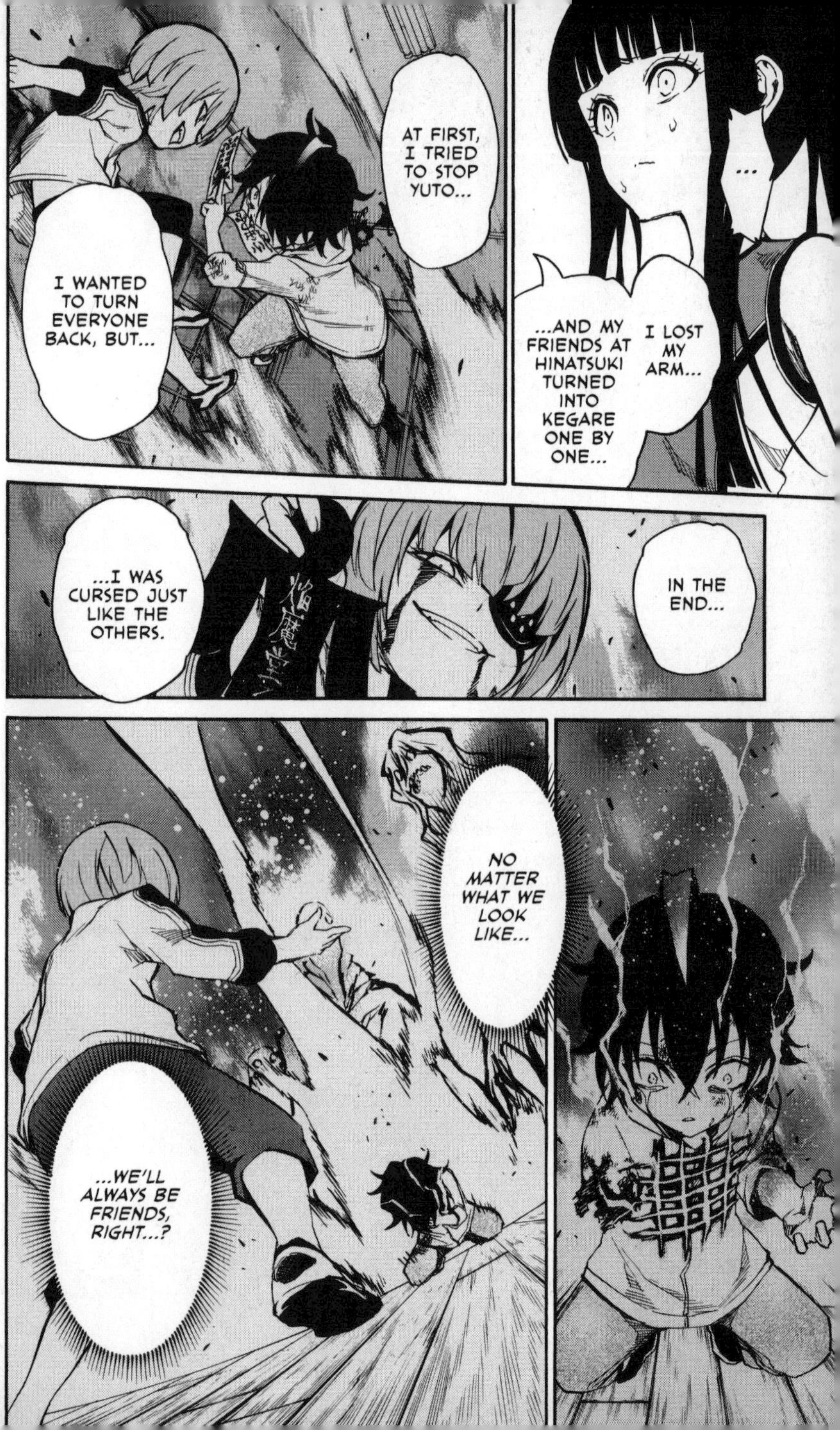
...
I LOST MY ARM...
...AND MY FRIENDS AT HINATSUKI TURNED INTO KEGARE ONE BY ONE...
AT FIRST, I TRIED TO STOP YUTO...
I WANTED TO TURN EVERYONE BACK, BUT...
IN THE END...
...I WAS CURSED JUST LIKE THE OTHERS.
NO MATTER WHAT WE LOOK LIKE...
...WE'LL ALWAYS BE FRIENDS, RIGHT...?

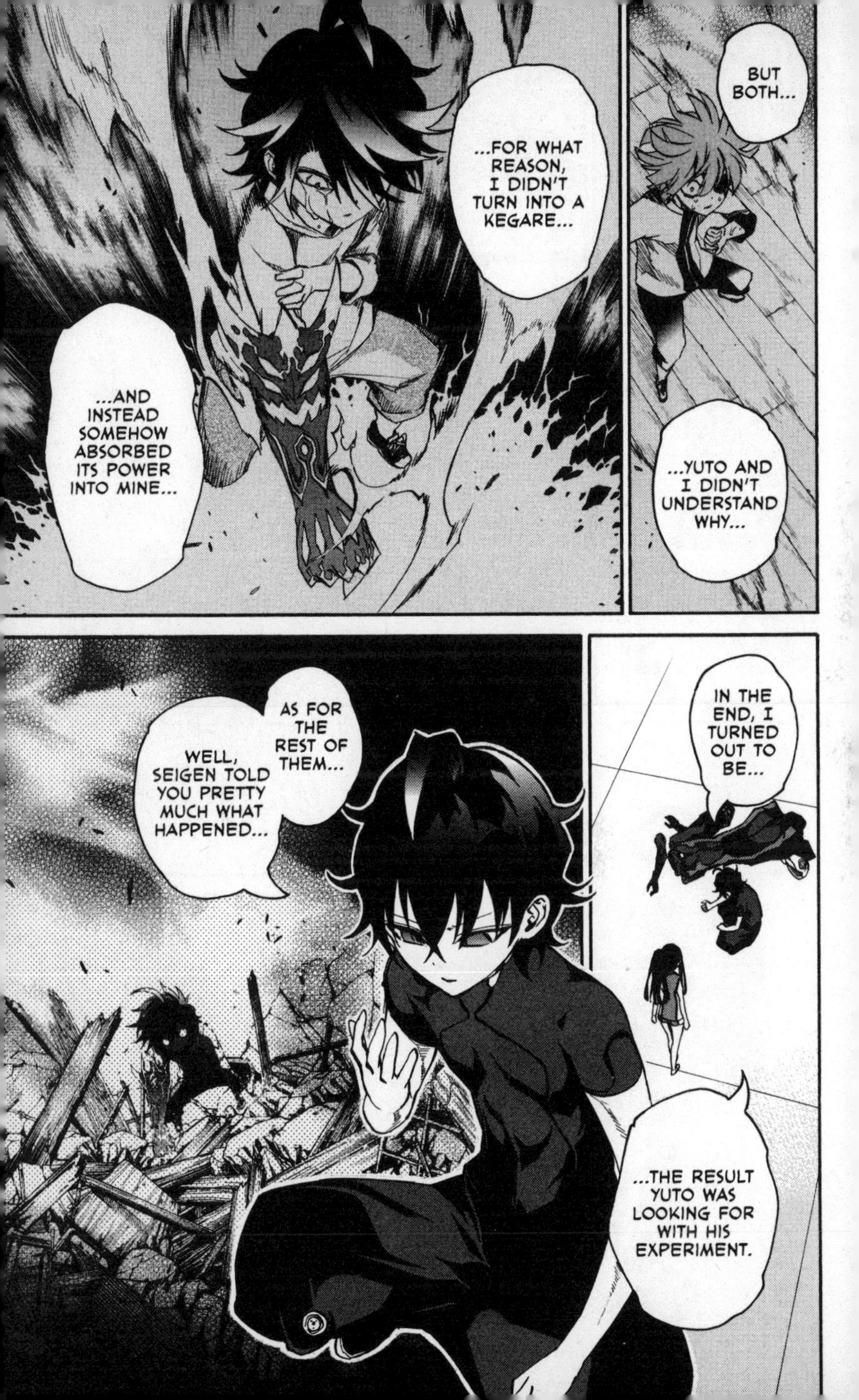
BUT BOTH...
...YUTO AND I DIDN'T UNDERSTAND WHY...
...FOR WHAT REASON, I DIDN'T TURN INTO A KEGARE...
...AND INSTEAD SOMEHOW ABSORBED ITS POWER INTO MINE...
IN THE END, I TURNED OUT TO BE...
...THE RESULT YUTO WAS LOOKING FOR WITH HIS EXPERIMENT.
AS FOR THE REST OF THEM...
WELL, SEIGEN TOLD YOU PRETTY MUCH WHAT HAPPENED...

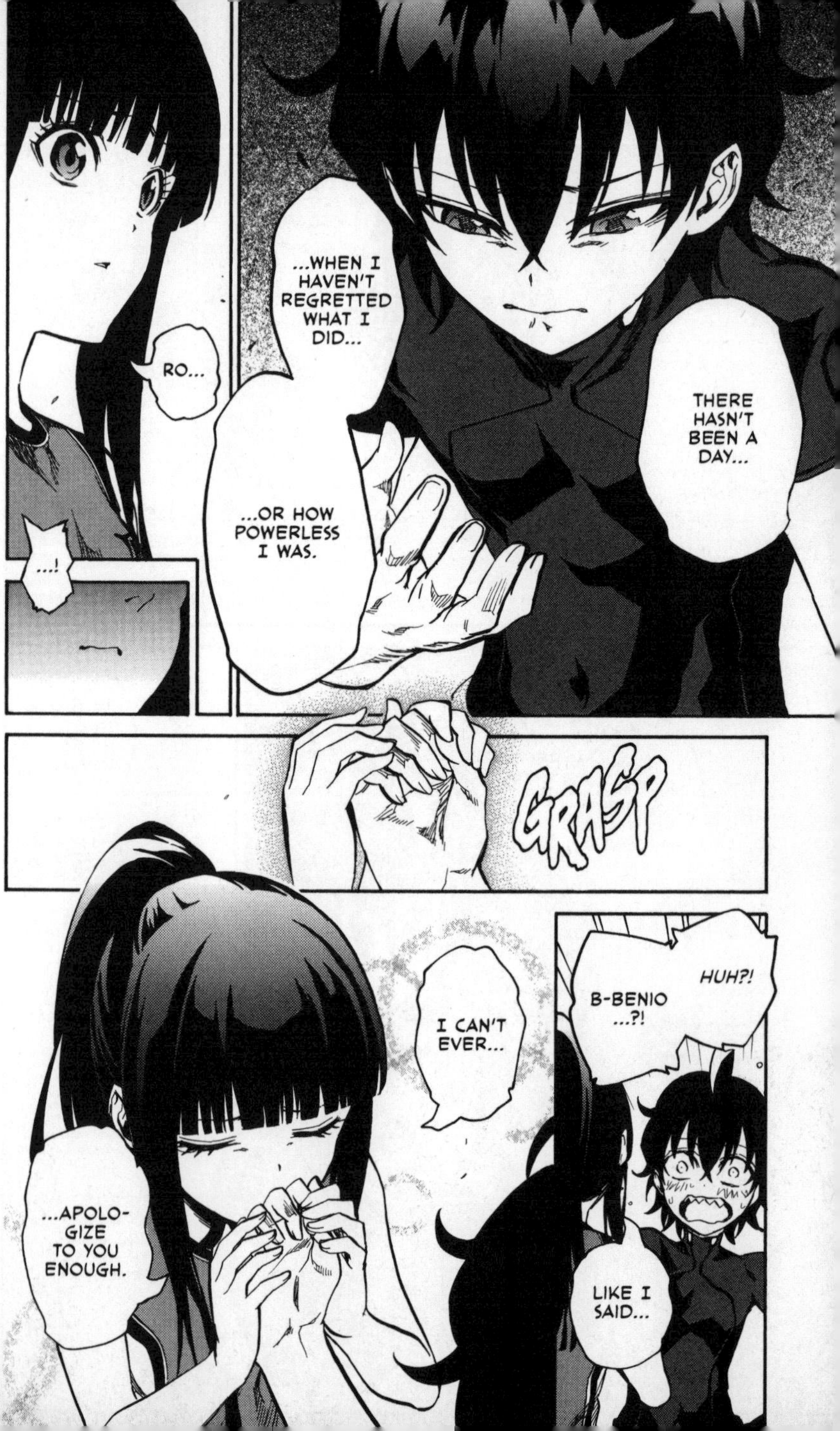
THERE HASN'T BEEN A DAY...
...WHEN I HAVEN'T REGRETTED WHAT I DID...
...OR HOW POWERLESS I WAS.
RO...
...!
GRASP
HUH?!
B-BENIO ...?!
LIKE I SAID...
I CAN'T EVER...
...APOLO-GIZE TO YOU ENOUGH.

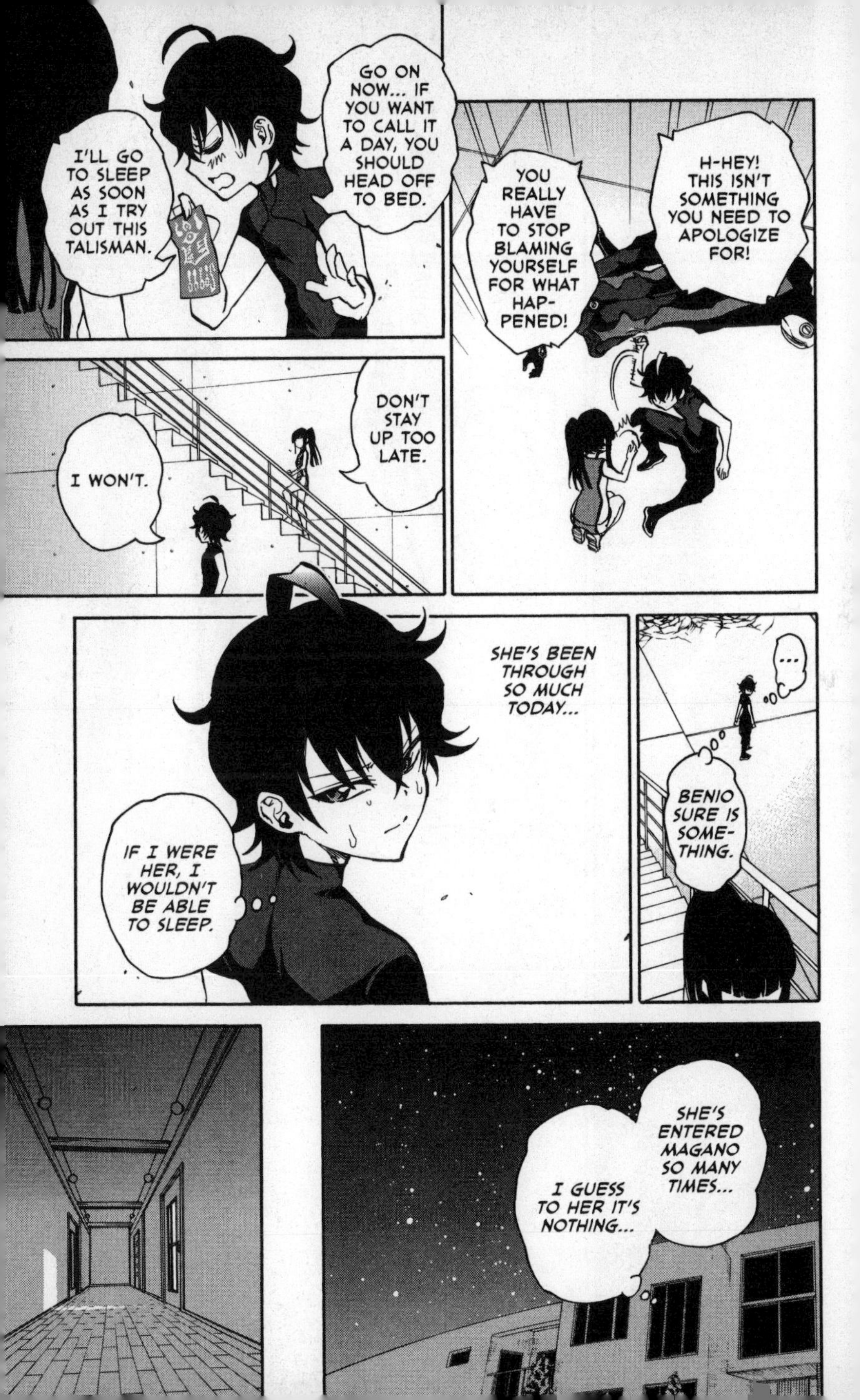
H-HEY! THIS ISN'T SOMETHING YOU NEED TO APOLOGIZE FOR!
YOU REALLY HAVE TO STOP BLAMING YOURSELF FOR WHAT HAP-PENED!
GO ON NOW... IF YOU WANT TO CALL IT A DAY, YOU SHOULD HEAD OFF TO BED.
I'LL GO TO SLEEP AS SOON AS I TRY OUT THIS TALISMAN.
DON'T STAY UP TOO LATE.
I WON'T.
...
BENIO SURE IS SOME-THING.
SHE'S BEEN THROUGH SO MUCH TODAY...
IF I WERE HER, I WOULDN'T BE ABLE TO SLEEP.
SHE'S ENTERED MAGANO SO MANY TIMES...
I GUESS TO HER IT'S NOTHING...

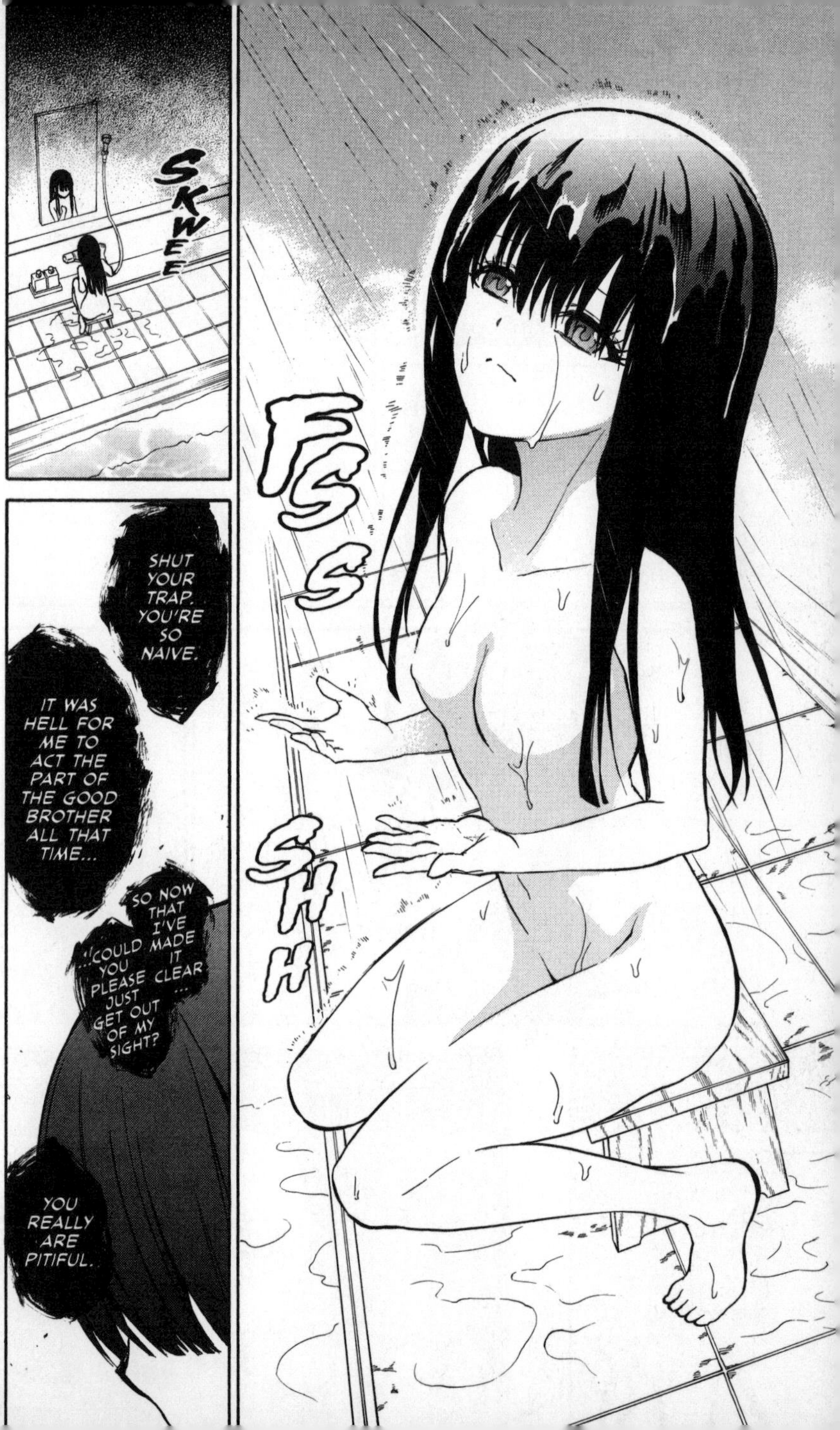
FSS
SHH
SKWEE
SHUT YOUR TRAP. YOU'RE SO NAIVE.
IT WAS HELL FOR ME TO ACT THE PART OF THE GOOD BROTHER ALL THAT TIME...
SO NOW THAT I'VE MADE IT CLEAR...
...COULD YOU PLEASE JUST GET OUT OF MY SIGHT?
YOU REALLY ARE PITIFUL.

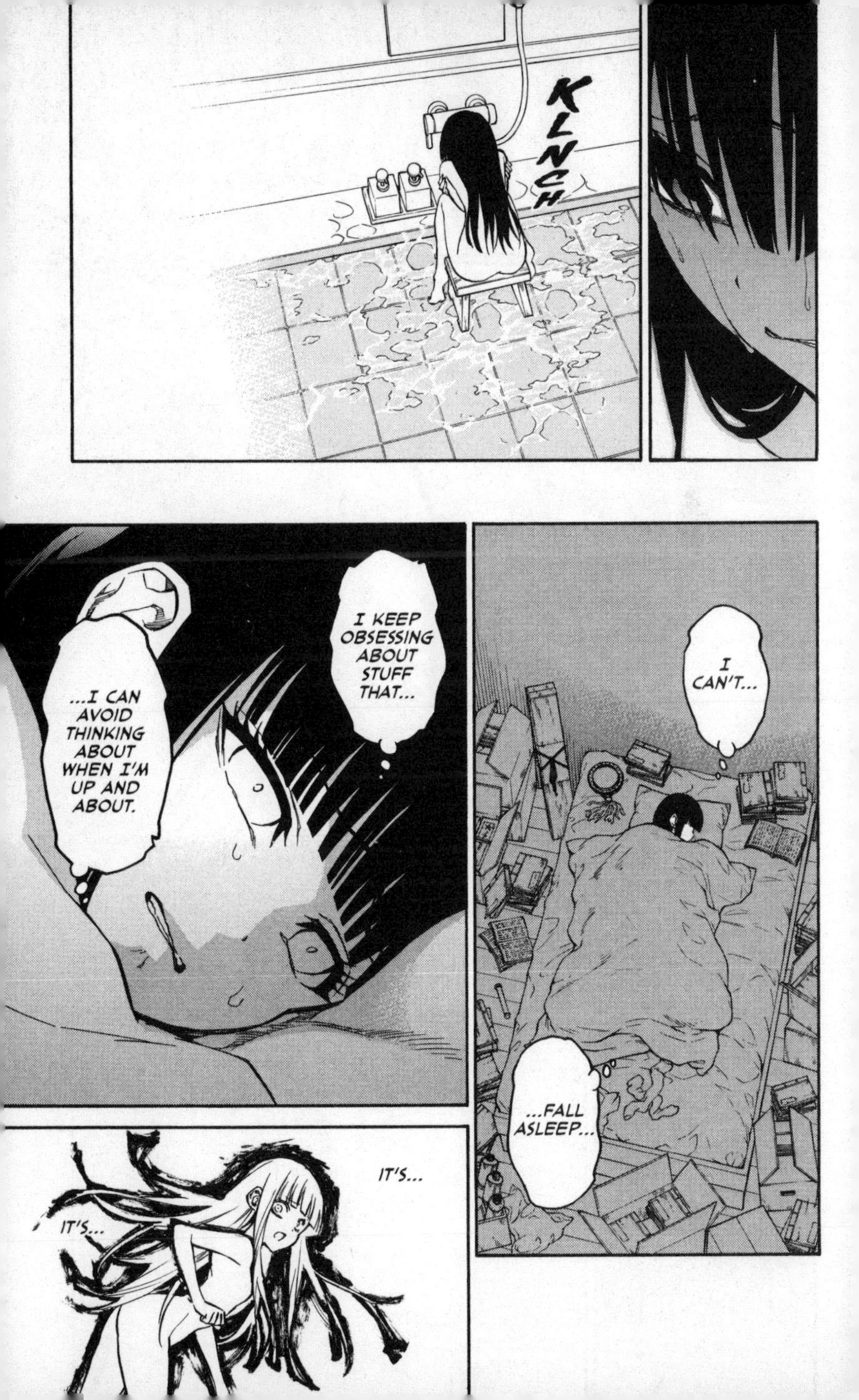
KLNCH
I CAN'T...
...FALL ASLEEP...
I KEEP OBSESSING ABOUT STUFF THAT...
...I CAN AVOID THINKING ABOUT WHEN I'M UP AND ABOUT.
IT'S...
IT'S...

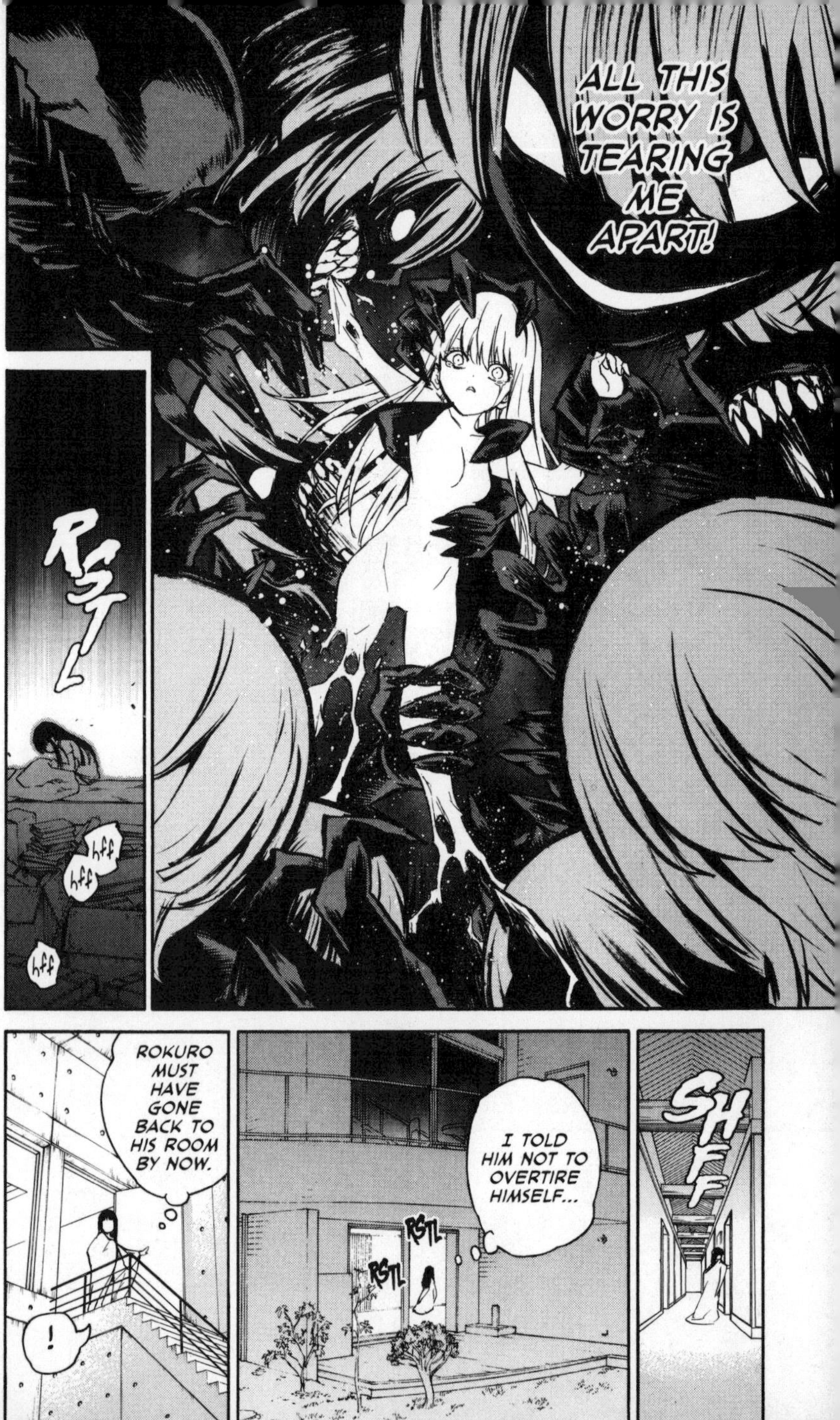
ALL THIS WORRY IS TEARING ME APART!
RSTL
hff
hff
hff
SHFF
I TOLD HIM NOT TO OVERTIRE HIMSELF...
RSTL
RSTL
ROKURO MUST HAVE GONE BACK TO HIS ROOM BY NOW.
!

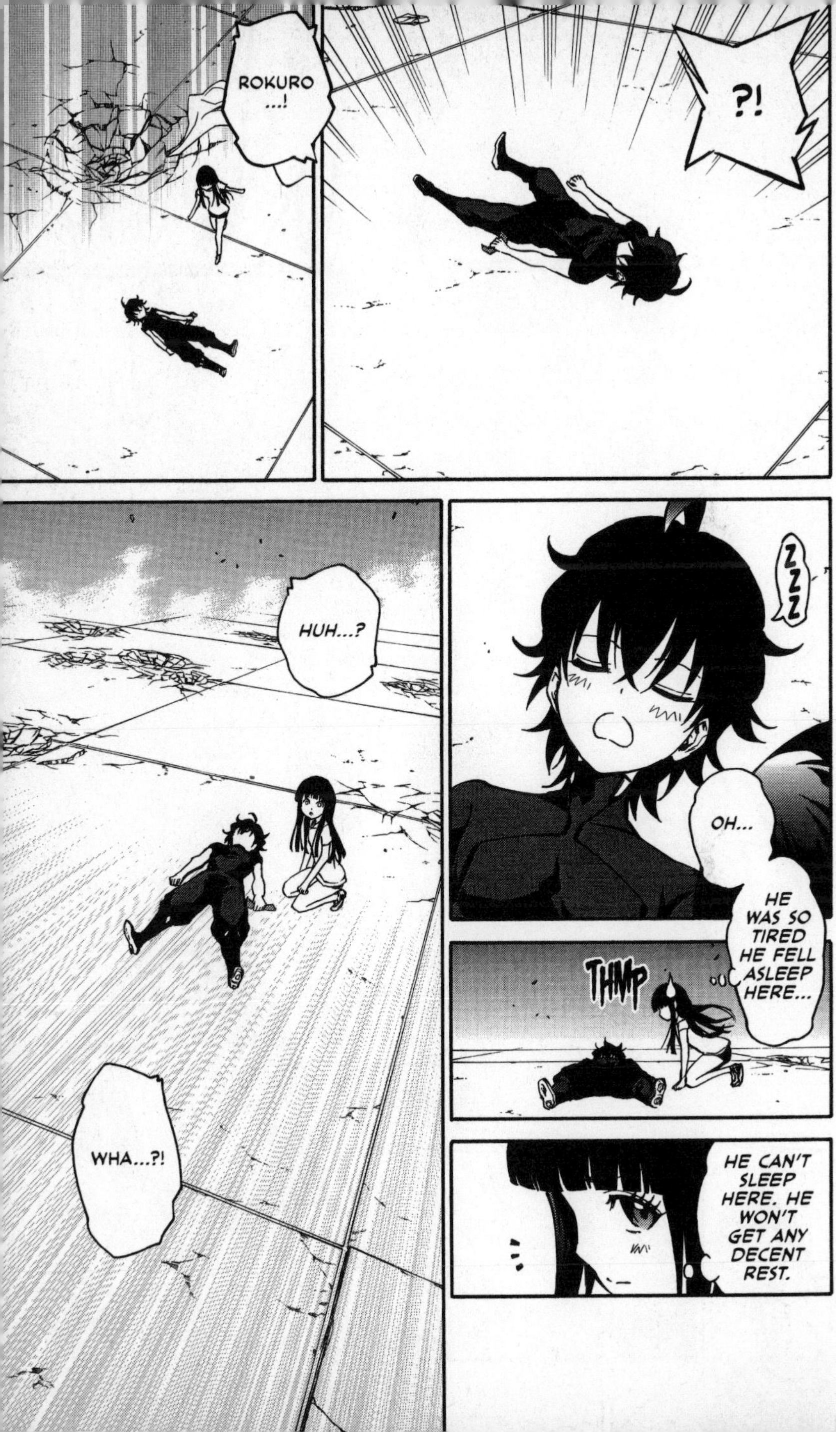
?!
ROKURO ...!
ZZZ
OH...
HE WAS SO TIRED HE FELL ASLEEP HERE...
THMP
HE CAN'T SLEEP HERE. HE WON'T GET ANY DECENT REST.
HUH...?
WHA...?!

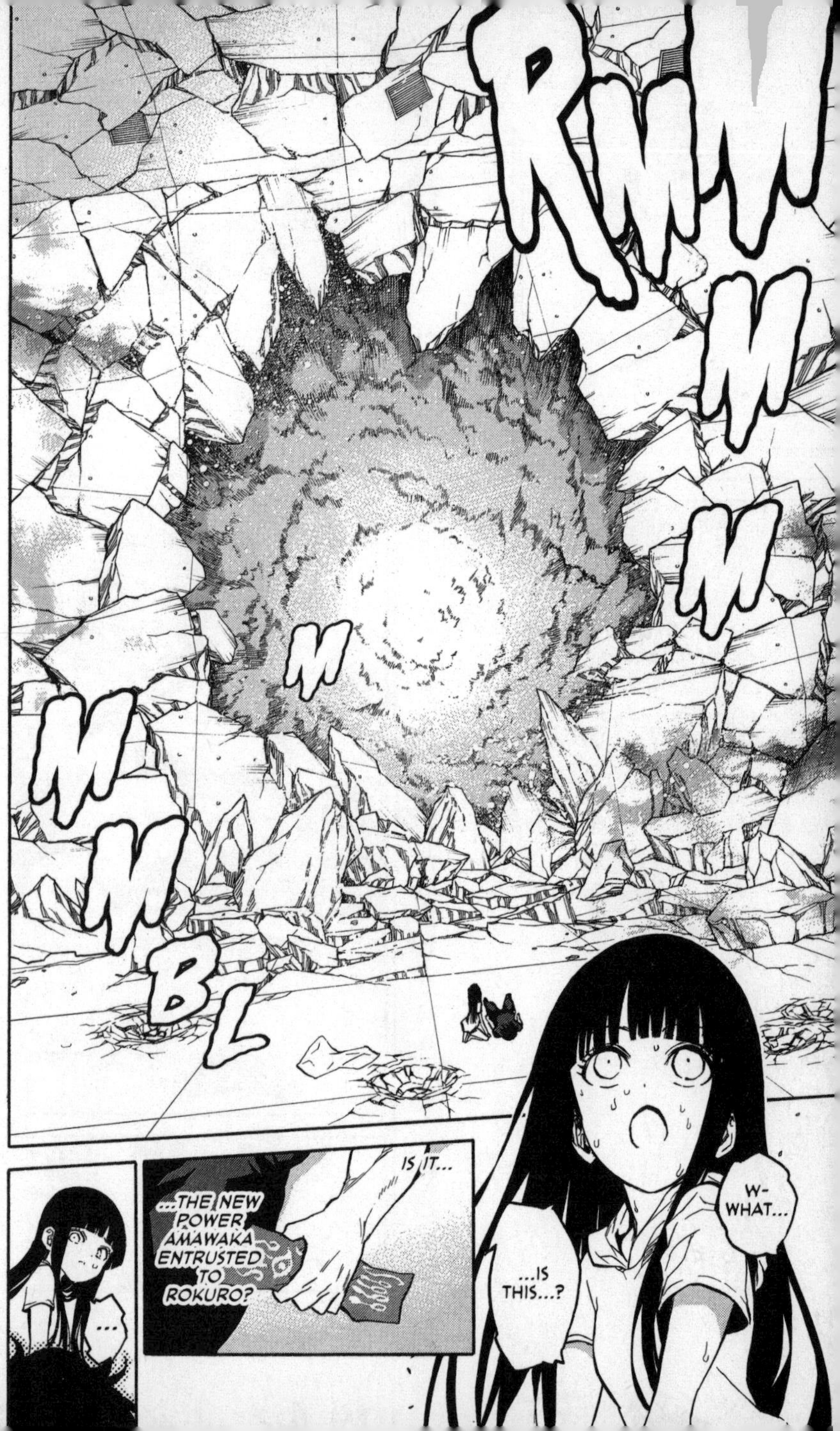
RMMMMMMMBL
W-WHAT...
...IS THIS...?
IS IT...
...THE NEW POWER AMAWAKA ENTRUSTED TO ROKURO?
...

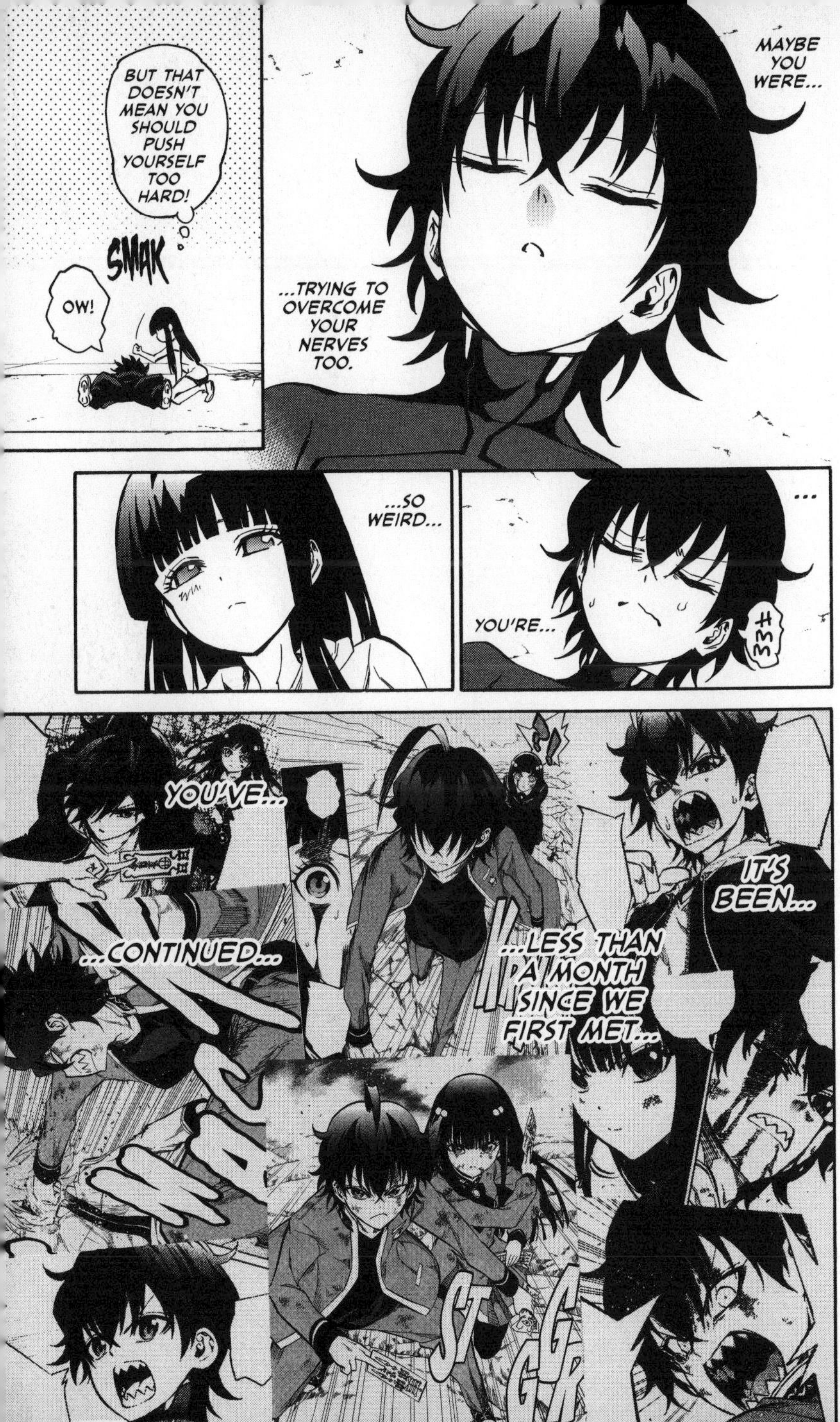
MAYBE YOU WERE...
...TRYING TO OVERCOME YOUR NERVES TOO.
BUT THAT DOESN'T MEAN YOU SHOULD PUSH YOURSELF TOO HARD!
SMAK
OW!
...
YOU'RE...
...SO WEIRD...
IT'S BEEN...
...LESS THAN A MONTH SINCE WE FIRST MET...
YOU'VE...
...CONTINUED...

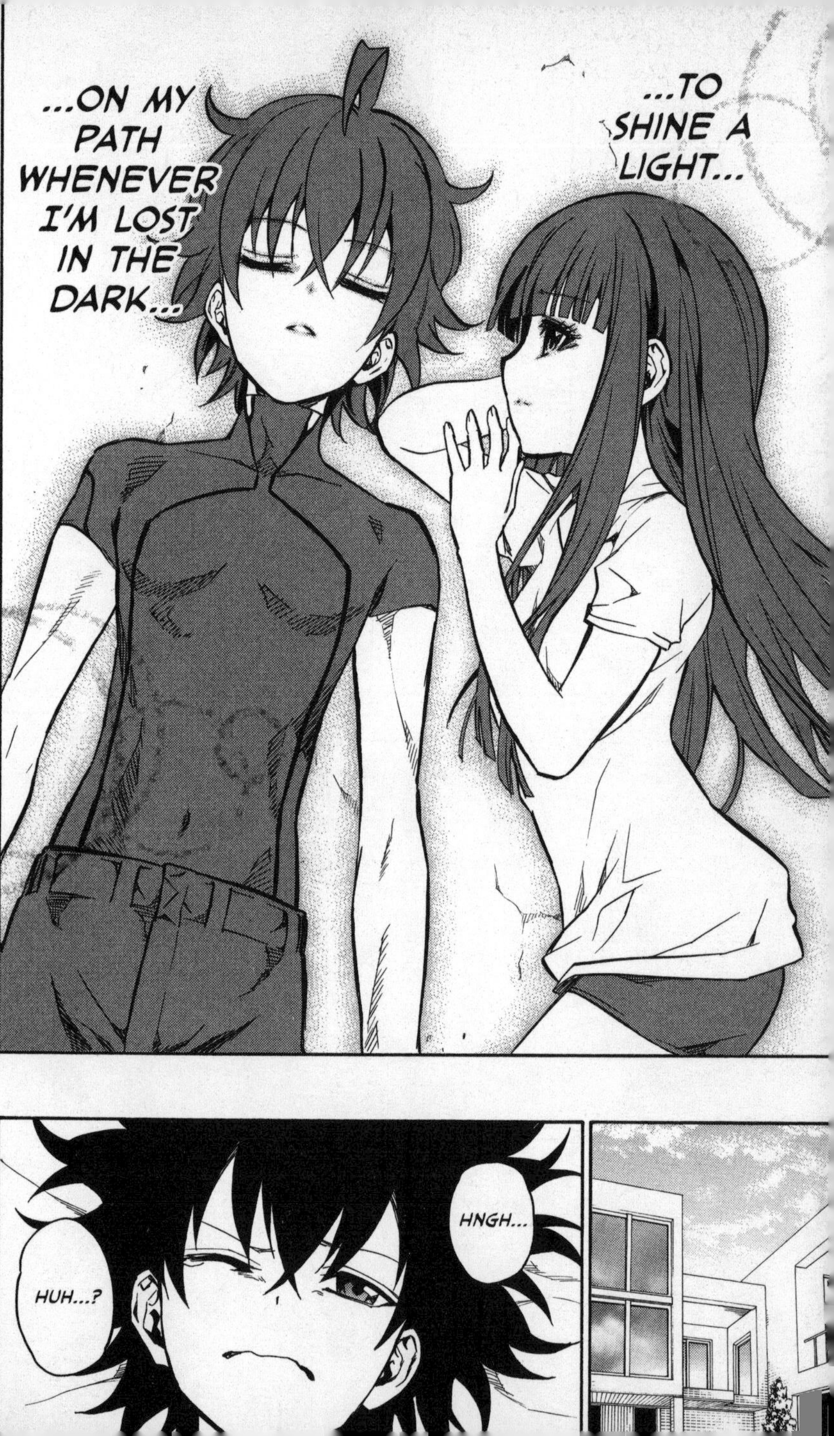
...TO SHINE A LIGHT...
...ON MY PATH WHENEVER I'M LOST IN THE DARK...
HNGH...
HUH...?

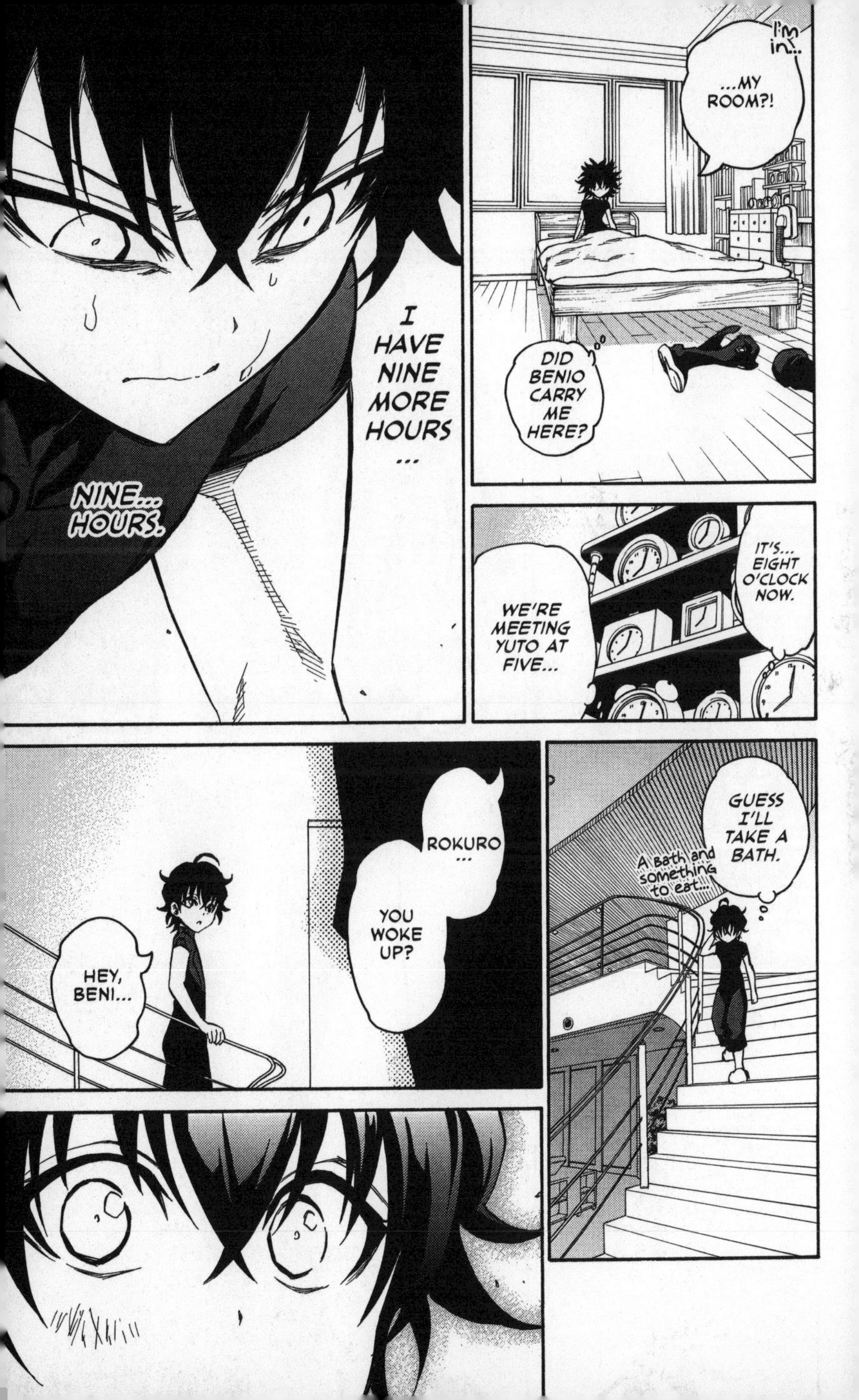
I'm in...
...MY ROOM?!
DID BENIO CARRY ME HERE?
IT'S... EIGHT O'CLOCK NOW.
WE'RE MEETING YUTO AT FIVE...
I HAVE NINE MORE HOURS...
NINE... HOURS.
GUESS I'LL TAKE A BATH.
A bath and something to eat...
ROKURO...
YOU WOKE UP?
HEY, BENI...

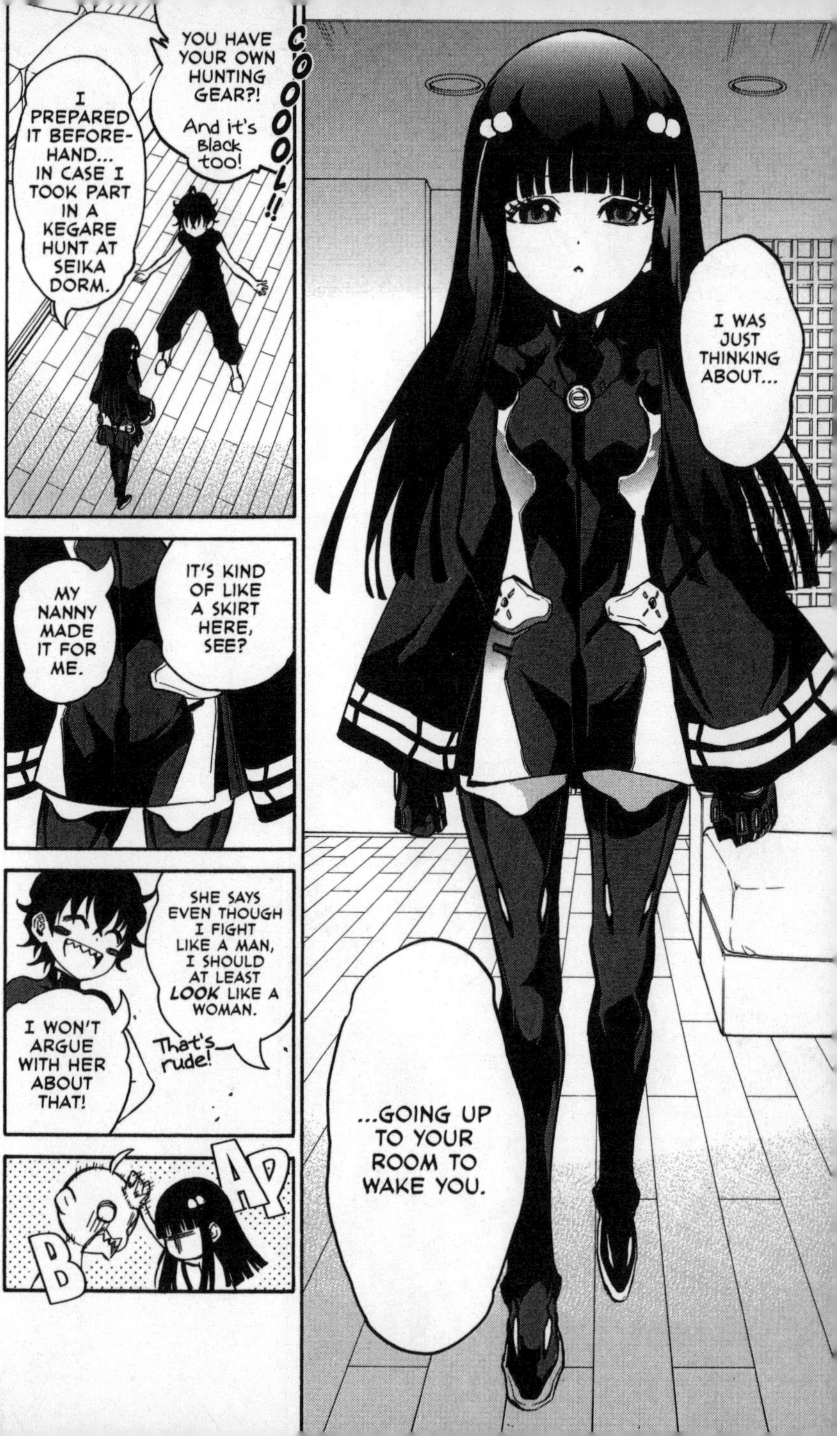

I WAS JUST THINKING ABOUT...
...GOING UP TO YOUR ROOM TO WAKE YOU.
COOOOOL!!
YOU HAVE YOUR OWN HUNTING GEAR?!
And it's black too!
I PREPARED IT BEFORE-HAND... IN CASE I TOOK PART IN A KEGARE HUNT AT SEIKA DORM.
IT'S KIND OF LIKE A SKIRT HERE, SEE?
MY NANNY MADE IT FOR ME.
SHE SAYS EVEN THOUGH I FIGHT LIKE A MAN, I SHOULD AT LEAST *LOOK* LIKE A WOMAN.
That's rude!
I WON'T ARGUE WITH HER ABOUT THAT!
BAP

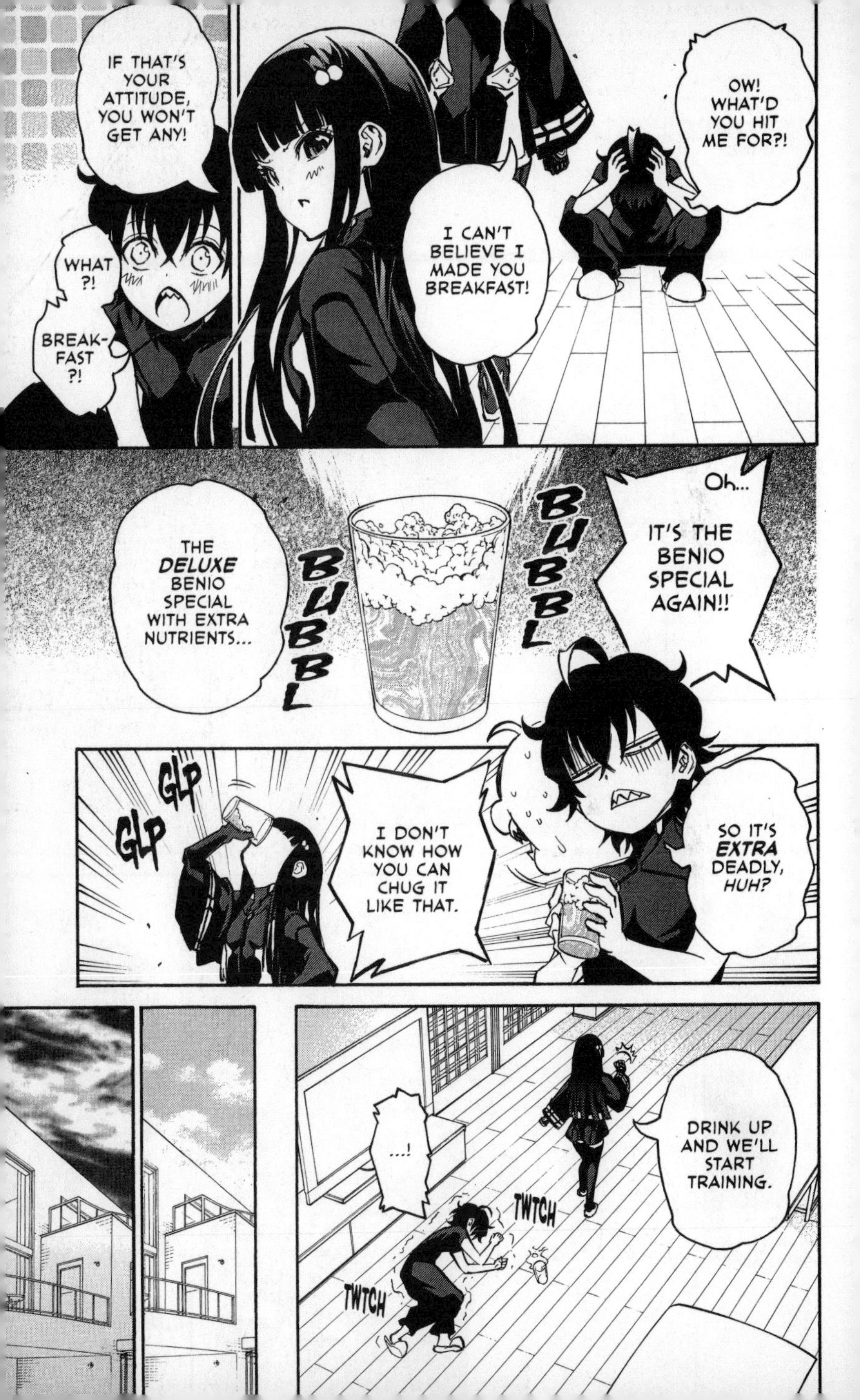
OW! WHAT'D YOU HIT ME FOR?!
I CAN'T BELIEVE I MADE YOU BREAKFAST!
IF THAT'S YOUR ATTITUDE, YOU WON'T GET ANY!
WHAT ?!
BREAK- FAST ?!
Oh...
IT'S THE BENIO SPECIAL AGAIN!!
BUBBL
BUBBL
THE *DELUXE* BENIO SPECIAL WITH EXTRA NUTRIENTS...
SO IT'S *EXTRA* DEADLY, *HUH?*
I DON'T KNOW HOW YOU CAN CHUG IT LIKE THAT.
GLP
GLP
DRINK UP AND WE'LL START TRAINING.
...!
TWTCH
TWTCH

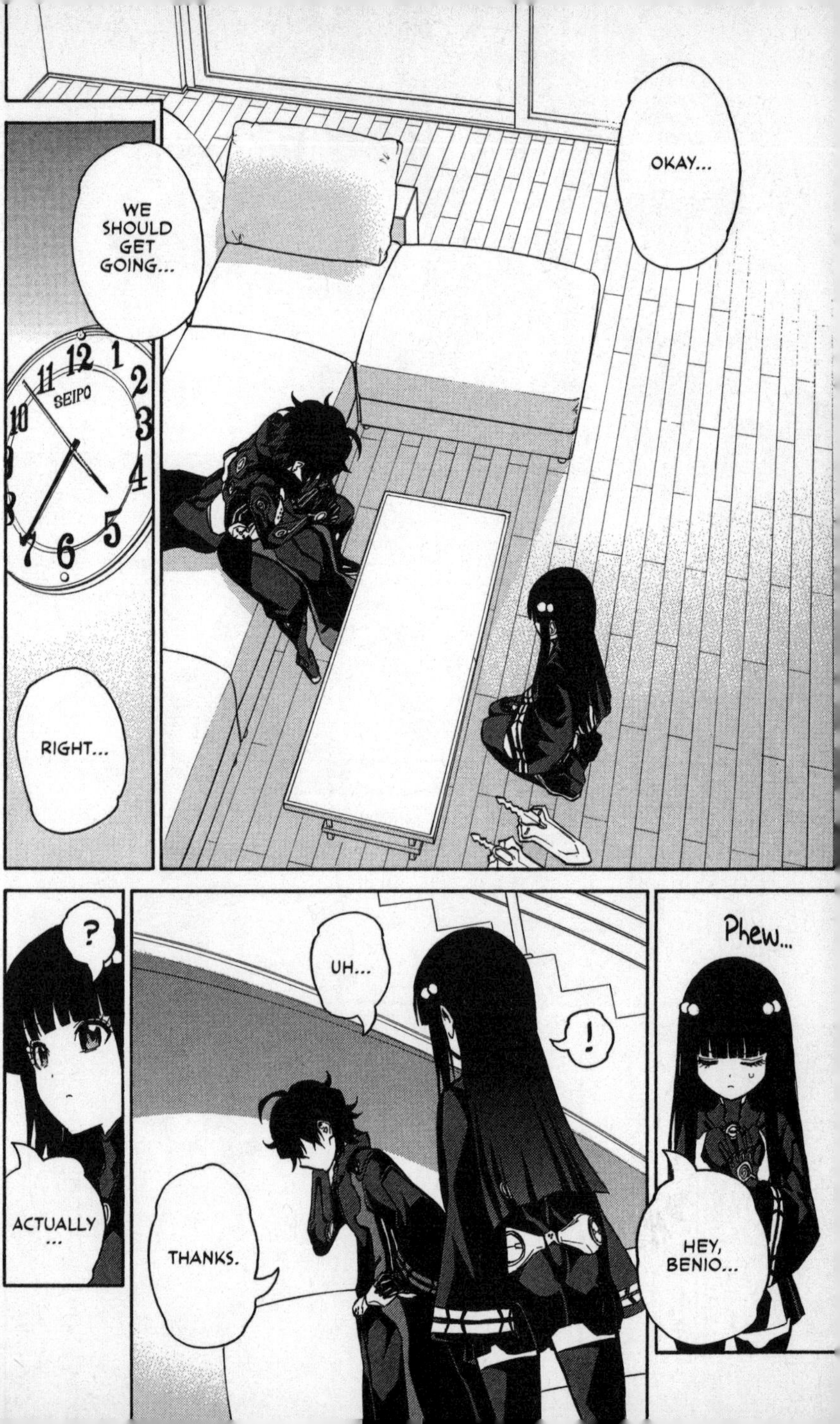
OKAY...
WE SHOULD GET GOING...
RIGHT...
SEIPO
Phew...
HEY, BENIO...
UH...
!
THANKS.
?
ACTUALLY...

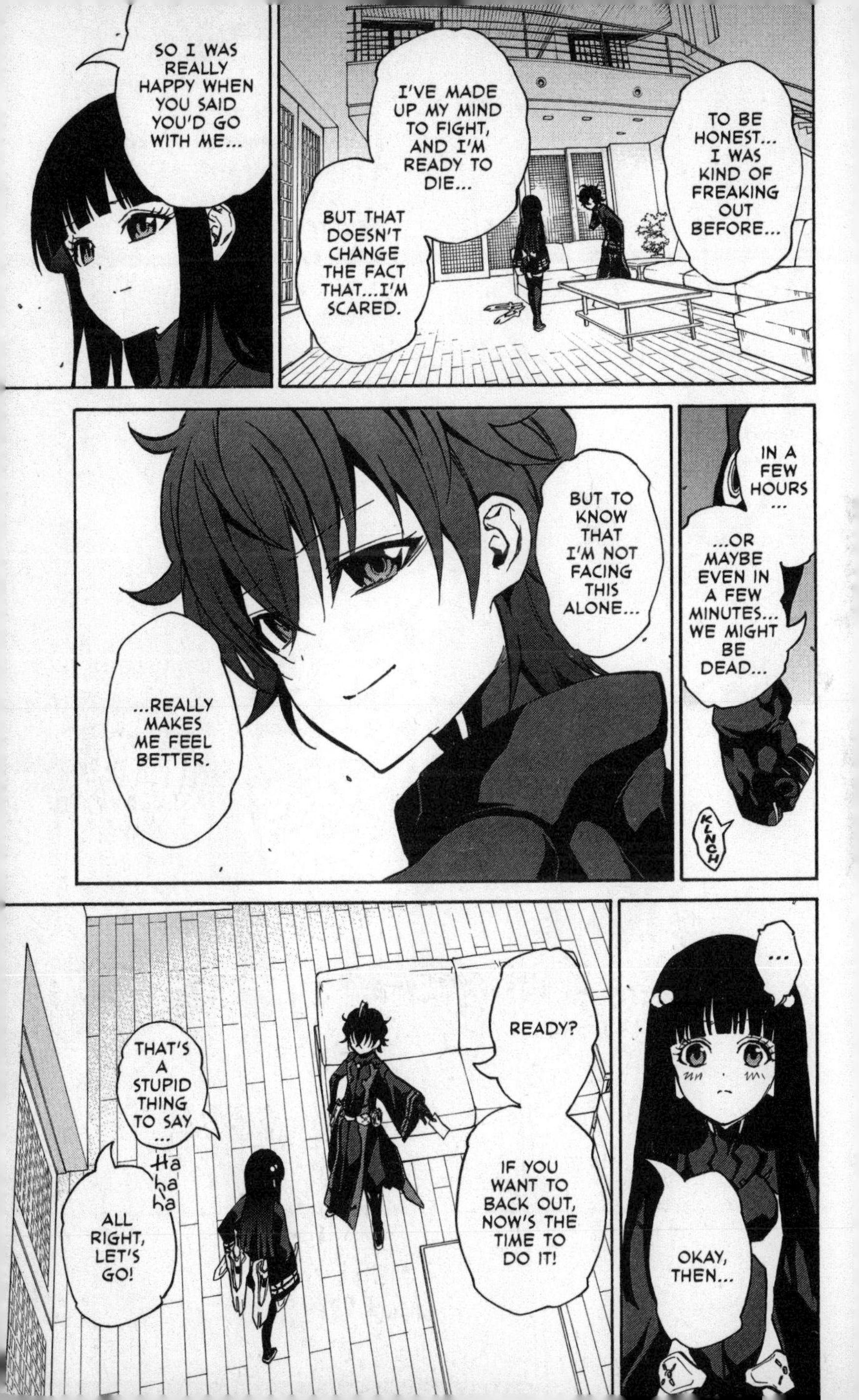
TO BE HONEST... I WAS KIND OF FREAKING OUT BEFORE...
I'VE MADE UP MY MIND TO FIGHT, AND I'M READY TO DIE...
BUT THAT DOESN'T CHANGE THE FACT THAT...I'M SCARED.
SO I WAS REALLY HAPPY WHEN YOU SAID YOU'D GO WITH ME...
IN A FEW HOURS ...
...OR MAYBE EVEN IN A FEW MINUTES... WE MIGHT BE DEAD...
KLNCH
BUT TO KNOW THAT I'M NOT FACING THIS ALONE...
...REALLY MAKES ME FEEL BETTER.
...
OKAY, THEN...
READY?
IF YOU WANT TO BACK OUT, NOW'S THE TIME TO DO IT!
THAT'S A STUPID THING TO SAY ...
Ha ha ha
ALL RIGHT, LET'S GO!

I humbly and respect-fully...
...beg your forgiveness... Please grant my humble request...
...to enter through the gates of the gods!
喼急如律令
LET'S END THIS... YUTO!
THIS WILL BE THE MAIDEN BATTLE OF...
Open the gates of Ma-gano.
Kyu-kyu-nyo-ritsu-ryo!
...THE TWIN-STAR EXORCISTS!

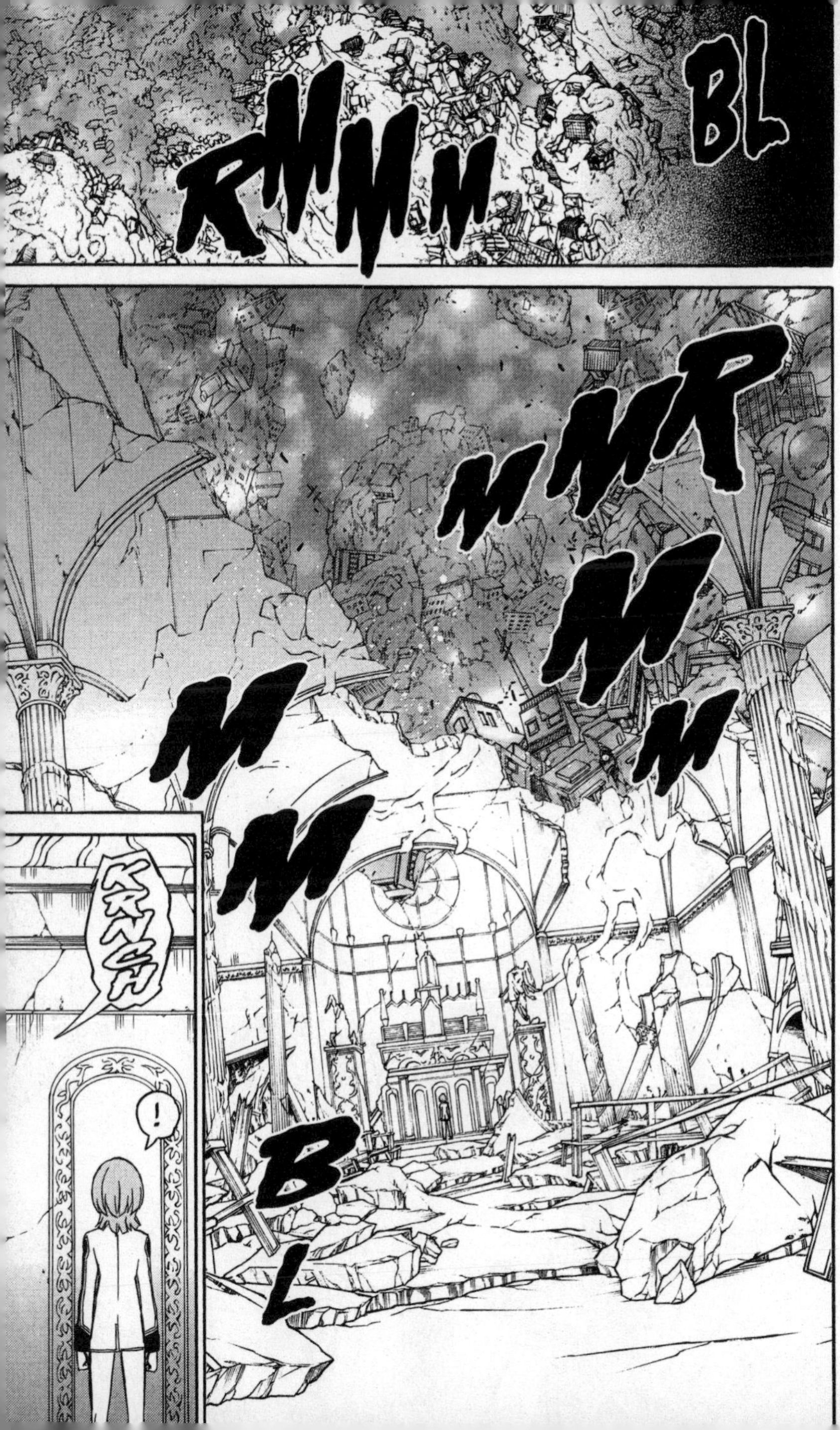
BL
RMMMM
MMMR
MMM
MM
MM
BL
KRNCH
!

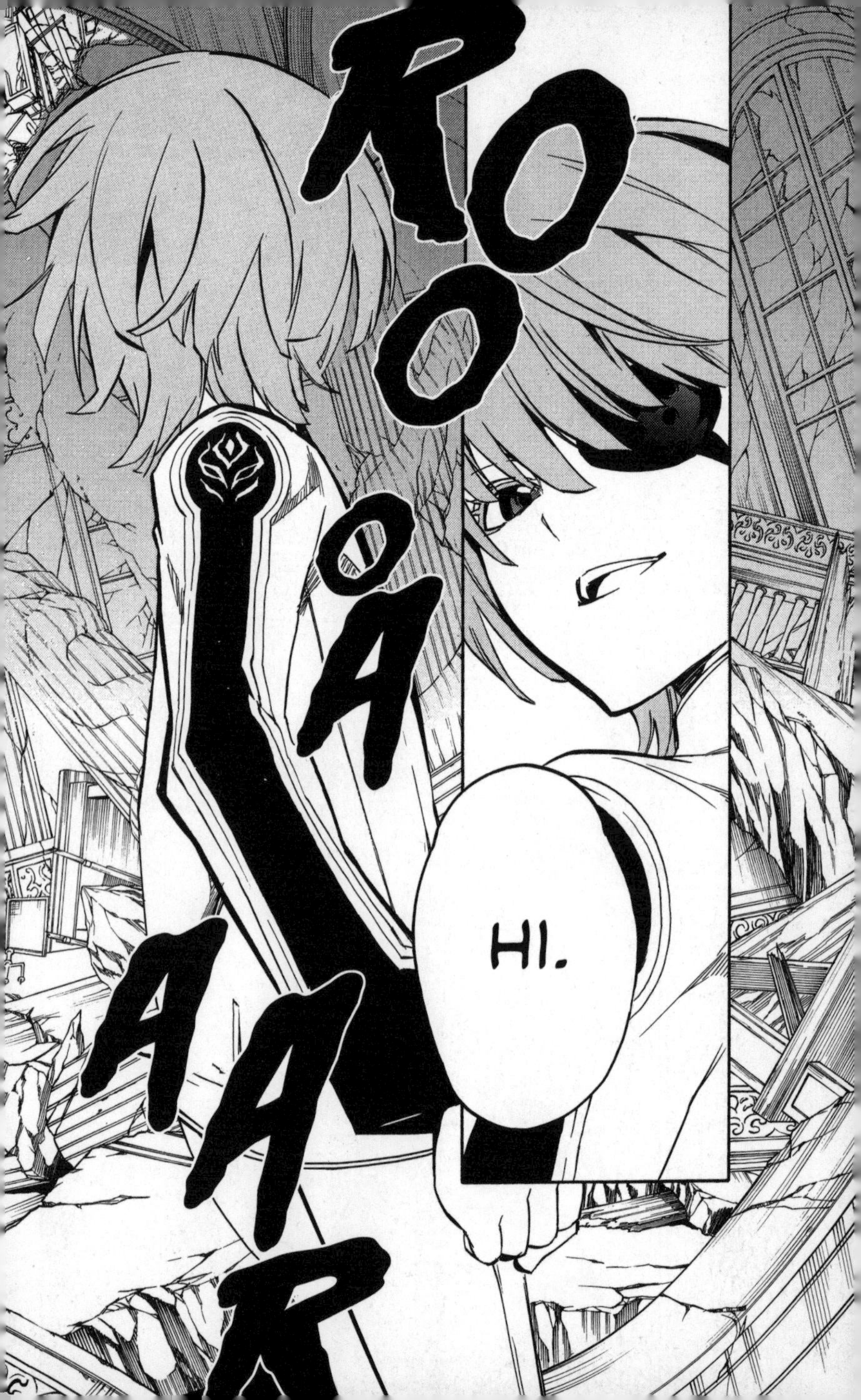
ROOOAAAR
HI.

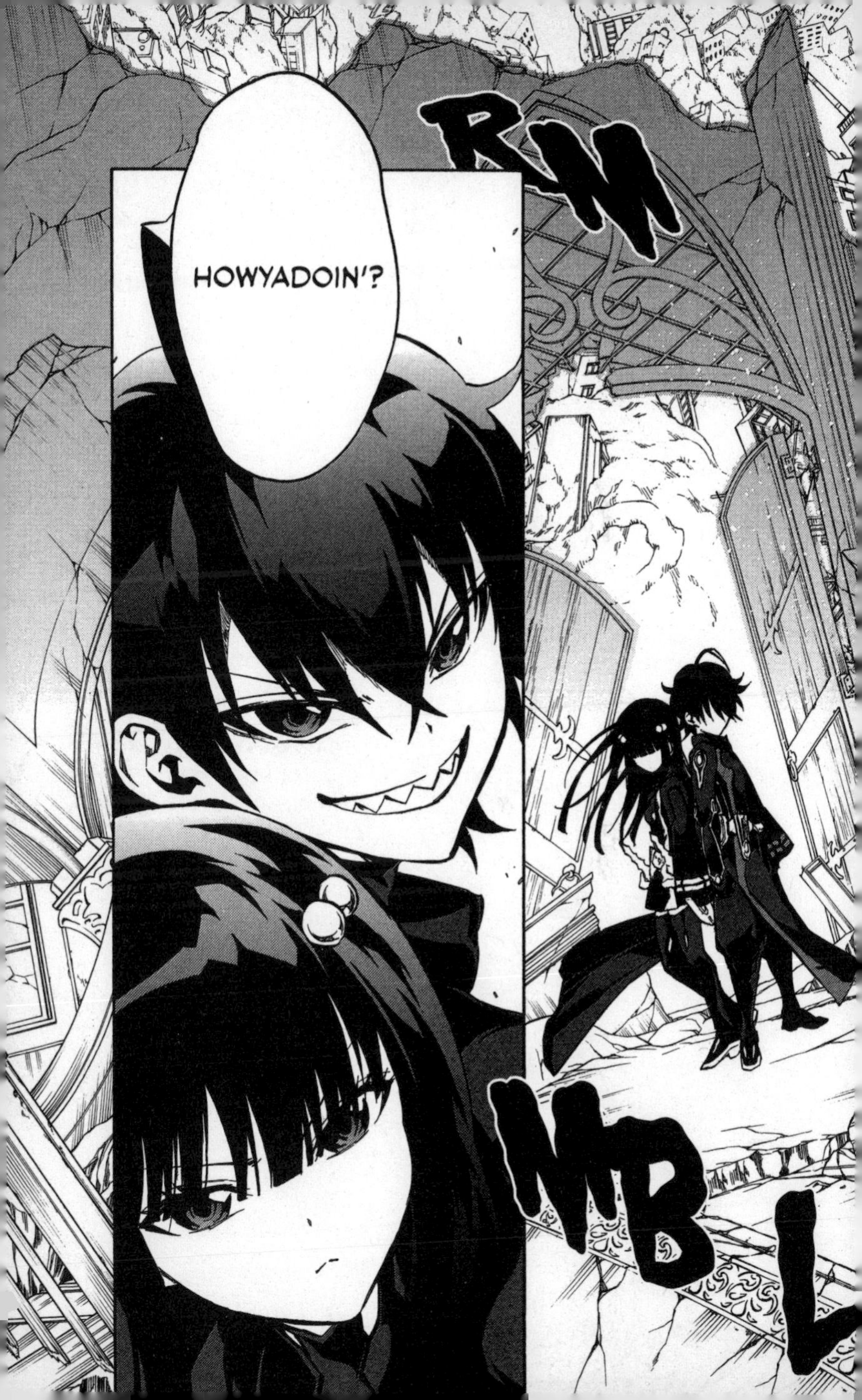
RM
HOWYADOIN'?
MB
L

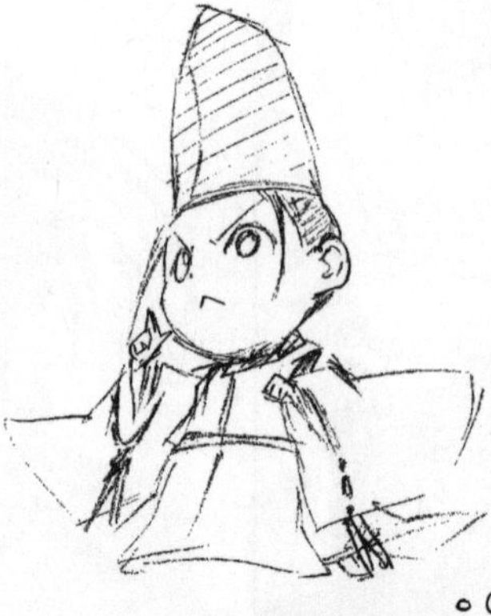

Column 9: Hunting Gear

This was the everyday wear of the Heian era nobles, worn when they went out to hunt or play. But there are no existing documents left from the time of Abeno Seimei, and all the images of Seimei were created afterwards. So these are basically clothes that are thought to have been worn by people back then.

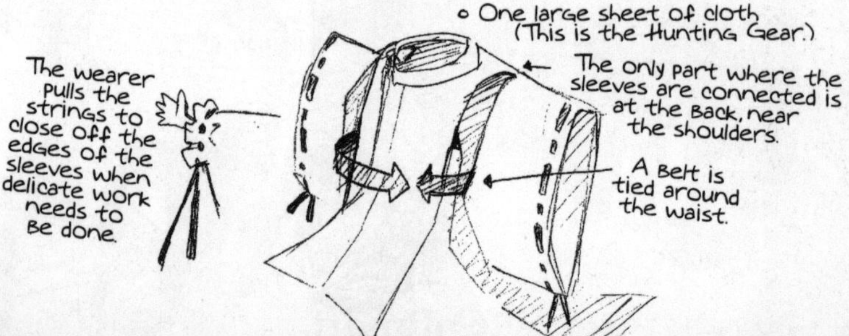

○ One large sheet of cloth (This is the Hunting Gear.)
The wearer pulls the strings to close off the edges of the sleeves when delicate work needs to be done.
The only part where the sleeves are connected is at the back, near the shoulders.
A belt is tied around the waist.

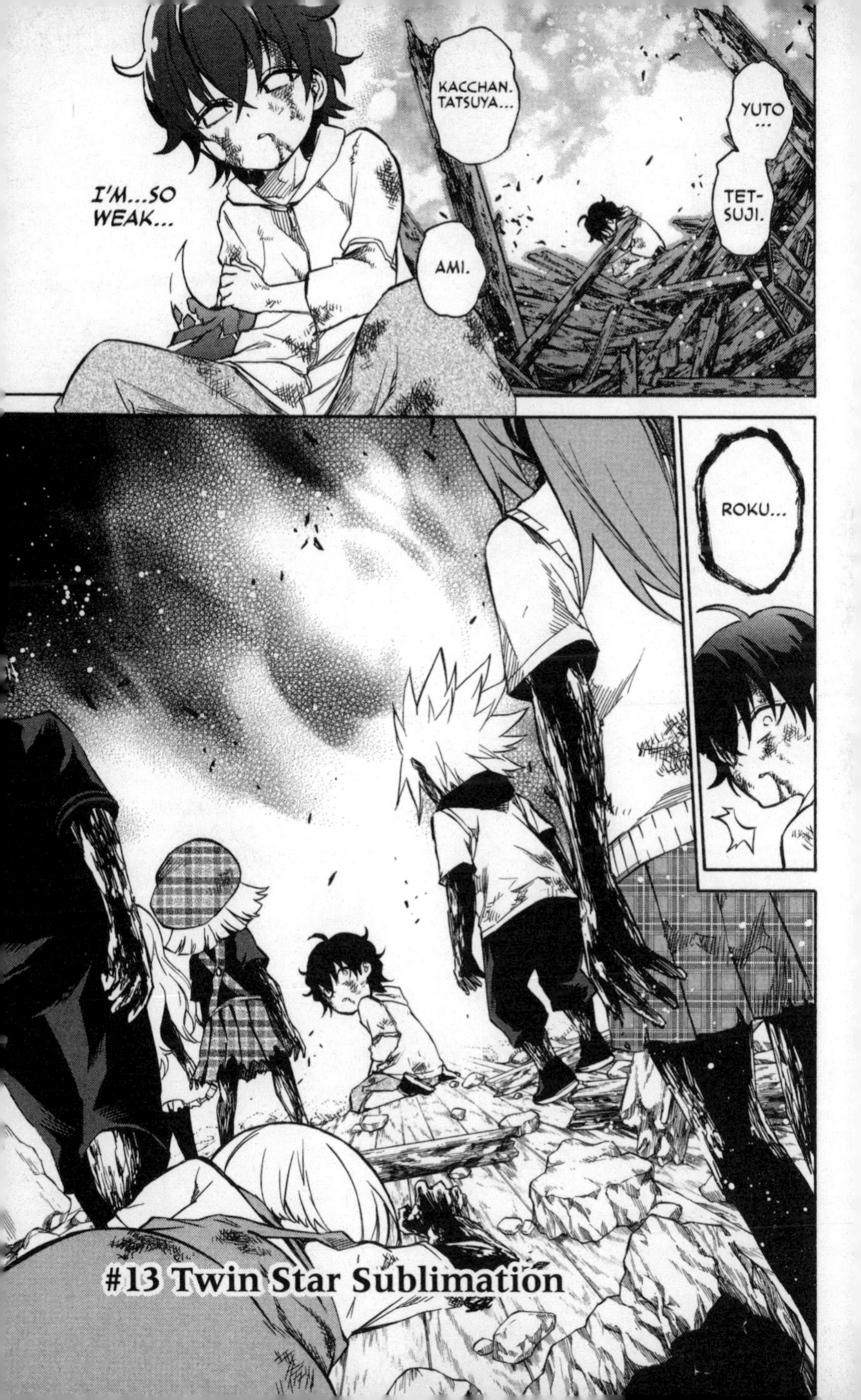
KACCHAN. TATSUYA...
YUTO...
TET-SUJI.
AMI.
I'M...SO WEAK...
ROKU...
#13 Twin Star Sublimation

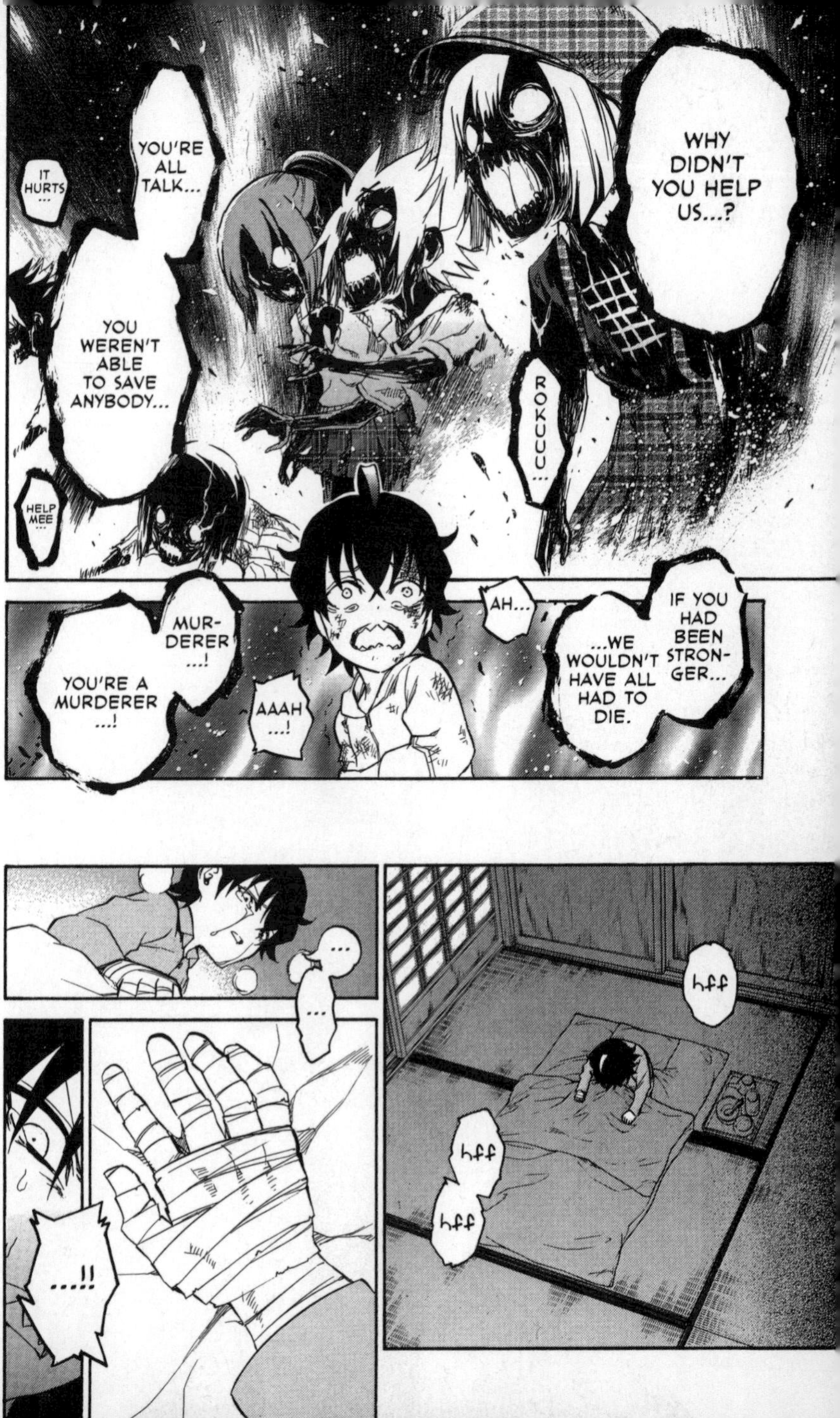
WHY DIDN'T YOU HELP US...?
ROKUUU...
YOU'RE ALL TALK...
IT HURTS...
YOU WEREN'T ABLE TO SAVE ANYBODY...
HELP MEE...
IF YOU HAD BEEN STRONGER...
...WE WOULDN'T HAVE ALL HAD TO DIE.
AH...
MURDERER...!
YOU'RE A MURDERER...!
AAAH...!
hff
hff
hff
...
...
...!!

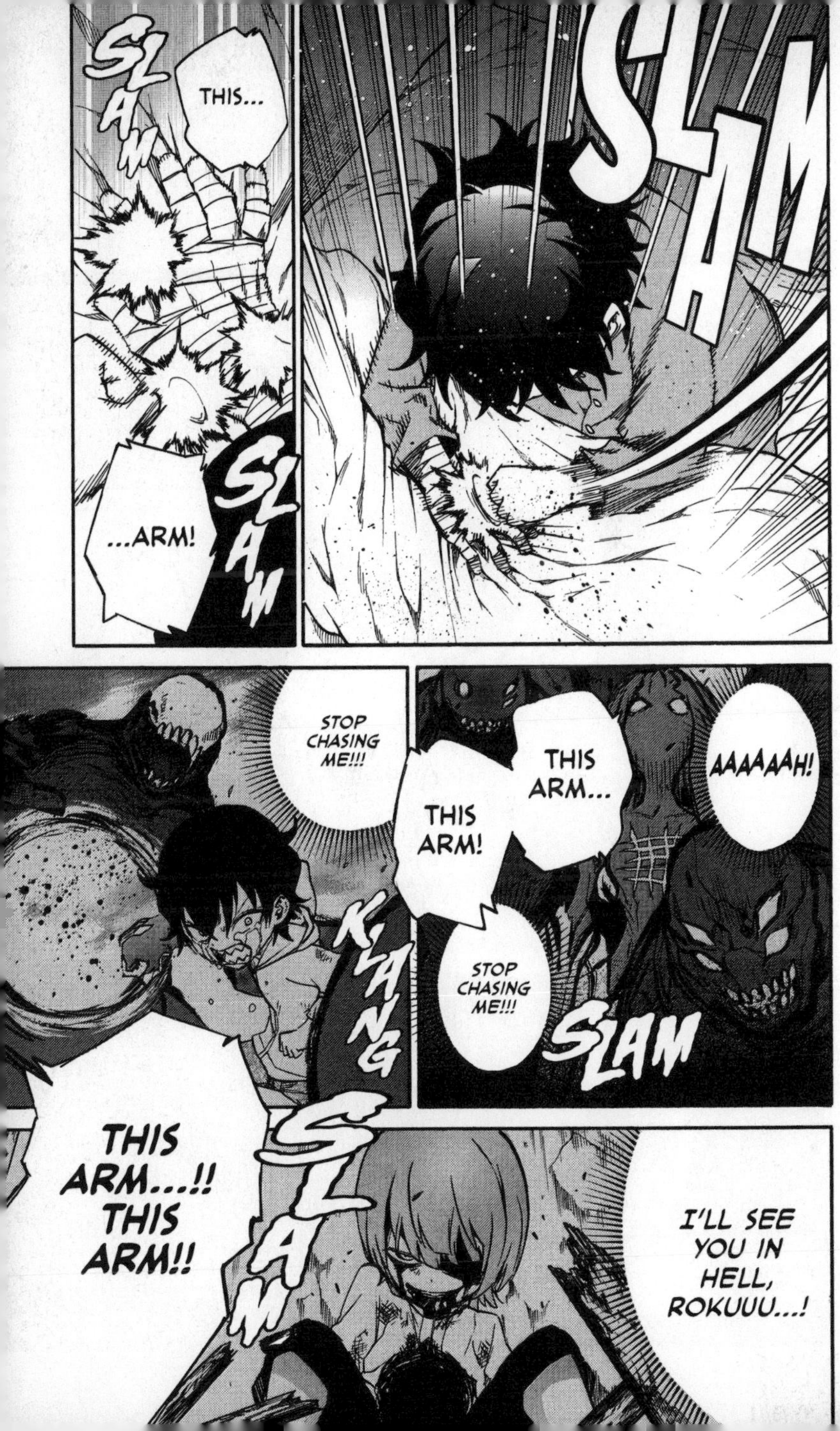
SLAM
SLAM
THIS...
...ARM!
SLAM
AAAAAAH!
THIS ARM...
THIS ARM!
STOP CHASING ME!!!
SLAM
STOP CHASING ME!!!
KLANG
I'LL SEE YOU IN HELL, ROKUUU...!
THIS ARM...!! THIS ARM!!
SLAM

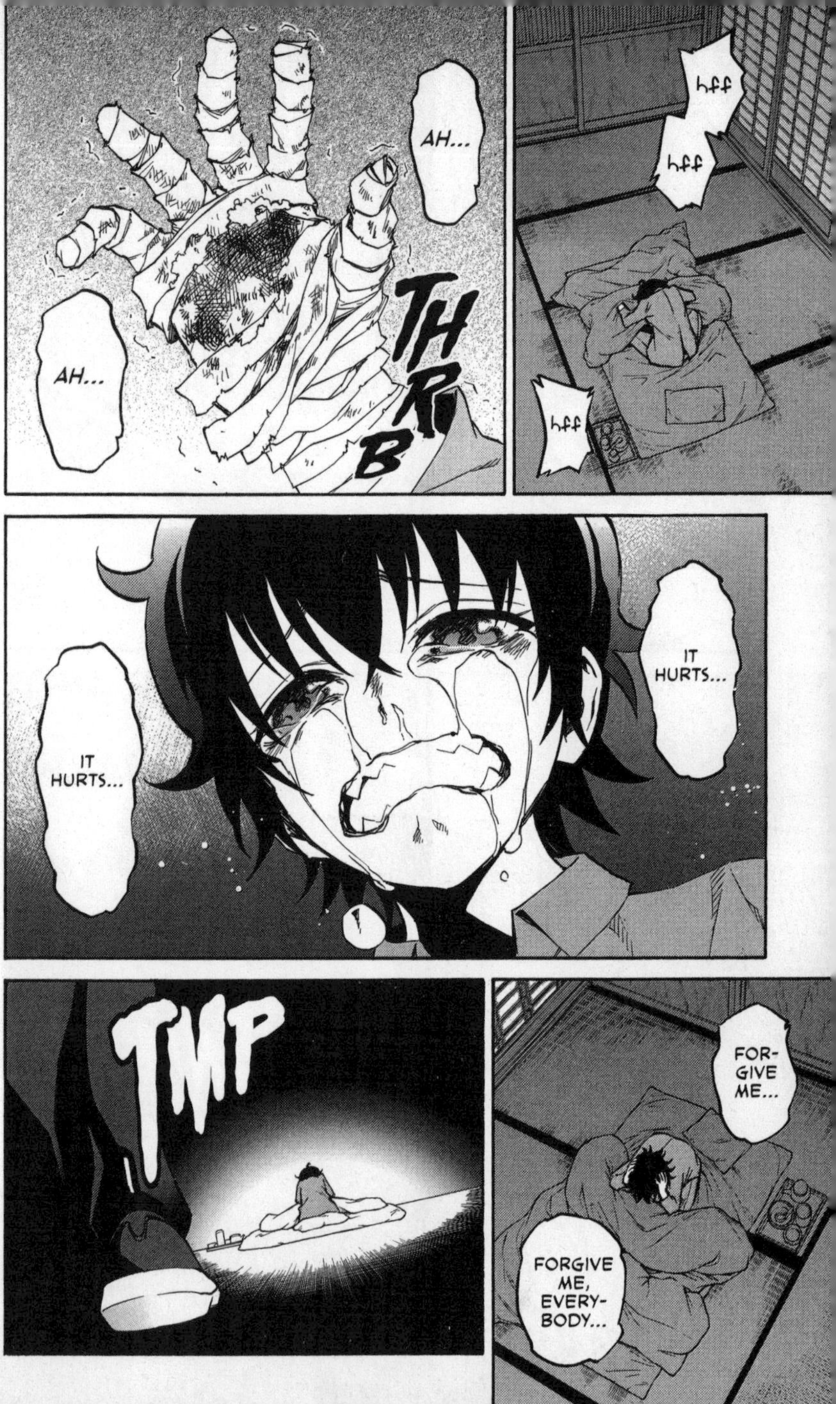
hff
hff
hff
AH...
THRB
AH...
IT HURTS...
IT HURTS...
FOR-GIVE ME...
FORGIVE ME, EVERY-BODY...
TMP

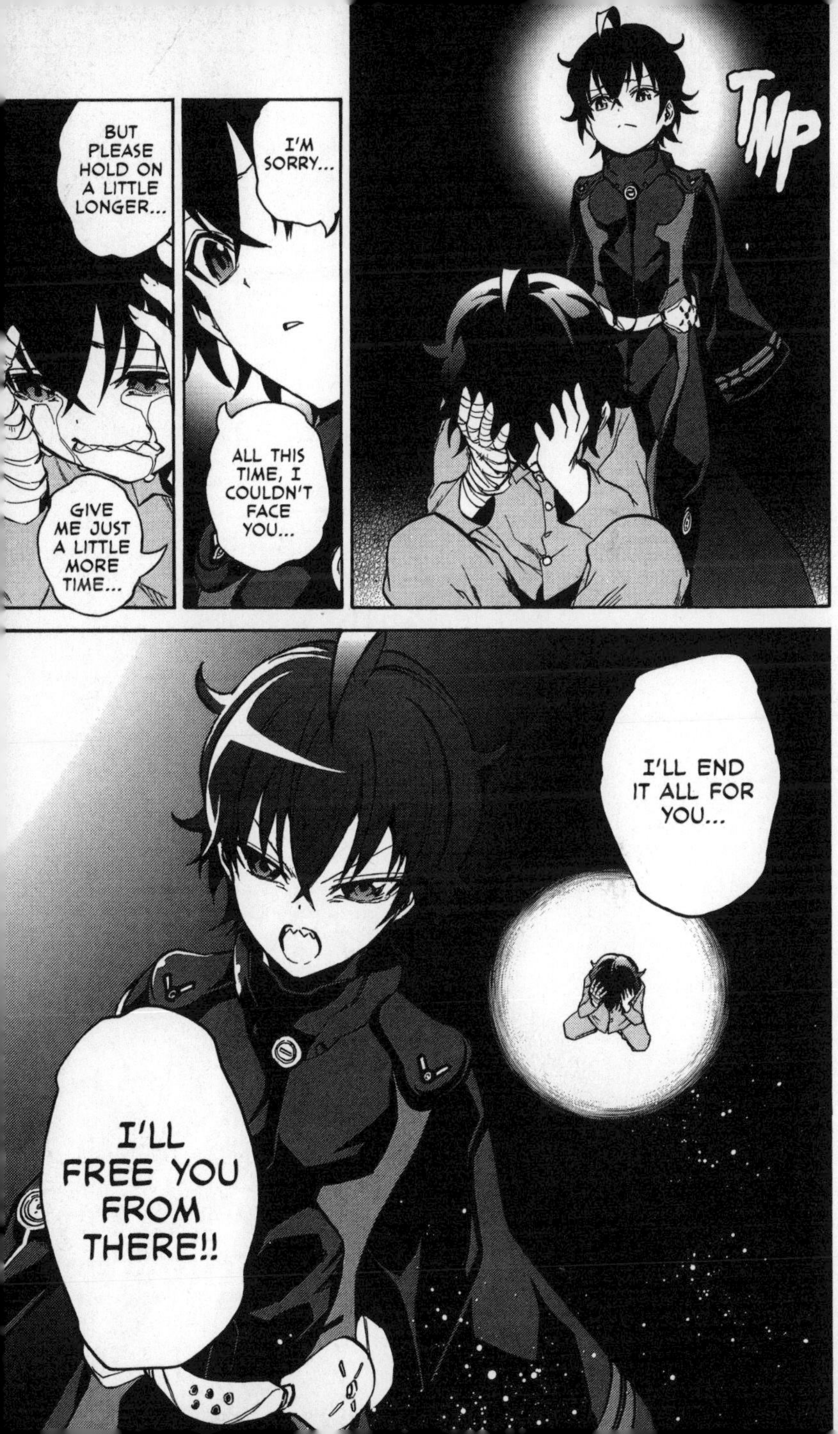
TMP
I'M SORRY...
ALL THIS TIME, I COULDN'T FACE YOU...
BUT PLEASE HOLD ON A LITTLE LONGER...
GIVE ME JUST A LITTLE MORE TIME...
I'LL END IT ALL FOR YOU...
I'LL FREE YOU FROM THERE!!

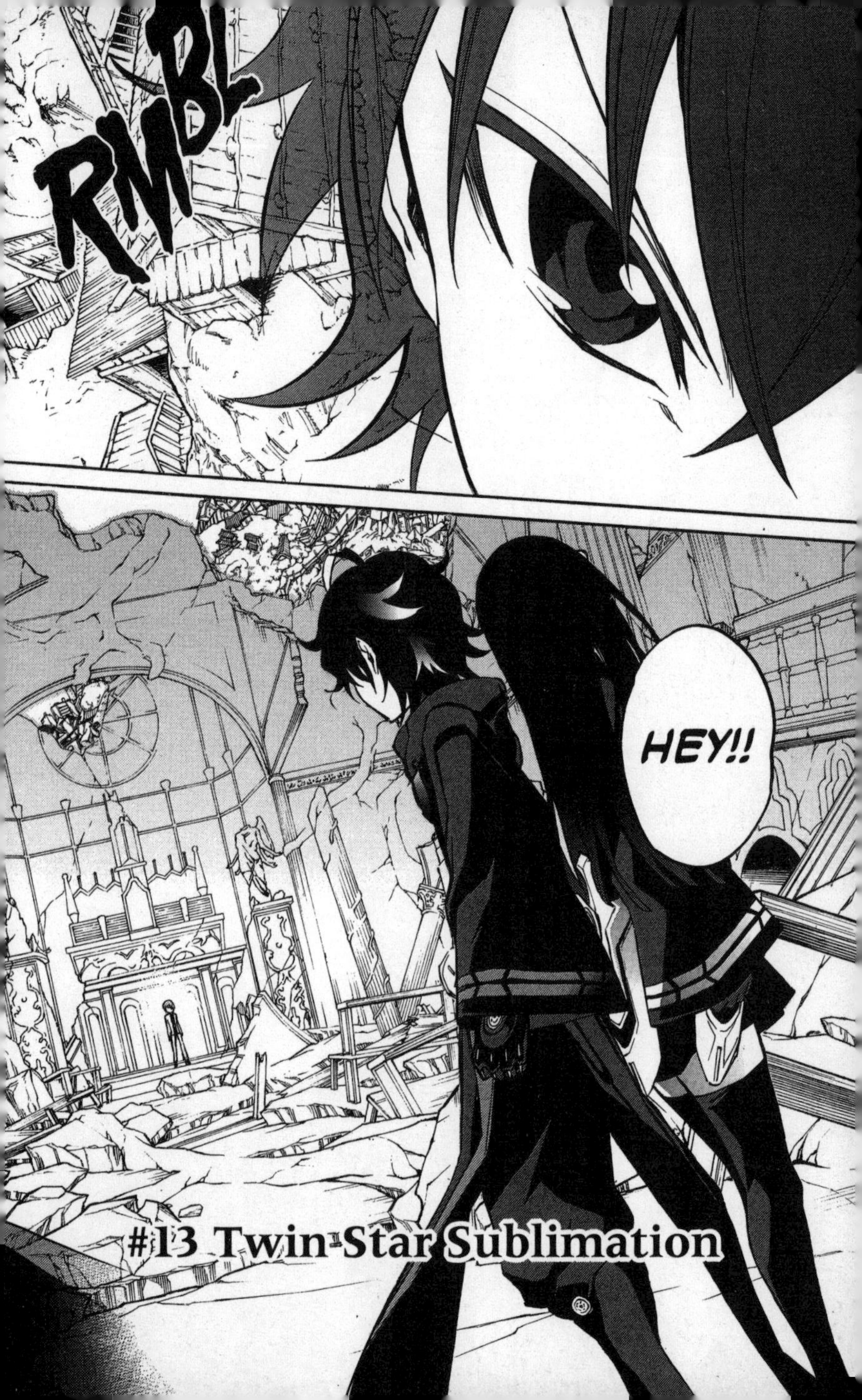
RMBL
HEY!!
#13 Twin-Star Sublimation

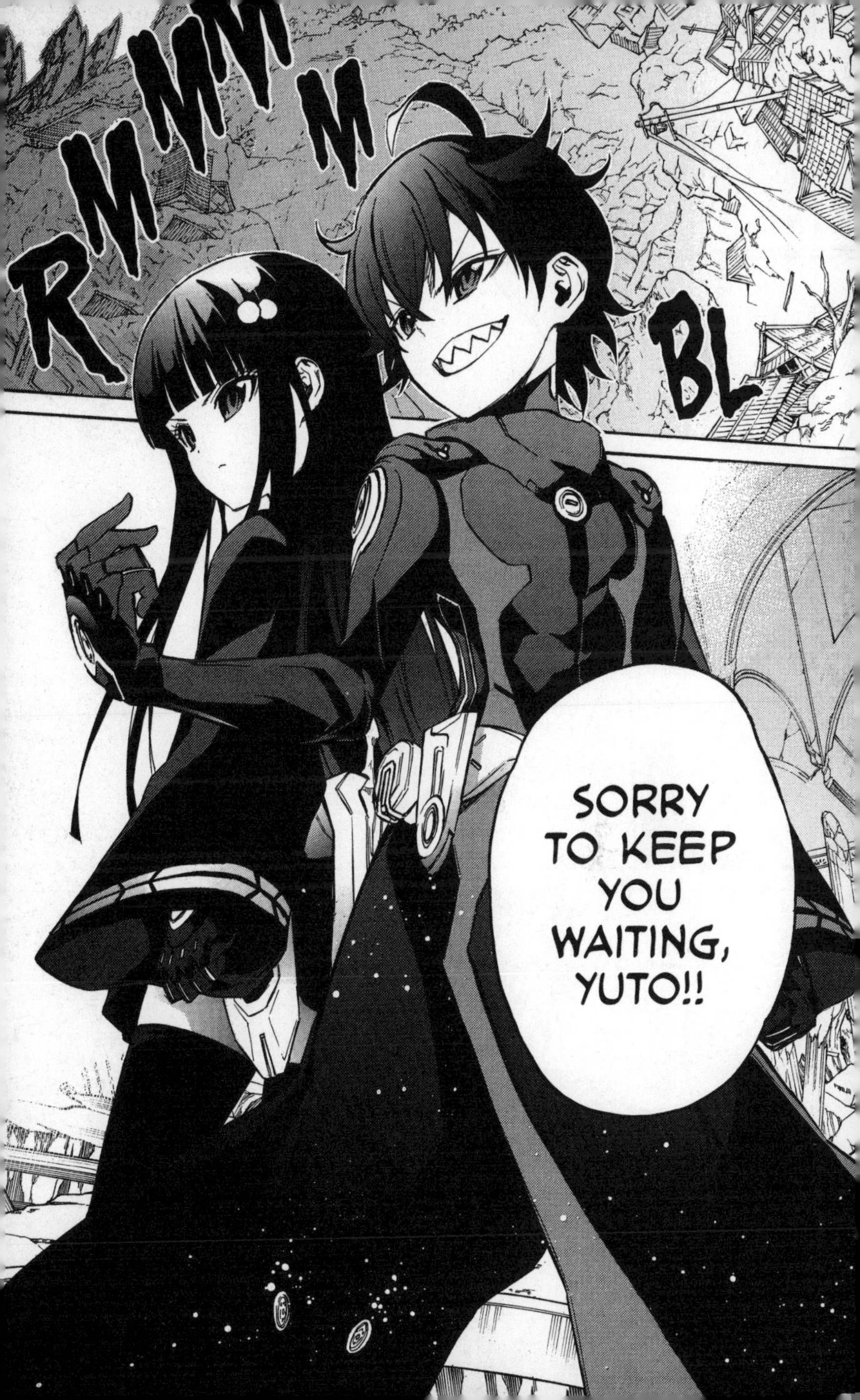
RMMMM
BL
SORRY TO KEEP YOU WAITING, YUTO!!

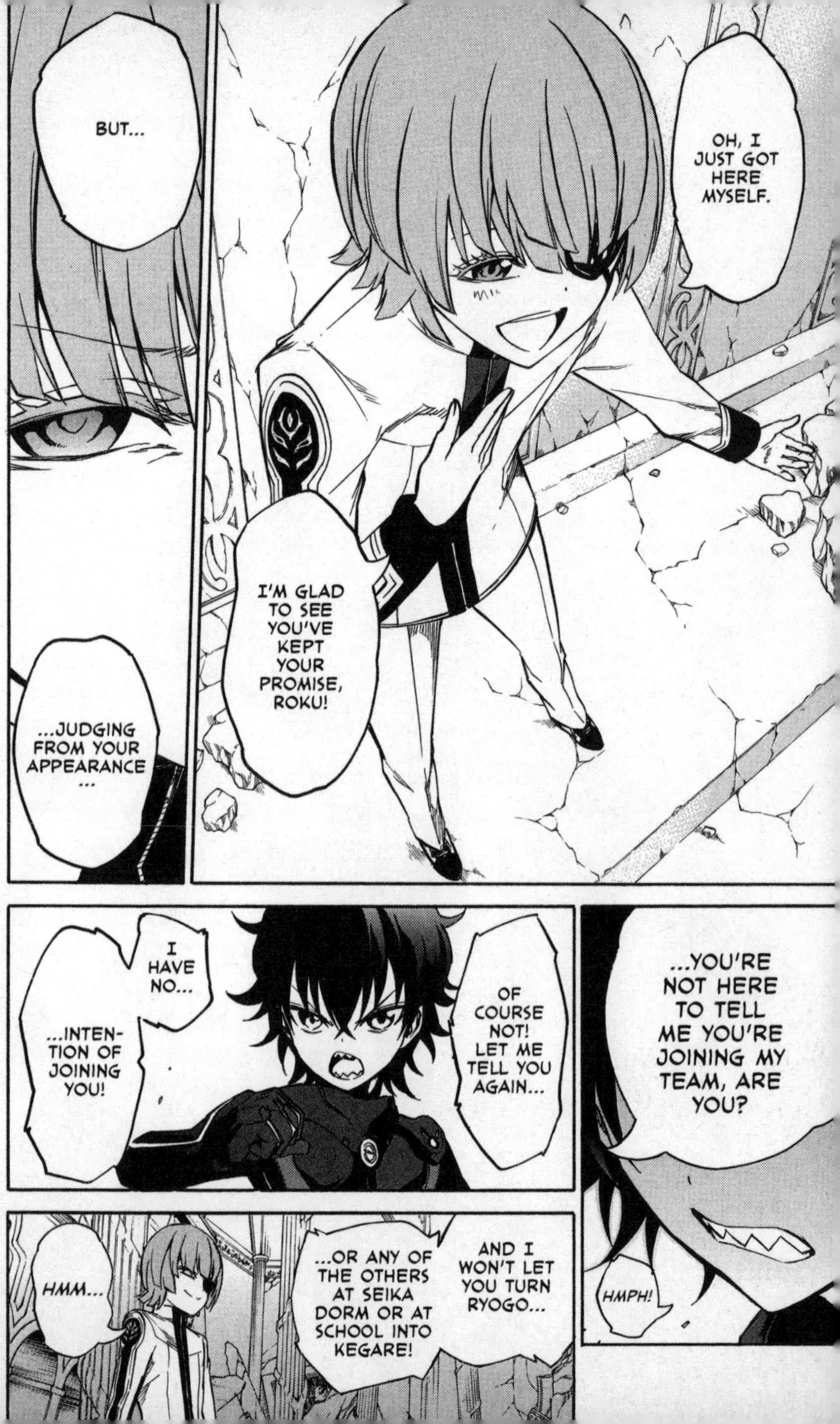
OH, I JUST GOT HERE MYSELF.
I'M GLAD TO SEE YOU'VE KEPT YOUR PROMISE, ROKU!
BUT...
...JUDGING FROM YOUR APPEARANCE ...
...YOU'RE NOT HERE TO TELL ME YOU'RE JOINING MY TEAM, ARE YOU?
HMPH!
OF COURSE NOT! LET ME TELL YOU AGAIN...
I HAVE NO...
...INTEN-TION OF JOINING YOU!
AND I WON'T LET YOU TURN RYOGO...
...OR ANY OF THE OTHERS AT SEIKA DORM OR AT SCHOOL INTO KEGARE!
HMM...

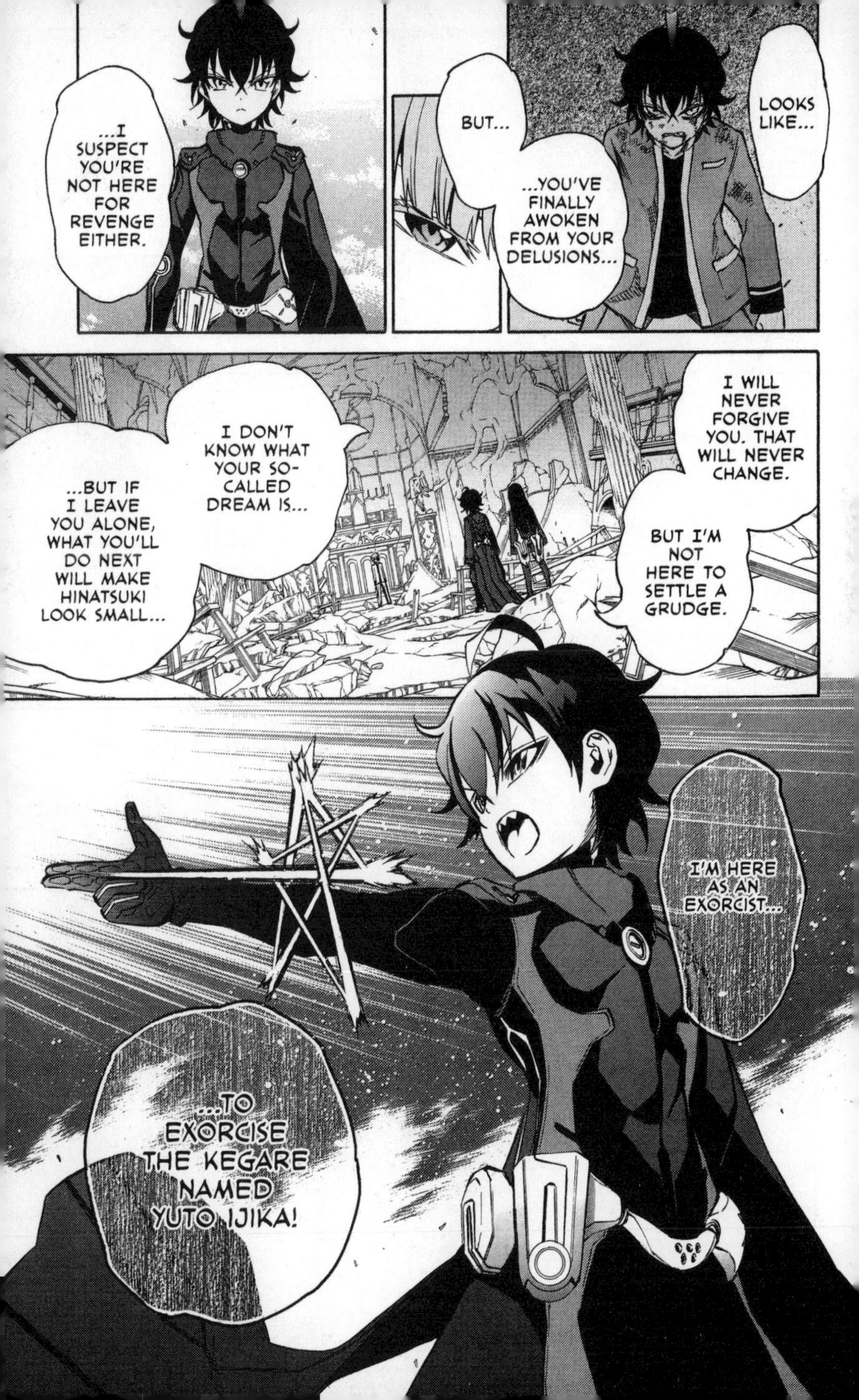
LOOKS LIKE...
BUT...
...YOU'VE FINALLY AWOKEN FROM YOUR DELUSIONS...
...I SUSPECT YOU'RE NOT HERE FOR REVENGE EITHER.
I WILL NEVER FORGIVE YOU. THAT WILL NEVER CHANGE.
BUT I'M NOT HERE TO SETTLE A GRUDGE.
I DON'T KNOW WHAT YOUR SO-CALLED DREAM IS...
...BUT IF I LEAVE YOU ALONE, WHAT YOU'LL DO NEXT WILL MAKE HINATSUKI LOOK SMALL...
I'M HERE AS AN EXORCIST...
...TO EXORCISE THE KEGARE NAMED YUTO IJIKA!

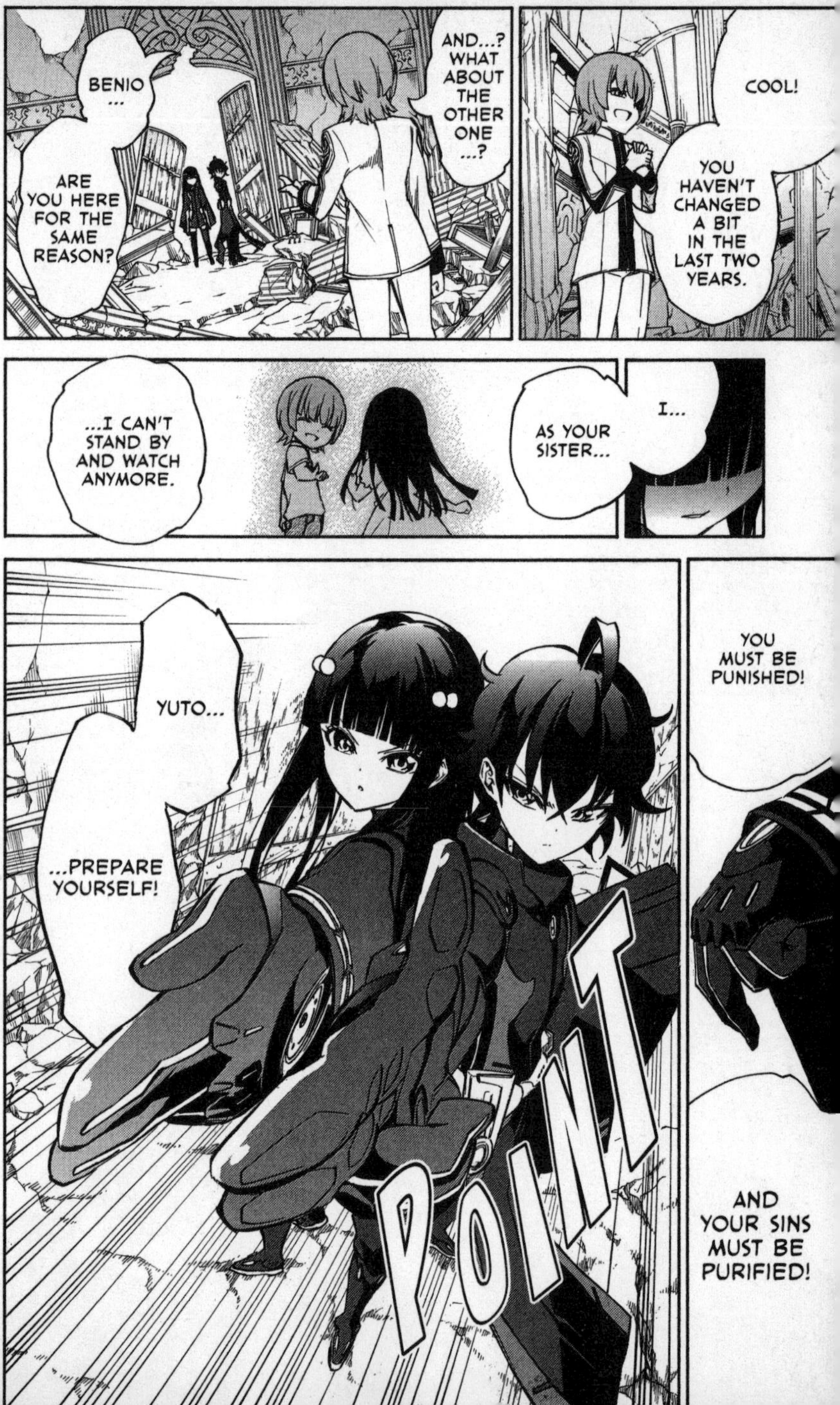
COOL!
YOU HAVEN'T CHANGED A BIT IN THE LAST TWO YEARS.
AND...? WHAT ABOUT THE OTHER ONE ...?
BENIO ...
ARE YOU HERE FOR THE SAME REASON?
I...
AS YOUR SISTER...
...I CAN'T STAND BY AND WATCH ANYMORE.
YOU MUST BE PUNISHED!
AND YOUR SINS MUST BE PURIFIED!
YUTO...
...PREPARE YOURSELF!
POINT

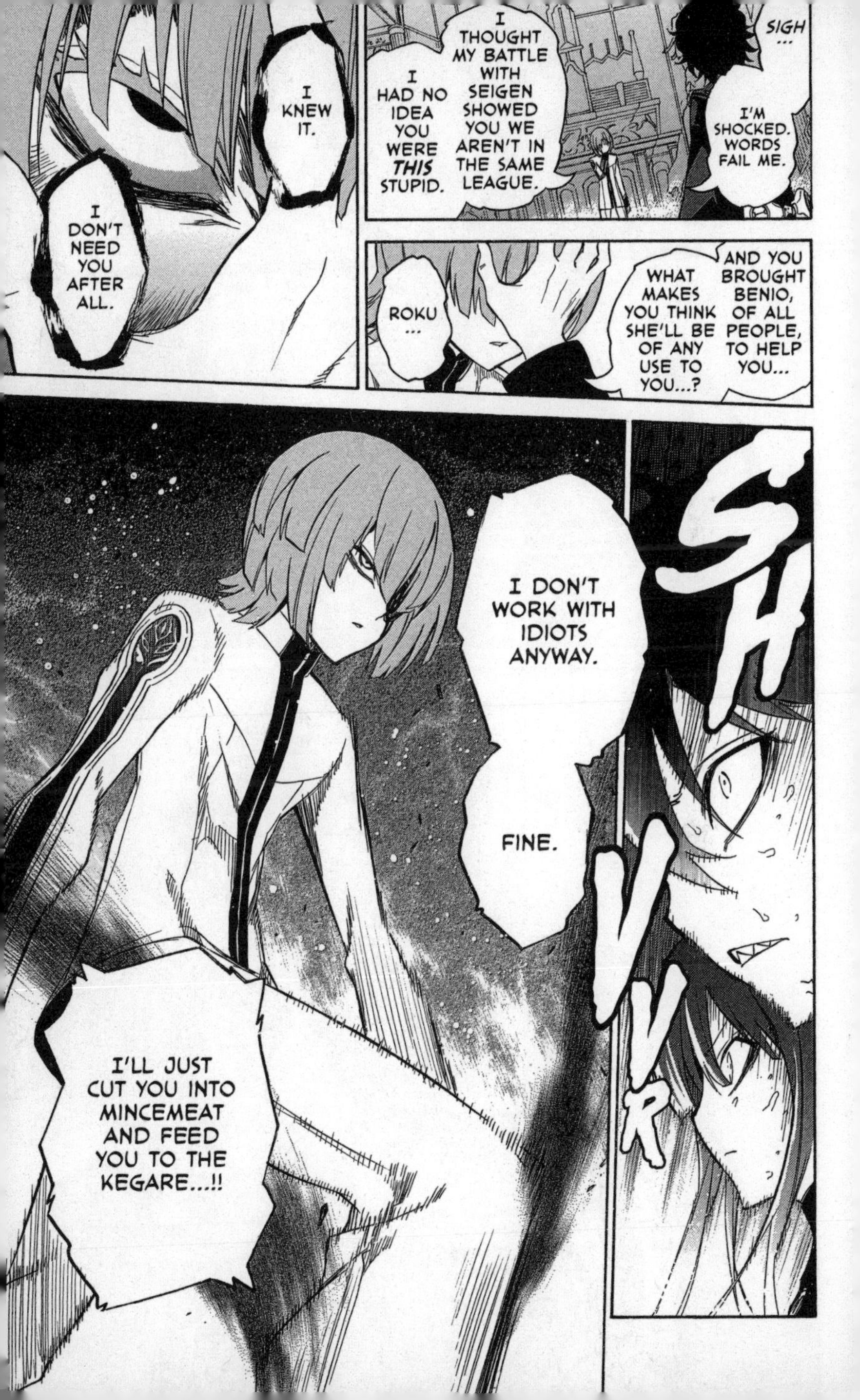
SIGH...
I'M SHOCKED. WORDS FAIL ME.
I THOUGHT MY BATTLE WITH SEIGEN SHOWED YOU WE AREN'T IN THE SAME LEAGUE.
I HAD NO IDEA YOU WERE *THIS* STUPID.
AND YOU BROUGHT BENIO, OF ALL PEOPLE, TO HELP YOU...
WHAT MAKES YOU THINK SHE'LL BE OF ANY USE TO YOU...?
ROKU...
I KNEW IT.
I DON'T NEED YOU AFTER ALL.
SHVVR
I DON'T WORK WITH IDIOTS ANYWAY.
FINE.
I'LL JUST CUT YOU INTO MINCEMEAT AND FEED YOU TO THE KEGARE...!!

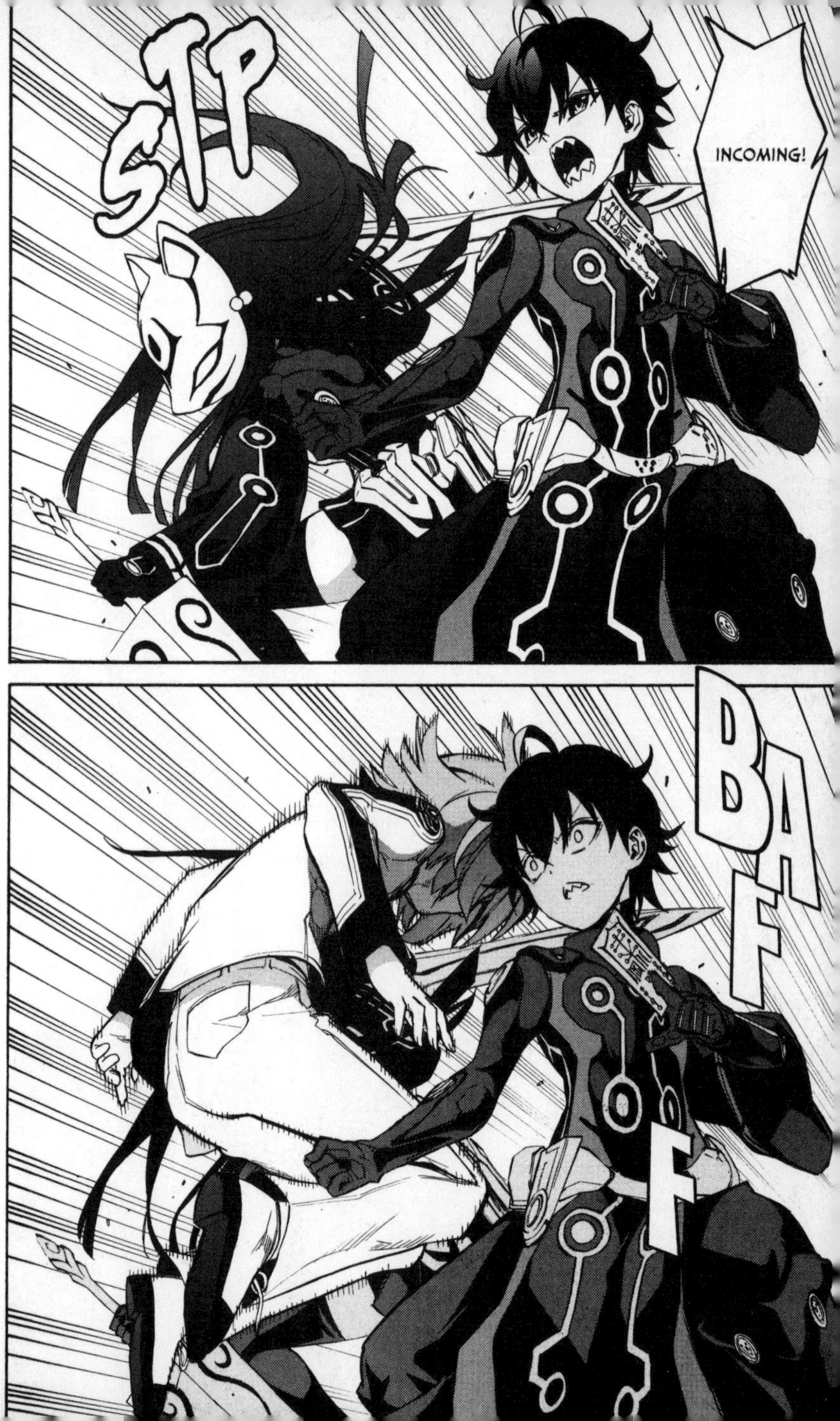
INCOMING!
STP
BAFF

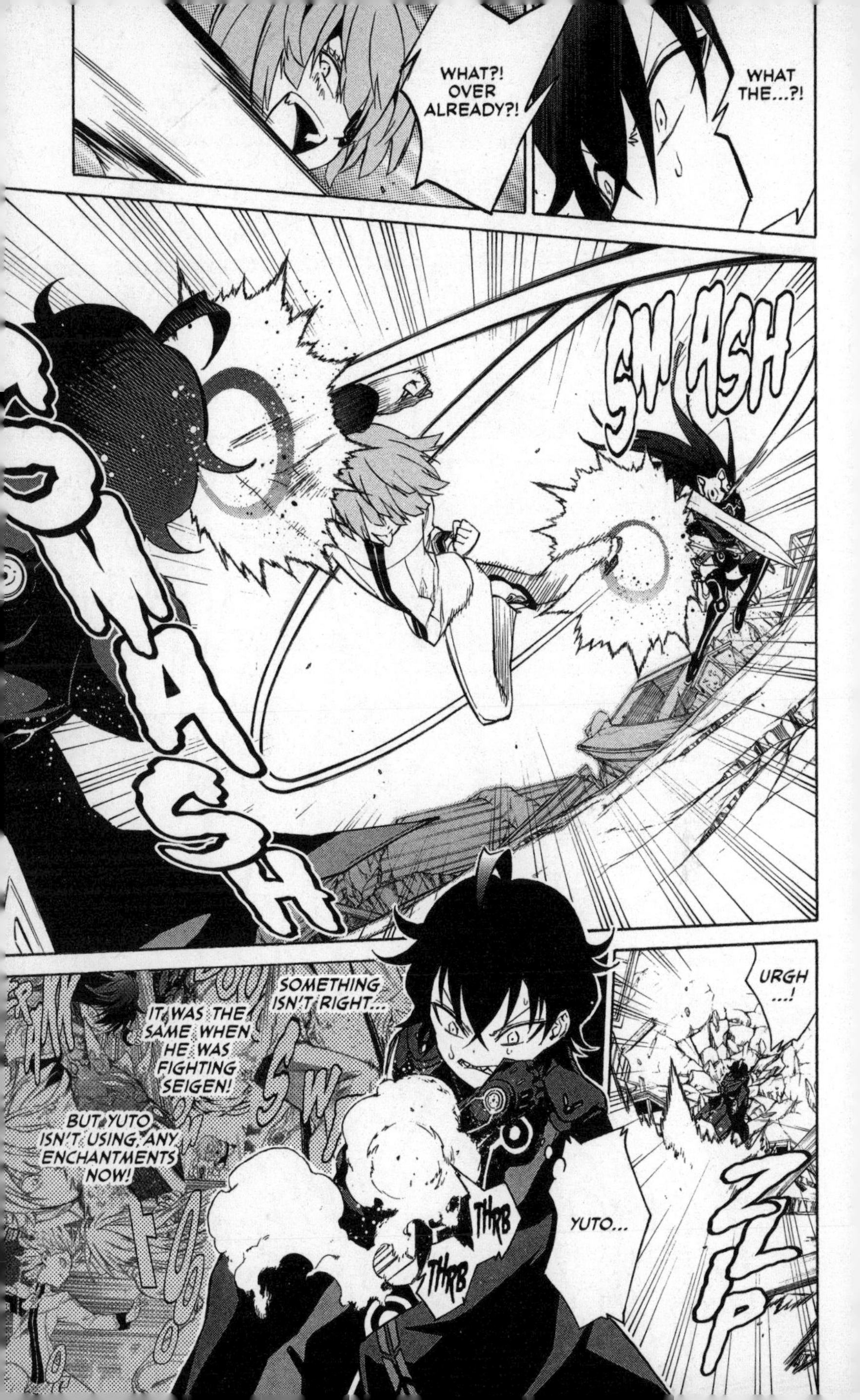
WHAT THE...?!
WHAT?! OVER ALREADY?!
SMASH
SMASH
URGH ...!
SOMETHING ISN'T RIGHT...
IT WAS THE SAME WHEN HE WAS FIGHTING SEIGEN!
BUT YUTO ISN'T USING ANY ENCHANTMENTS NOW!
ZZIP
YUTO...
THRB
THRB

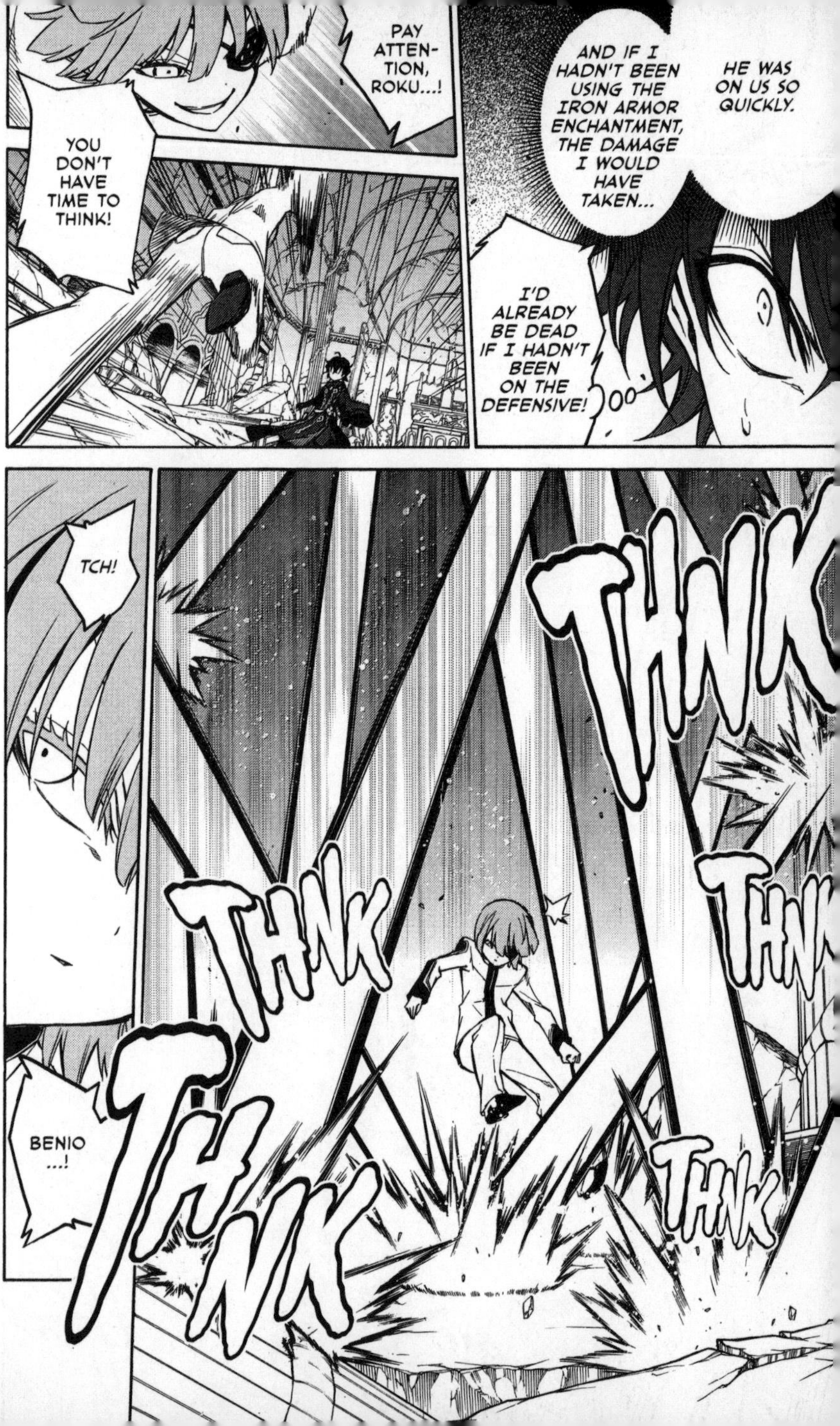
HE WAS ON US SO QUICKLY.
AND IF I HADN'T BEEN USING THE IRON ARMOR ENCHANTMENT, THE DAMAGE I WOULD HAVE TAKEN...
I'D ALREADY BE DEAD IF I HADN'T BEEN ON THE DEFENSIVE!
PAY ATTENTION, ROKU...!
YOU DON'T HAVE TIME TO THINK!
THNK
THNK
THNK
THNK
THNK
TCH!
BENIO ...!

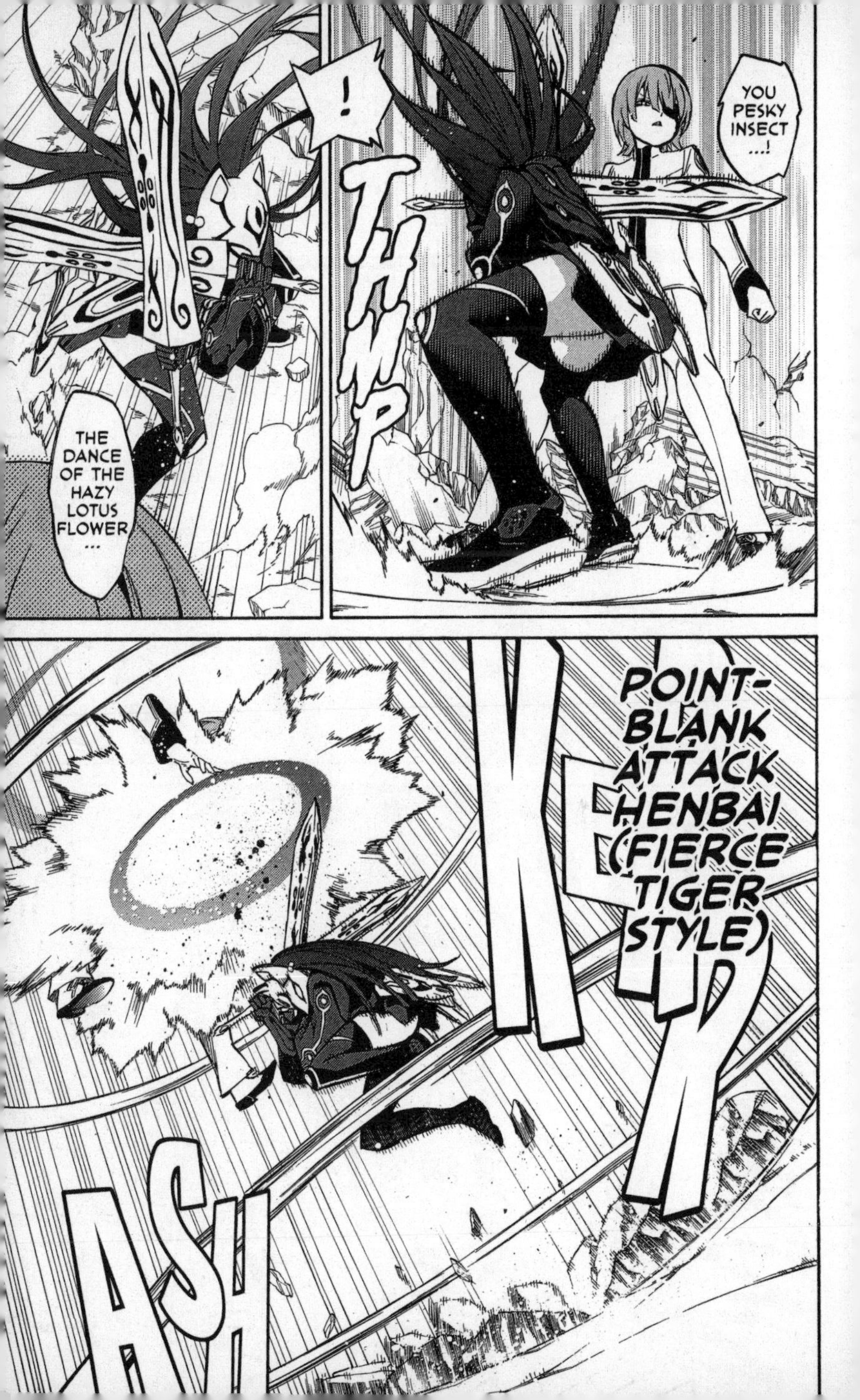
YOU PESKY INSECT ...!
THUMP
!
THE DANCE OF THE HAZY LOTUS FLOWER ...
POINT-BLANK ATTACK HENBAI (FIERCE TIGER STYLE)

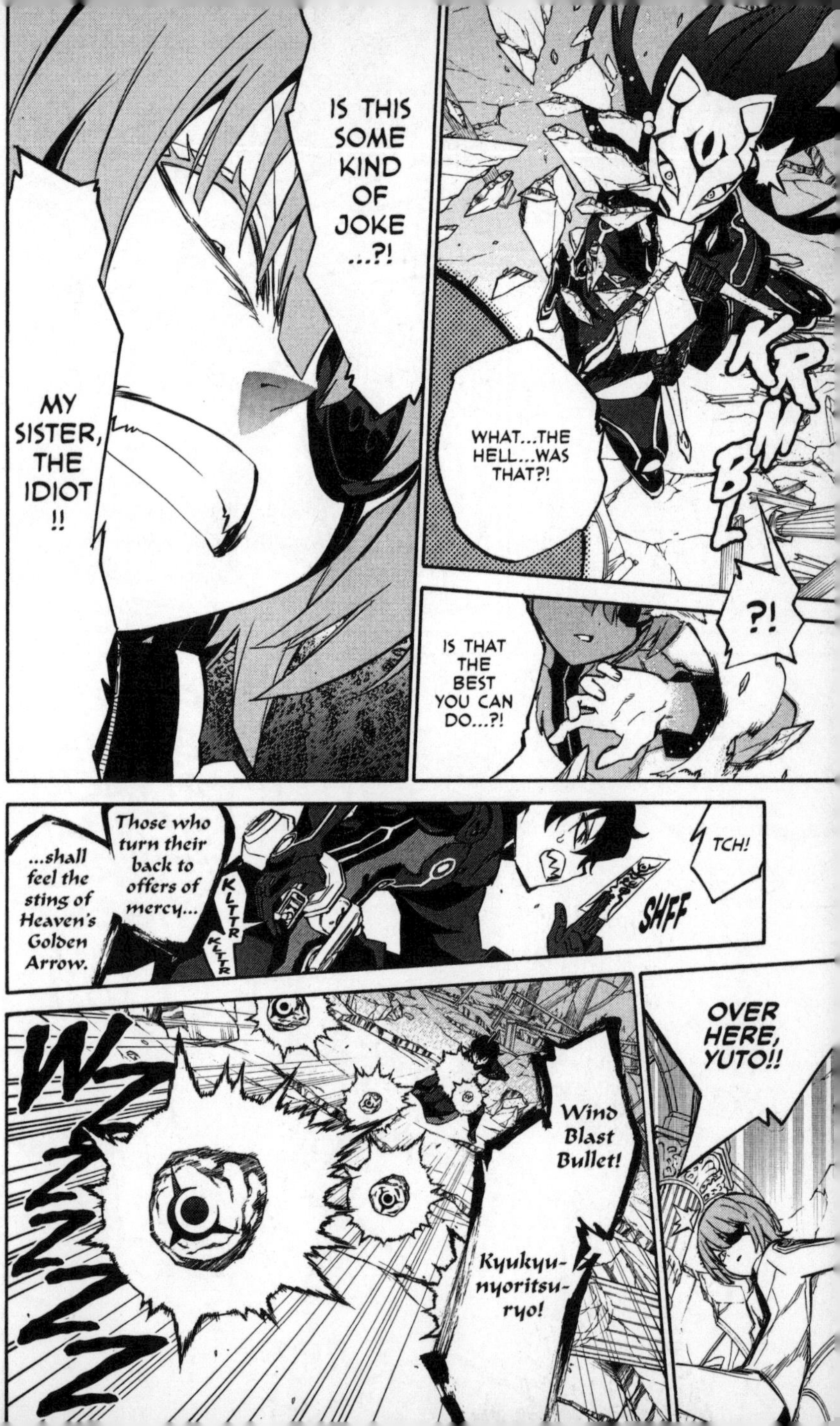
WHAT...THE HELL...WAS THAT?!
KRMBL
?!
IS THAT THE BEST YOU CAN DO...?!
IS THIS SOME KIND OF JOKE...?!
MY SISTER, THE IDIOT!!
TCH!
SHFF
Those who turn their back to offers of mercy...
KLTTR KLTTR
...shall feel the sting of Heaven's Golden Arrow.
OVER HERE, YUTO!!
Wind Blast Bullet!
Kyukyu-nyoritsu-ryo!

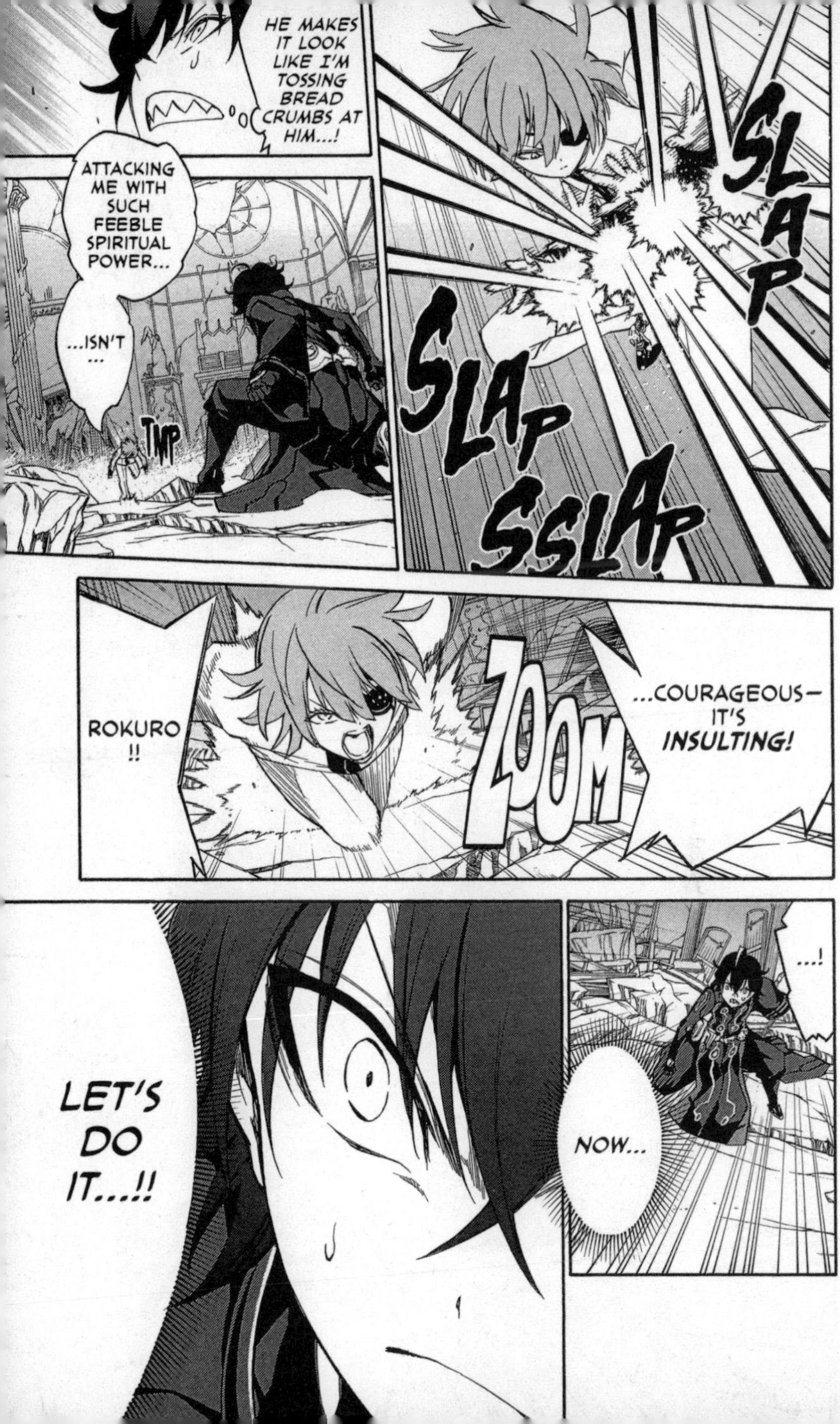
SLAP
SLAP
SSLAP
HE MAKES IT LOOK LIKE I'M TOSSING BREAD CRUMBS AT HIM...!
ATTACKING ME WITH SUCH FEEBLE SPIRITUAL POWER...
...ISN'T ...
TMP
...COURAGEOUS— IT'S INSULTING!
ZOOM
ROKURO !!
...!
NOW...
LET'S DO IT...!!

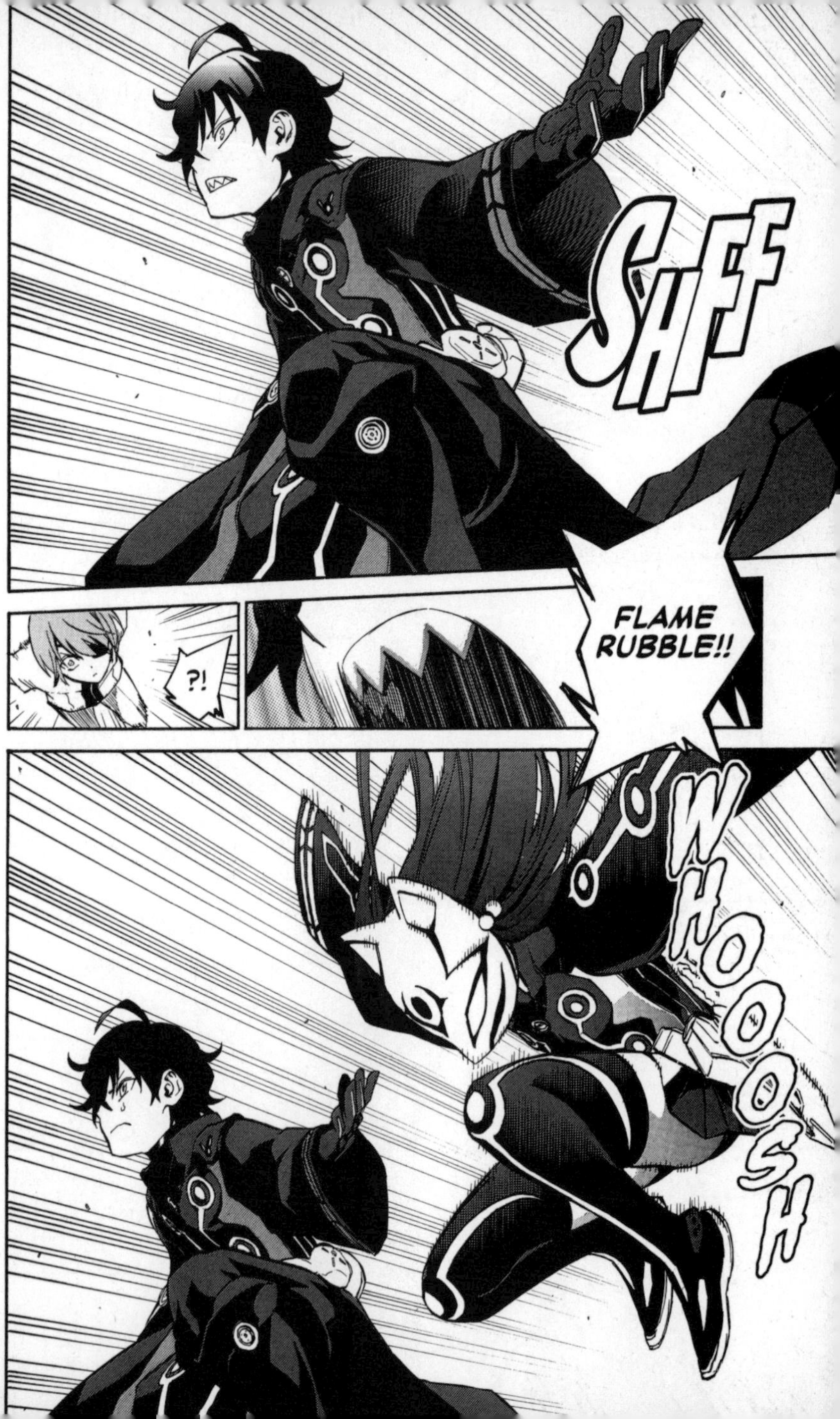
SHFF
FLAME RUBBLE!!
?!
WHOOOOSH

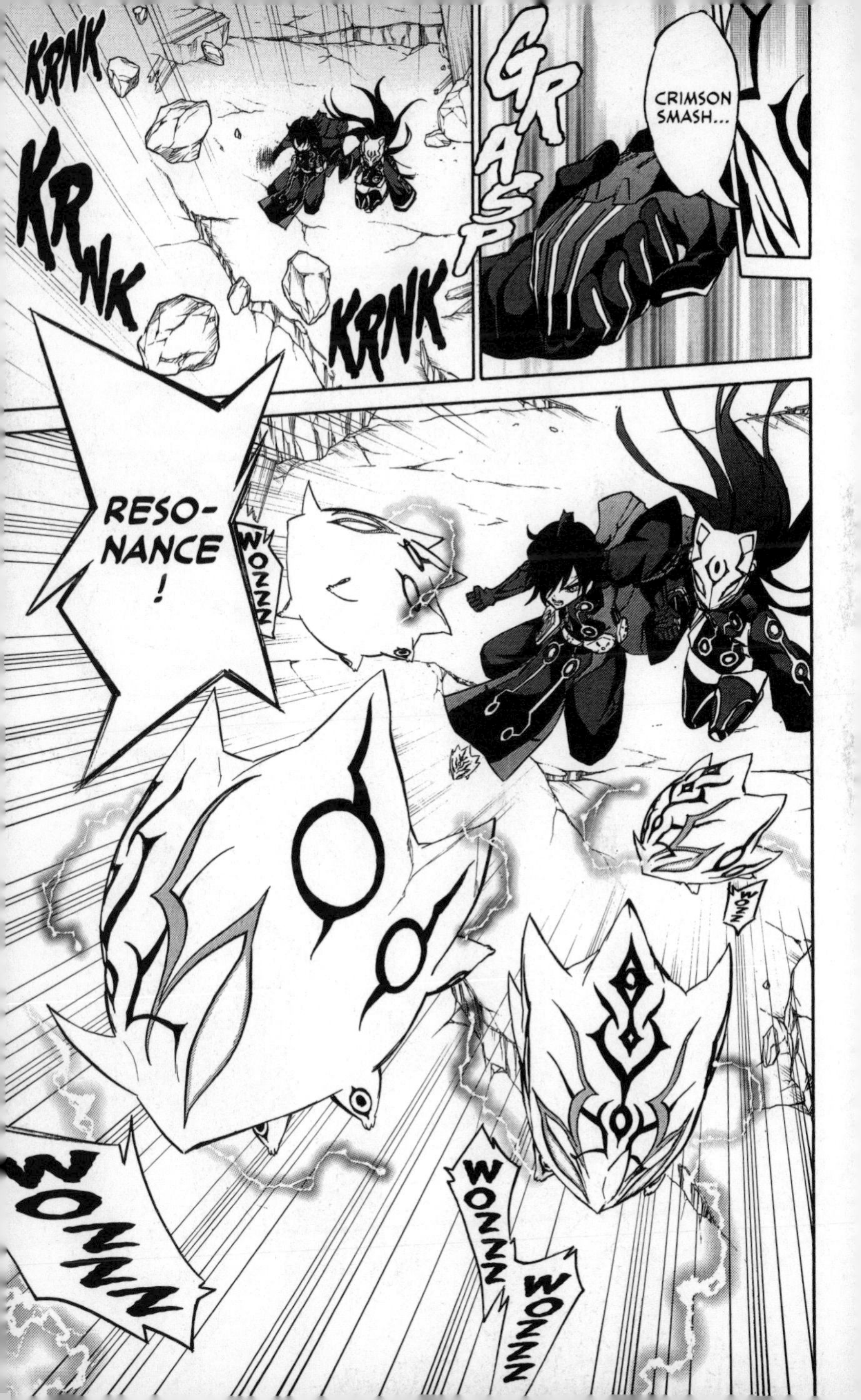
CRIMSON SMASH...
GRASP
KRNK
KRNK
KRNK
WOZZ
RESO-NANCE!
WONNN
WONNN
WOZZZ
WONNN

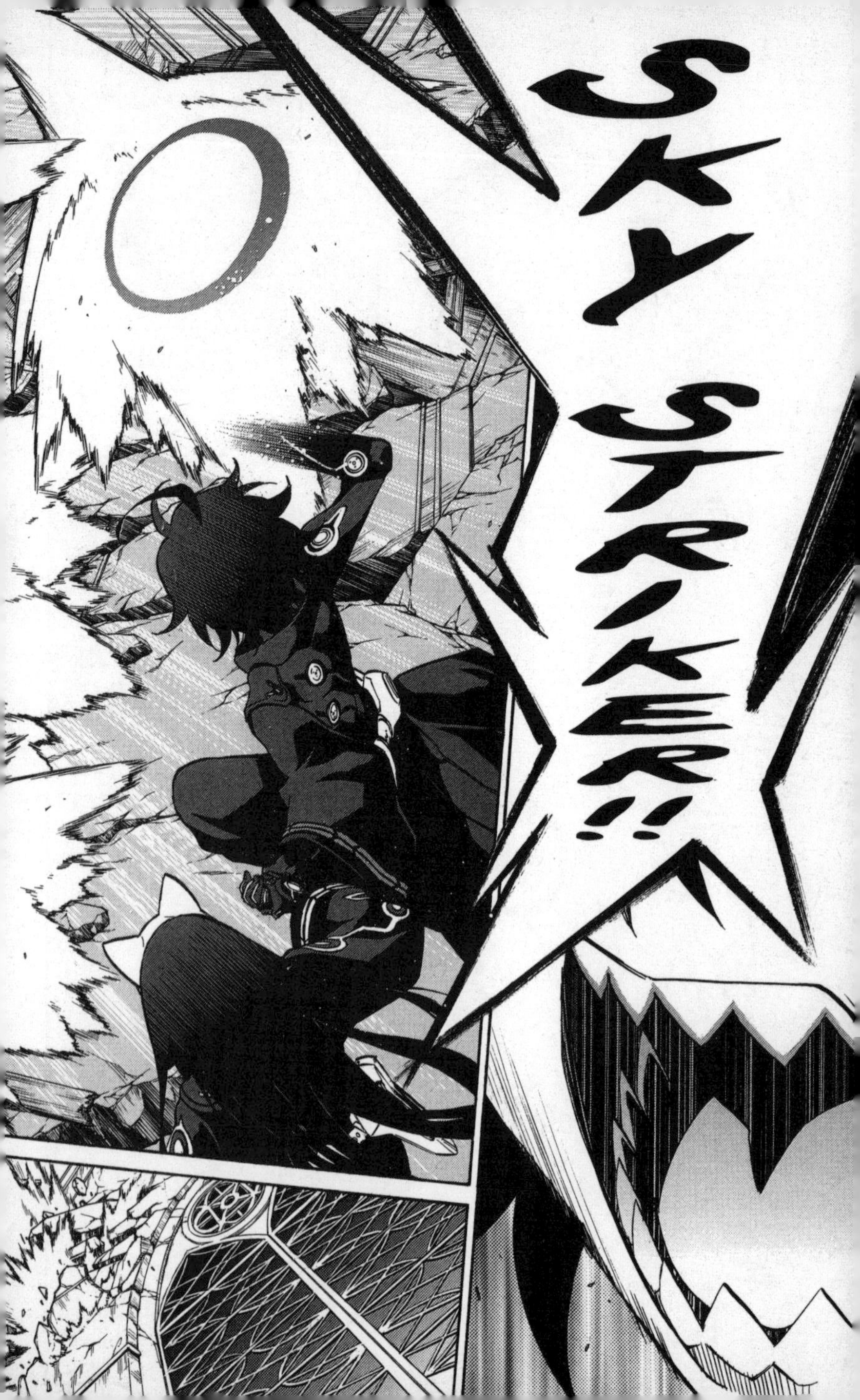
SKY STRIKER!!

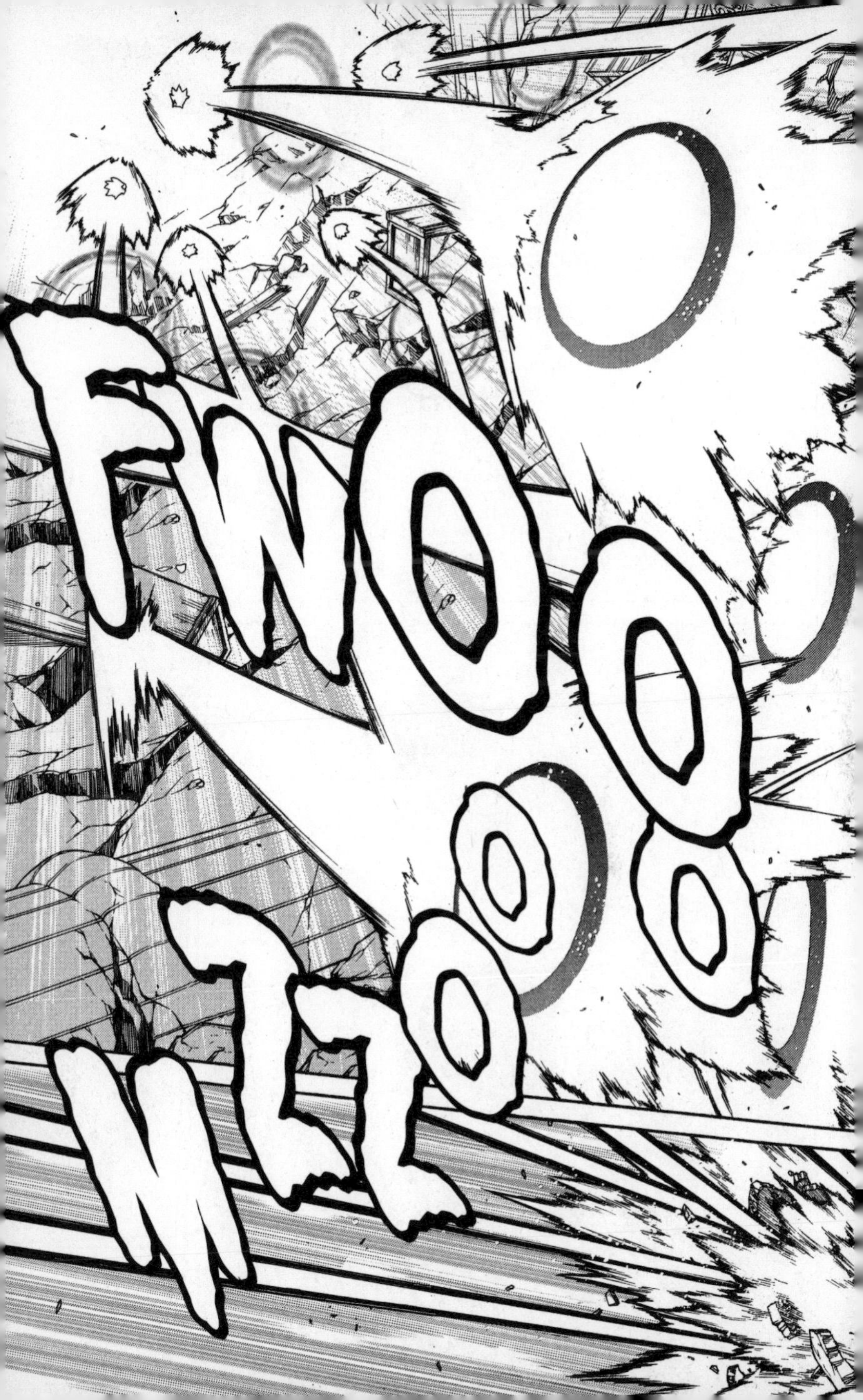
FWOOOO

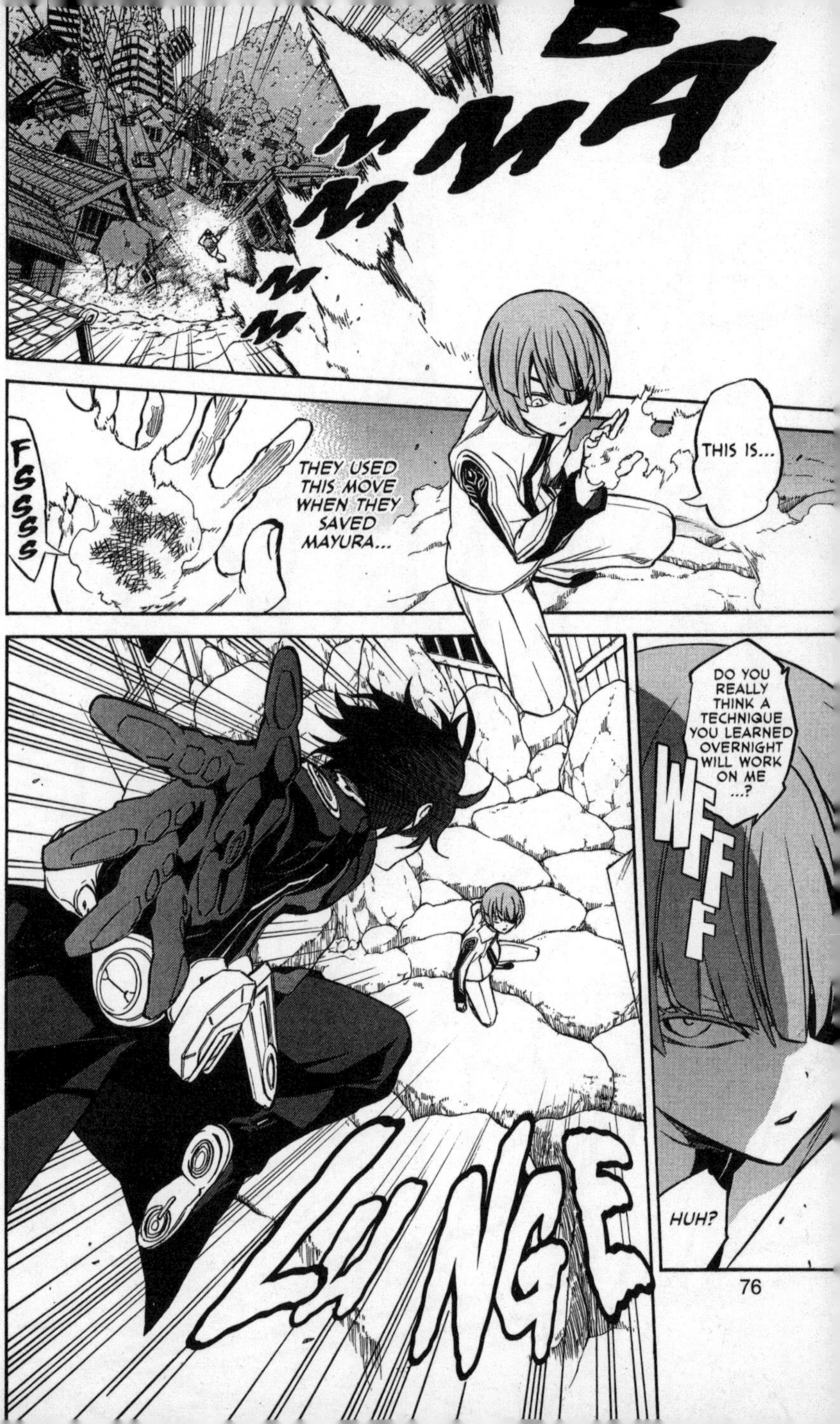
BAMMMMMM
THIS IS...
THEY USED THIS MOVE WHEN THEY SAVED MAYURA...
FSSSS
DO YOU REALLY THINK A TECHNIQUE YOU LEARNED OVERNIGHT WILL WORK ON ME ...?
WFFF
HUH?
LUNGE

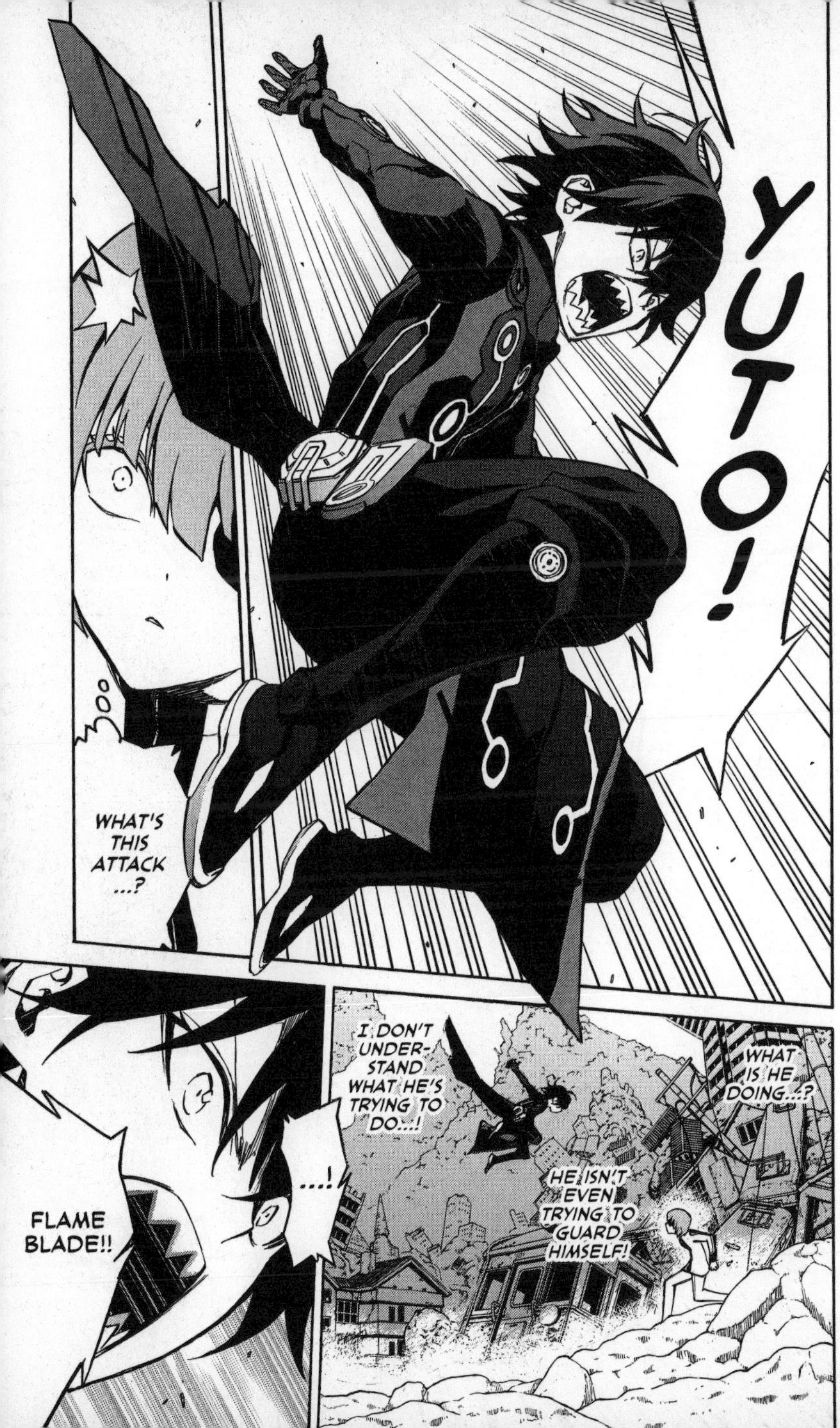
YUTO!!
WHAT'S THIS ATTACK ...?
WHAT IS HE DOING...?
I DON'T UNDER-STAND WHAT HE'S TRYING TO DO...!
HE ISN'T EVEN TRYING TO GUARD HIMSELF!
...!
FLAME BLADE!!

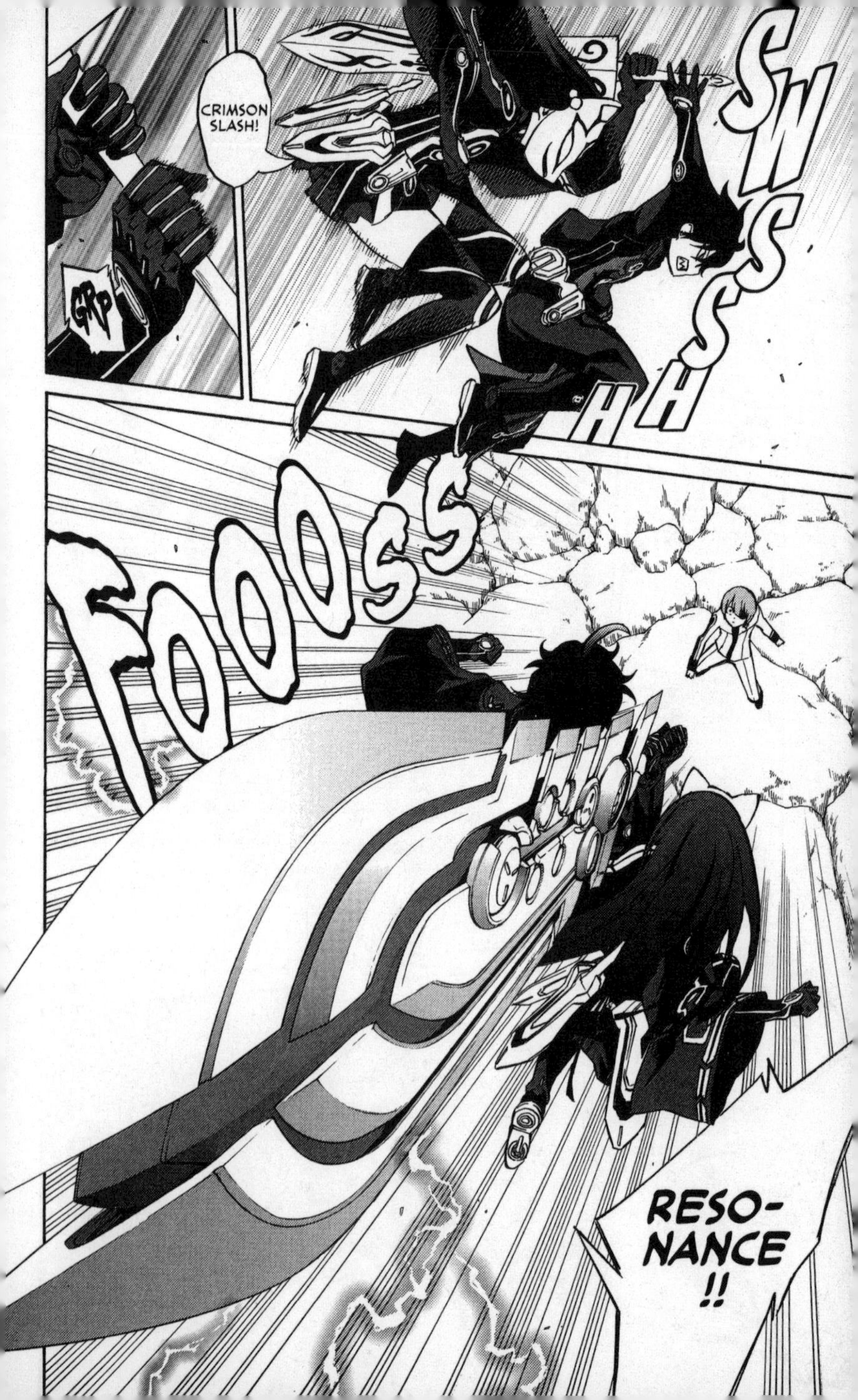
SWSSHH
CRIMSON SLASH!
GRP
FOOOSS
RESONANCE!!

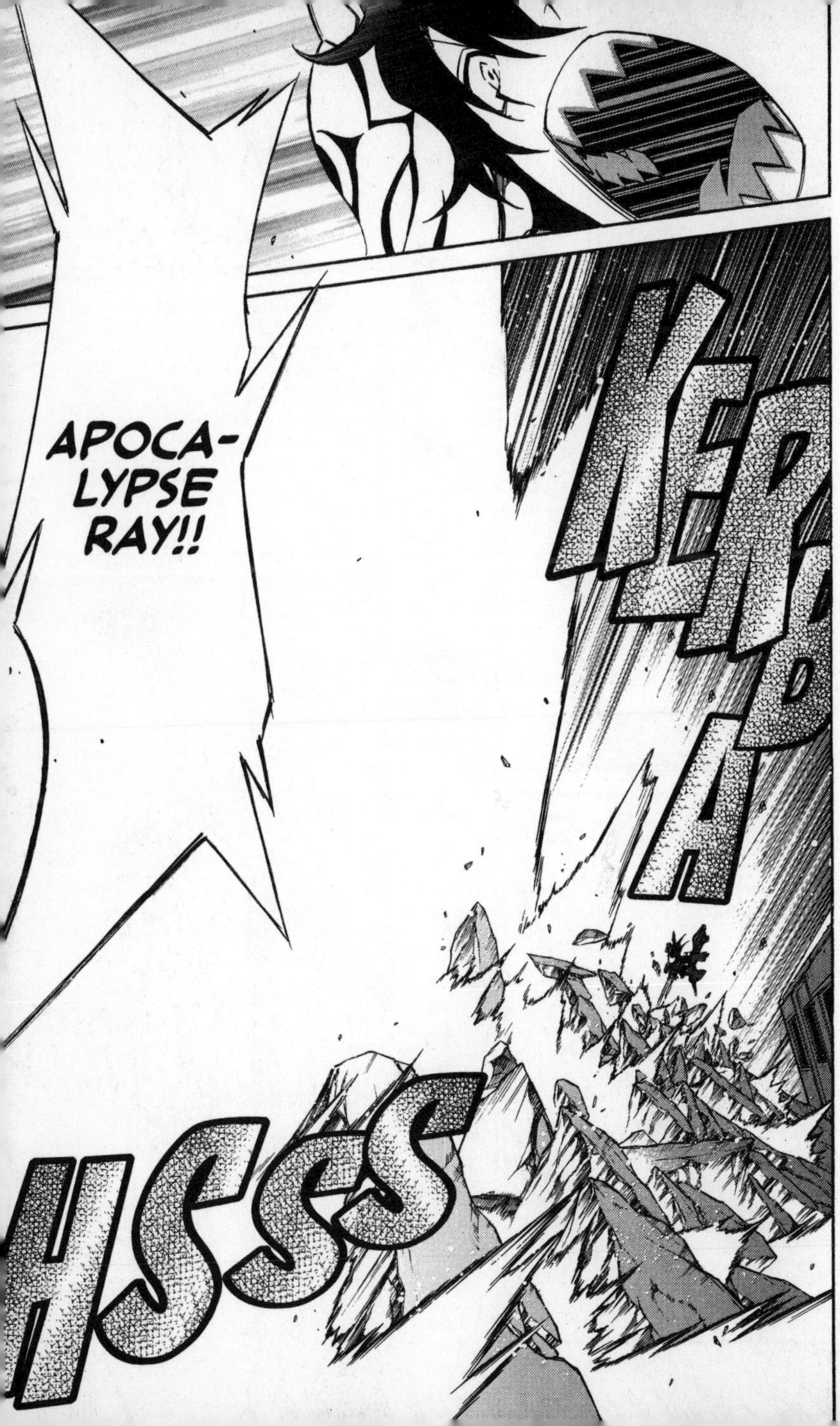
KERBA
APOCA-LYPSE RAY!!
HSSS

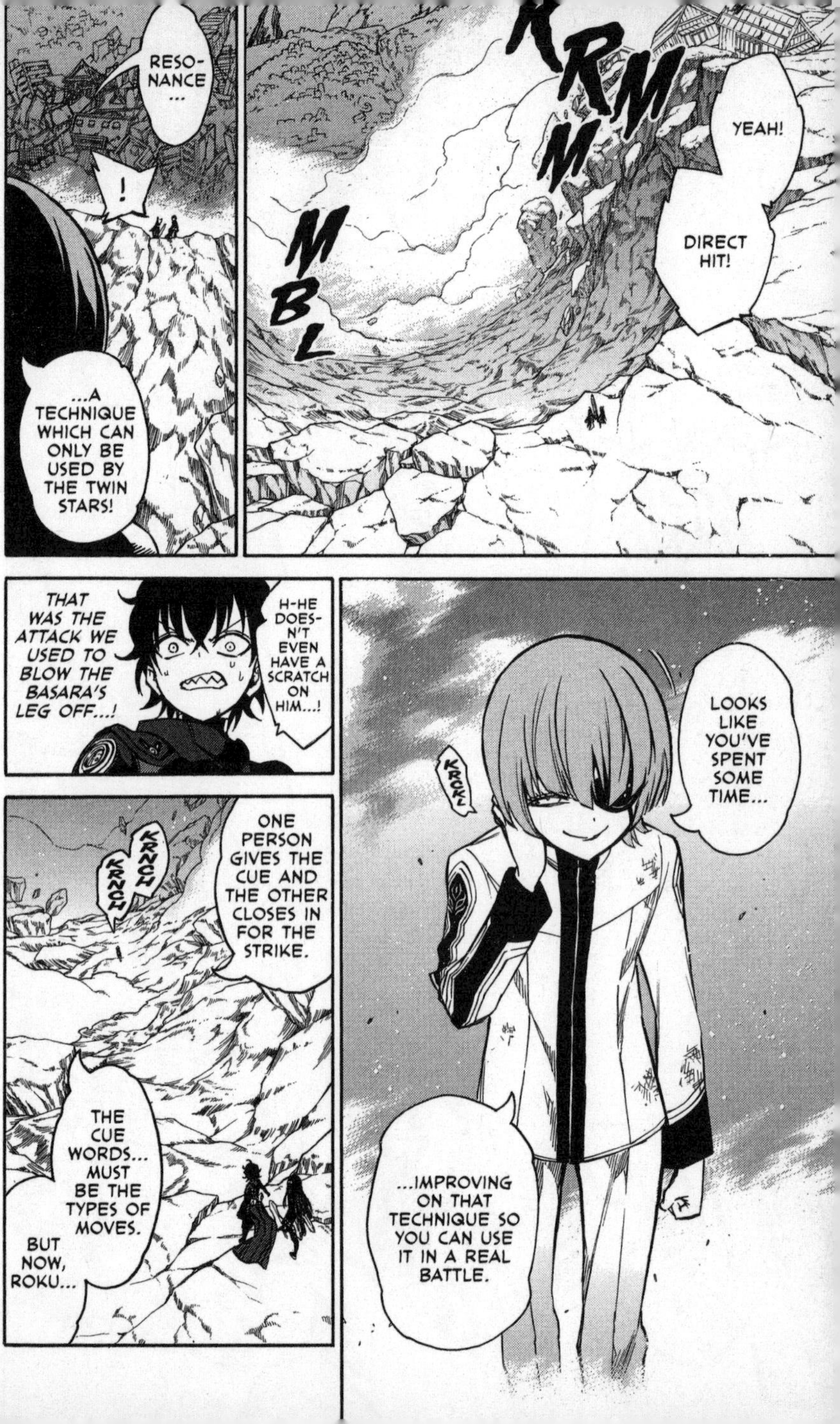
KRMMMMBL
YEAH!
DIRECT HIT!
RESONANCE...
!
...A TECHNIQUE WHICH CAN ONLY BE USED BY THE TWIN STARS!
LOOKS LIKE YOU'VE SPENT SOME TIME...
KRCKL
...IMPROVING ON THAT TECHNIQUE SO YOU CAN USE IT IN A REAL BATTLE.
H-HE DOESN'T EVEN HAVE A SCRATCH ON HIM...!
THAT WAS THE ATTACK WE USED TO BLOW THE BASARA'S LEG OFF...!
ONE PERSON GIVES THE CUE AND THE OTHER CLOSES IN FOR THE STRIKE.
KRNCH
KRNCH
THE CUE WORDS... MUST BE THE TYPES OF MOVES.
BUT NOW, ROKU...

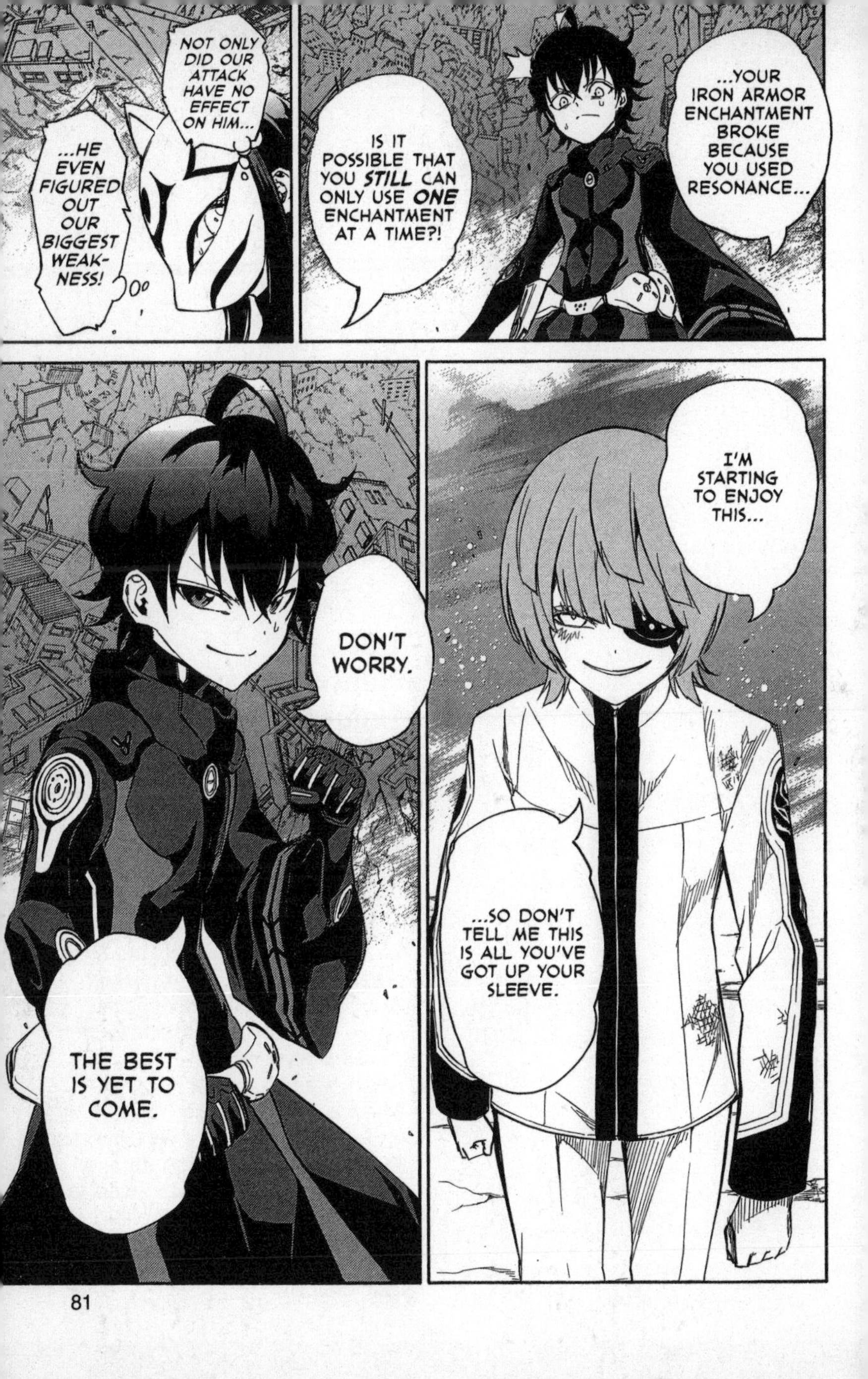
...YOUR IRON ARMOR ENCHANTMENT BROKE BECAUSE YOU USED RESONANCE...
IS IT POSSIBLE THAT YOU *STILL* CAN ONLY USE *ONE* ENCHANTMENT AT A TIME?!
NOT ONLY DID OUR ATTACK HAVE NO EFFECT ON HIM...
...HE EVEN FIGURED OUT OUR BIGGEST WEAK-NESS!
I'M STARTING TO ENJOY THIS...
...SO DON'T TELL ME THIS IS ALL YOU'VE GOT UP YOUR SLEEVE.
DON'T WORRY.
THE BEST IS YET TO COME.

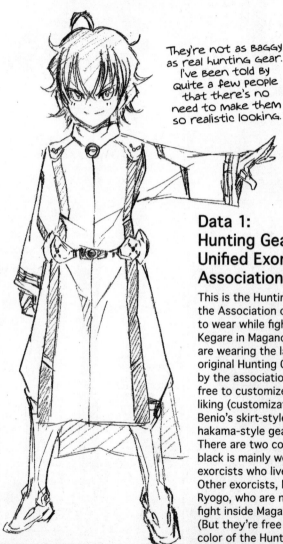

They're not as baggy as real hunting gear. I've been told by quite a few people that there's no need to make them so realistic looking.

Data 1:
Hunting Gear:
Unified Exorcist
Association Style

This is the Hunting Gear refined by the Association of Unified Exorcists to wear while fighting against Kegare in Magano. Rokuro and Benio are wearing the latest version. The original Hunting Gear is supplied by the association. Exorcists are free to customize them to their liking (customization examples: Benio's skirt-style gear and Seigen's hakama-style gear).

There are two colors. In general, black is mainly worn by a group of exorcists who live in a certain area. Other exorcists, like Rokuro and Ryogo, who are not authorized to fight inside Magano, wear white. (But they're free to customize the color of the Hunting Gear they are supplied with.)

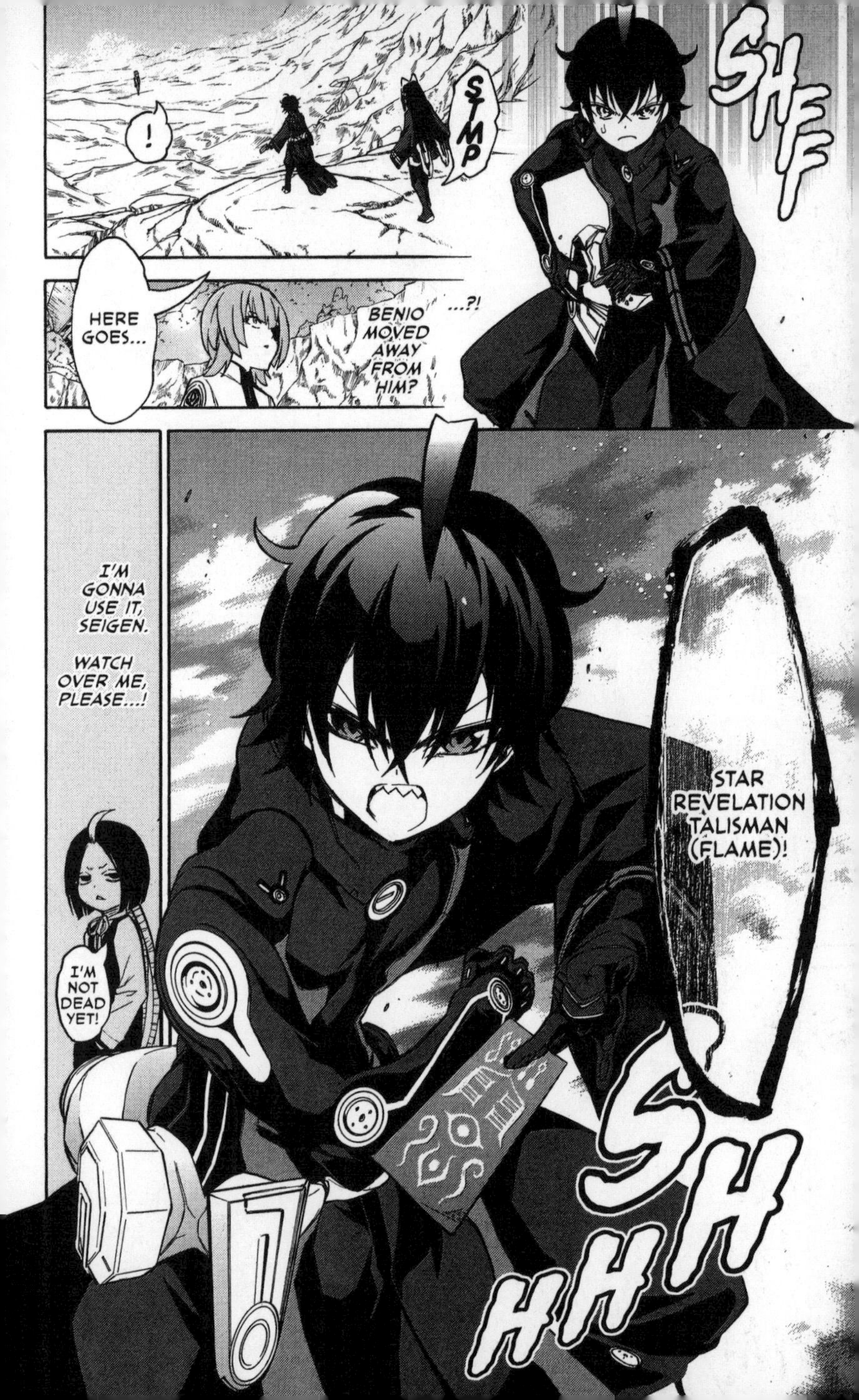
SHFF
...?!
STMP
!
BENIO MOVED AWAY FROM HIM?
HERE GOES...
STAR REVELATION TALISMAN (FLAME)!
SHHHH
I'M GONNA USE IT, SEIGEN.
WATCH OVER ME, PLEASE...!
I'M NOT DEAD YET!

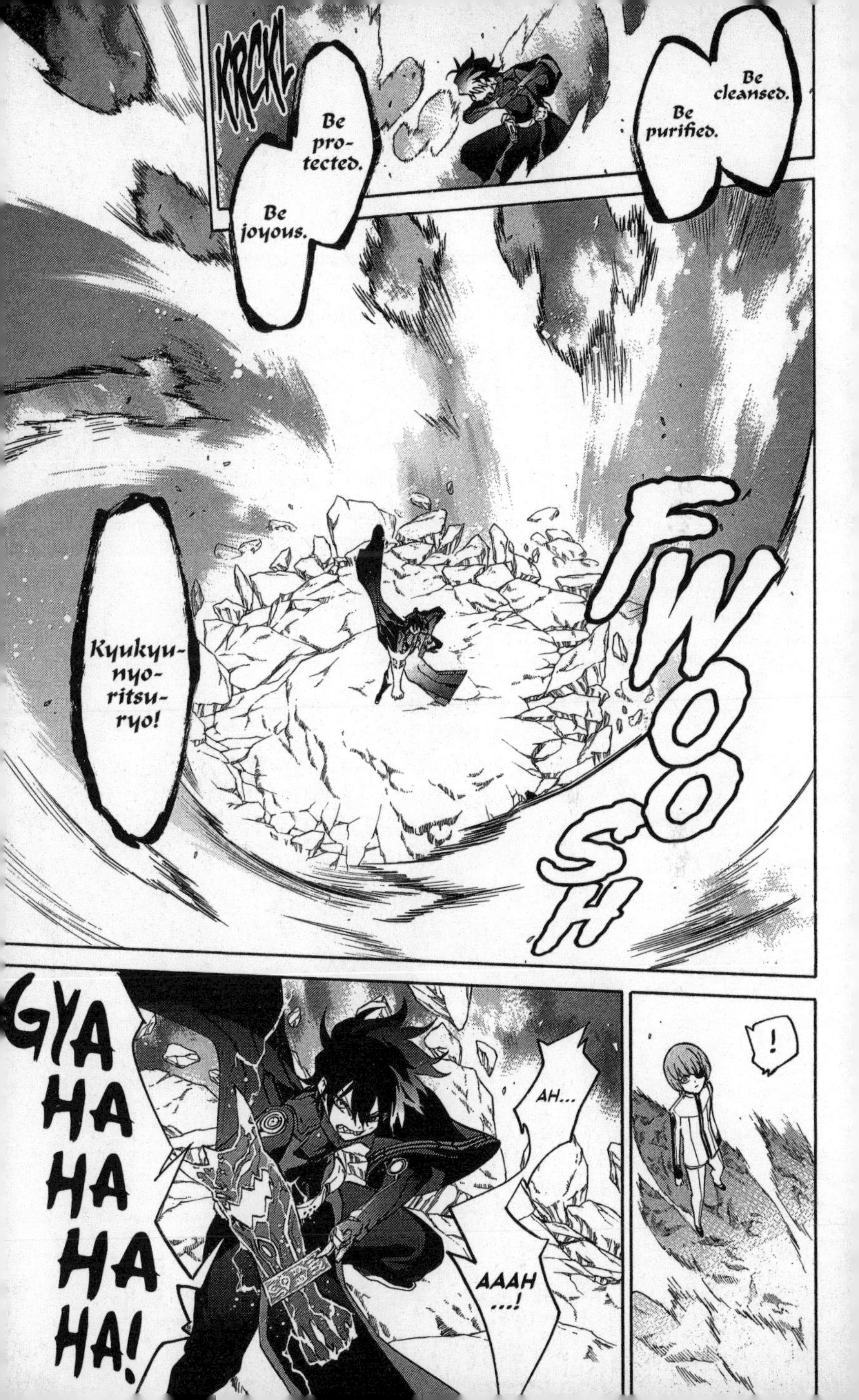
Be cleansed.
Be purified.
Be protected.
Be joyous.
KRCKL
FWOOSH
Kyukyu-nyo-ritsu-ryo!
!
AH...
AAAH...!
GYA HA HA HA HA HA!

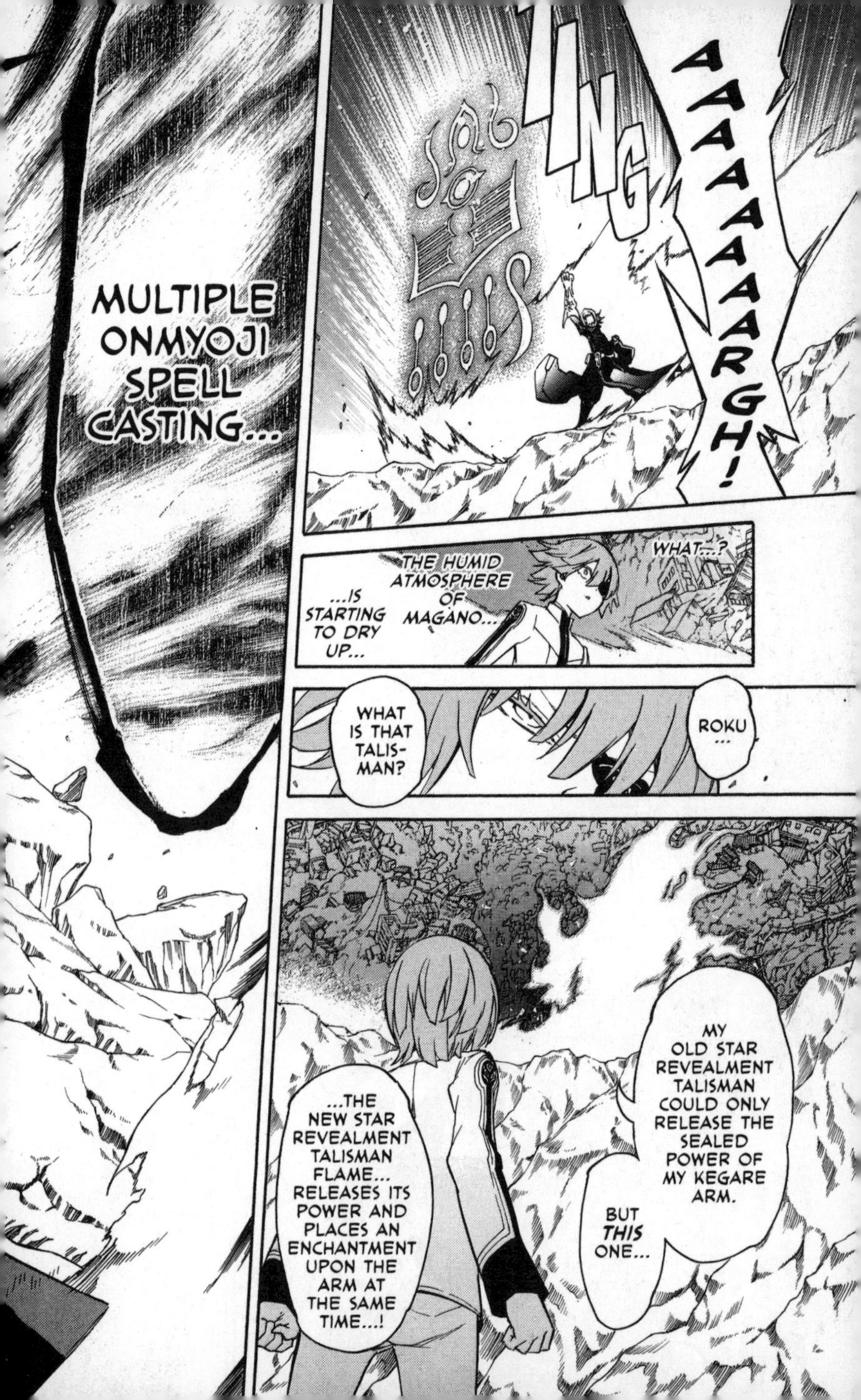
AAAAAAARGH!
ING
WHAT...?
THE HUMID ATMOSPHERE OF MAGANO...
...IS STARTING TO DRY UP...
ROKU...
WHAT IS THAT TALISMAN?
MY OLD STAR REVEALMENT TALISMAN COULD ONLY RELEASE THE SEALED POWER OF MY KEGARE ARM.
BUT *THIS* ONE...
...THE NEW STAR REVEALMENT TALISMAN FLAME... RELEASES ITS POWER AND PLACES AN ENCHANTMENT UPON THE ARM AT THE SAME TIME...!
MULTIPLE ONMYOJI SPELL CASTING...

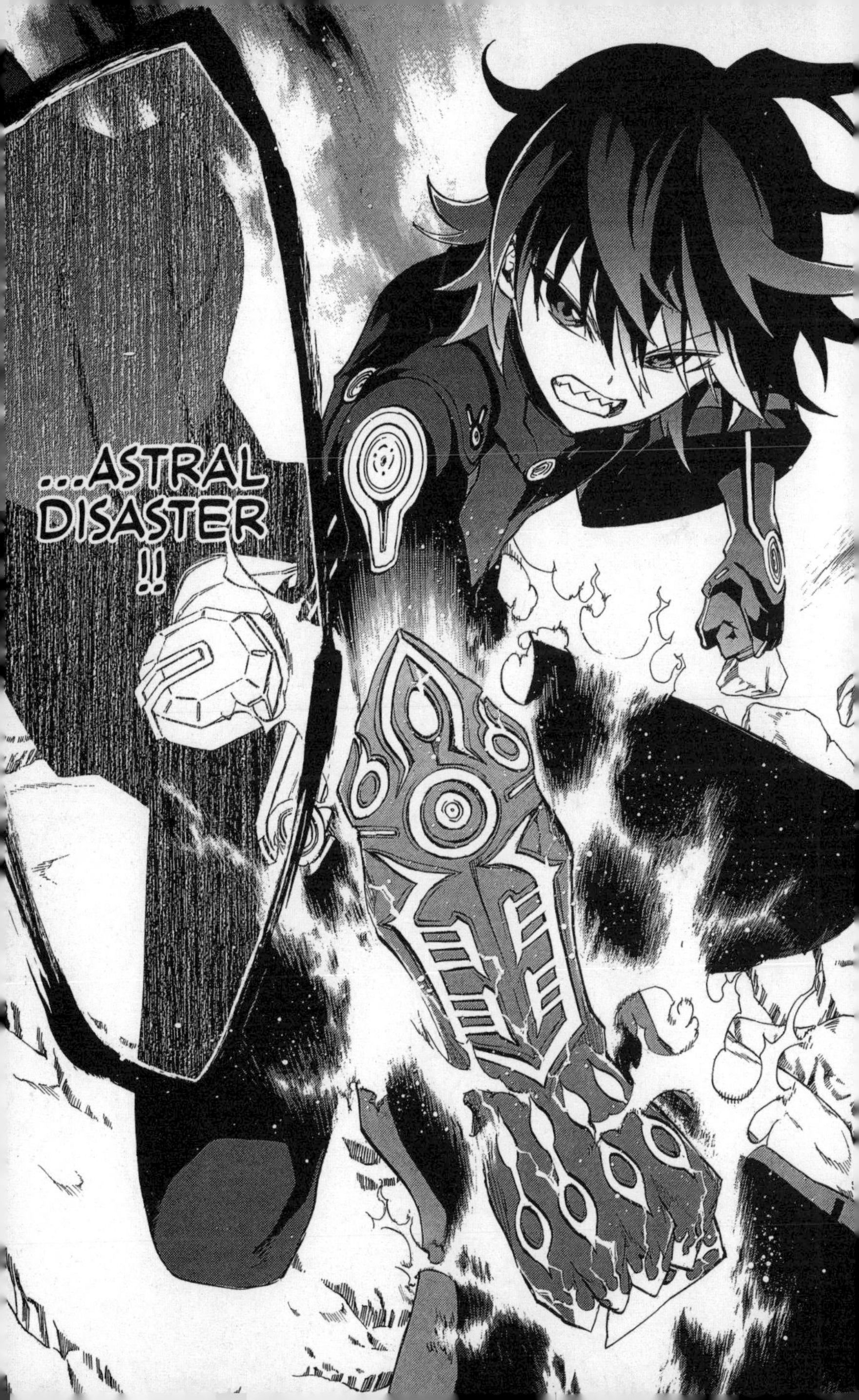
...ASTRAL DISASTER !!

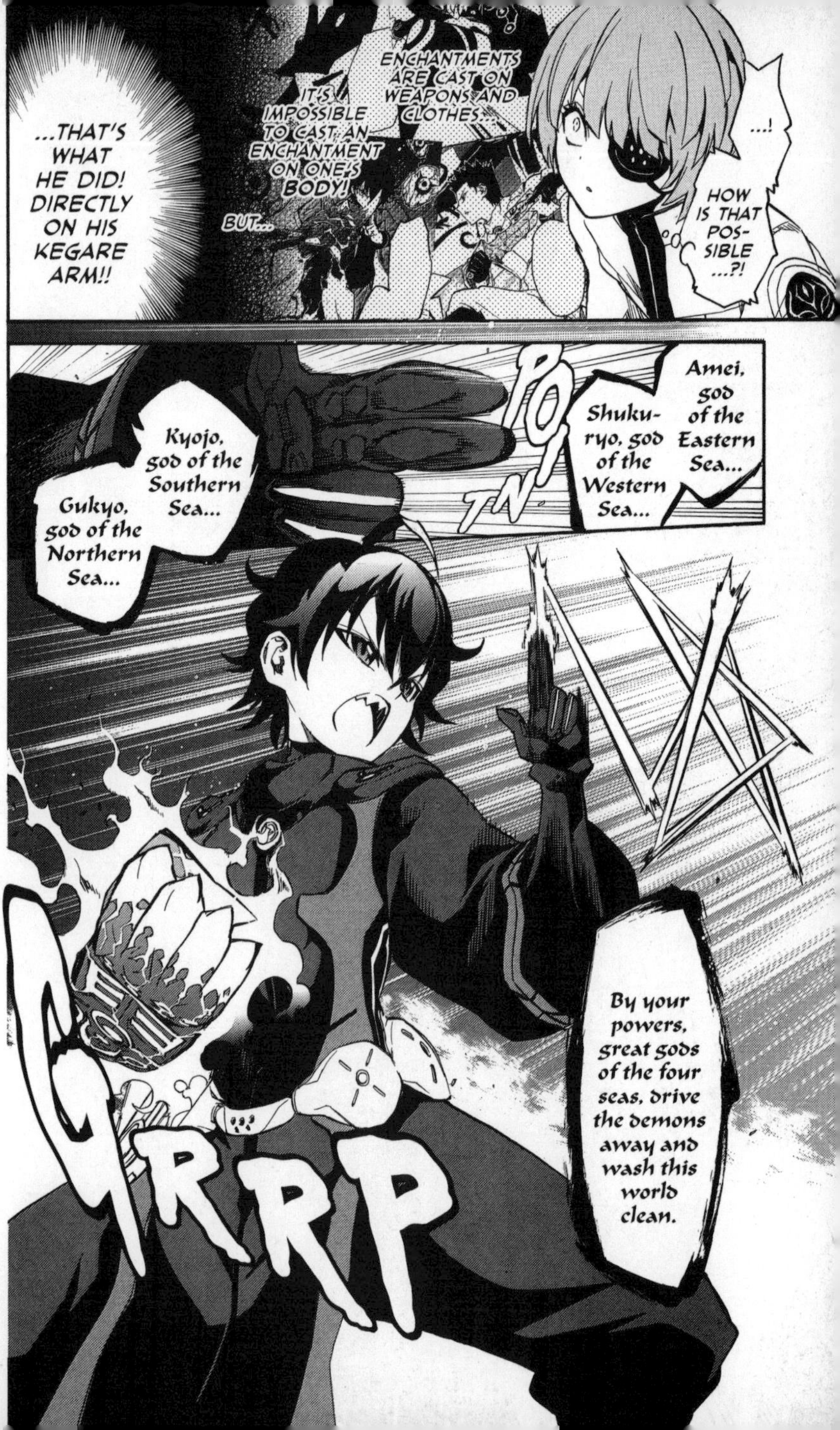
...!
HOW IS THAT POS-SIBLE ...?!
ENCHANTMENTS ARE CAST ON WEAPONS AND CLOTHES...
IT'S IMPOSSIBLE TO CAST AN ENCHANTMENT ON ONE'S BODY!
BUT...
...THAT'S WHAT HE DID! DIRECTLY ON HIS KEGARE ARM!!
Amei, god of the Eastern Sea...
Shuku-ryo, god of the Western Sea...
Kyojo, god of the Southern Sea...
Gukyo, god of the Northern Sea...
By your powers, great gods of the four seas, drive the demons away and wash this world clean.
GRRP

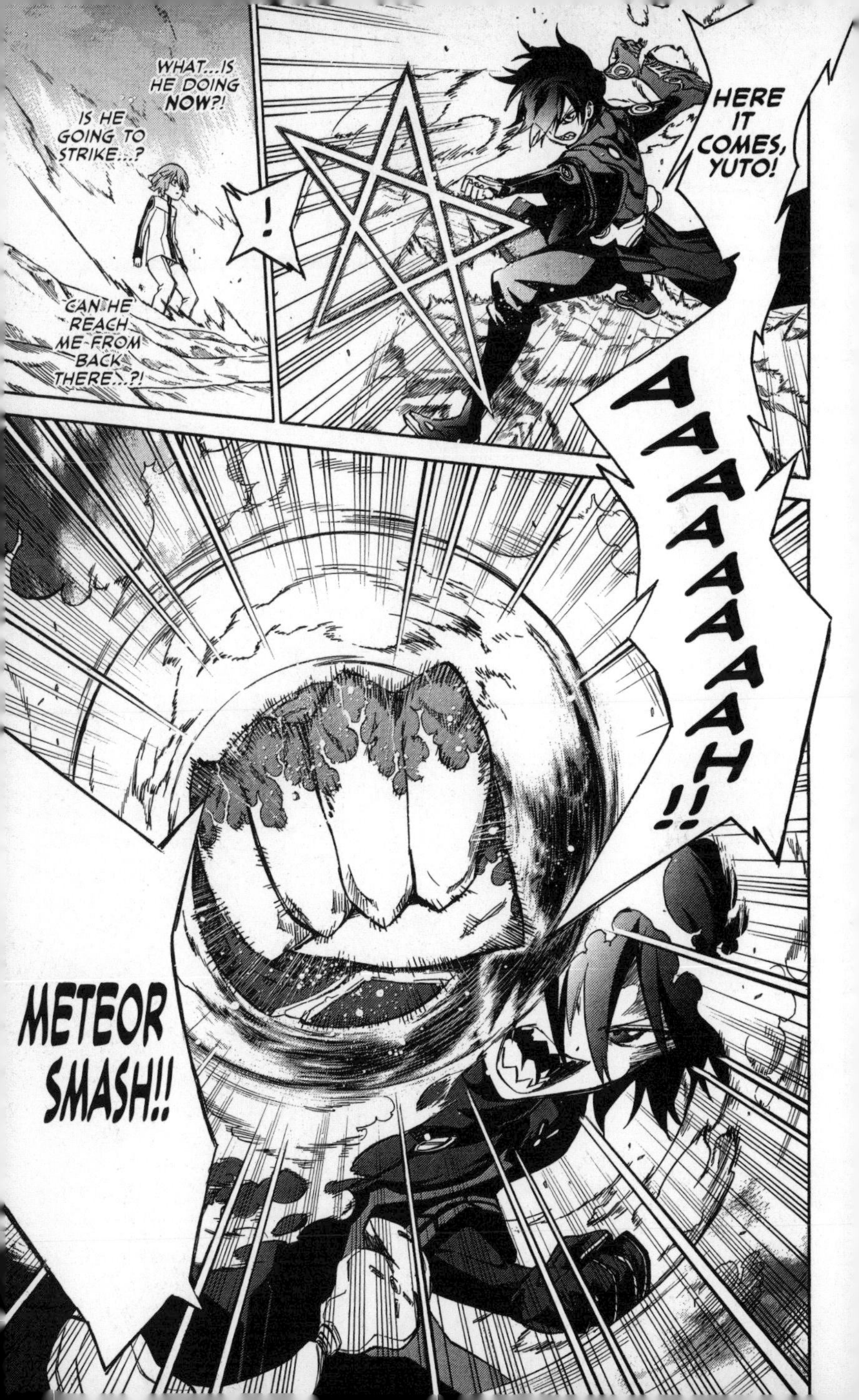
HERE IT COMES, YUTO!
!
WHAT...IS HE DOING NOW?!
IS HE GOING TO STRIKE...?
CAN HE REACH ME FROM BACK THERE...?!
AAAAAAAH!!
METEOR SMASH!!

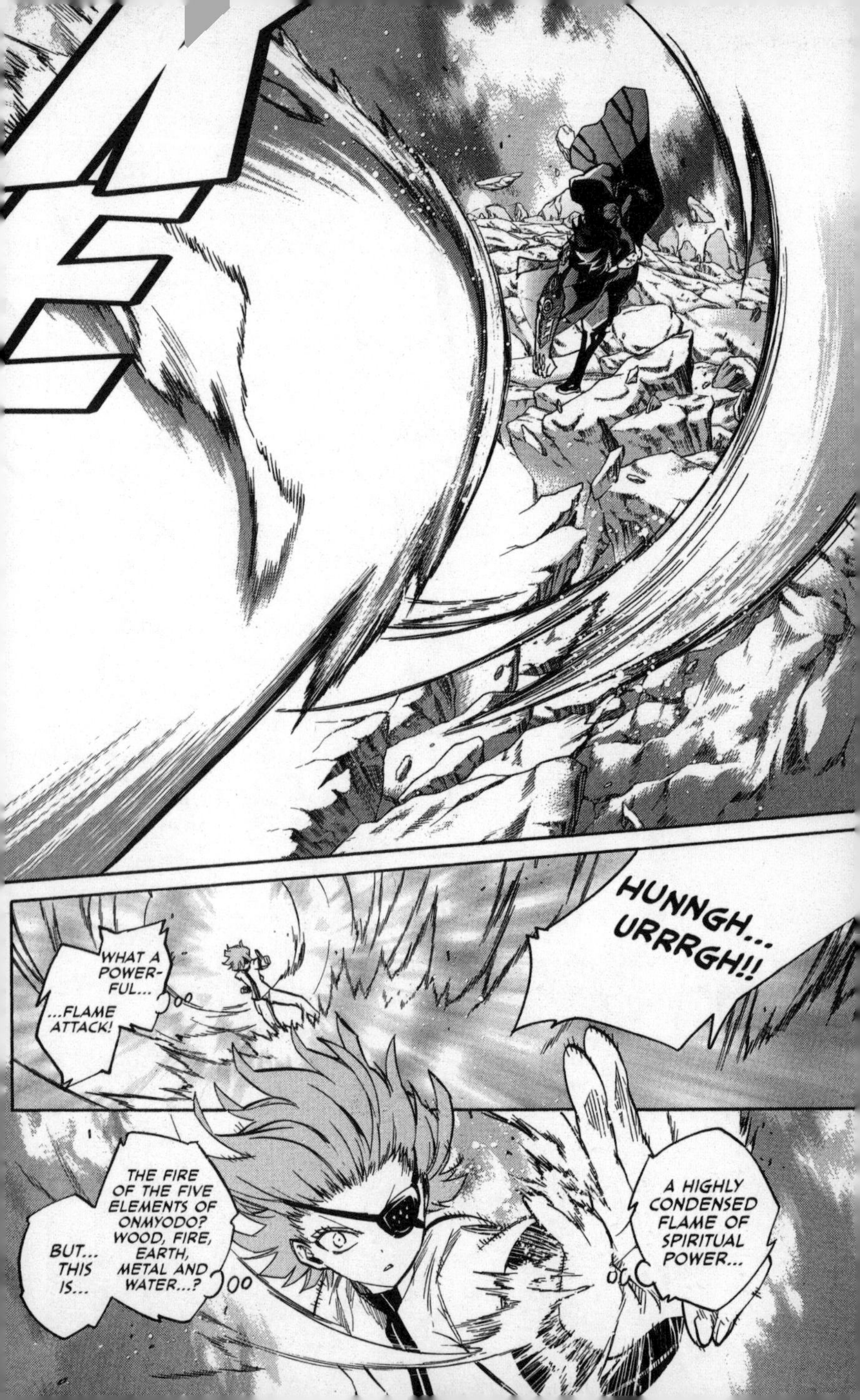
HUNNGH... URRRGH!!
WHAT A POWERFUL...
...FLAME ATTACK!
A HIGHLY CONDENSED FLAME OF SPIRITUAL POWER...
THE FIRE OF THE FIVE ELEMENTS OF ONMYODO? WOOD, FIRE, EARTH, METAL AND WATER...?
BUT... THIS IS...

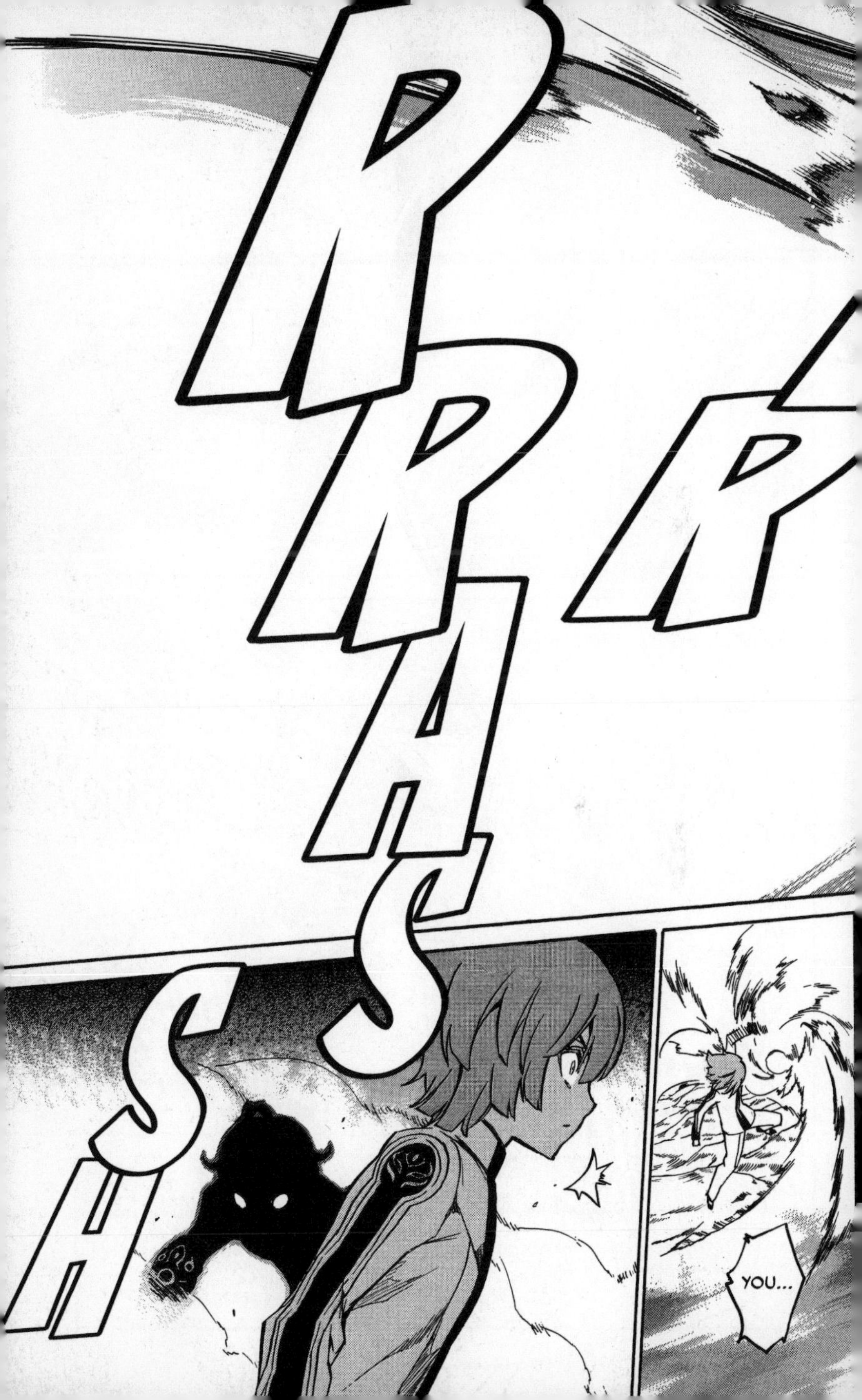
RRRASSH
YOU...

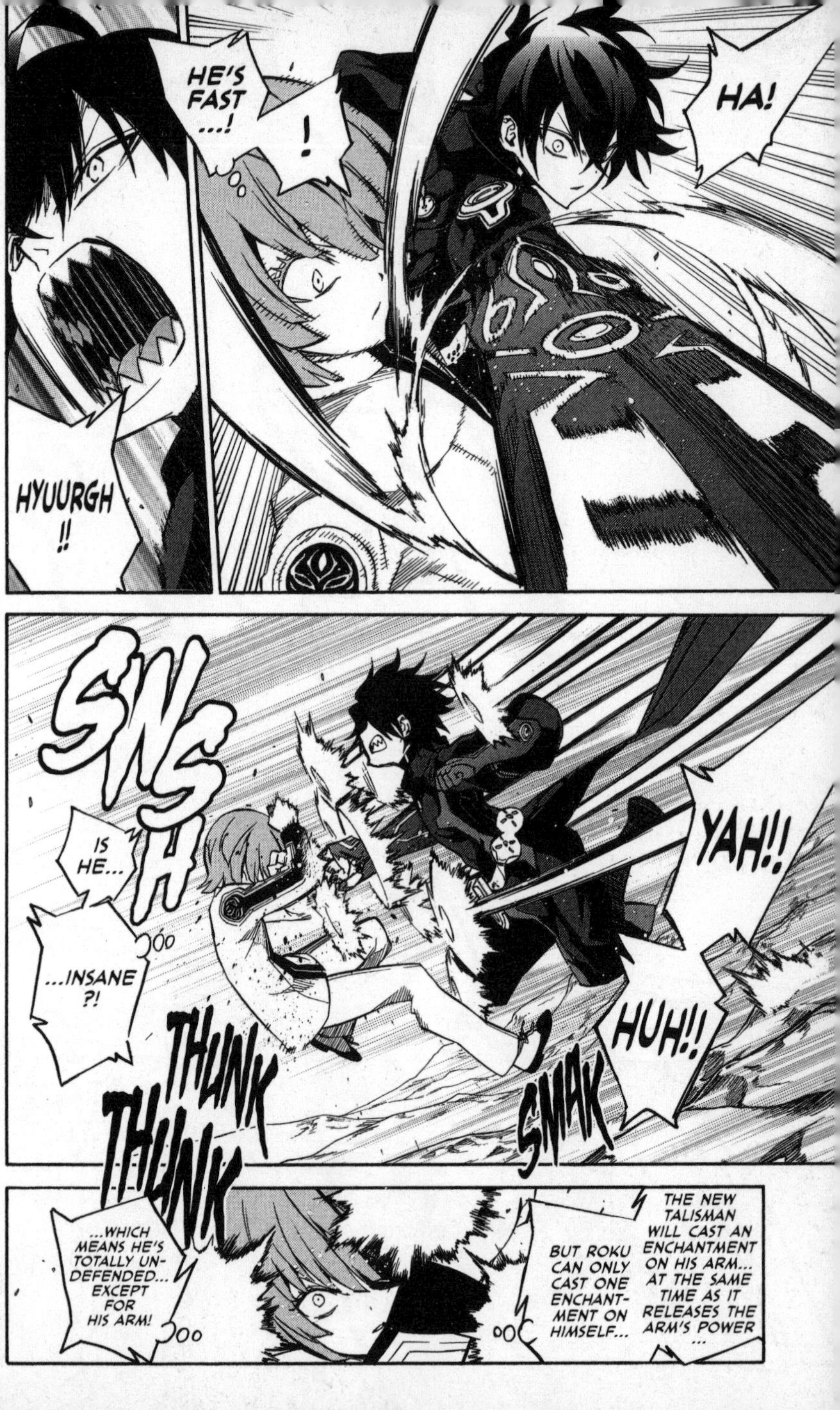
HA!
!
HE'S FAST ...!
HYUURGH !!
SNSH
YAH!!
IS HE...
...INSANE ?!
HUH!!
SMAK
THUNK
THUNK
THE NEW TALISMAN WILL CAST AN ENCHANTMENT ON HIS ARM... AT THE SAME TIME AS IT RELEASES THE ARM'S POWER ...
BUT ROKU CAN ONLY CAST ONE ENCHANT-MENT ON HIMSELF...
...WHICH MEANS HE'S TOTALLY UN-DEFENDED... EXCEPT FOR HIS ARM!

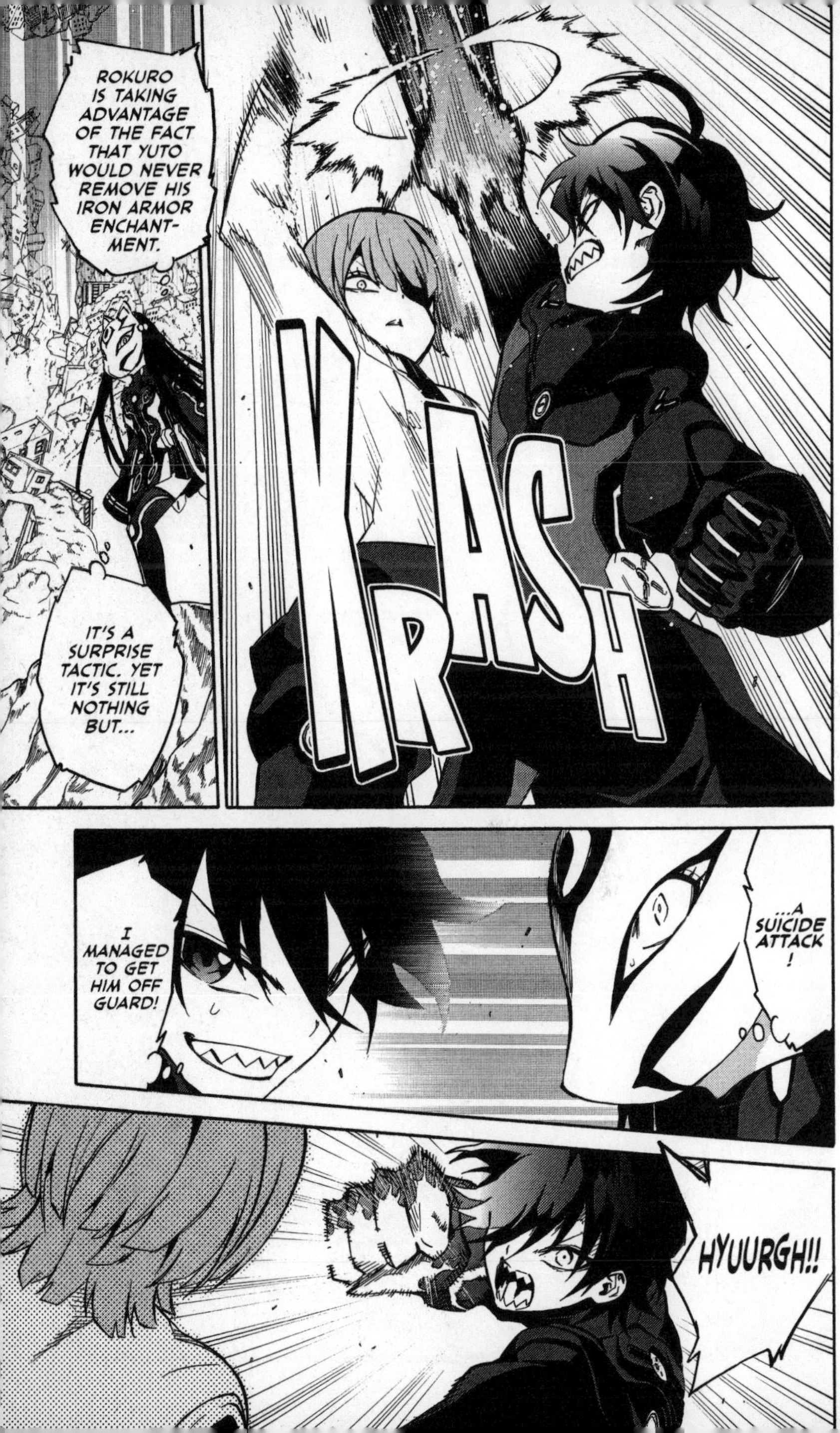
KRASH
ROKURO IS TAKING ADVANTAGE OF THE FACT THAT YUTO WOULD NEVER REMOVE HIS IRON ARMOR ENCHANT-MENT.
IT'S A SURPRISE TACTIC. YET IT'S STILL NOTHING BUT...
...A SUICIDE ATTACK!
I MANAGED TO GET HIM OFF GUARD!
HYUURGH!!

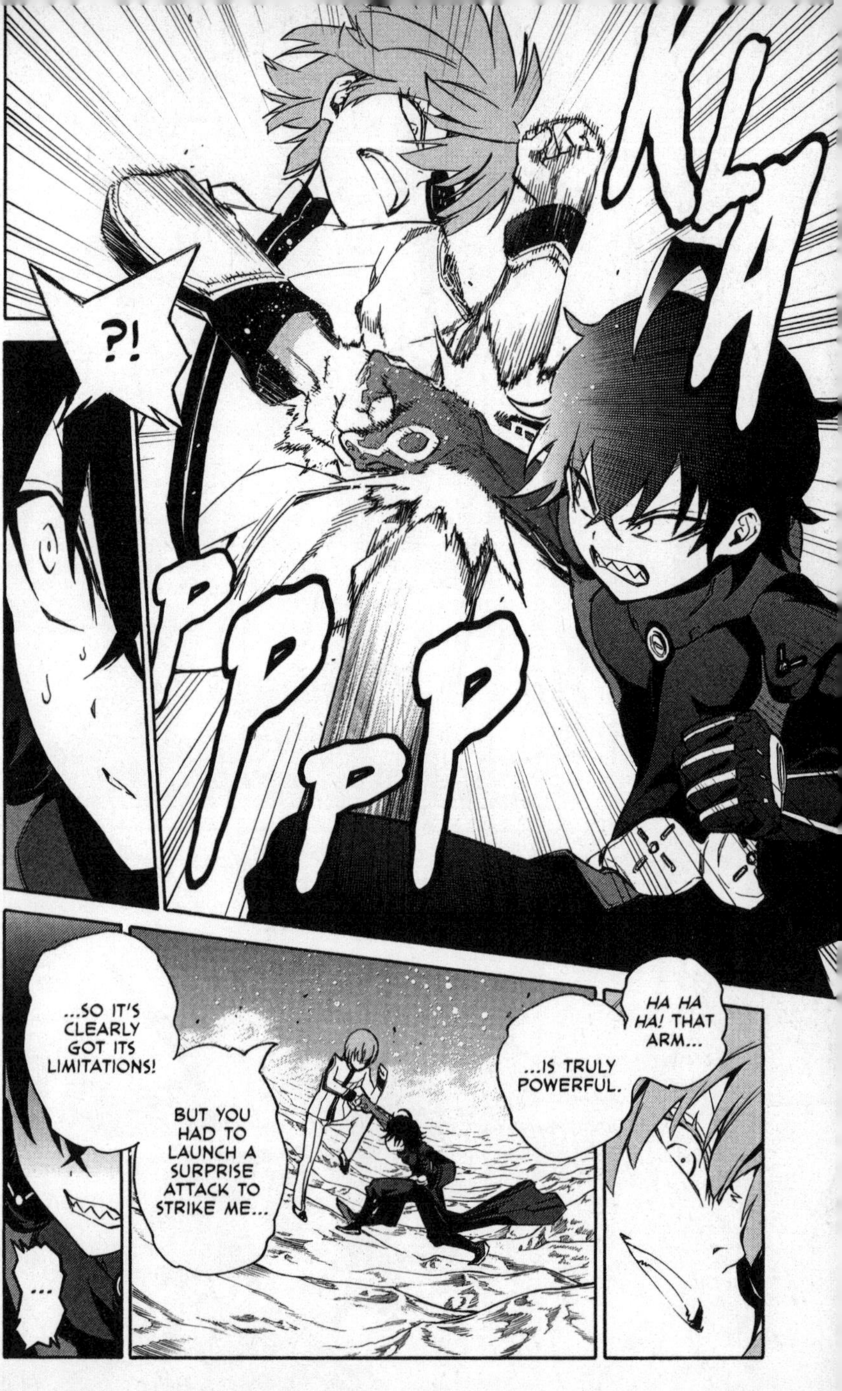
?!
PPPP
HA HA HA! THAT ARM...
...IS TRULY POWERFUL.
BUT YOU HAD TO LAUNCH A SURPRISE ATTACK TO STRIKE ME...
...SO IT'S CLEARLY GOT ITS LIMITATIONS!
...

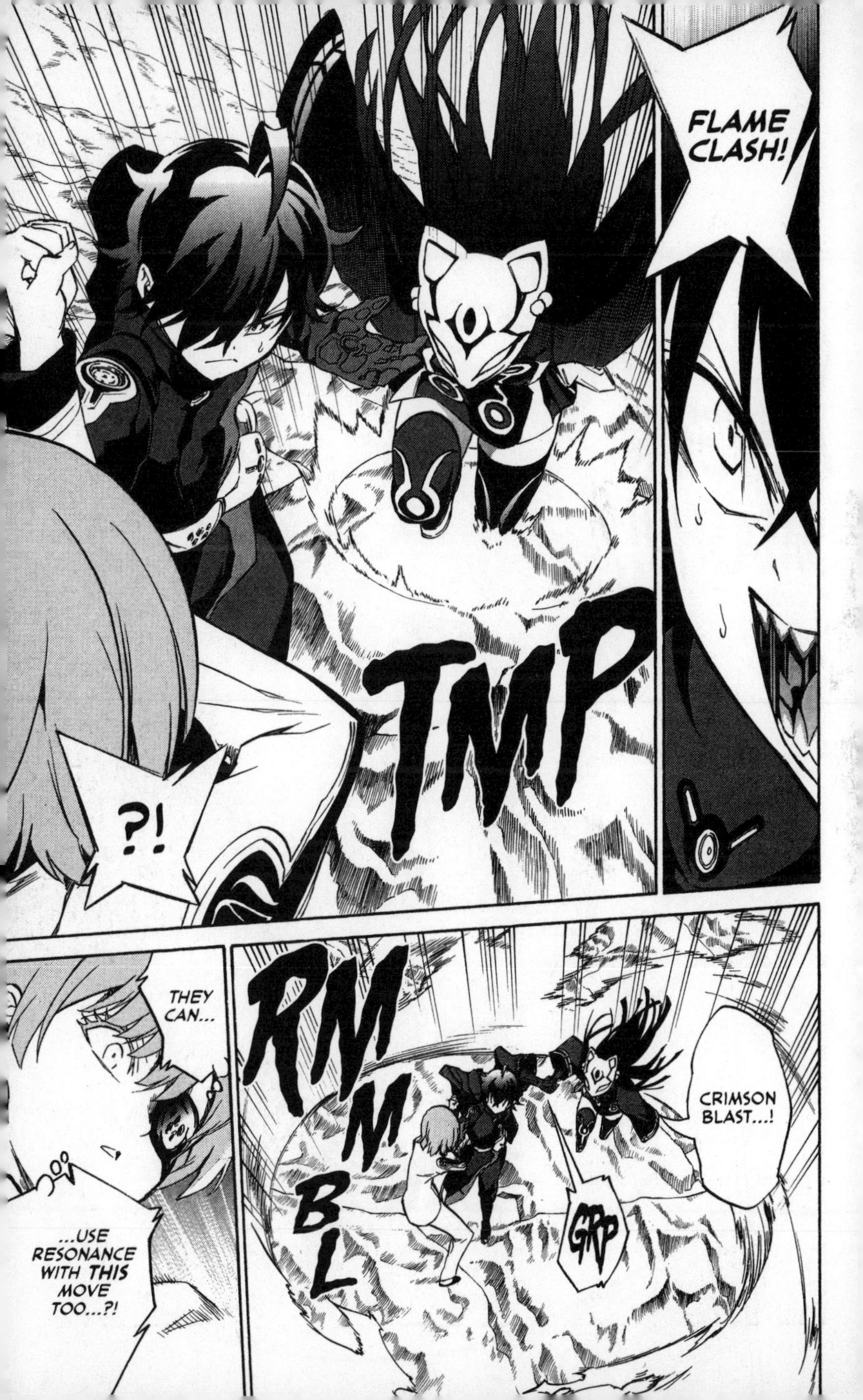
FLAME CLASH!
TMP
?!
CRIMSON BLAST...!
RMMBL
GRP
THEY CAN...
...USE RESONANCE WITH THIS MOVE TOO...?!

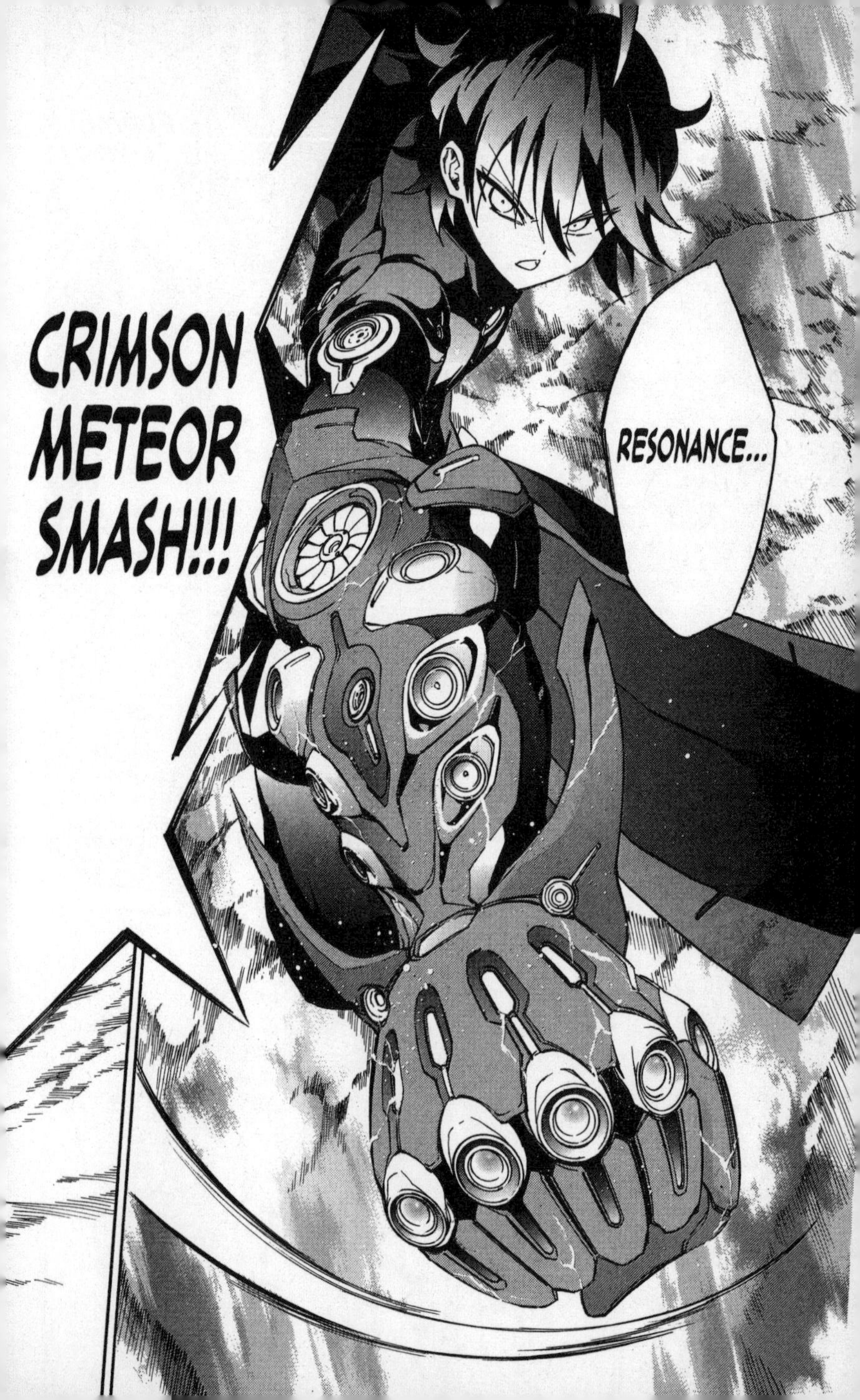
RESONANCE...
CRIMSON METEOR SMASH!!!

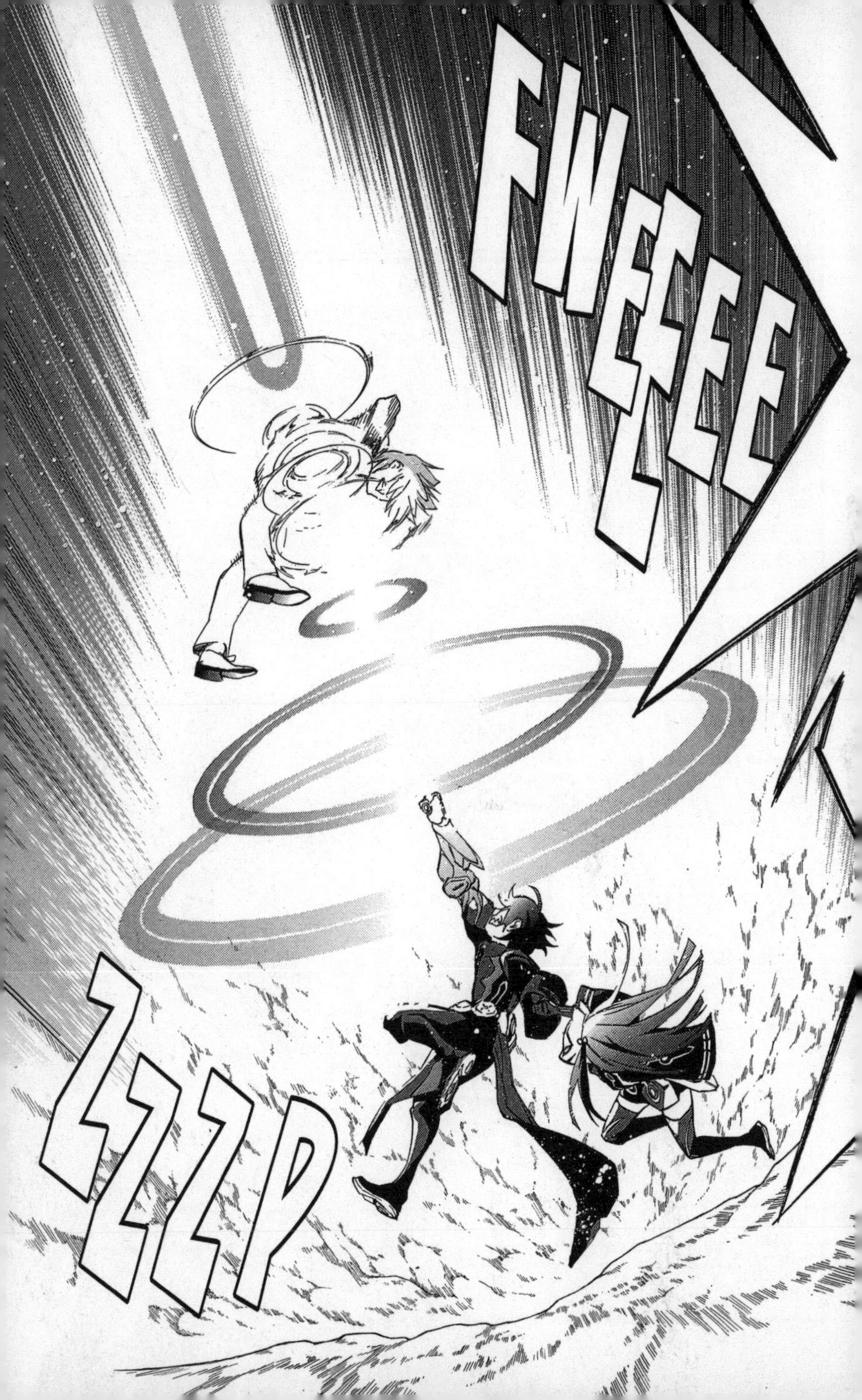
FWEEEE
ZZZP

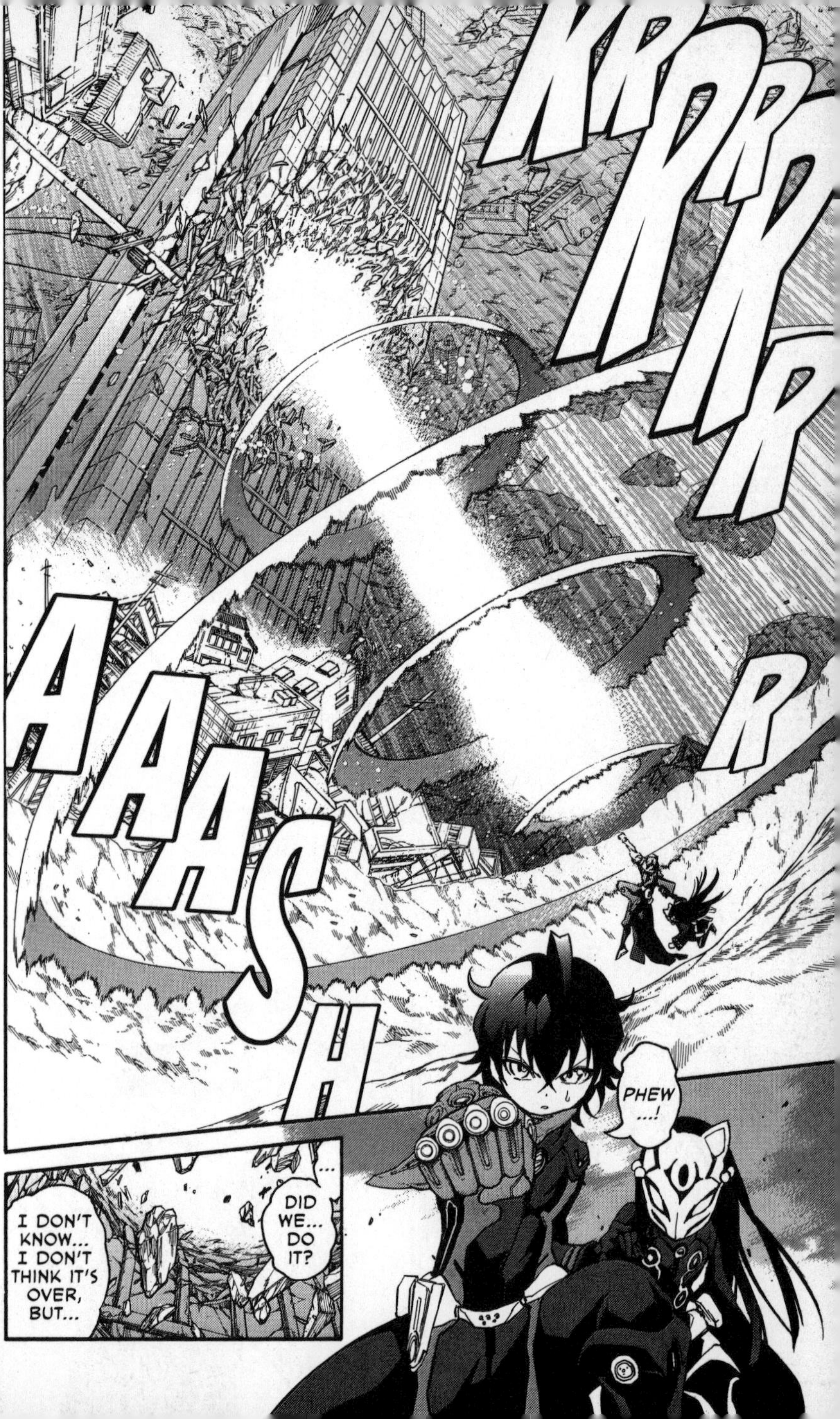
KRRRRRR
R
AAAASH
PHEW...!
...
DID WE... DO IT?
I DON'T KNOW... I DON'T THINK IT'S OVER, BUT...

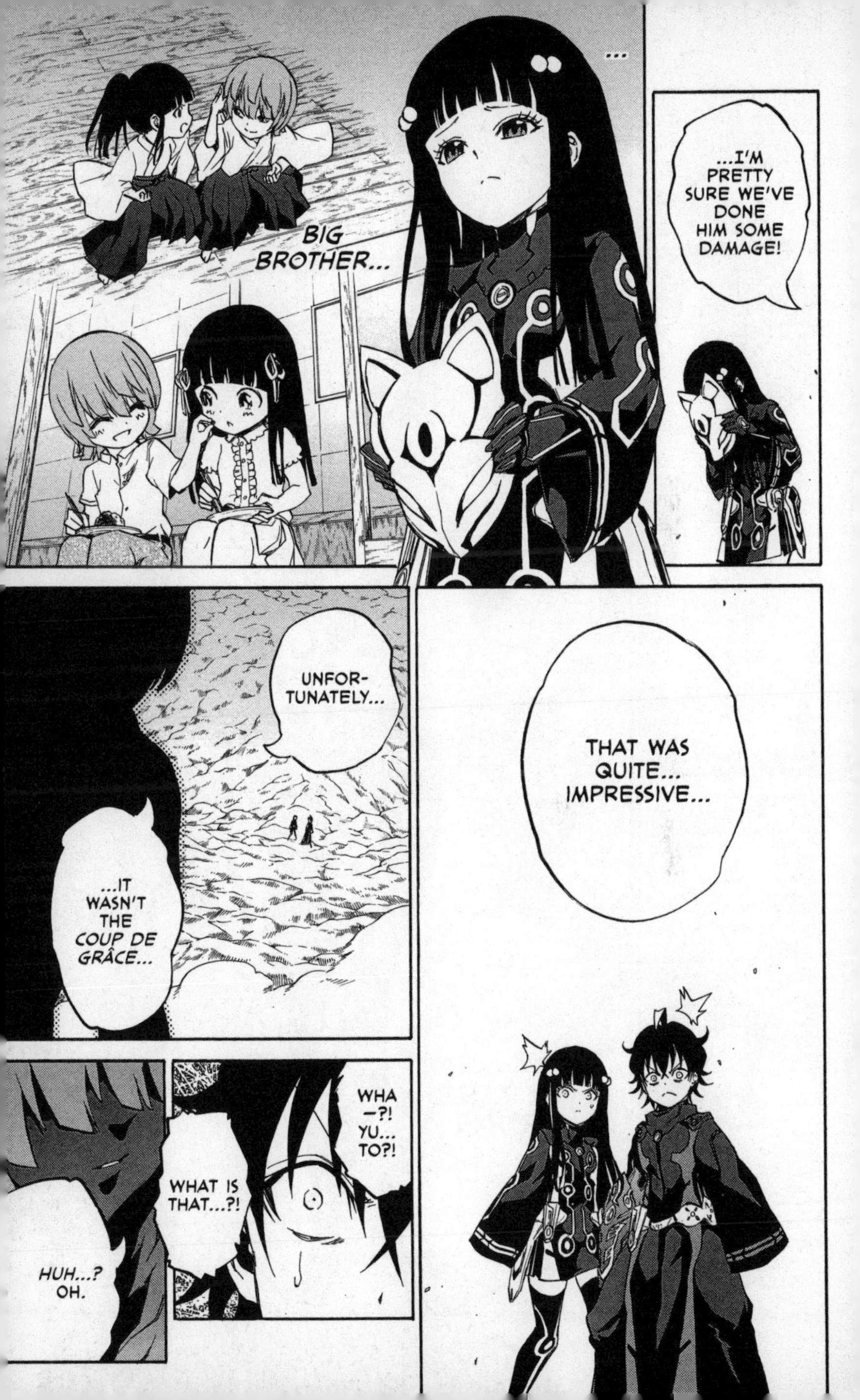
...I'M PRETTY SURE WE'VE DONE HIM SOME DAMAGE!
...
BIG BROTHER...
THAT WAS QUITE... IMPRESSIVE...
UNFORTUNATELY...
...IT WASN'T THE COUP DE GRÂCE...
WHA—?! YU... TO?!
WHAT IS THAT...?!
HUH...? OH.

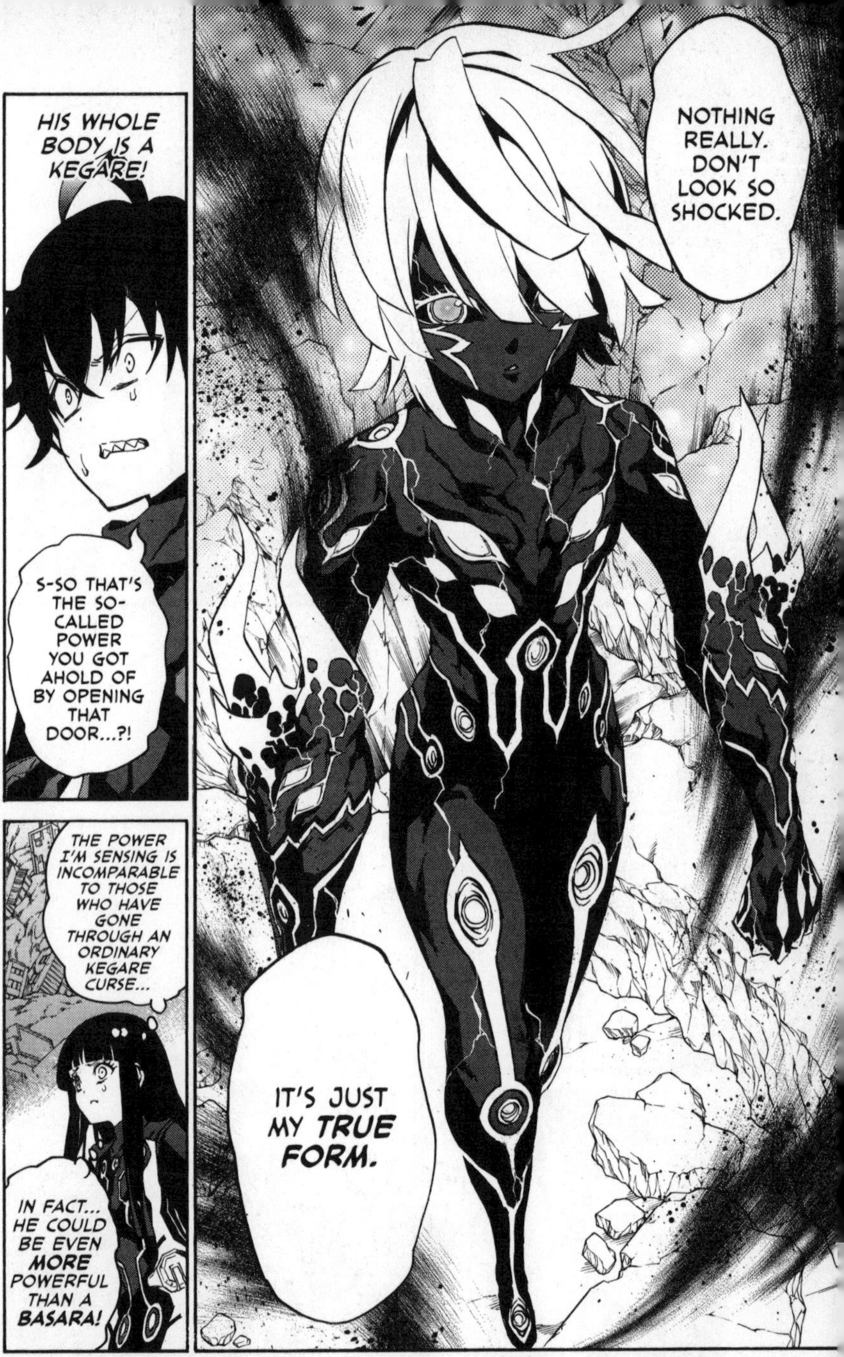
NOTHING REALLY. DON'T LOOK SO SHOCKED.
IT'S JUST MY **TRUE FORM.**
HIS WHOLE BODY IS A KEGARE!
S-SO THAT'S THE SO-CALLED POWER YOU GOT AHOLD OF BY OPENING THAT DOOR...?!
THE POWER I'M SENSING IS INCOMPARABLE TO THOSE WHO HAVE GONE THROUGH AN ORDINARY KEGARE CURSE...
IN FACT... HE COULD BE EVEN **MORE** POWERFUL THAN A **BASARA!**

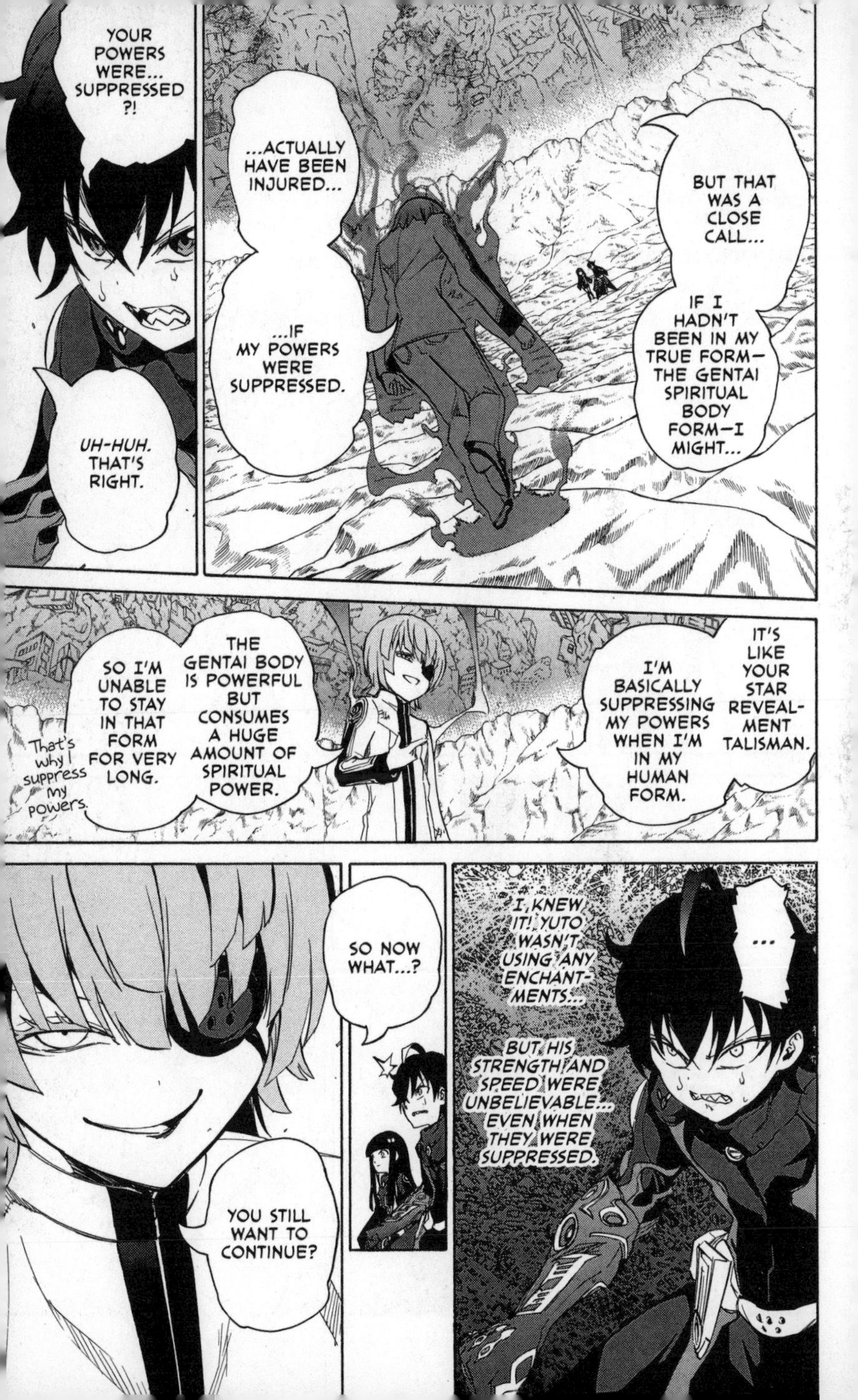
BUT THAT WAS A CLOSE CALL...
IF I HADN'T BEEN IN MY TRUE FORM—THE GENTAI SPIRITUAL BODY FORM—I MIGHT...
...ACTUALLY HAVE BEEN INJURED...
...IF MY POWERS WERE SUPPRESSED.
YOUR POWERS WERE... SUPPRESSED?!
UH-HUH. THAT'S RIGHT.
IT'S LIKE YOUR STAR REVEAL-MENT TALISMAN.
I'M BASICALLY SUPPRESSING MY POWERS WHEN I'M IN MY HUMAN FORM.
THE GENTAI BODY IS POWERFUL BUT CONSUMES A HUGE AMOUNT OF SPIRITUAL POWER.
SO I'M UNABLE TO STAY IN THAT FORM FOR VERY LONG.
That's why I suppress my powers.
...
I KNEW IT! YUTO WASN'T USING ANY ENCHANT-MENTS...
BUT HIS STRENGTH AND SPEED WERE UNBELIEVABLE... EVEN WHEN THEY WERE SUPPRESSED.
SO NOW WHAT...?
YOU STILL WANT TO CONTINUE?

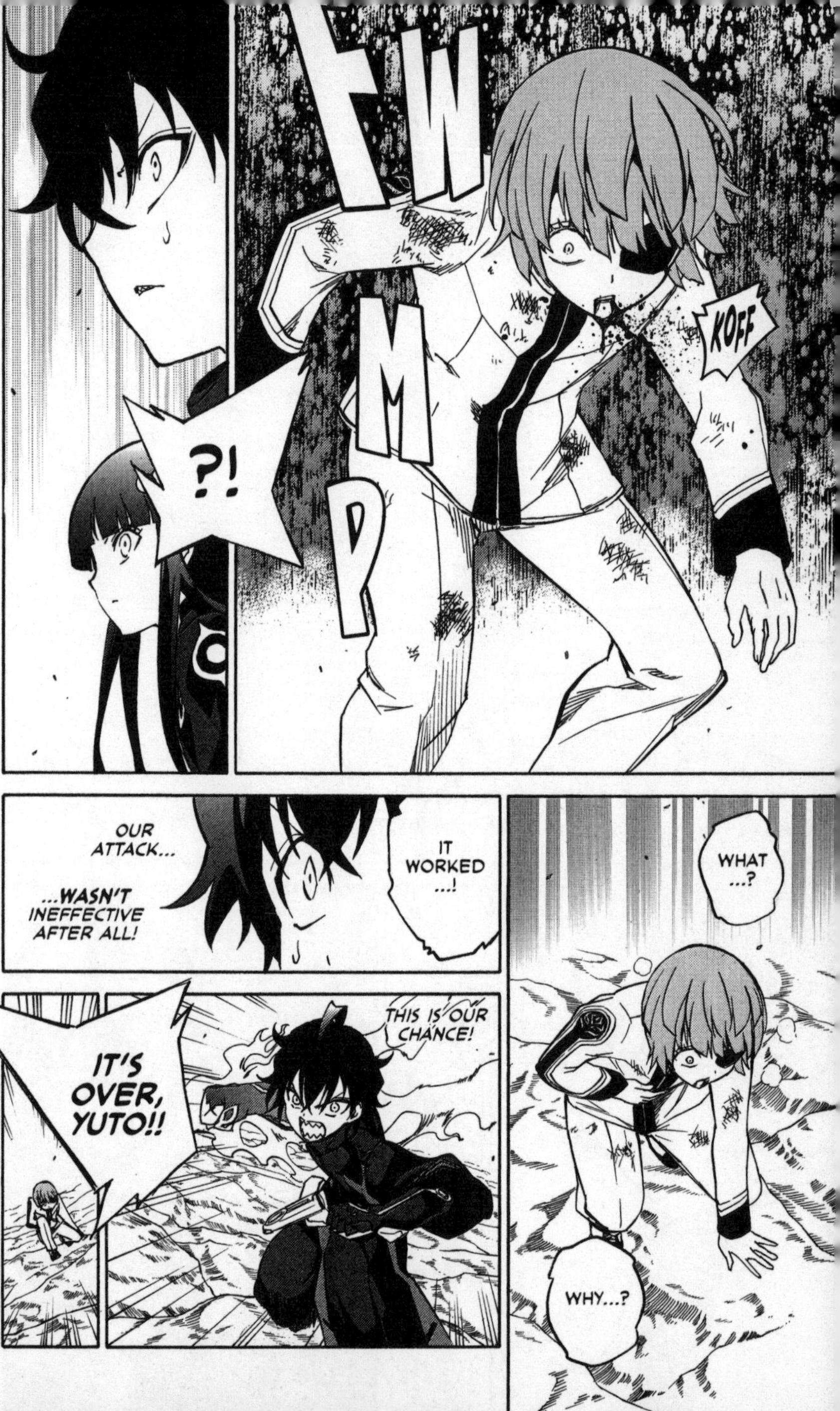
FWMP
KOFF
?!
WHAT ...?
WHY...?
IT WORKED ...!
OUR ATTACK...
...WASN'T INEFFECTIVE AFTER ALL!
THIS IS OUR CHANCE!
IT'S OVER, YUTO!!

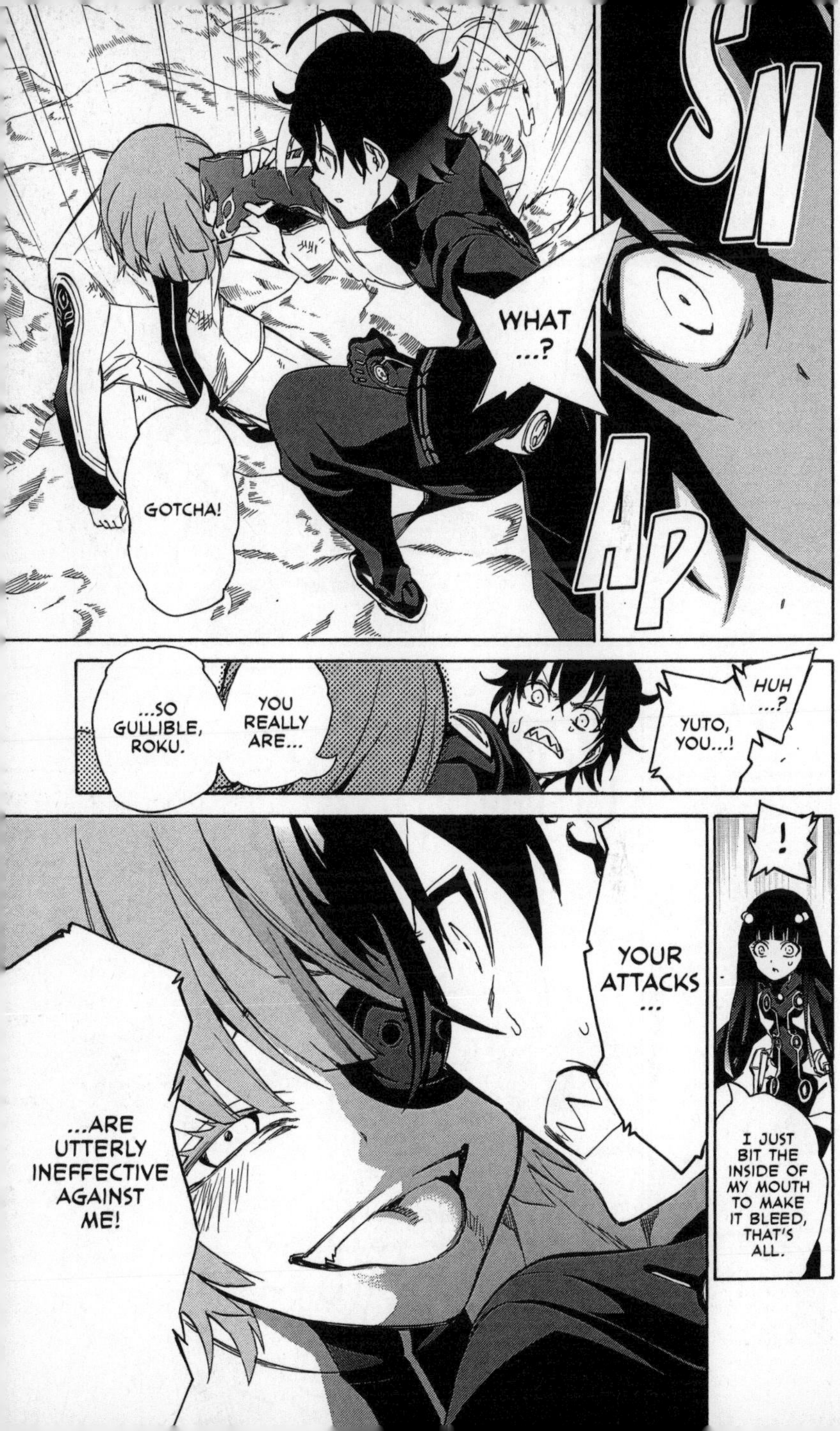
SNAP
WHAT ...?
GOTCHA!
HUH ...?
YUTO, YOU...!
YOU REALLY ARE...
...SO GULLIBLE, ROKU.
!
I JUST BIT THE INSIDE OF MY MOUTH TO MAKE IT BLEED, THAT'S ALL.
YOUR ATTACKS ...
...ARE UTTERLY INEFFECTIVE AGAINST ME!

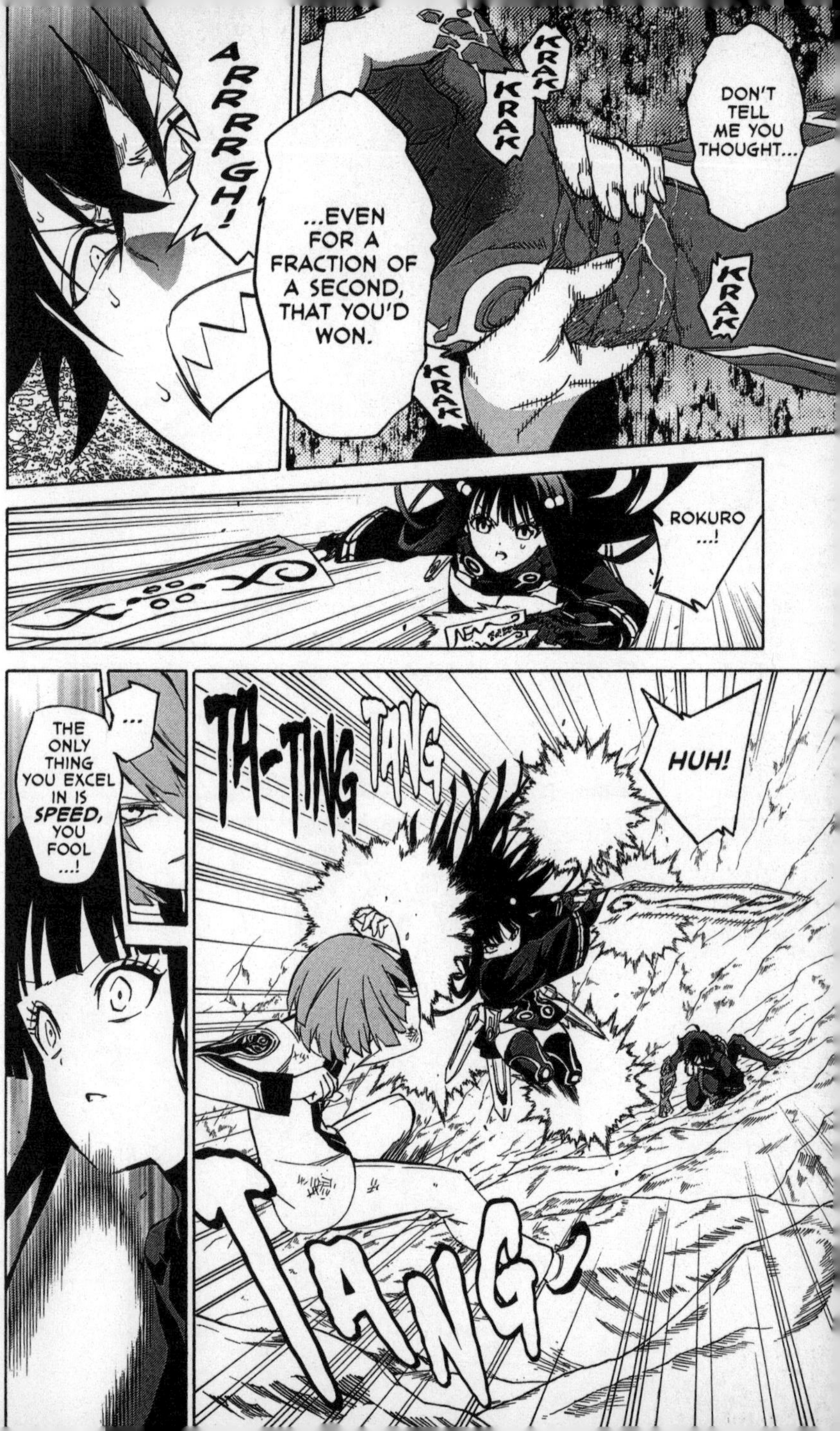
DON'T TELL ME YOU THOUGHT...
KRAK KRAK
KRAK KRAK
...EVEN FOR A FRACTION OF A SECOND, THAT YOU'D WON.
KRAK KRAK
ARRRGH!
ROKURO ...!
HUH!
TA-TING TANG
TANG
...
THE ONLY THING YOU EXCEL IN IS *SPEED*, YOU FOOL ...!

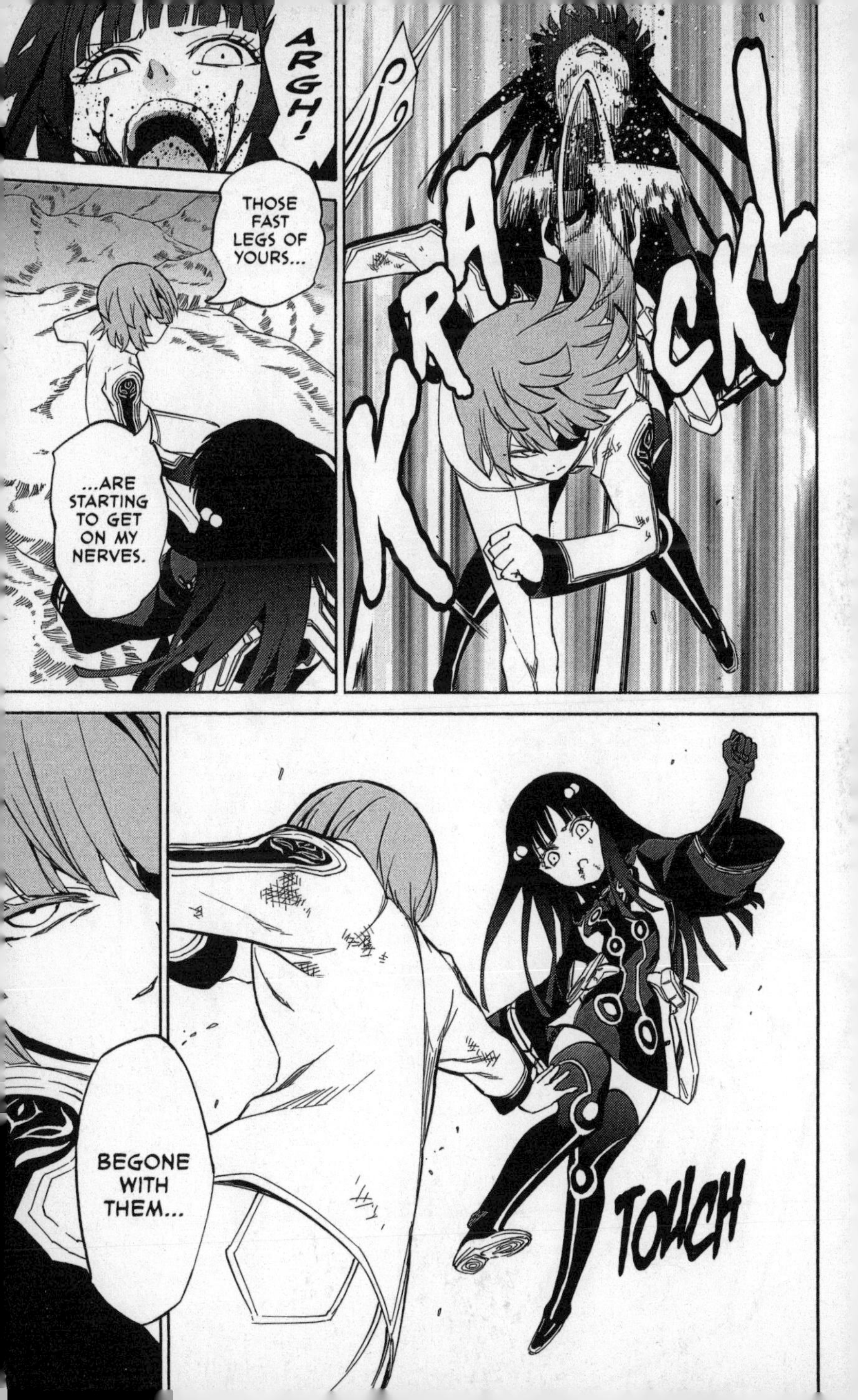
KRACKL
ARGH!
THOSE FAST LEGS OF YOURS...
...ARE STARTING TO GET ON MY NERVES.
TOUCH
BEGONE WITH THEM...

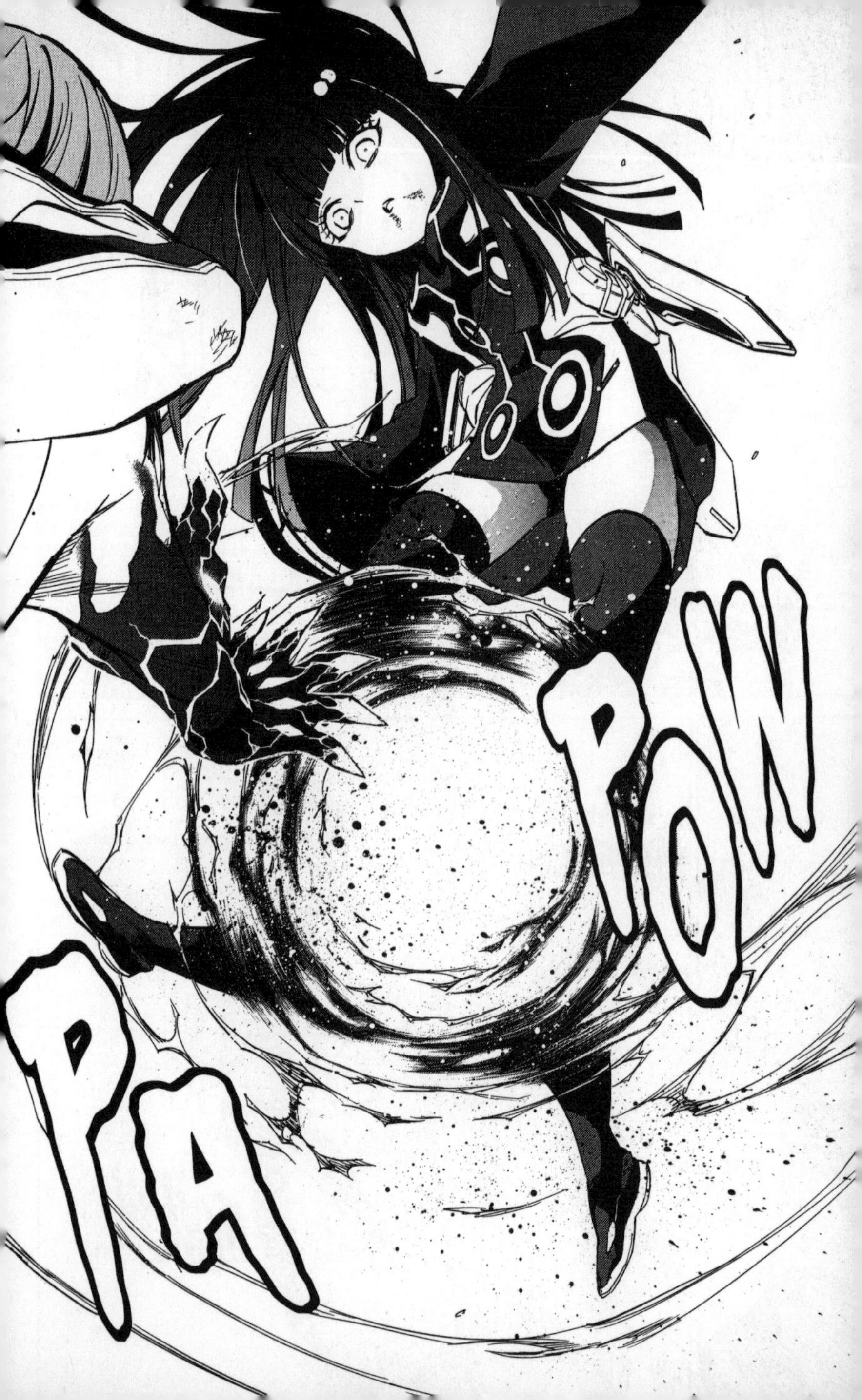
PA
POW

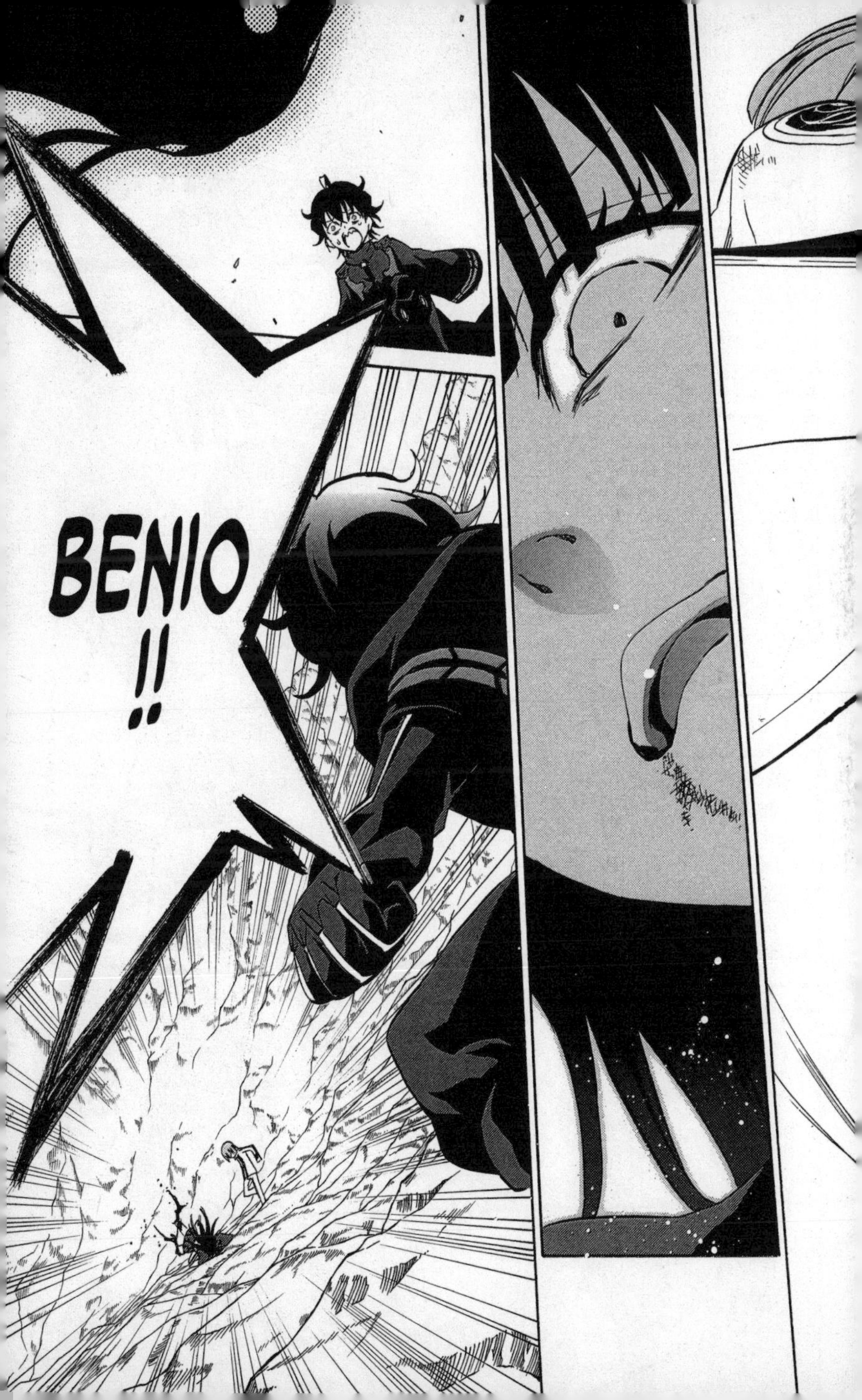
BENIO !!

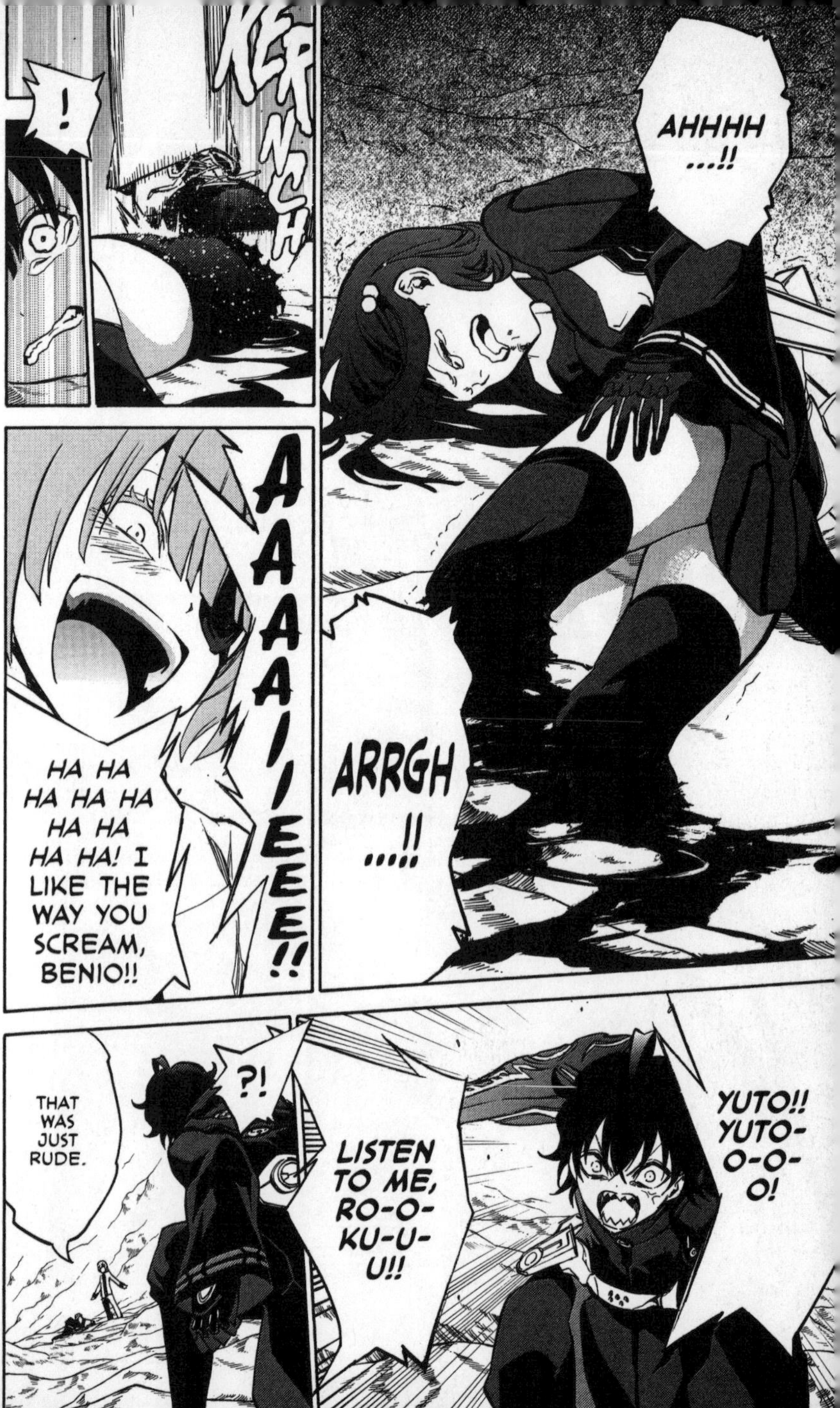
AHHHH ...!!
ARRGH ...!!
KERNCH
!
AAAAIIEEEE!!
HA HA HA HA HA HA HA HA HA! I LIKE THE WAY YOU SCREAM, BENIO!!
YUTO!! YUTO-O-O-O!
LISTEN TO ME, RO-O-KU-U-U!!
?!
THAT WAS JUST RUDE.

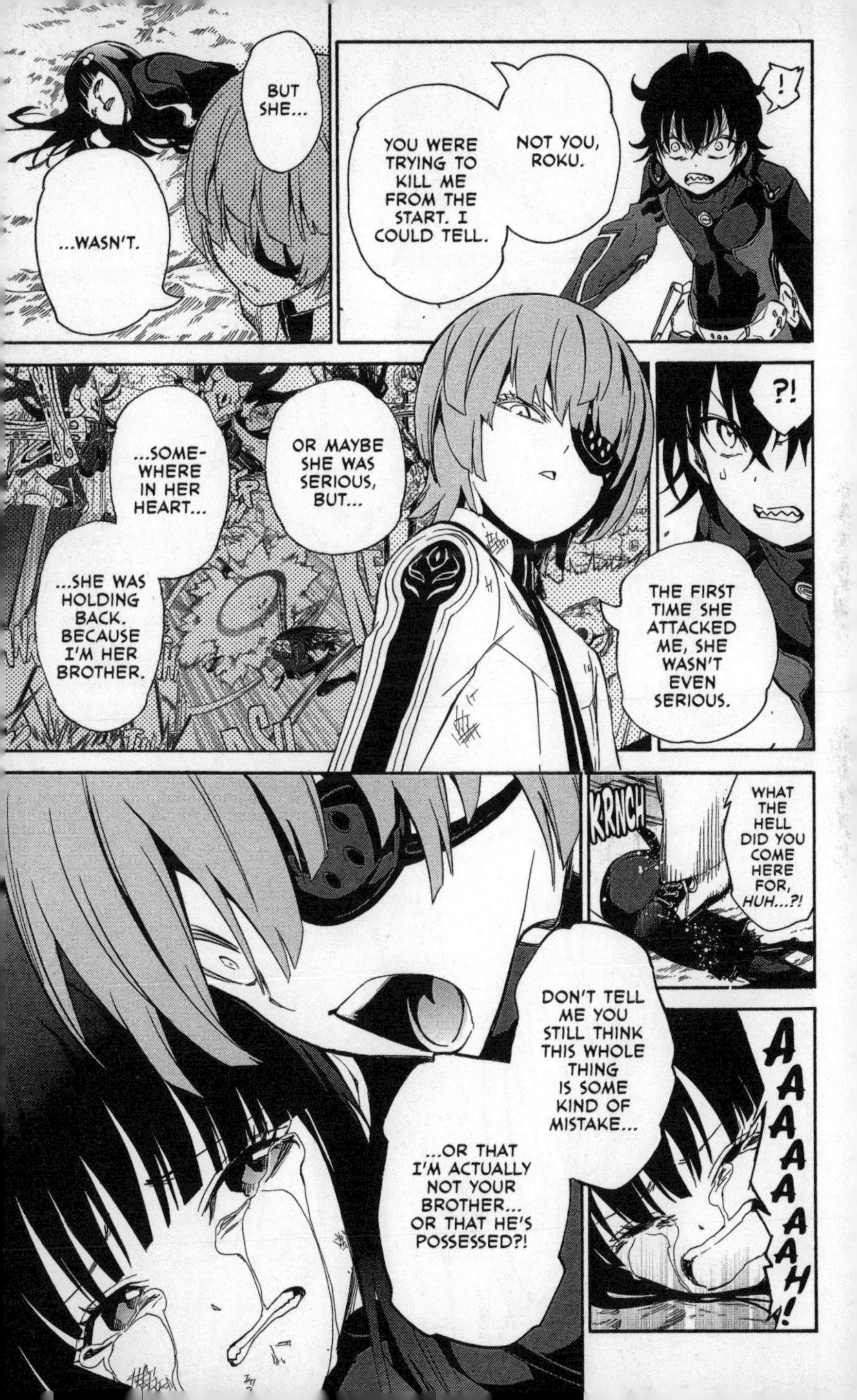

!
NOT YOU, ROKU.
YOU WERE TRYING TO KILL ME FROM THE START. I COULD TELL.
BUT SHE...
...WASN'T.
?!
THE FIRST TIME SHE ATTACKED ME, SHE WASN'T EVEN SERIOUS.
OR MAYBE SHE WAS SERIOUS, BUT...
...SOME-WHERE IN HER HEART...
...SHE WAS HOLDING BACK. BECAUSE I'M HER BROTHER.
KRNCH
WHAT THE HELL DID YOU COME HERE FOR, HUH...?!
AAAAAAAH!
DON'T TELL ME YOU STILL THINK THIS WHOLE THING IS SOME KIND OF MISTAKE...
...OR THAT I'M ACTUALLY NOT YOUR BROTHER... OR THAT HE'S POSSESSED?!

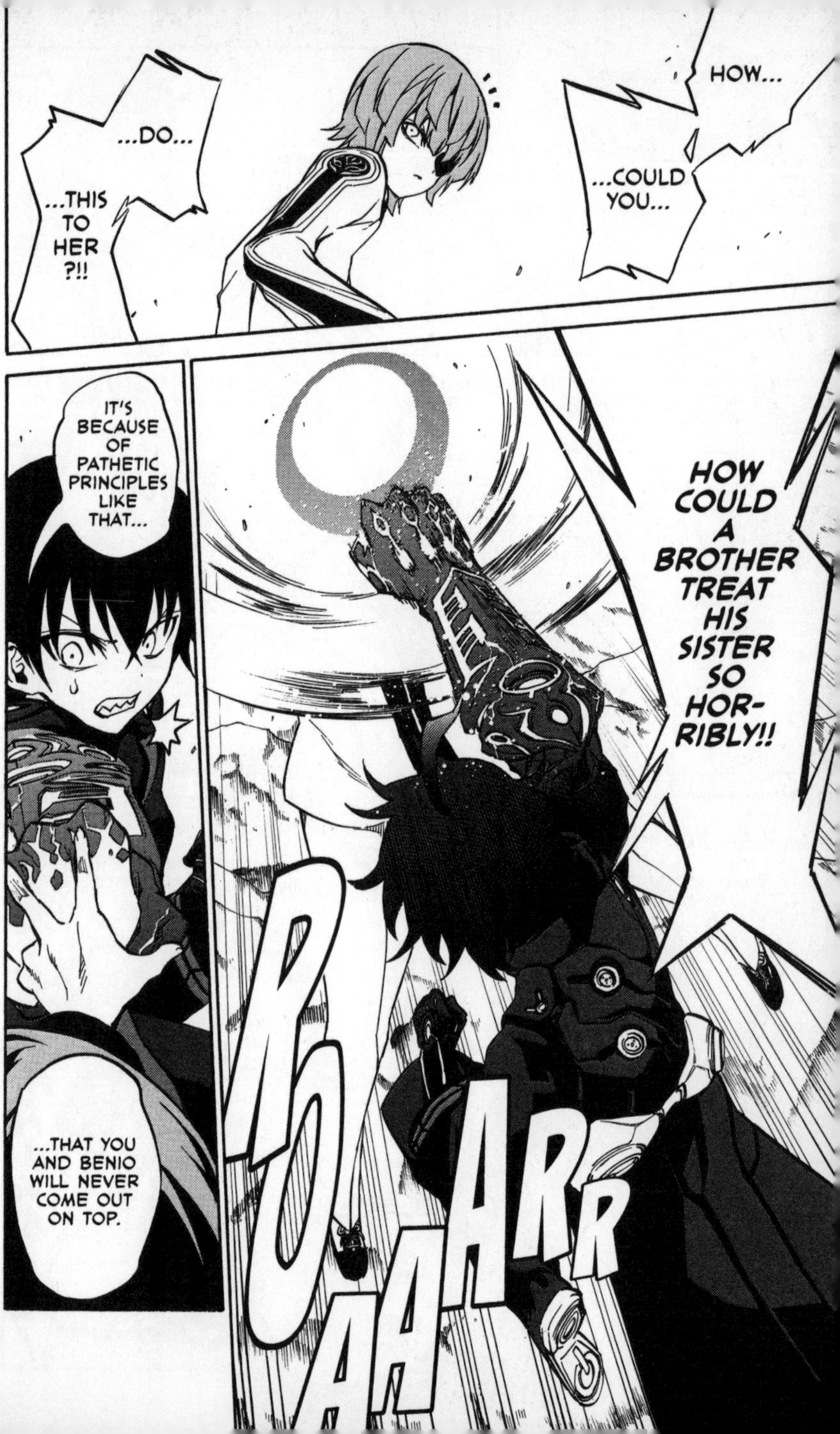
HOW... ...COULD YOU...
...DO... ...THIS TO HER ?!!
HOW COULD A BROTHER TREAT HIS SISTER SO HOR-RIBLY!!
ROAAARR
IT'S BECAUSE OF PATHETIC PRINCIPLES LIKE THAT...
...THAT YOU AND BENIO WILL NEVER COME OUT ON TOP.

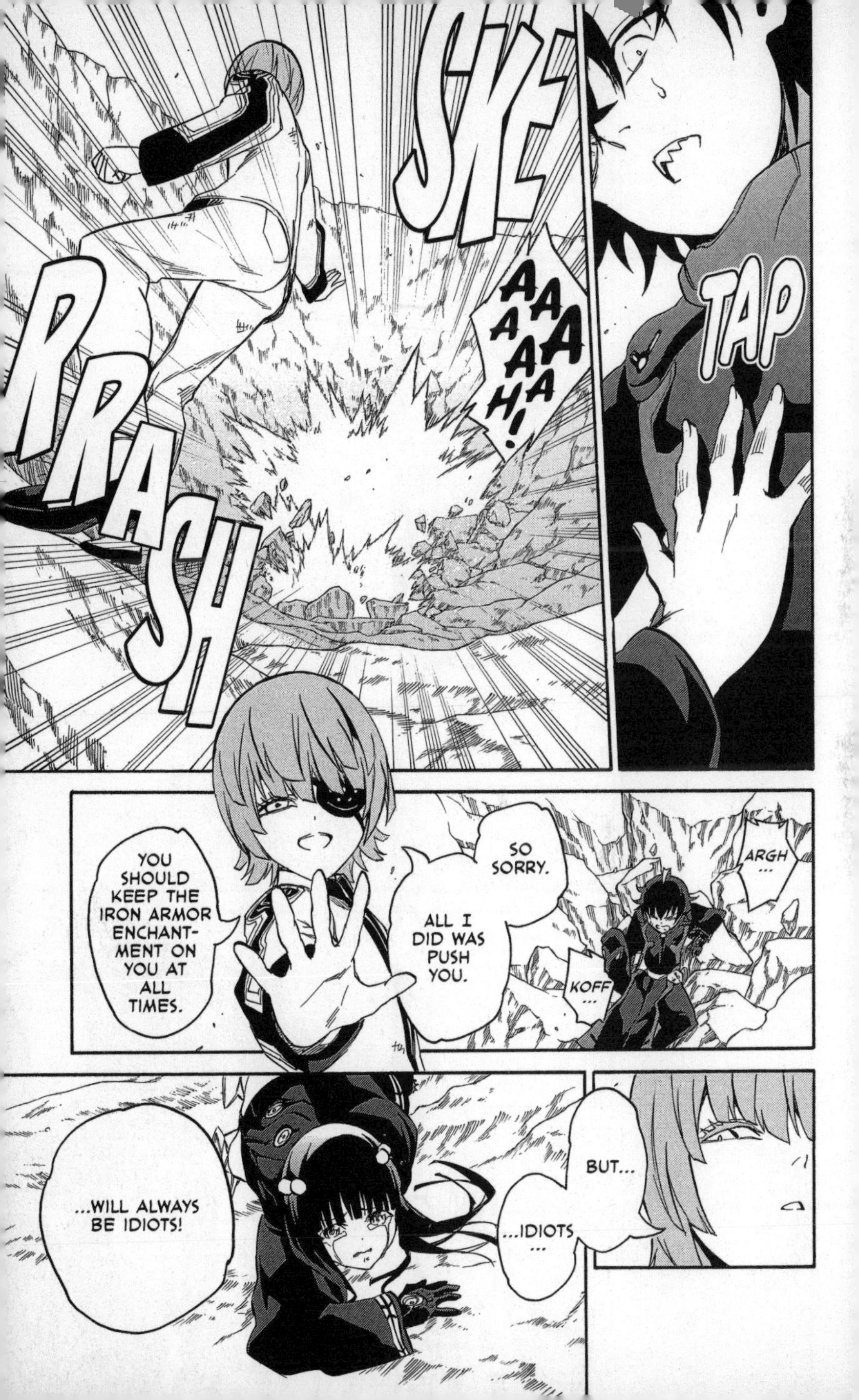
TAP
SKE
AAAAAAAH!
KRASH
ARGH...
KOFF...
SO SORRY.
ALL I DID WAS PUSH YOU.
YOU SHOULD KEEP THE IRON ARMOR ENCHANTMENT ON YOU AT ALL TIMES.
BUT...
...IDIOTS...
...WILL ALWAYS BE IDIOTS!

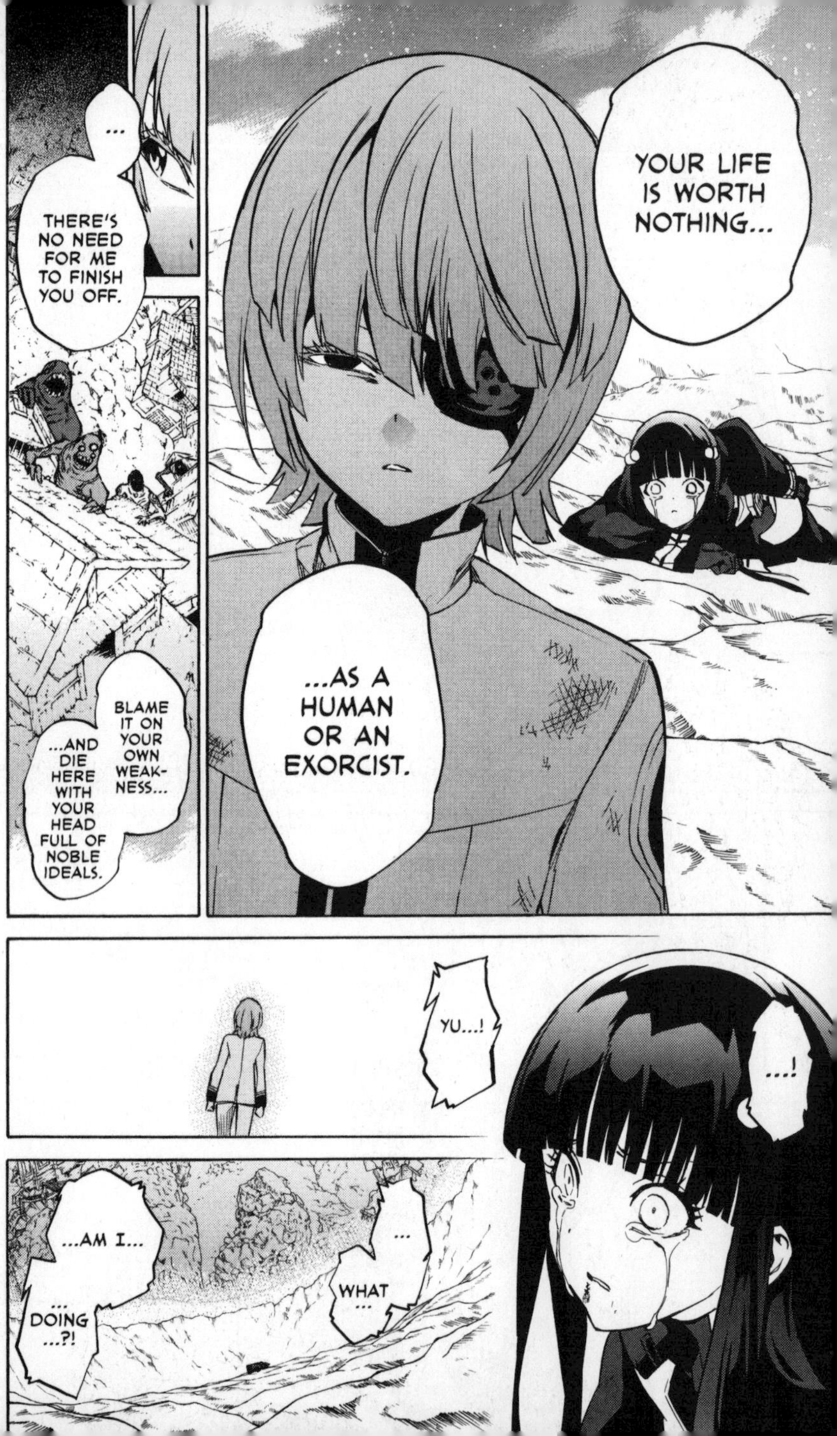
YOUR LIFE IS WORTH NOTHING...
...AS A HUMAN OR AN EXORCIST.
...
THERE'S NO NEED FOR ME TO FINISH YOU OFF.
BLAME IT ON YOUR OWN WEAK-NESS...
...AND DIE HERE WITH YOUR HEAD FULL OF NOBLE IDEALS.
...!
YU...!
...
WHAT ...
...AM I...
... DOING ...?!

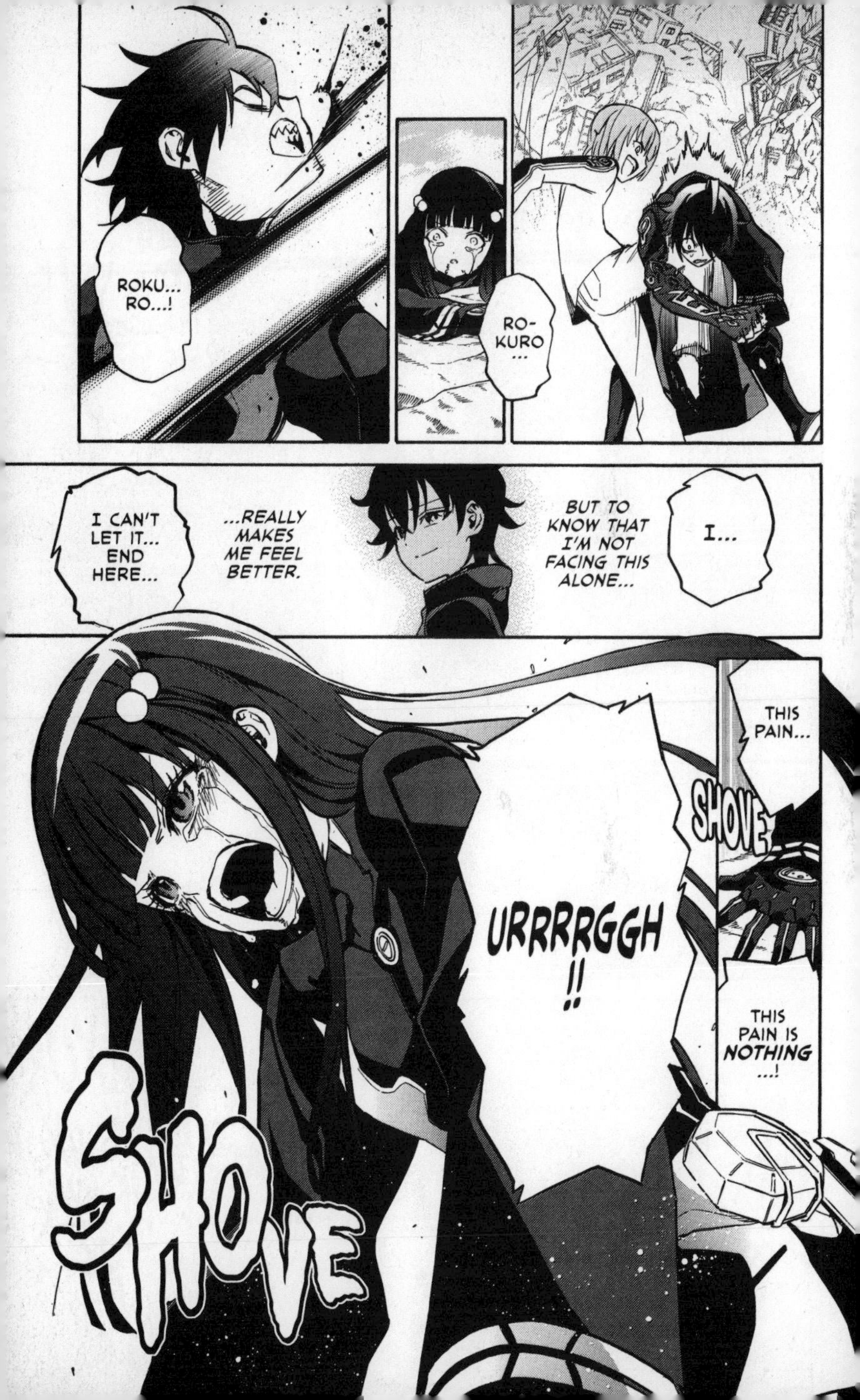
RO-KURO ...
ROKU... RO...!
I...
BUT TO KNOW THAT I'M NOT FACING THIS ALONE...
...REALLY MAKES ME FEEL BETTER.
I CAN'T LET IT... END HERE...
THIS PAIN...
SHOVE
THIS PAIN IS NOTHING ...!
URRRRGGH !!
SHOVE

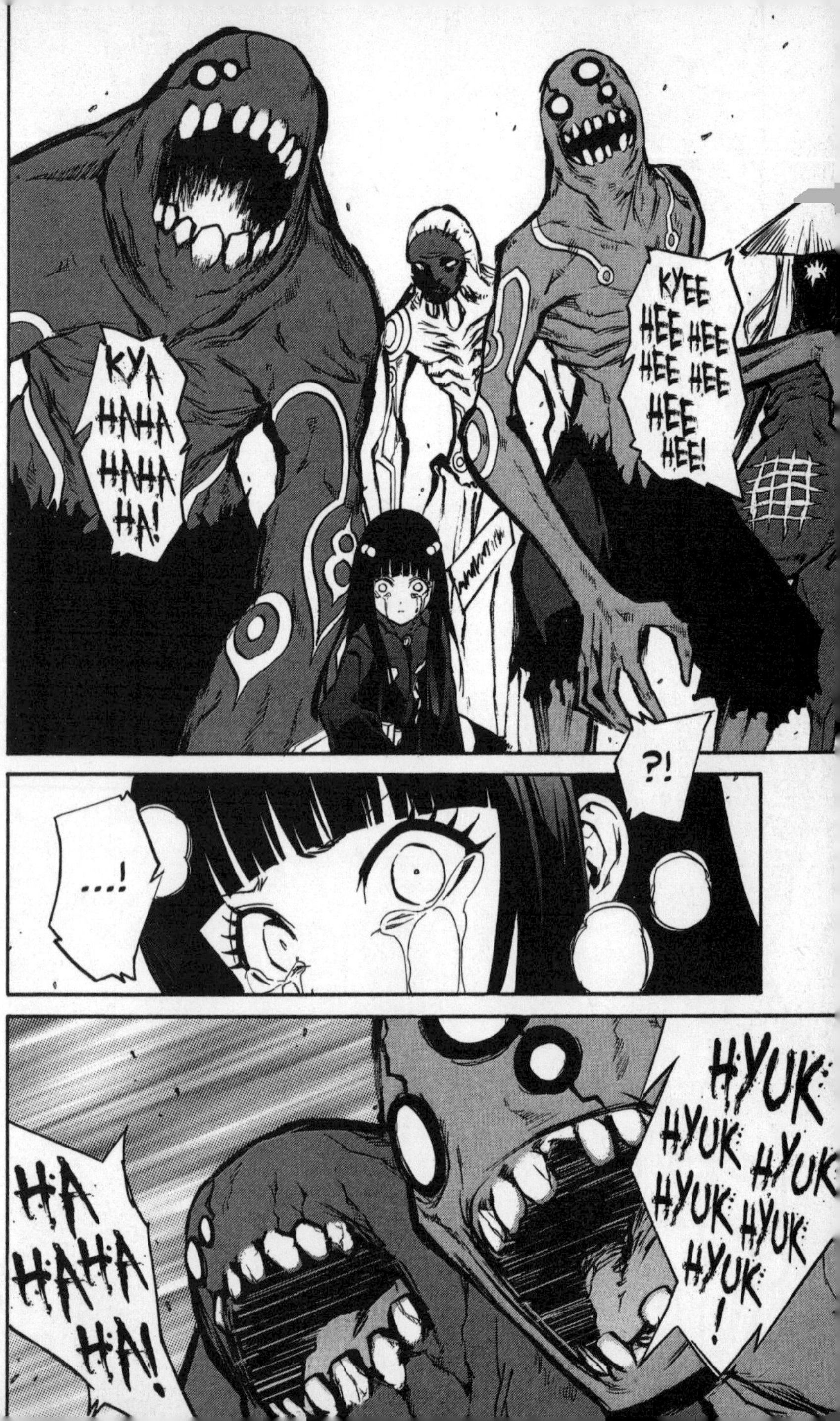
KYEE HEE HEE HEE HEE HEE HEE!
KYA HAHA HAHA HA!
?!
...!
HYUK HYUK HYUK HYUK HYUK HYUK!
HA HAHA HA!

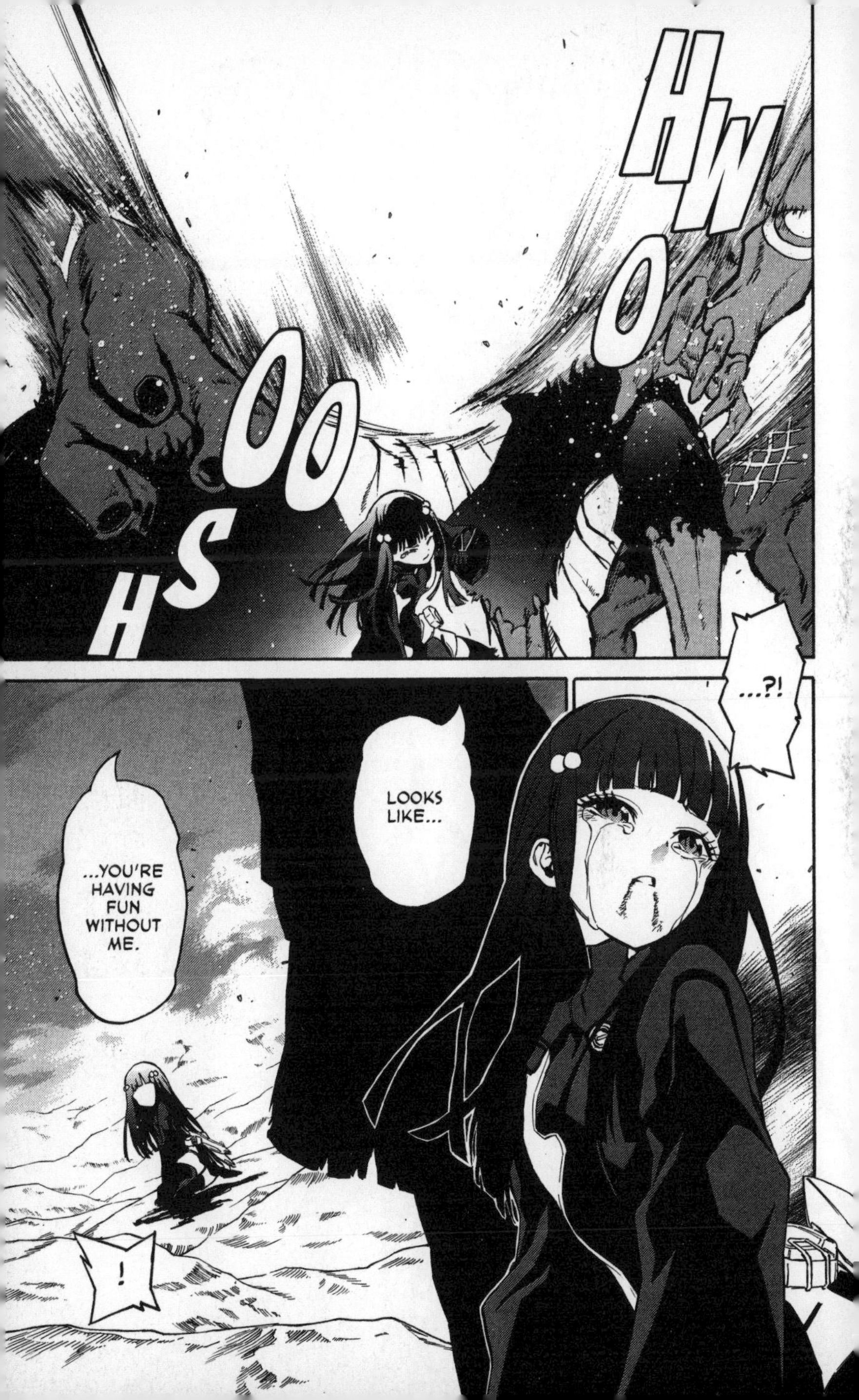
HWOOOSH
...?!
LOOKS LIKE...
...YOU'RE HAVING FUN WITHOUT ME.
!

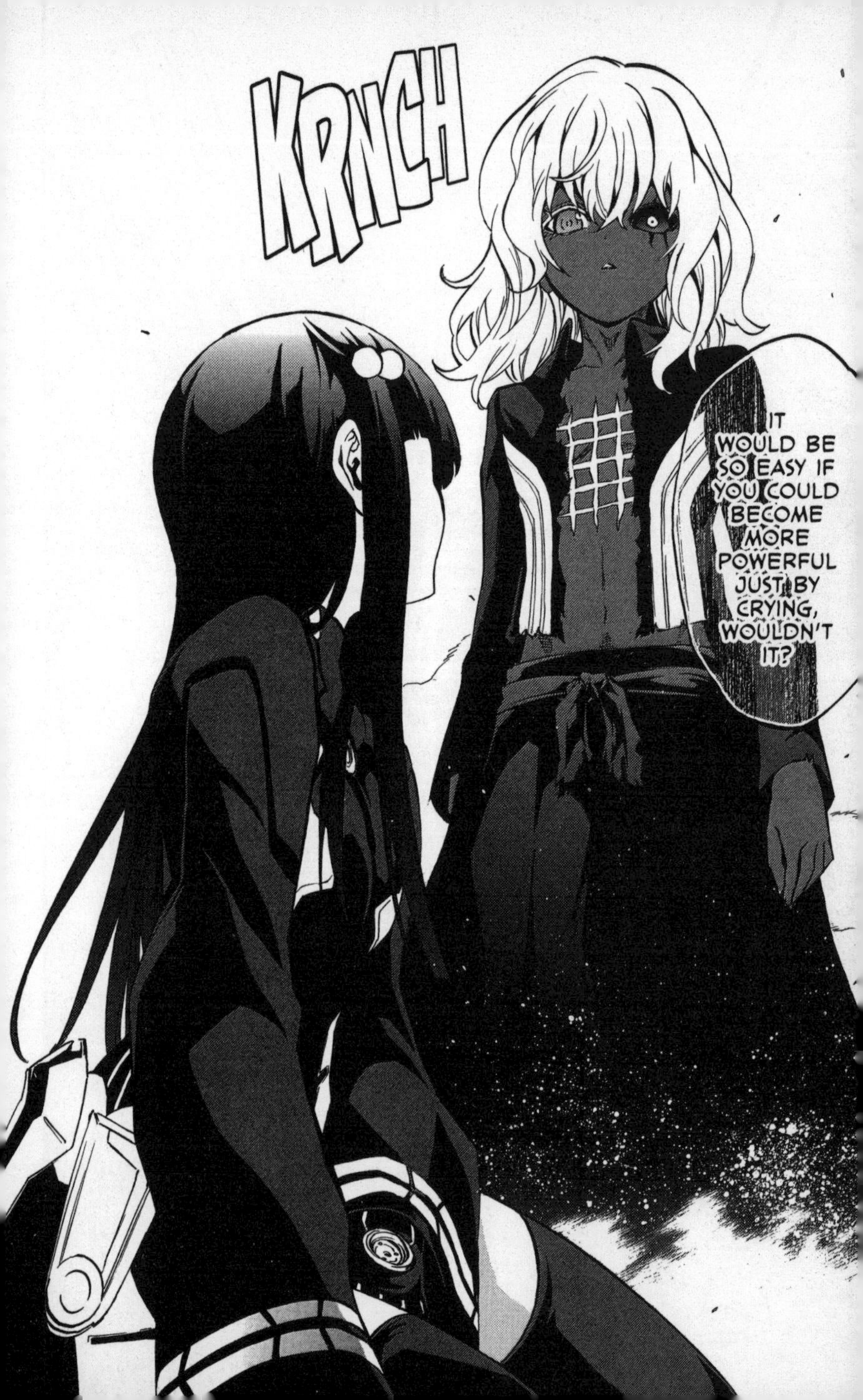
KRNCH
IT WOULD BE SO EASY IF YOU COULD BECOME MORE POWERFUL JUST BY CRYING, WOULDN'T IT?

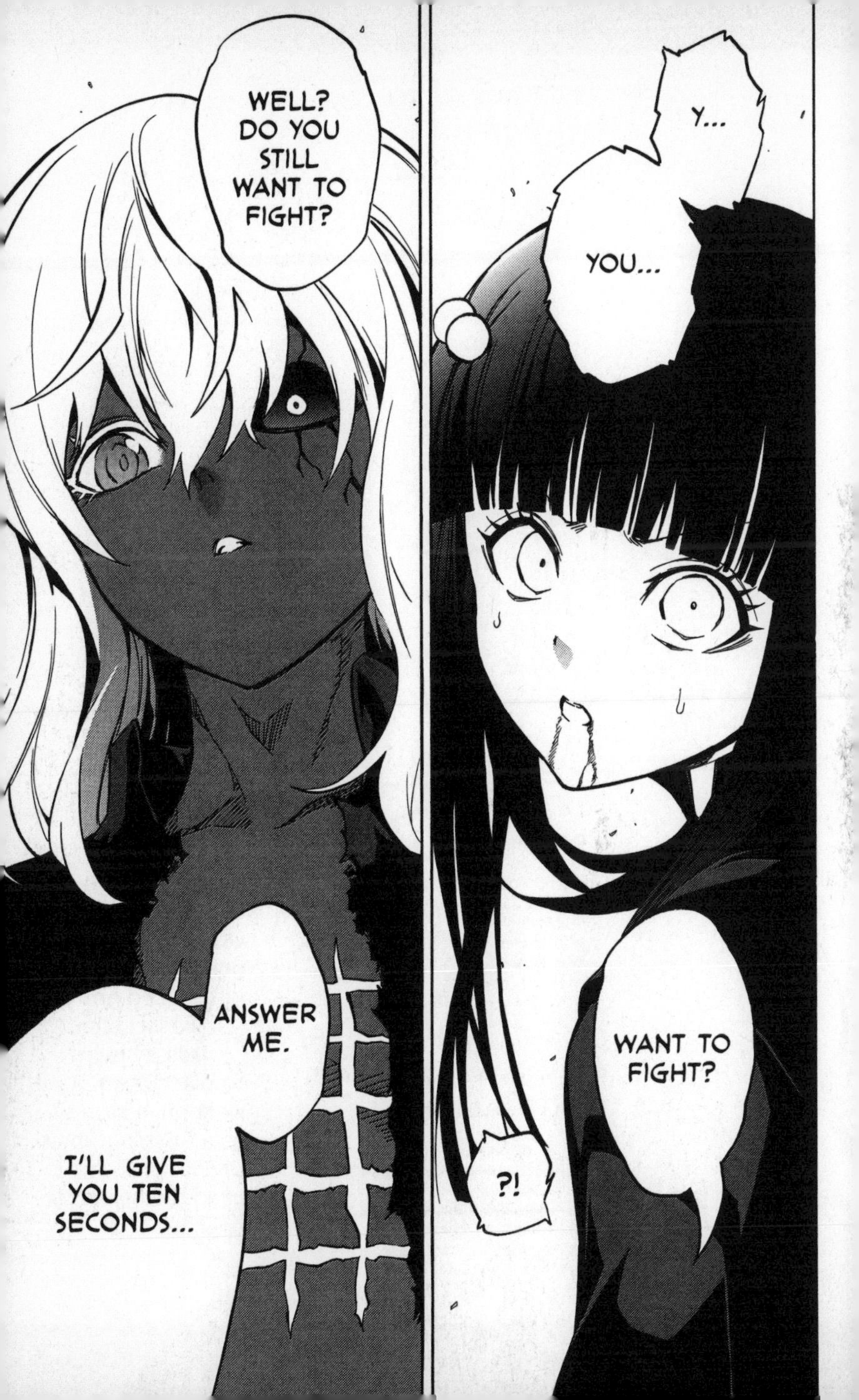
Y...
YOU...
WANT TO FIGHT?
?!
WELL? DO YOU STILL WANT TO FIGHT?
ANSWER ME.
I'LL GIVE YOU TEN SECONDS...

Data 2: Multi-Attachments

This is some of the equipment used for battling Kegare, exploring Magano, gathering geographic data and staying inside Magano for a long time. You can place up to six of these in the slots on the belt. Other than the equipment I've introduced on the left, there's also a sheath to place the weapon in as well as a Cosmographic Divination Board used to search for enemies.

Talisman Holder

A must-have attachment to fight Kegare. Those who specialize in supporting the front line fighters usually have more than two of these on them.

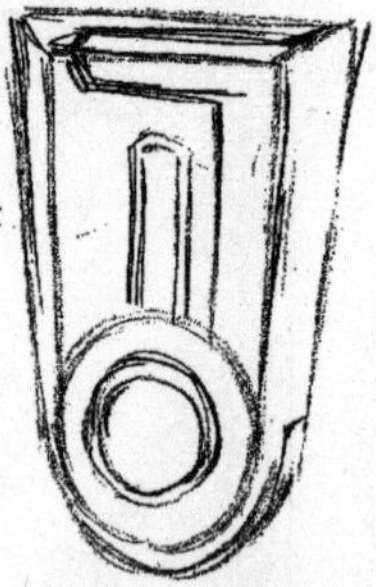

Press this and the holder opens up. Pull out the talisman and close the holder.

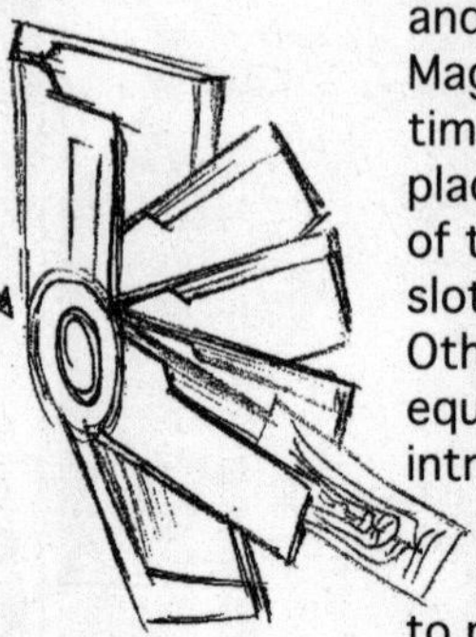

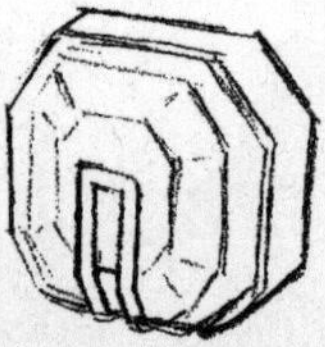

Medical Case

A container for herbs and pills. Rokuro places the pebbles he uses for Wind Blast Bullet in this.

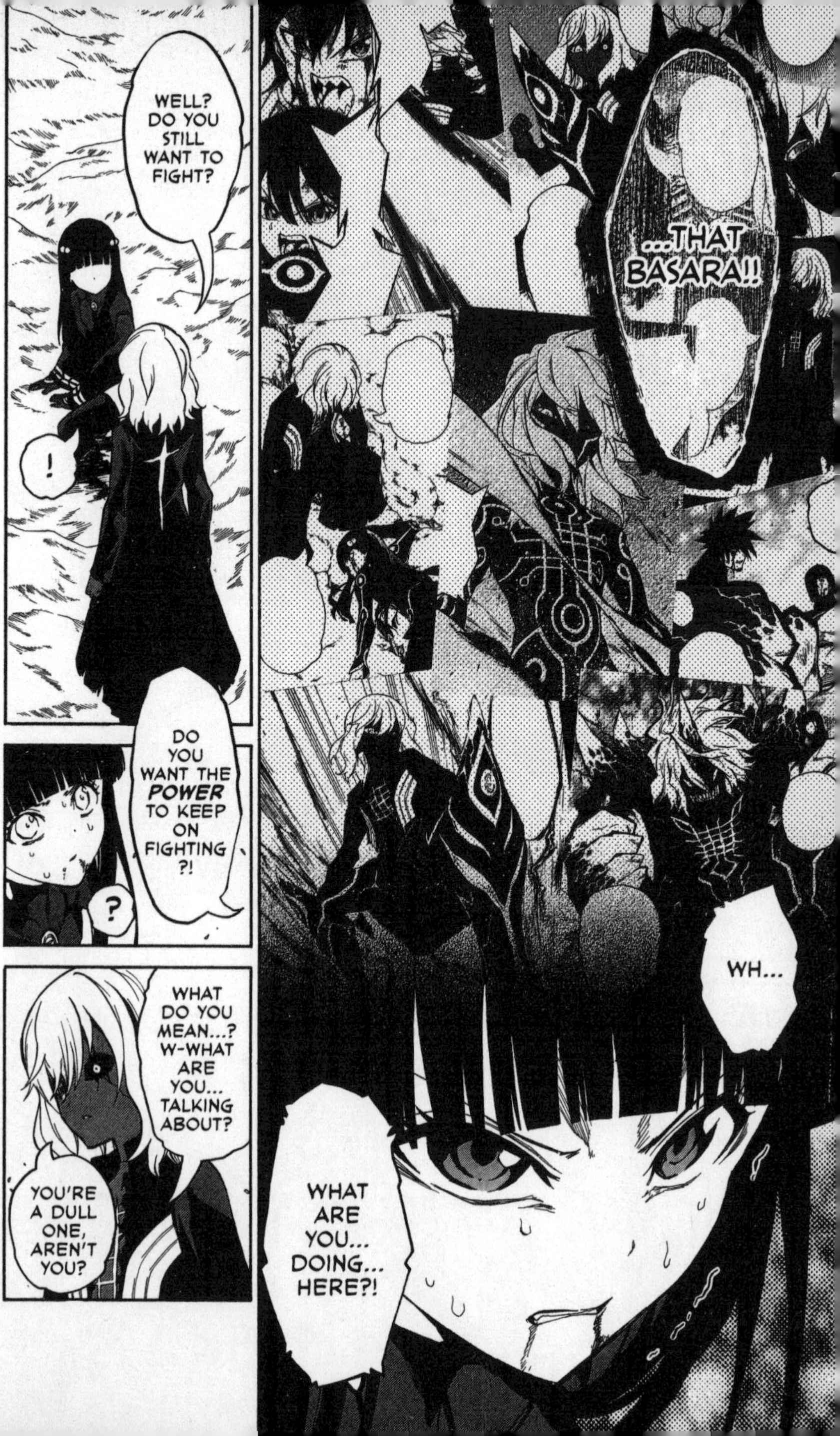
...THAT BASARA!!
WH...
WHAT ARE YOU... DOING... HERE?!
WELL? DO YOU STILL WANT TO FIGHT?
!
DO YOU WANT THE *POWER* TO KEEP ON FIGHTING?!
?
WHAT DO YOU MEAN...? W-WHAT ARE YOU... TALKING ABOUT?
YOU'RE A DULL ONE, AREN'T YOU?

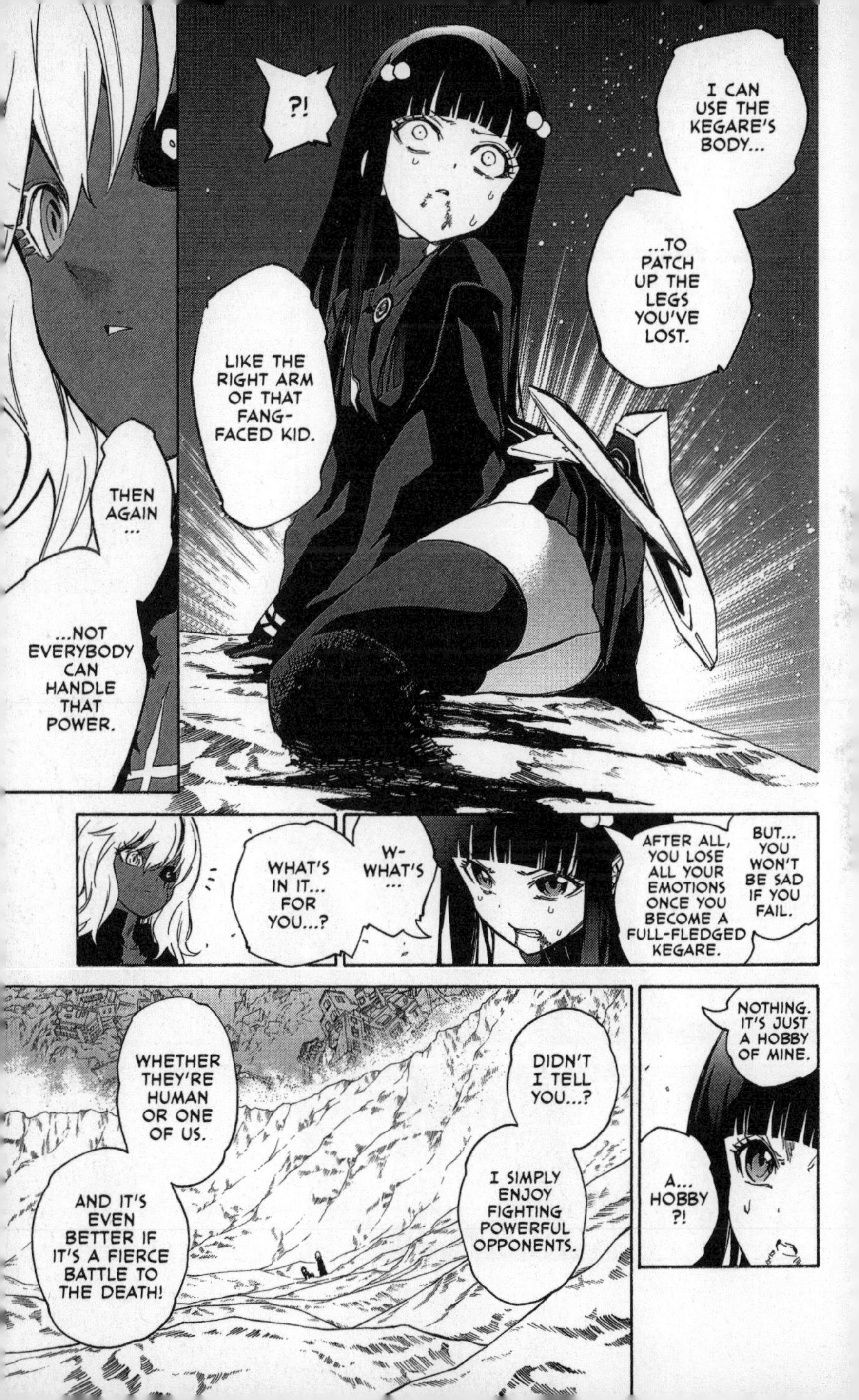

I CAN USE THE KEGARE'S BODY...
...TO PATCH UP THE LEGS YOU'VE LOST.
?!
LIKE THE RIGHT ARM OF THAT FANG-FACED KID.
THEN AGAIN...
...NOT EVERYBODY CAN HANDLE THAT POWER.
BUT... YOU WON'T BE SAD IF YOU FAIL.
AFTER ALL, YOU LOSE ALL YOUR EMOTIONS ONCE YOU BECOME A FULL-FLEDGED KEGARE.
W-WHAT'S...
WHAT'S IN IT... FOR YOU...?
NOTHING. IT'S JUST A HOBBY OF MINE.
A... HOBBY?!
DIDN'T I TELL YOU...?
WHETHER THEY'RE HUMAN OR ONE OF US.
I SIMPLY ENJOY FIGHTING POWERFUL OPPONENTS.
AND IT'S EVEN BETTER IF IT'S A FIERCE BATTLE TO THE DEATH!

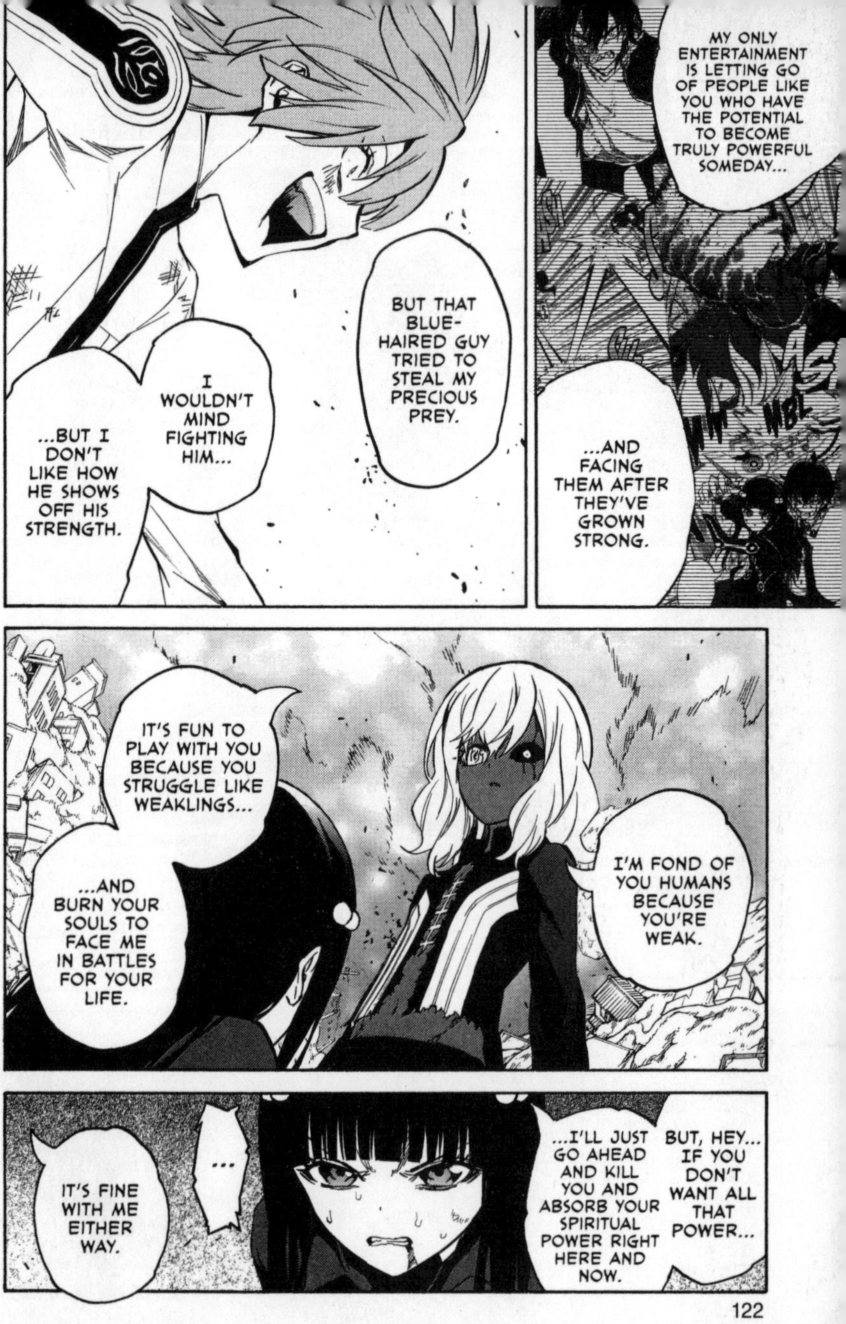
MY ONLY ENTERTAINMENT IS LETTING GO OF PEOPLE LIKE YOU WHO HAVE THE POTENTIAL TO BECOME TRULY POWERFUL SOMEDAY...
...AND FACING THEM AFTER THEY'VE GROWN STRONG.
BUT THAT BLUE-HAIRED GUY TRIED TO STEAL MY PRECIOUS PREY.
I WOULDN'T MIND FIGHTING HIM...
...BUT I DON'T LIKE HOW HE SHOWS OFF HIS STRENGTH.
I'M FOND OF YOU HUMANS BECAUSE YOU'RE WEAK.
IT'S FUN TO PLAY WITH YOU BECAUSE YOU STRUGGLE LIKE WEAKLINGS...
...AND BURN YOUR SOULS TO FACE ME IN BATTLES FOR YOUR LIFE.
BUT, HEY... IF YOU DON'T WANT ALL THAT POWER...
...I'LL JUST GO AHEAD AND KILL YOU AND ABSORB YOUR SPIRITUAL POWER RIGHT HERE AND NOW.
...
IT'S FINE WITH ME EITHER WAY.

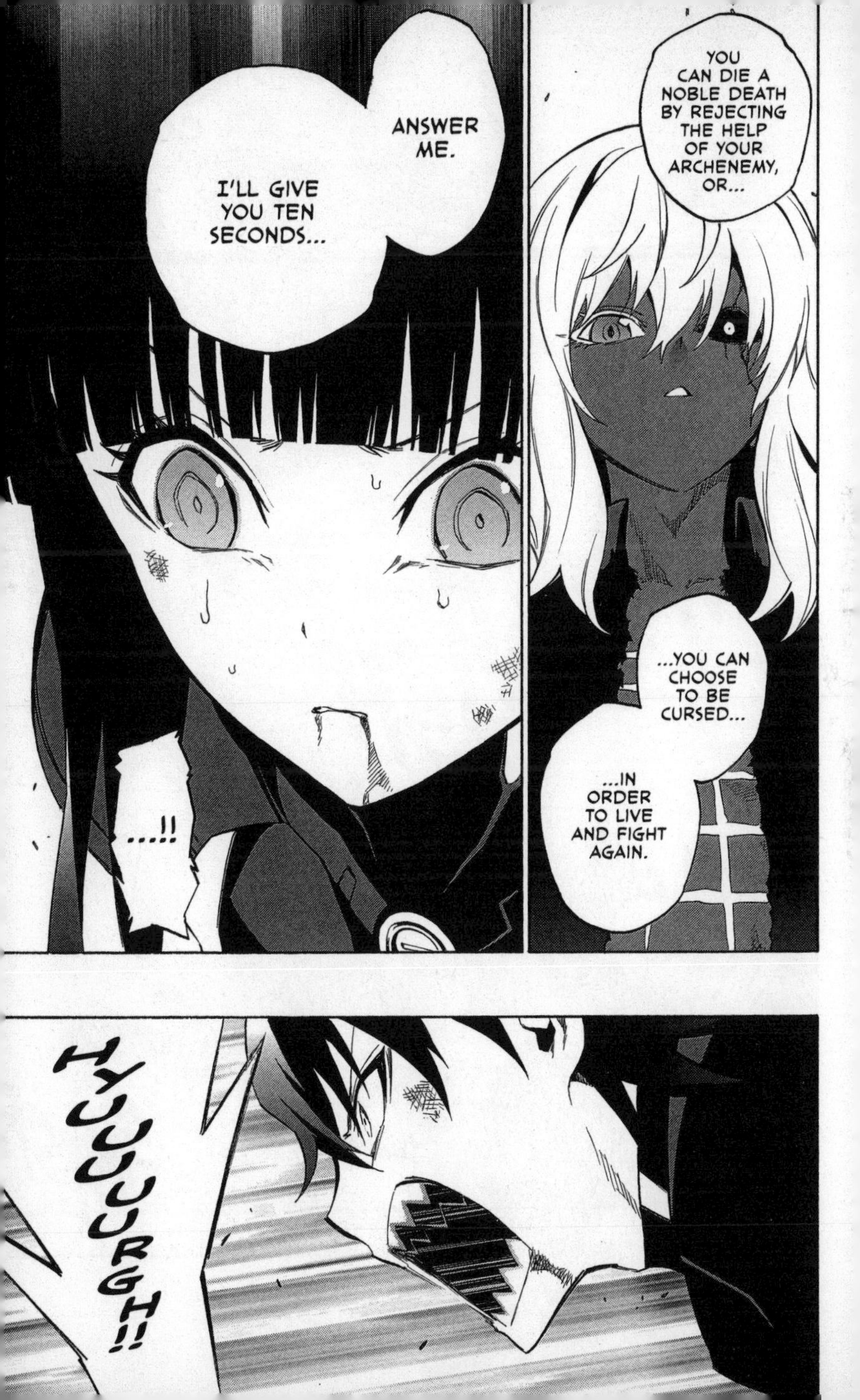
YOU CAN DIE A NOBLE DEATH BY REJECTING THE HELP OF YOUR ARCHENEMY, OR...
...YOU CAN CHOOSE TO BE CURSED...
...IN ORDER TO LIVE AND FIGHT AGAIN.
ANSWER ME.
I'LL GIVE YOU TEN SECONDS...
...!!
HYUUUURGH!!

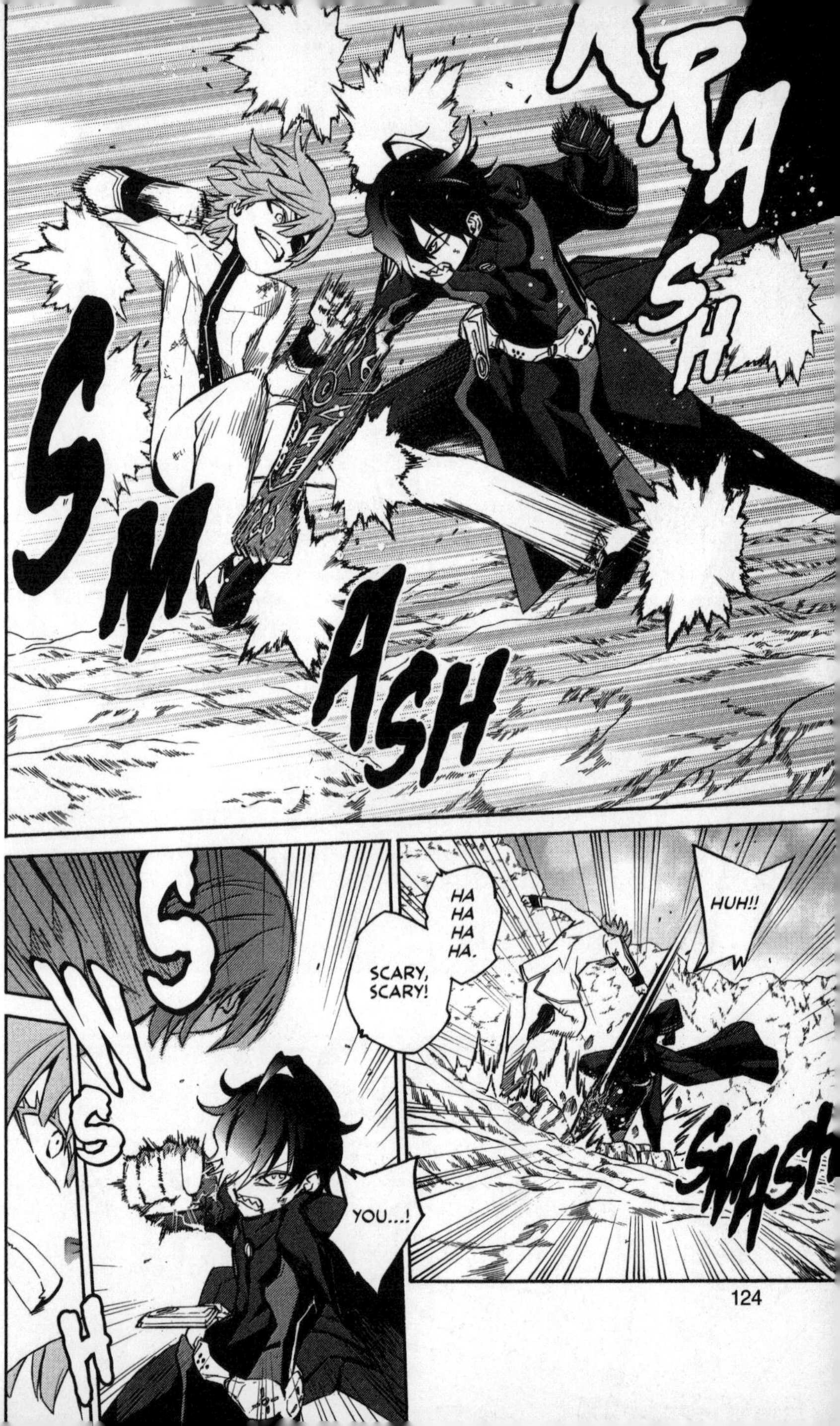
KRASH
SMASH
HUH!!
HA HA HA HA.
SCARY, SCARY!
SMASH
SWSH
YOU...!

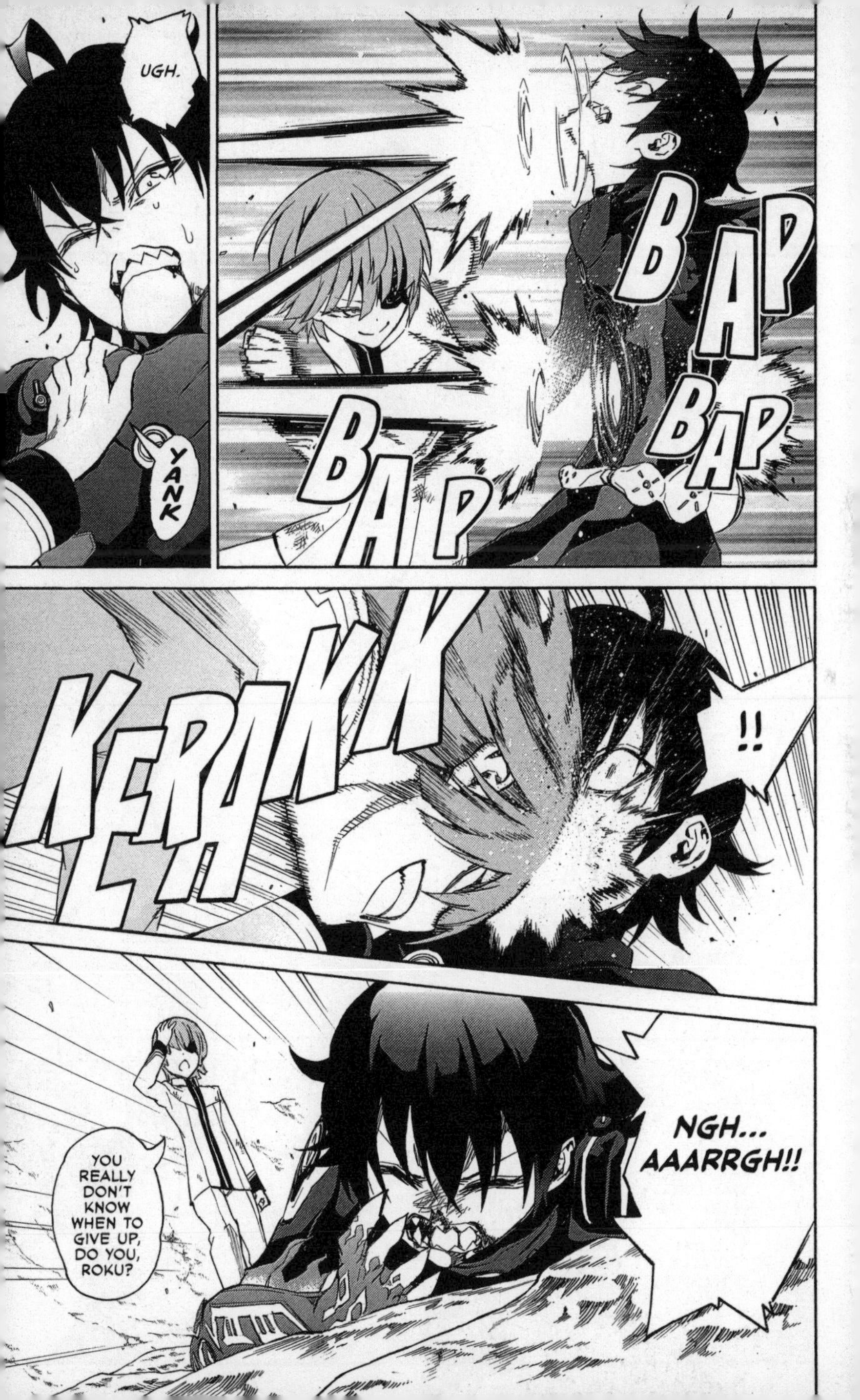
BAP
BAP
BAP
UGH.
YANK
KERAKKK
LA
!!
NGH... AAARRGH!!
YOU REALLY DON'T KNOW WHEN TO GIVE UP, DO YOU, ROKU?

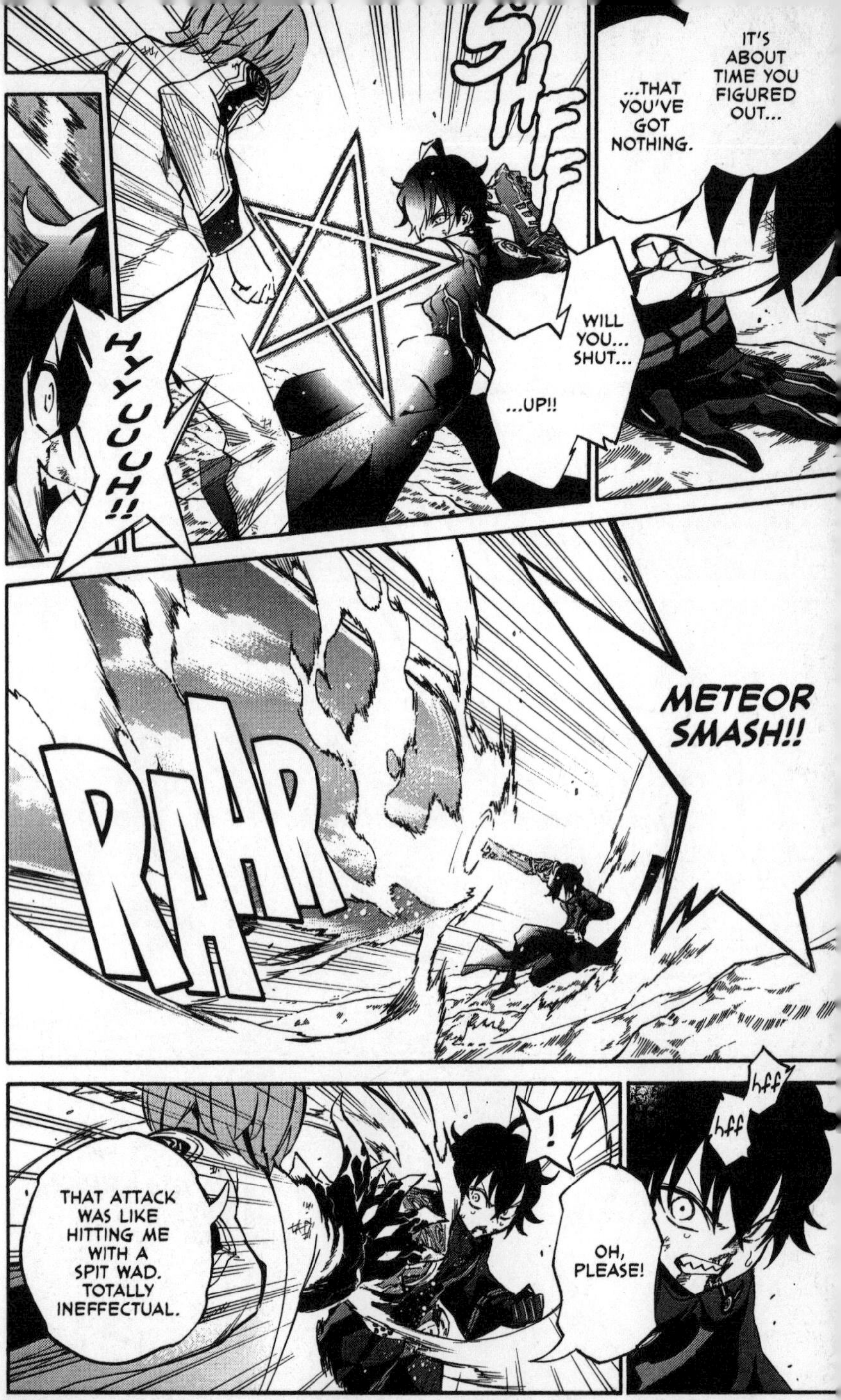
IT'S ABOUT TIME YOU FIGURED OUT...
...THAT YOU'VE GOT NOTHING.
SHF
WILL YOU... SHUT...
...UP!!
HYYUUUH!!
METEOR SMASH!!
RAAR
hff
hff
OH, PLEASE!
!
THAT ATTACK WAS LIKE HITTING ME WITH A SPIT WAD. TOTALLY INEFFECTUAL.

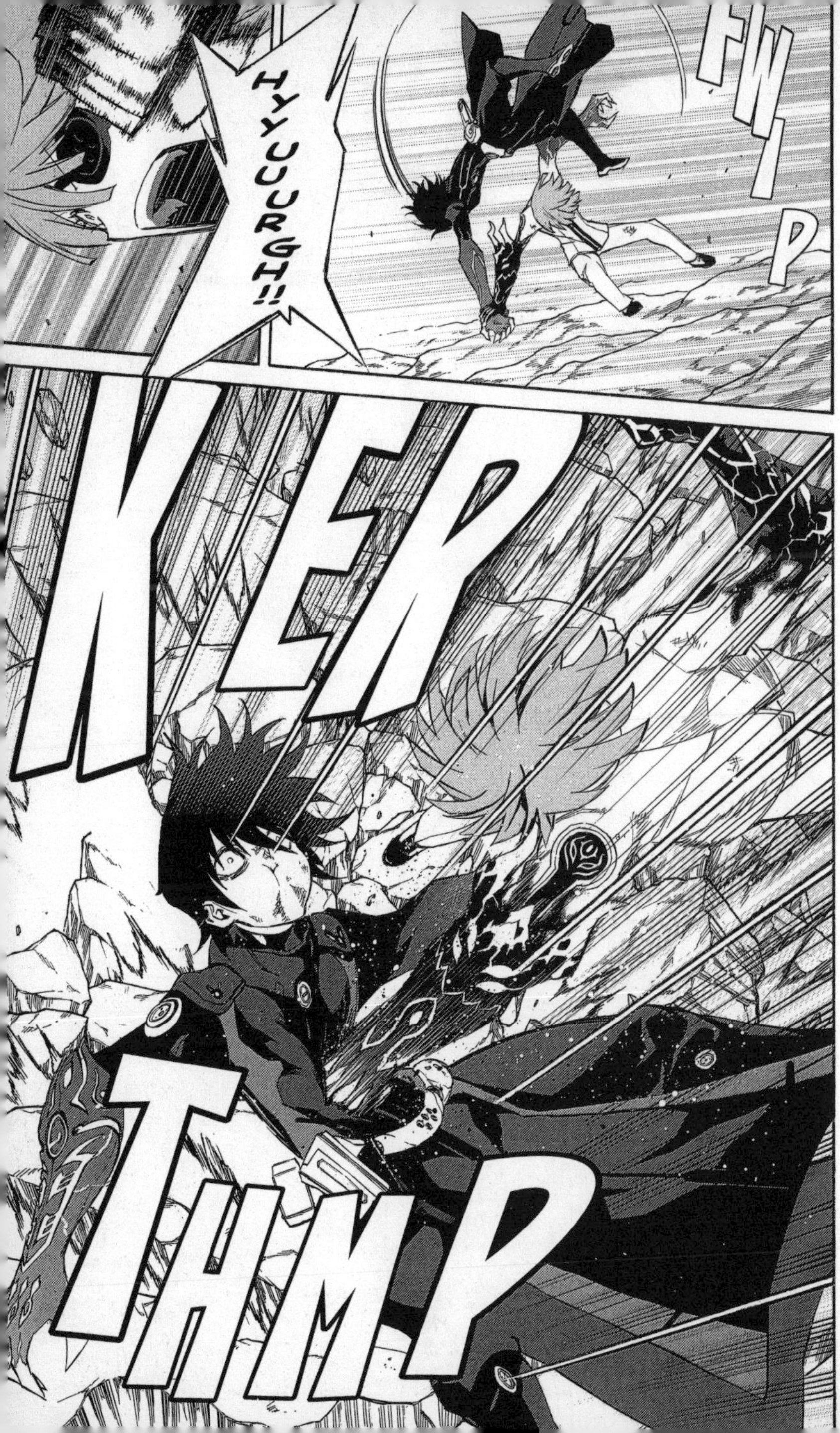
FWIP
HYYUUURGH!!
KER
THMP

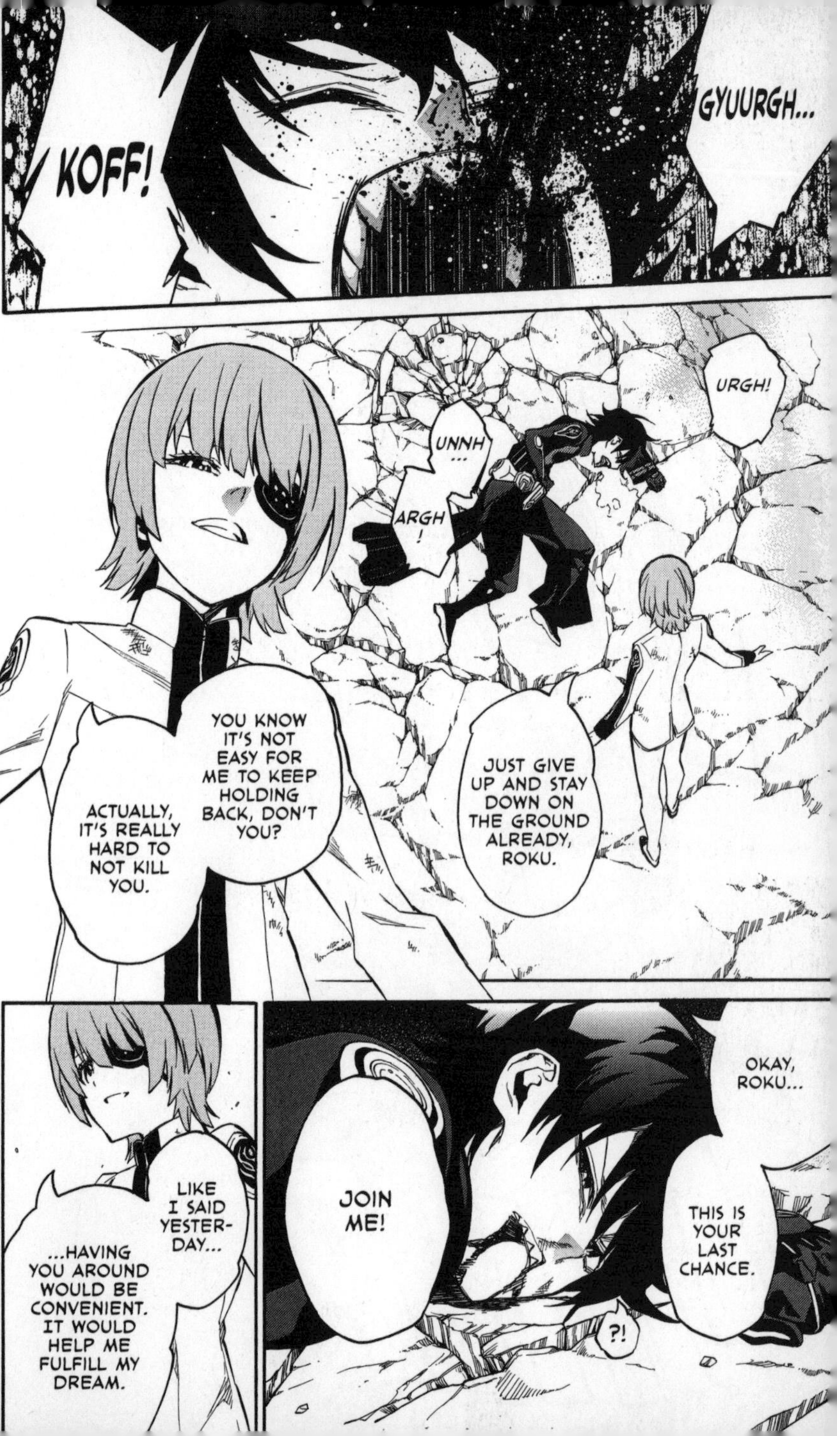
GYUURGH...
KOFF!
URGH!
UNNH...
ARGH!
JUST GIVE UP AND STAY DOWN ON THE GROUND ALREADY, ROKU.
YOU KNOW IT'S NOT EASY FOR ME TO KEEP HOLDING BACK, DON'T YOU?
ACTUALLY, IT'S REALLY HARD TO NOT KILL YOU.
OKAY, ROKU...
THIS IS YOUR LAST CHANCE.
JOIN ME!
?!
LIKE I SAID YESTER-DAY...
...HAVING YOU AROUND WOULD BE CONVENIENT. IT WOULD HELP ME FULFILL MY DREAM.

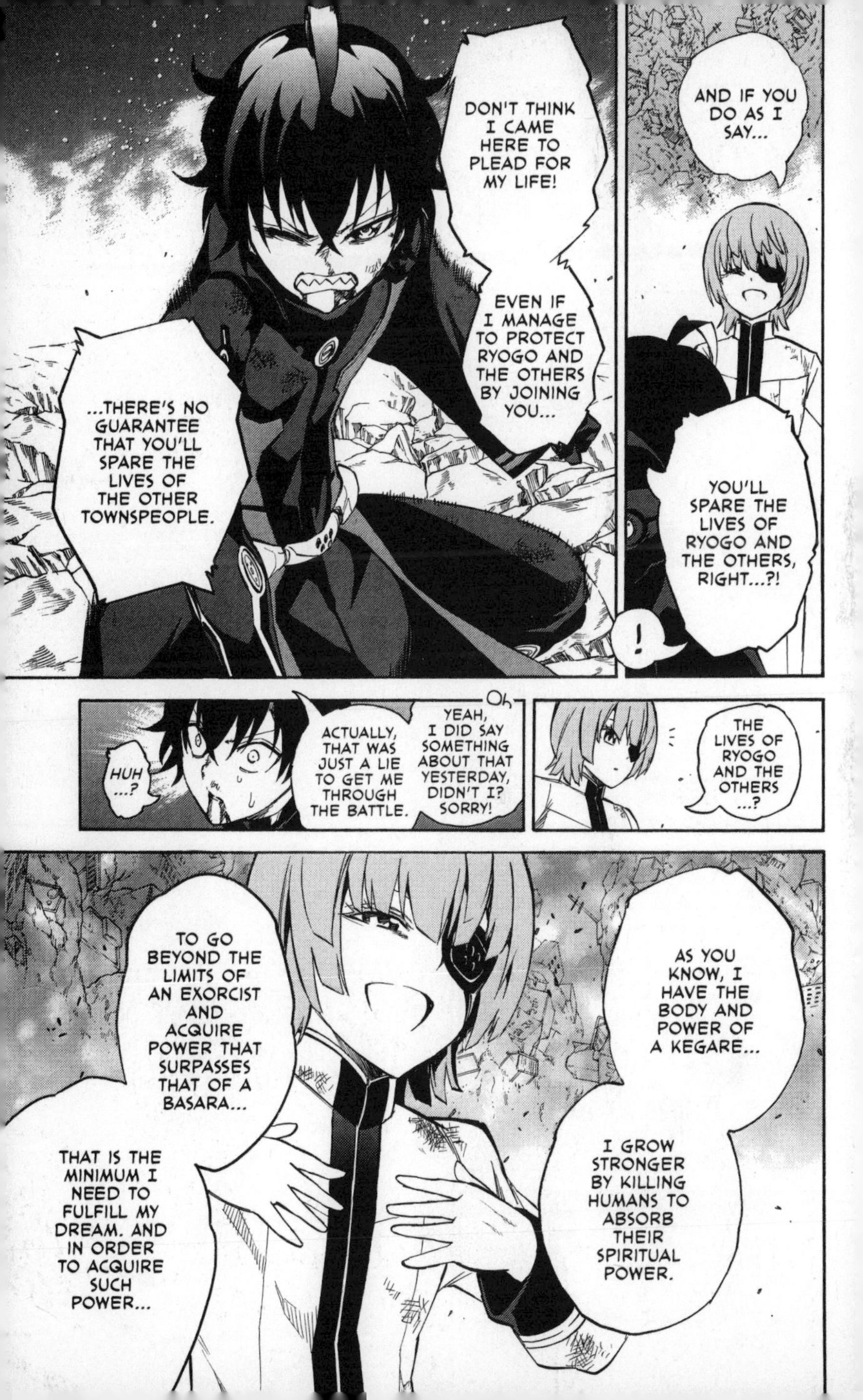
AND IF YOU DO AS I SAY...
YOU'LL SPARE THE LIVES OF RYOGO AND THE OTHERS, RIGHT...?!
!
DON'T THINK I CAME HERE TO PLEAD FOR MY LIFE!
EVEN IF I MANAGE TO PROTECT RYOGO AND THE OTHERS BY JOINING YOU...
...THERE'S NO GUARANTEE THAT YOU'LL SPARE THE LIVES OF THE OTHER TOWNSPEOPLE.
THE LIVES OF RYOGO AND THE OTHERS ...?
Oh
YEAH, I DID SAY SOMETHING ABOUT THAT YESTERDAY, DIDN'T I? SORRY!
ACTUALLY, THAT WAS JUST A LIE TO GET ME THROUGH THE BATTLE.
HUH ...?
AS YOU KNOW, I HAVE THE BODY AND POWER OF A KEGARE...
I GROW STRONGER BY KILLING HUMANS TO ABSORB THEIR SPIRITUAL POWER.
TO GO BEYOND THE LIMITS OF AN EXORCIST AND ACQUIRE POWER THAT SURPASSES THAT OF A BASARA...
THAT IS THE MINIMUM I NEED TO FULFILL MY DREAM. AND IN ORDER TO ACQUIRE SUCH POWER...

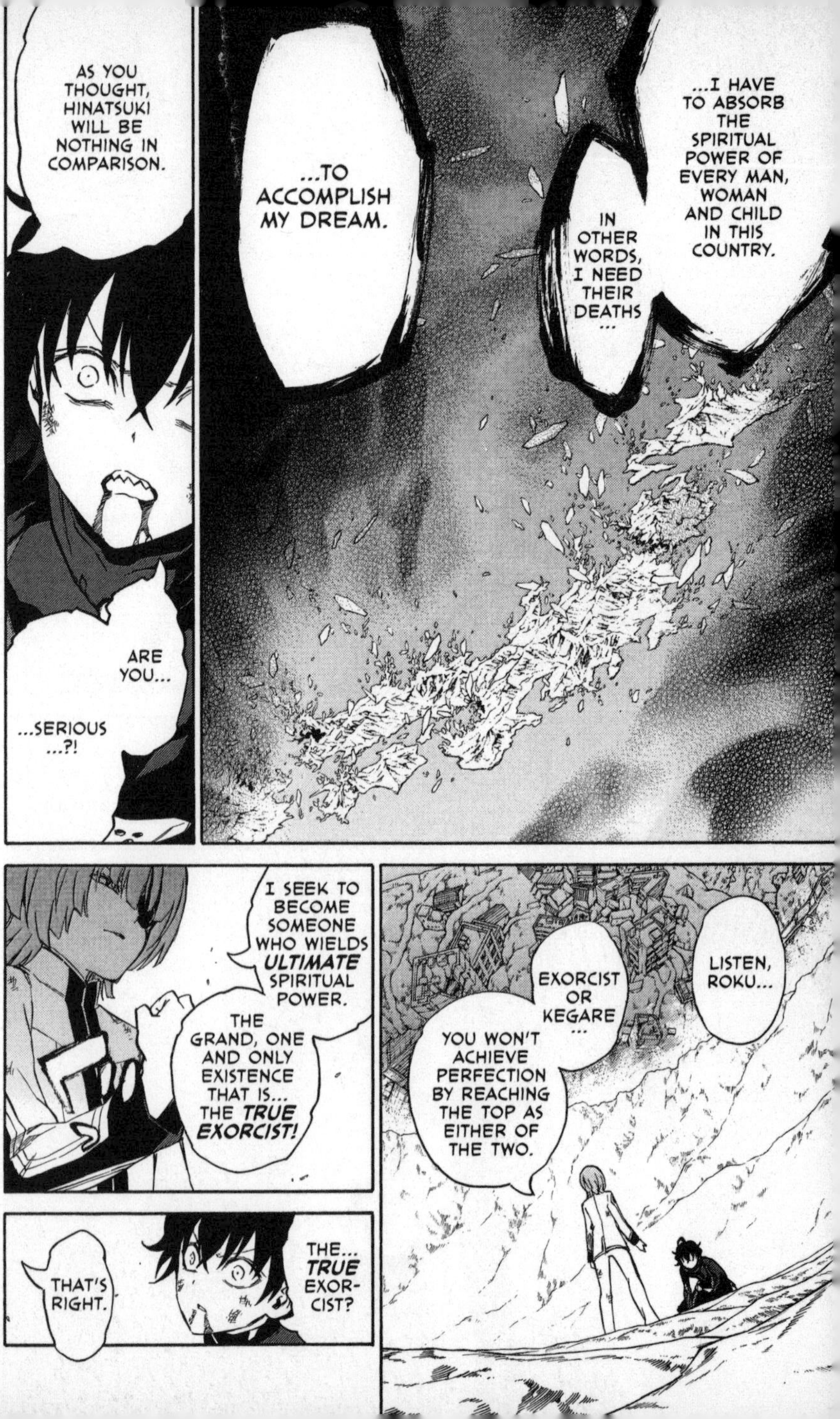
...I HAVE TO ABSORB THE SPIRITUAL POWER OF EVERY MAN, WOMAN AND CHILD IN THIS COUNTRY.
IN OTHER WORDS, I NEED THEIR DEATHS...
...TO ACCOMPLISH MY DREAM.
AS YOU THOUGHT, HINATSUKI WILL BE NOTHING IN COMPARISON.
ARE YOU...
...SERIOUS...?!
LISTEN, ROKU...
EXORCIST OR KEGARE...
YOU WON'T ACHIEVE PERFECTION BY REACHING THE TOP AS EITHER OF THE TWO.
I SEEK TO BECOME SOMEONE WHO WIELDS *ULTIMATE* SPIRITUAL POWER.
THE GRAND, ONE AND ONLY EXISTENCE THAT IS... THE *TRUE EXORCIST!*
THE... *TRUE* EXOR-CIST?
THAT'S RIGHT.

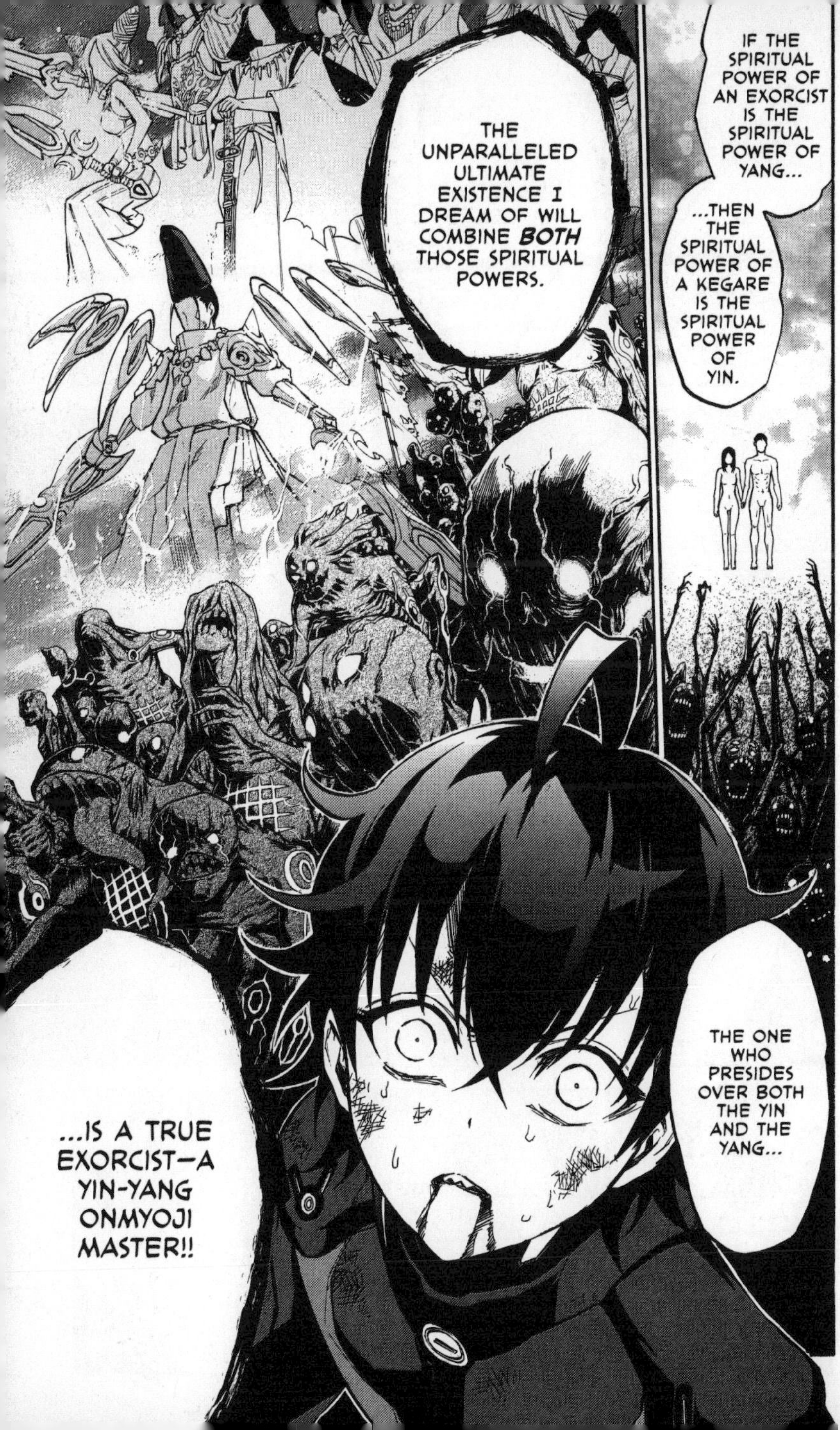
IF THE SPIRITUAL POWER OF AN EXORCIST IS THE SPIRITUAL POWER OF YANG...
...THEN THE SPIRITUAL POWER OF A KEGARE IS THE SPIRITUAL POWER OF YIN.
THE UNPARALLELED ULTIMATE EXISTENCE I DREAM OF WILL COMBINE BOTH THOSE SPIRITUAL POWERS.
THE ONE WHO PRESIDES OVER BOTH THE YIN AND THE YANG...
...IS A TRUE EXORCIST—A YIN-YANG ONMYOJI MASTER!!

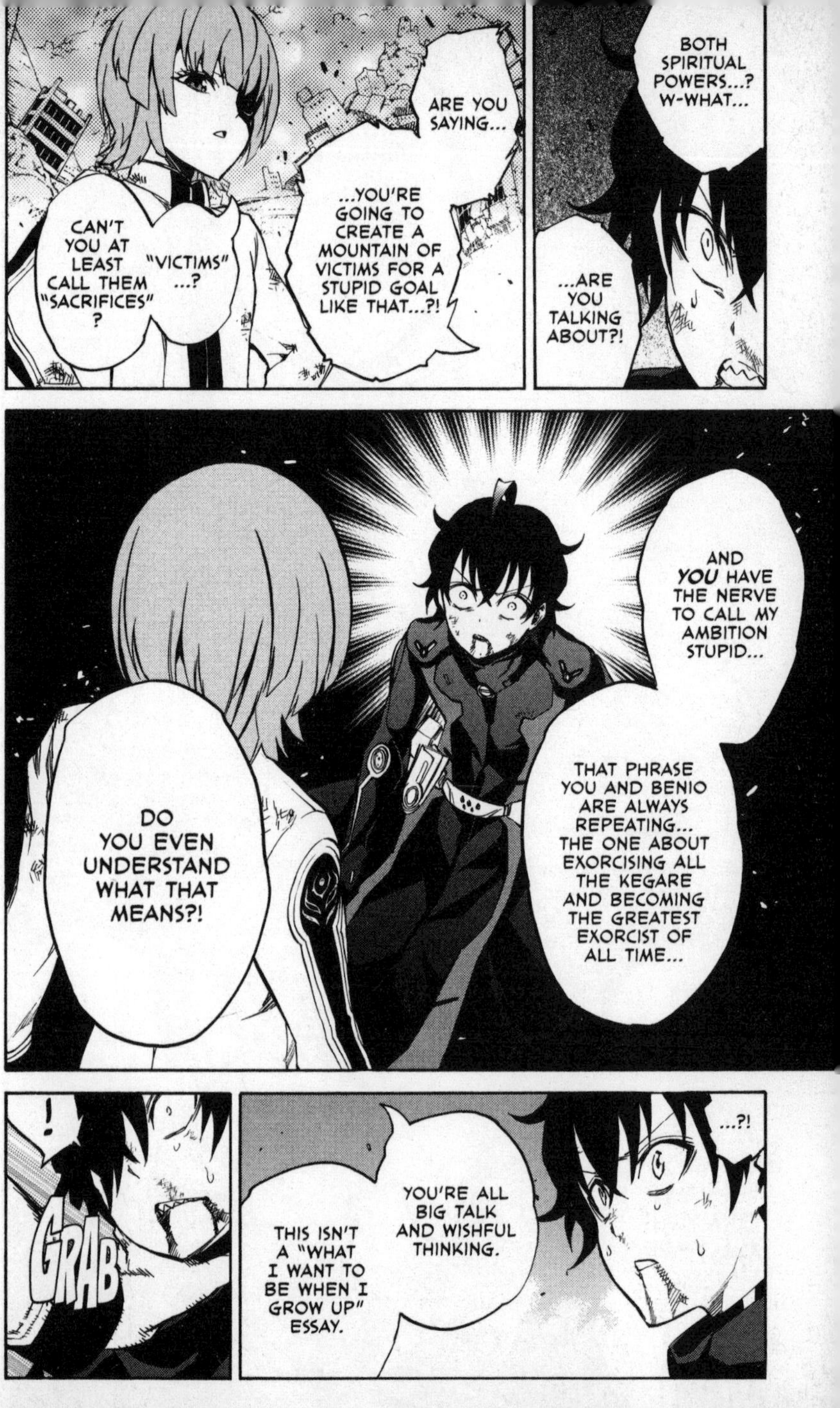
BOTH SPIRITUAL POWERS...? W-WHAT...
...ARE YOU TALKING ABOUT?!
ARE YOU SAYING...
...YOU'RE GOING TO CREATE A MOUNTAIN OF VICTIMS FOR A STUPID GOAL LIKE THAT...?!
"VICTIMS" ...? CAN'T YOU AT LEAST CALL THEM "SACRIFICES"?
AND *YOU* HAVE THE NERVE TO CALL MY AMBITION STUPID...
THAT PHRASE YOU AND BENIO ARE ALWAYS REPEATING... THE ONE ABOUT EXORCISING ALL THE KEGARE AND BECOMING THE GREATEST EXORCIST OF ALL TIME...
DO YOU EVEN UNDERSTAND WHAT THAT MEANS?!
...?!
YOU'RE ALL BIG TALK AND WISHFUL THINKING.
THIS ISN'T A "WHAT I WANT TO BE WHEN I GROW UP" ESSAY.
!
GRAB

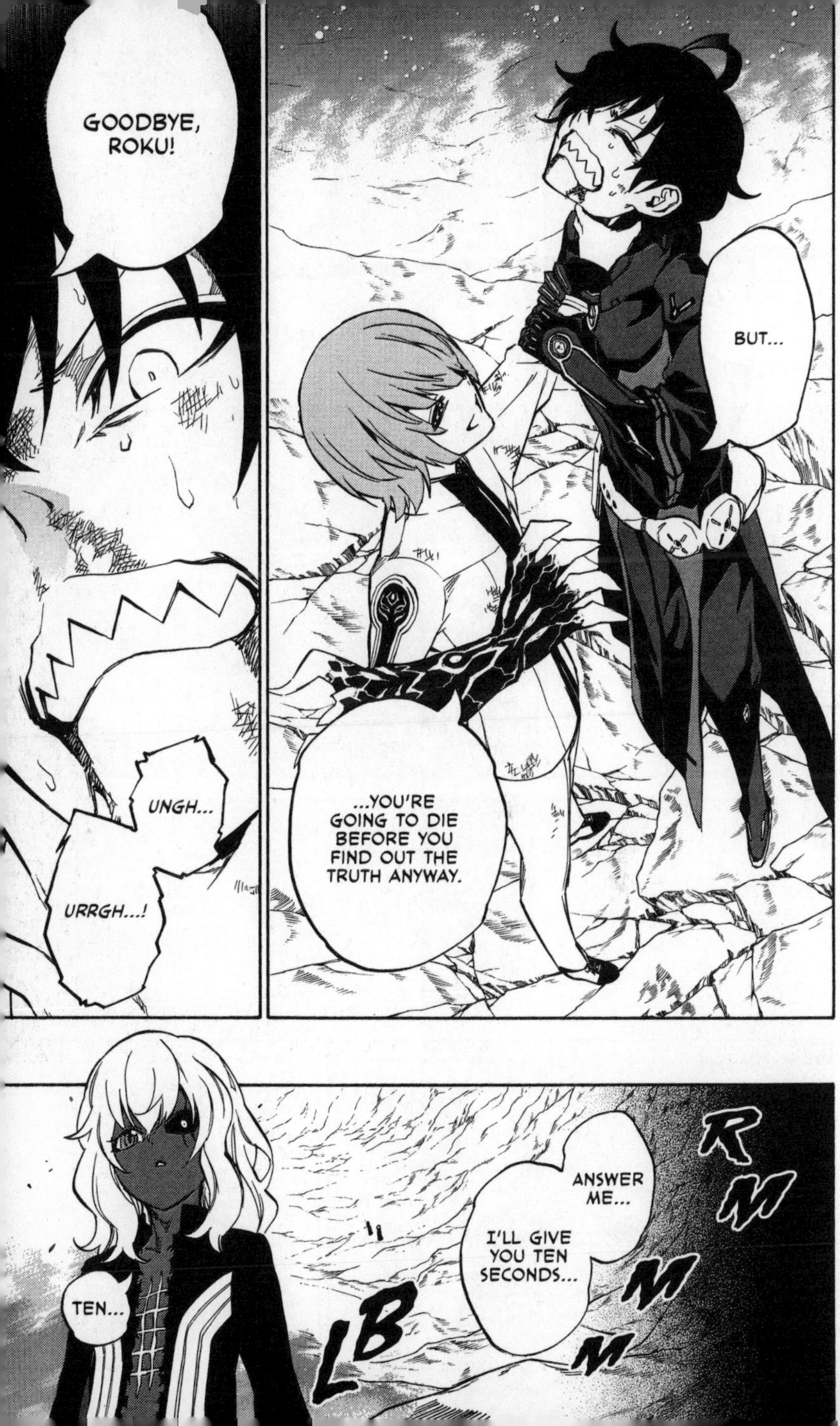
BUT...
...YOU'RE GOING TO DIE BEFORE YOU FIND OUT THE TRUTH ANYWAY.
GOODBYE, ROKU!
UNGH...
URRGH...!
RMMMM
ANSWER ME...
I'LL GIVE YOU TEN SECONDS...
LB
TEN...

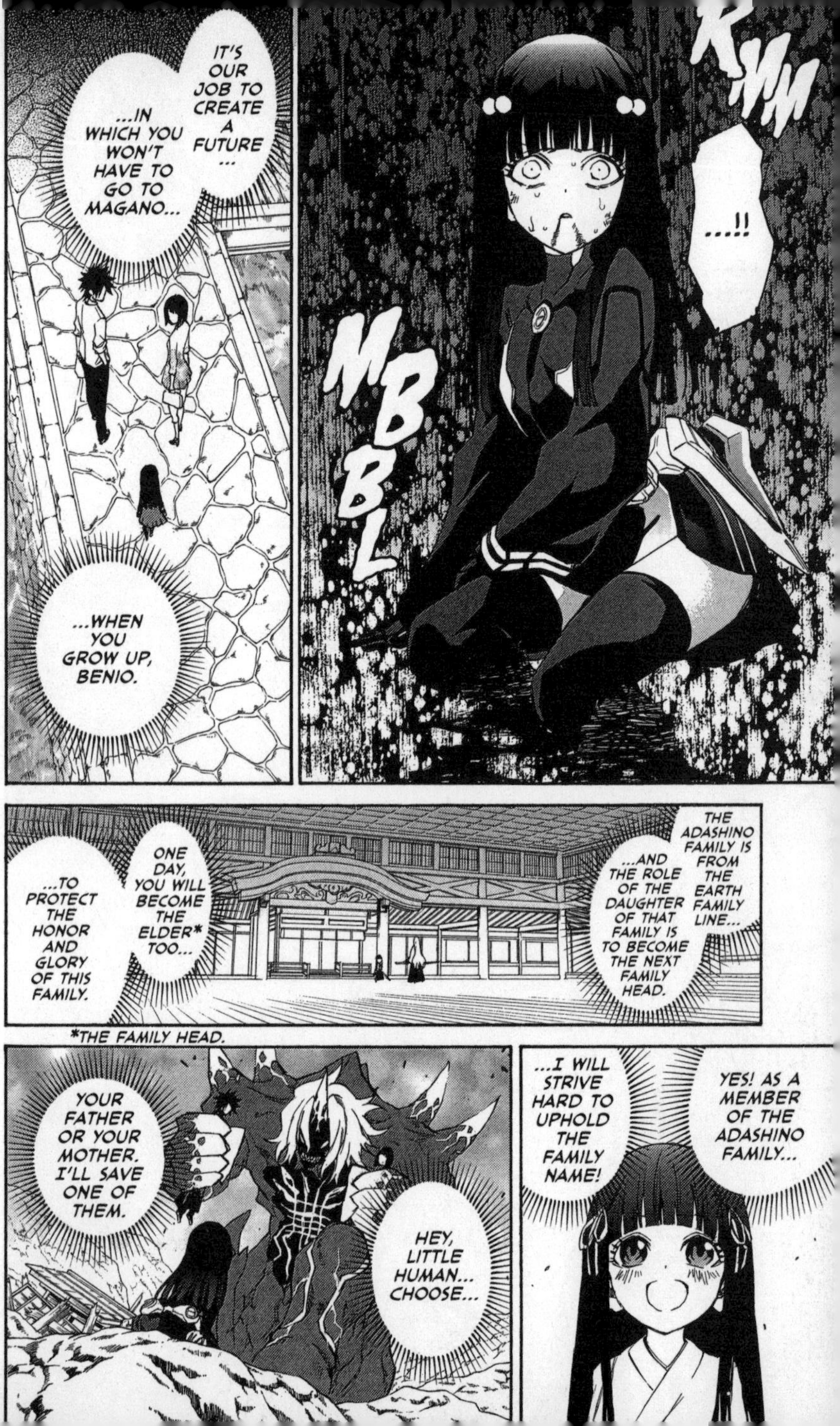
RMM
...!!
MBBL
IT'S OUR JOB TO CREATE A FUTURE...
...IN WHICH YOU WON'T HAVE TO GO TO MAGANO...
...WHEN YOU GROW UP, BENIO.
THE ADASHINO FAMILY IS FROM THE EARTH FAMILY LINE...
...AND THE ROLE OF THE DAUGHTER OF THAT FAMILY IS TO BECOME THE NEXT FAMILY HEAD.
ONE DAY, YOU WILL BECOME THE ELDER* TOO...
...TO PROTECT THE HONOR AND GLORY OF THIS FAMILY.
YES! AS A MEMBER OF THE ADASHINO FAMILY...
...I WILL STRIVE HARD TO UPHOLD THE FAMILY NAME!
HEY, LITTLE HUMAN... CHOOSE...
YOUR FATHER OR YOUR MOTHER. I'LL SAVE ONE OF THEM.

*THE FAMILY HEAD.

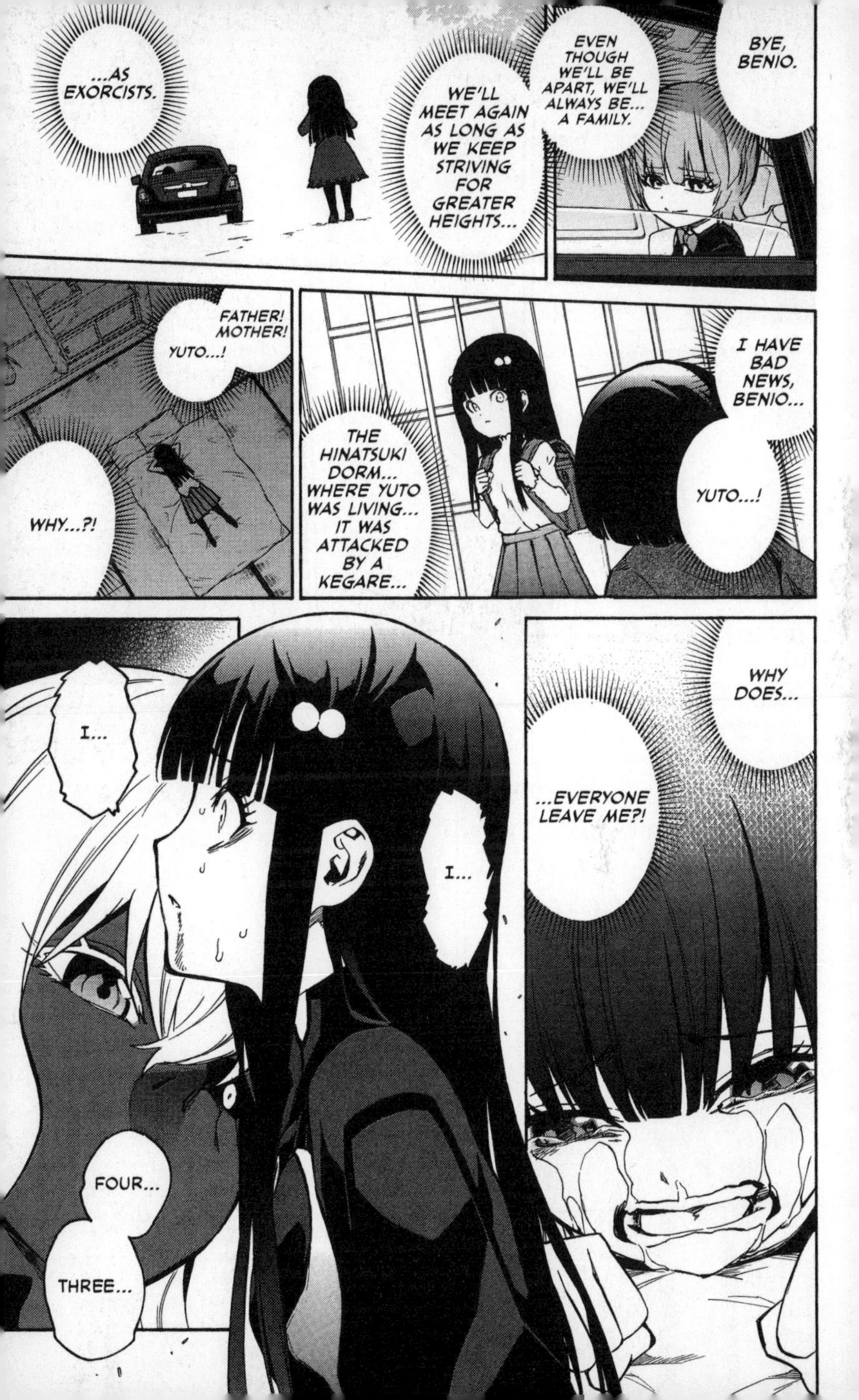
BYE, BENIO.
EVEN THOUGH WE'LL BE APART, WE'LL ALWAYS BE... A FAMILY.
WE'LL MEET AGAIN AS LONG AS WE KEEP STRIVING FOR GREATER HEIGHTS...
...AS EXORCISTS.
I HAVE BAD NEWS, BENIO...
THE HINATSUKI DORM... WHERE YUTO WAS LIVING... IT WAS ATTACKED BY A KEGARE...
YUTO...!
FATHER! MOTHER!
YUTO...!
WHY...?!
WHY DOES...
...EVERYONE LEAVE ME?!
I...
I...
FOUR...
THREE...

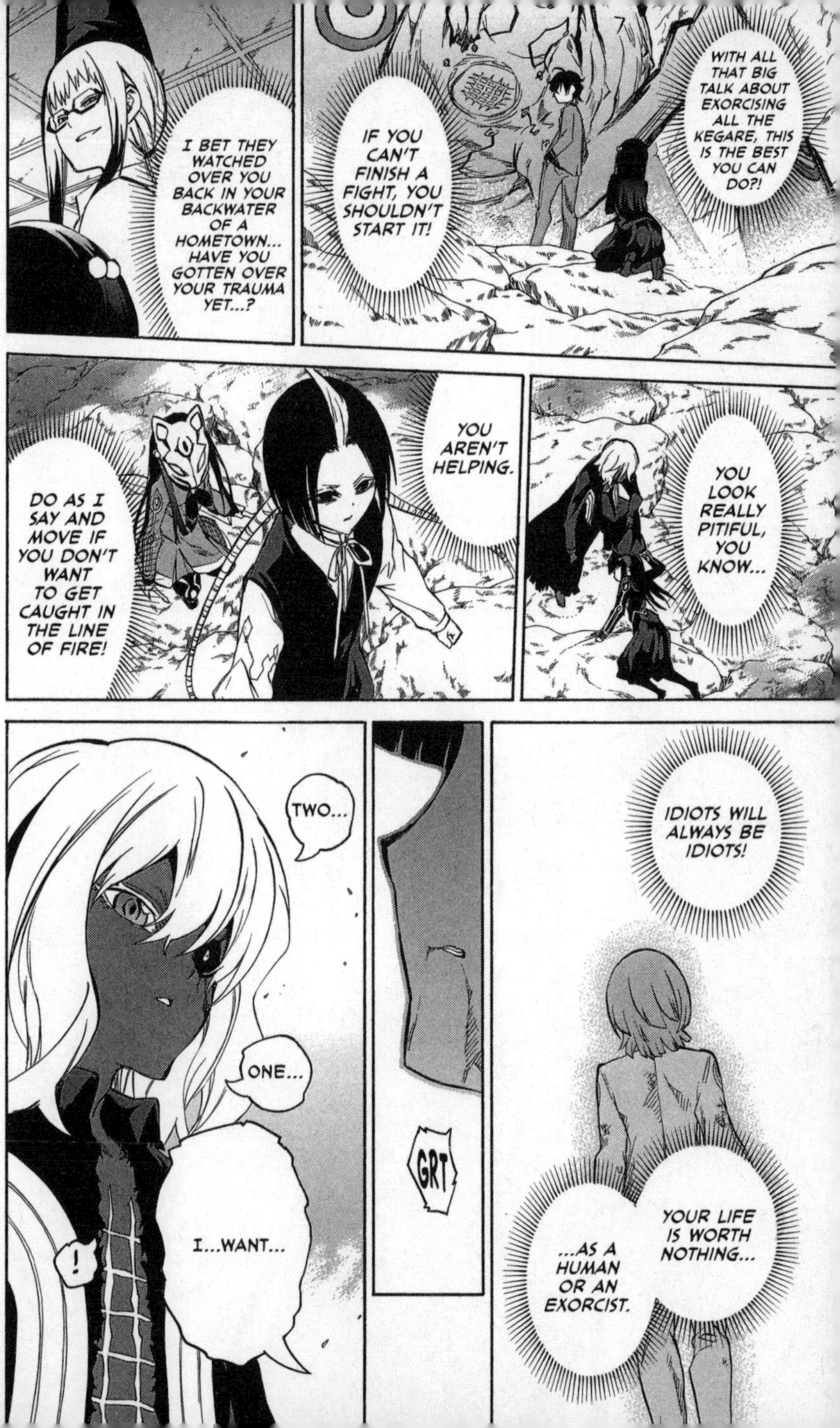
WITH ALL THAT BIG TALK ABOUT EXORCISING ALL THE KEGARE, THIS IS THE BEST YOU CAN DO?!
IF YOU CAN'T FINISH A FIGHT, YOU SHOULDN'T START IT!
I BET THEY WATCHED OVER YOU BACK IN YOUR BACKWATER OF A HOMETOWN... HAVE YOU GOTTEN OVER YOUR TRAUMA YET...?
YOU LOOK REALLY PITIFUL, YOU KNOW...
YOU AREN'T HELPING.
DO AS I SAY AND MOVE IF YOU DON'T WANT TO GET CAUGHT IN THE LINE OF FIRE!
IDIOTS WILL ALWAYS BE IDIOTS!
YOUR LIFE IS WORTH NOTHING...
...AS A HUMAN OR AN EXORCIST.
GRT
TWO...
ONE...
I...WANT...
!

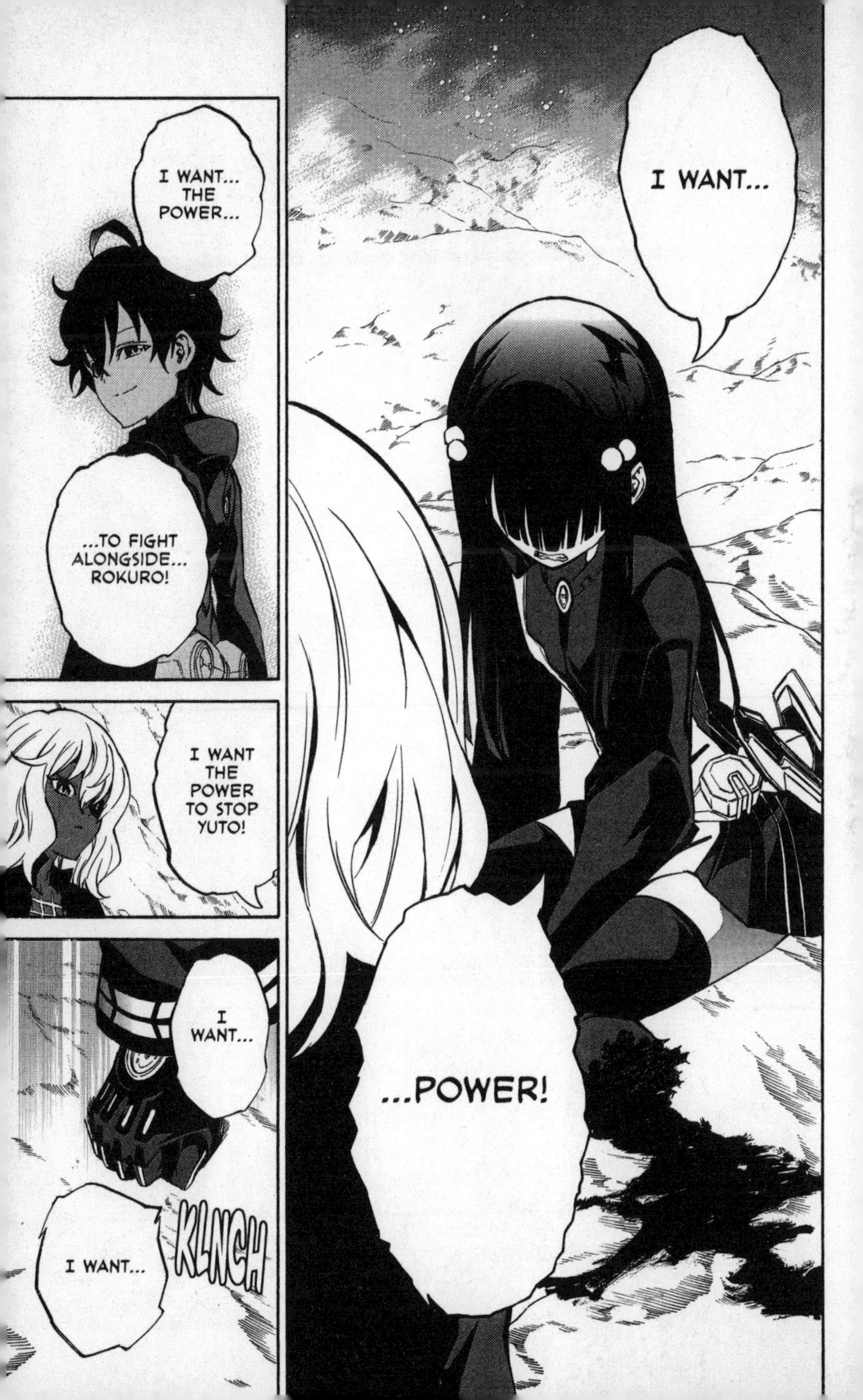
I WANT...
...POWER!
I WANT... THE POWER...
...TO FIGHT ALONGSIDE... ROKURO!
I WANT THE POWER TO STOP YUTO!
I WANT...
KLNCH
I WANT...

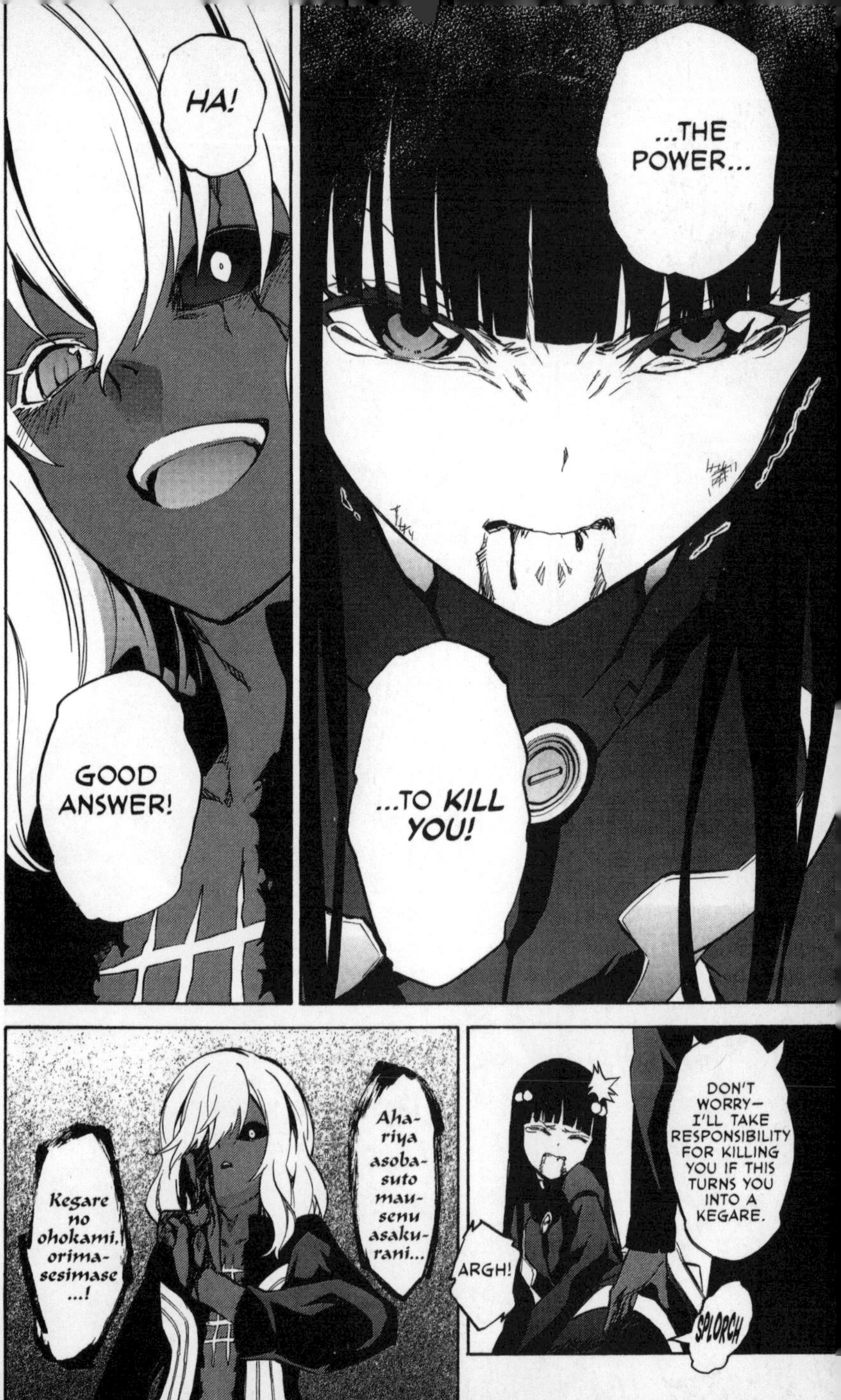
...THE POWER...
...TO KILL YOU!
HA!
GOOD ANSWER!
DON'T WORRY—I'LL TAKE RESPONSIBILITY FOR KILLING YOU IF THIS TURNS YOU INTO A KEGARE.
ARGH!
SPLORCH
Ahariya asobasuto mausenu asakurani...
Kegare no ohokami, orimasesimase...!

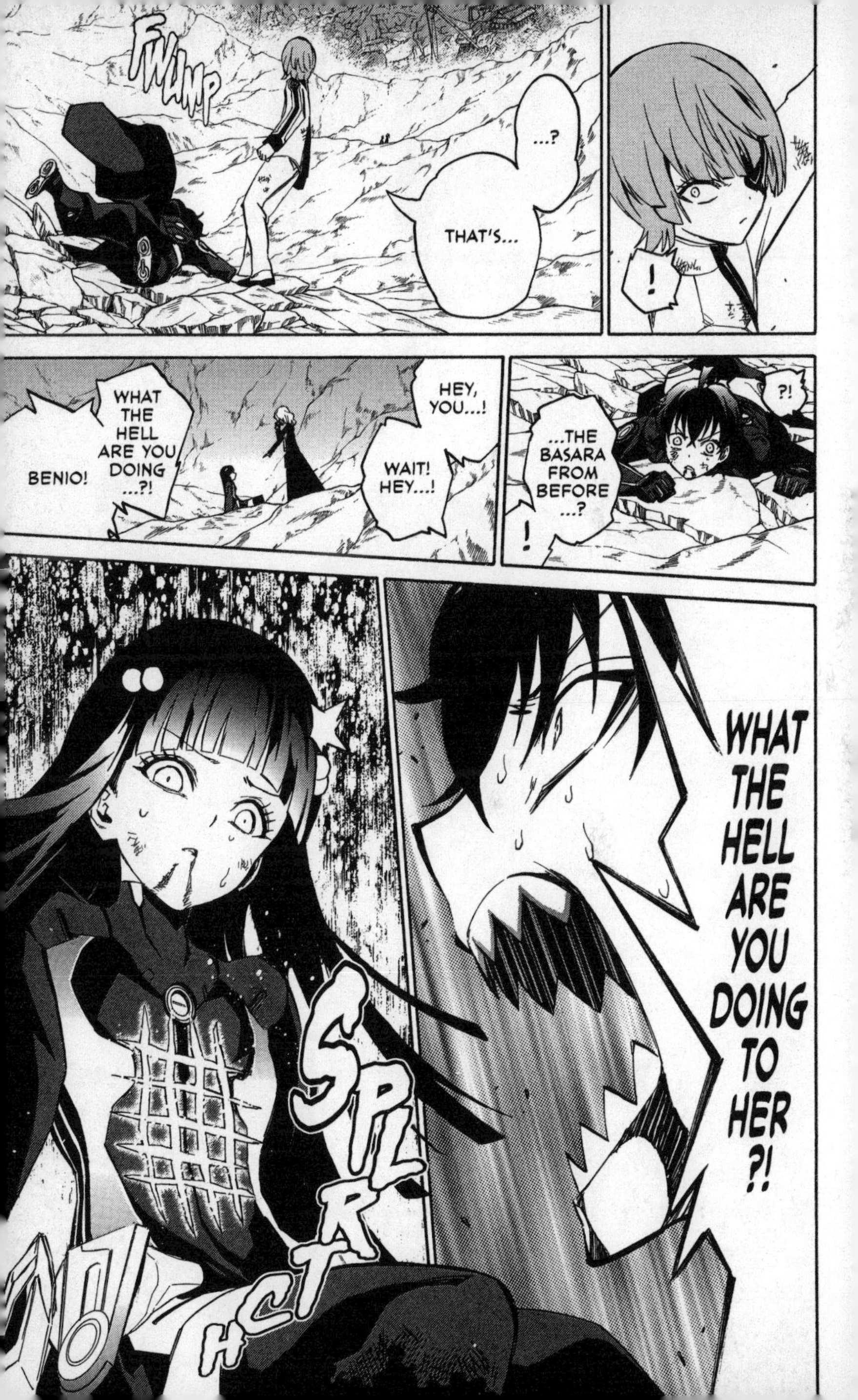
!
FWUMP
...?
THAT'S...
?!
...THE BASARA FROM BEFORE ...?
!
HEY, YOU...!
WAIT! HEY...!
WHAT THE HELL ARE YOU DOING ...?!
BENIO!
WHAT THE HELL ARE YOU DOING TO HER ?!
SPLRTCH

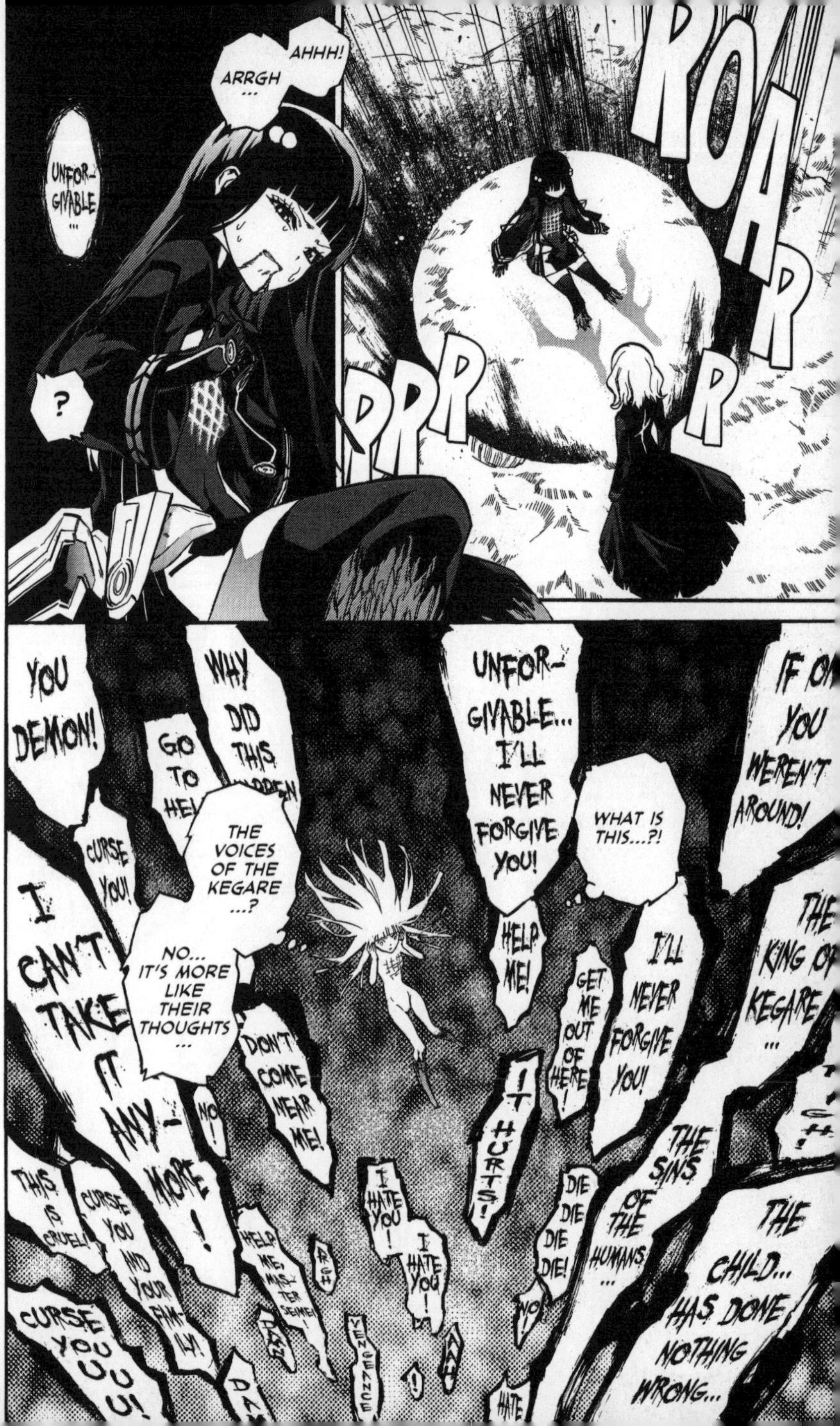
ROAR
DRR
AHHH! ARRGH...
UNFOR-GIVABLE...
?
IF ON
YOU WEREN'T AROUND!
UNFOR-GIVABLE... I'LL NEVER FORGIVE YOU!
WHAT IS THIS...?!
WHY DID THIS
YOU DEMON!
THE VOICES OF THE KEGARE...?
CURSE YOU!
NO... IT'S MORE LIKE THEIR THOUGHTS...
I CAN'T TAKE IT ANY-MORE!
THE KING OF KEGARE...
I'LL NEVER FORGIVE YOU!
HELP ME!
GET ME OUT OF HERE!
IT HURTS!
DON'T COME NEAR ME!
NO!
THE SINS OF THE HUMANS...
THE CHILD... HAS DONE NOTHING WRONG...
DIE DIE DIE DIE!
I HATE YOU!
I HATE YOU!
HELP ME, MASTER SEIMEI!
ARGH
THIS IS CRUEL!
CURSE YOU AND YOUR FAMILY!
CURSE YOUUUU!
VENGEANCE
NO!

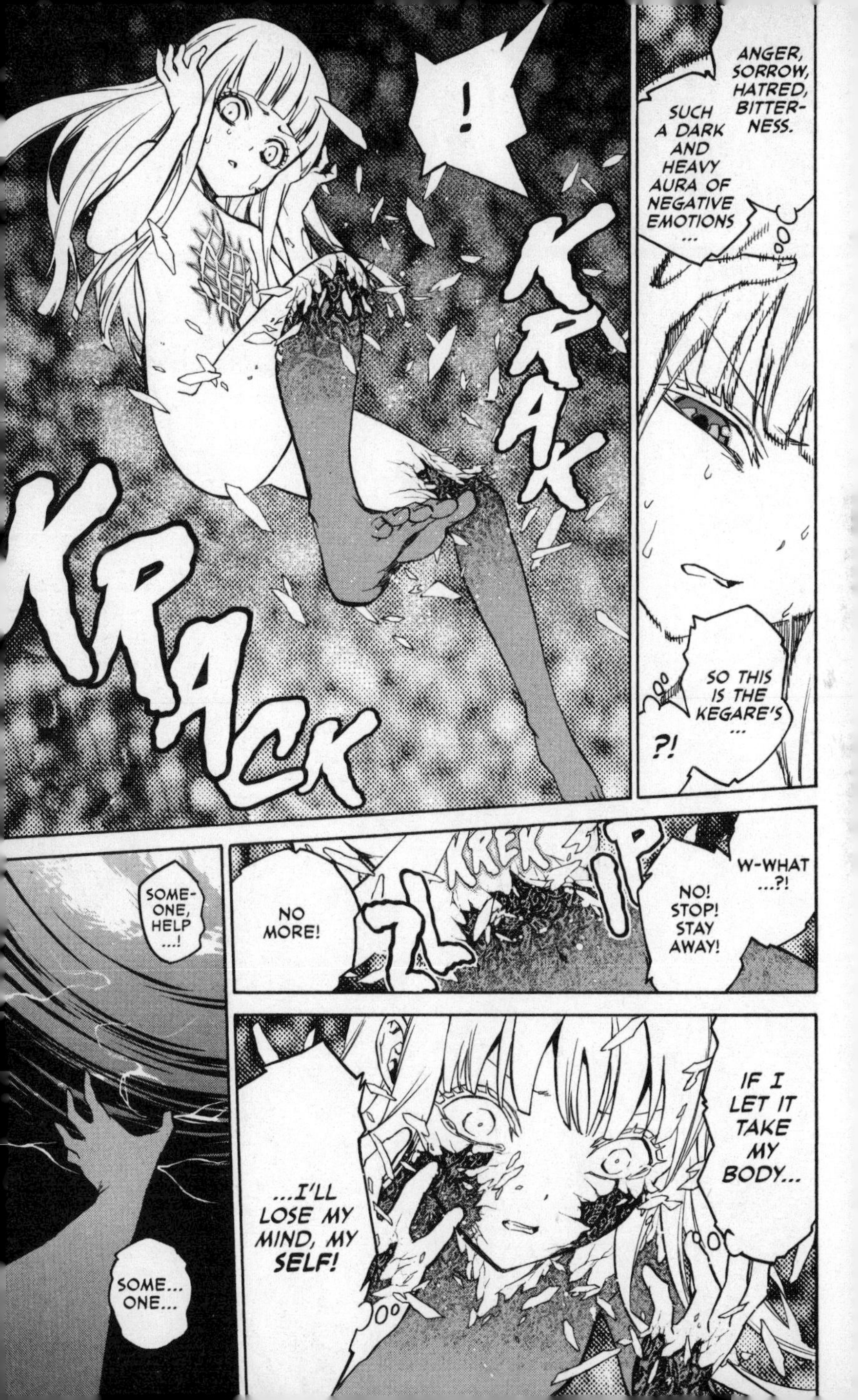
ANGER, SORROW, HATRED, BITTERNESS.
SUCH A DARK AND HEAVY AURA OF NEGATIVE EMOTIONS...
SO THIS IS THE KEGARE'S...
?!
!
KRAK
KRACK
W-WHAT...?!
NO! STOP! STAY AWAY!
KREK
ZLIP
NO MORE!
IF I LET IT TAKE MY BODY...
...I'LL LOSE MY MIND, MY SELF!
SOME-ONE, HELP...!
SOME... ONE...

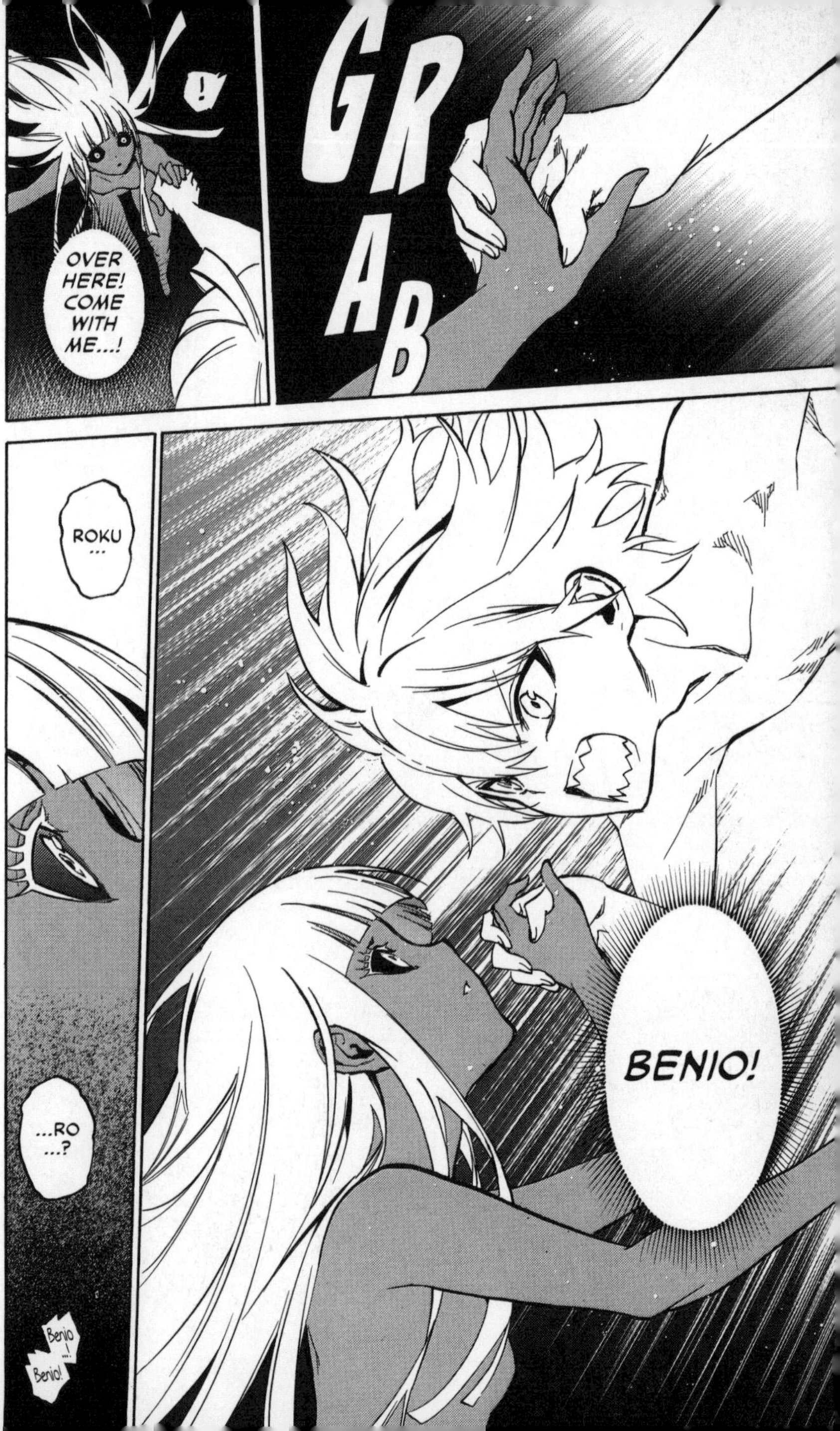
GRAB
!
OVER HERE! COME WITH ME...!
BENIO!
ROKU ...
...RO ...?
Benio ...!
Benio!

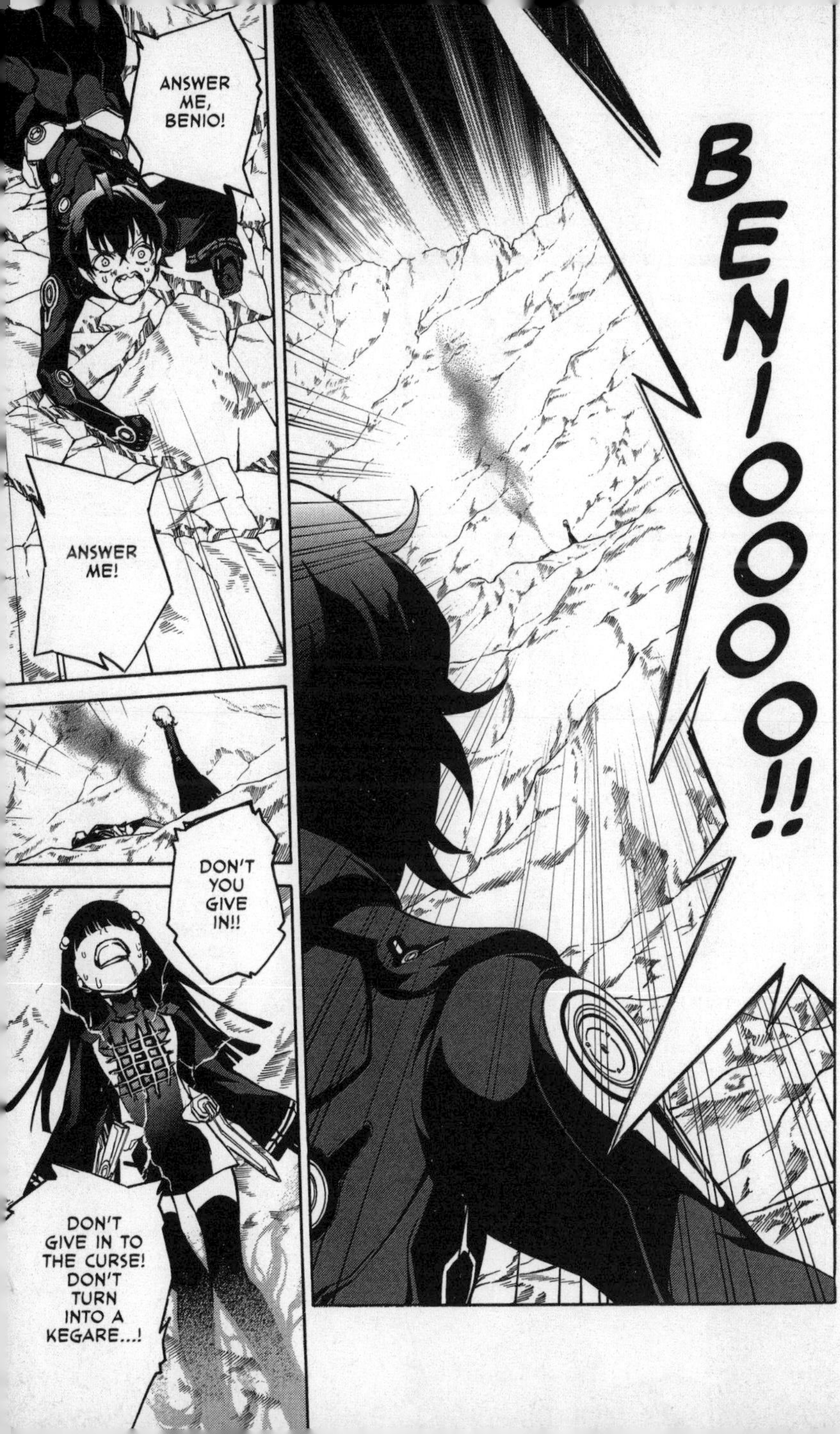
BENIOOOO!!
ANSWER ME, BENIO!
ANSWER ME!
DON'T YOU GIVE IN!!
DON'T GIVE IN TO THE CURSE! DON'T TURN INTO A KEGARE...!

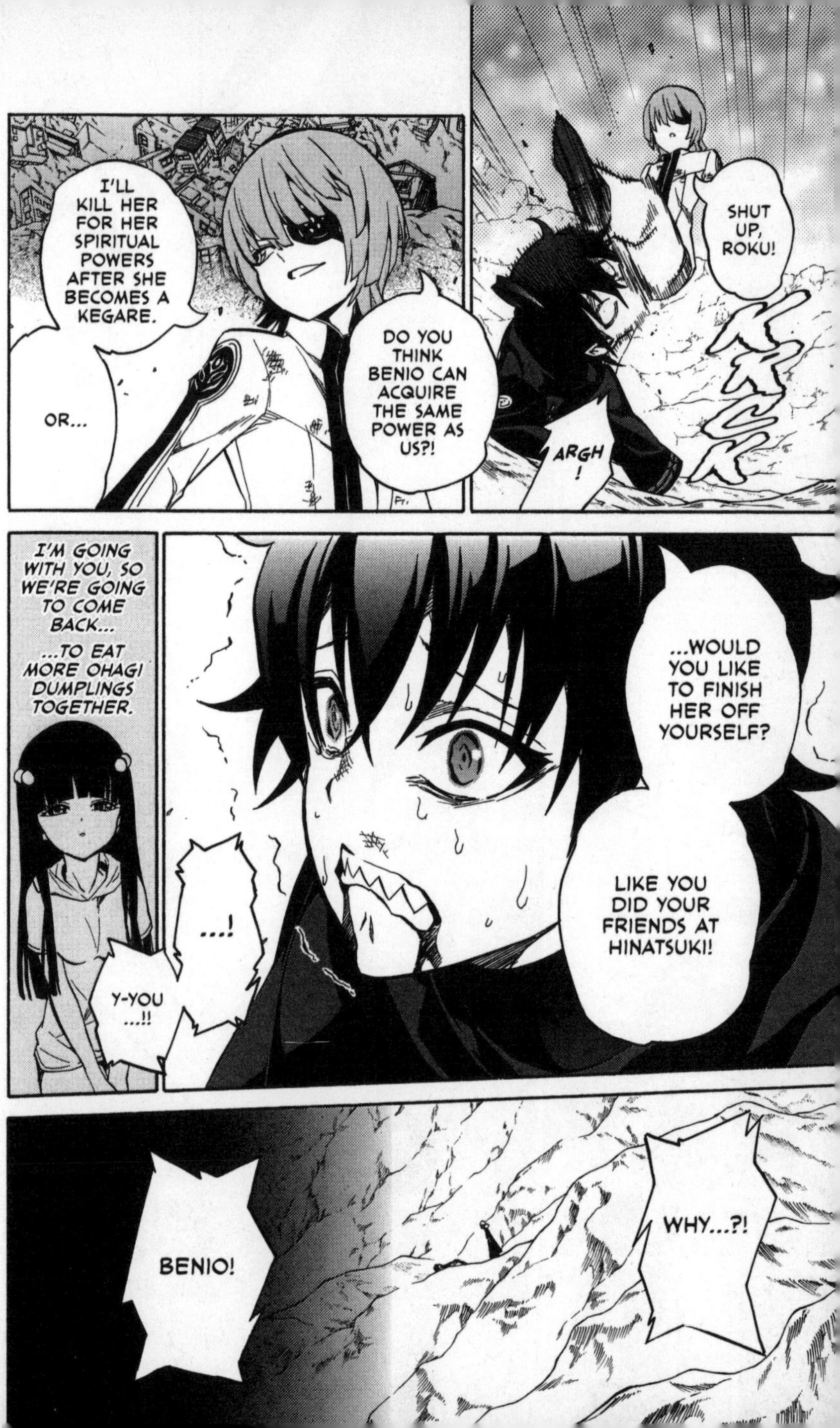

SHUT UP, ROKU!
KICK
ARGH!
I'LL KILL HER FOR HER SPIRITUAL POWERS AFTER SHE BECOMES A KEGARE.
DO YOU THINK BENIO CAN ACQUIRE THE SAME POWER AS US?!
OR...
...WOULD YOU LIKE TO FINISH HER OFF YOURSELF?
LIKE YOU DID YOUR FRIENDS AT HINATSUKI!
...!
Y-YOU ...!!
I'M GOING WITH YOU, SO WE'RE GOING TO COME BACK...
...TO EAT MORE OHAGI DUMPLINGS TOGETHER.
WHY...?!
BENIO!

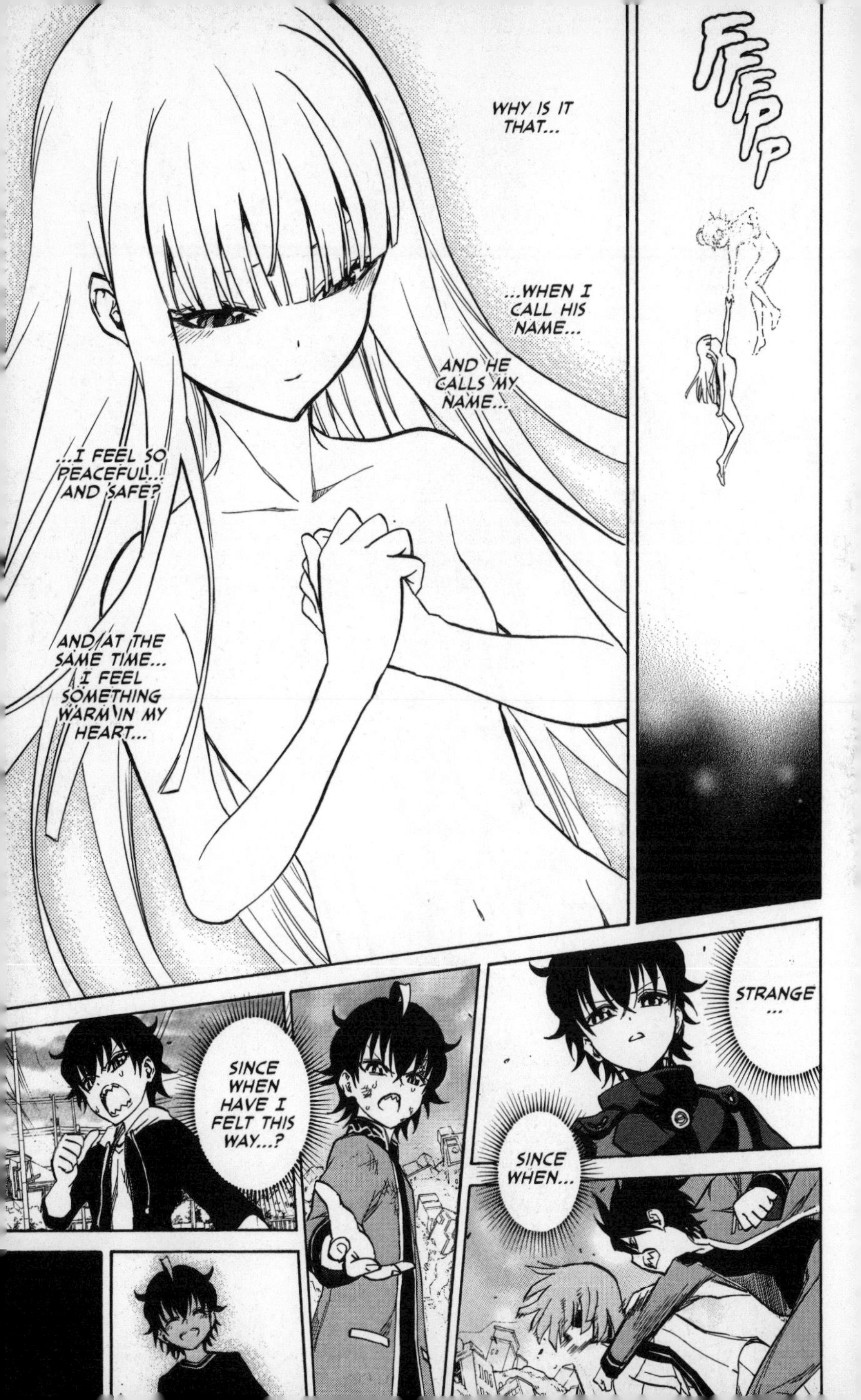
FFFP
WHY IS IT THAT...
...WHEN I CALL HIS NAME...
AND HE CALLS MY NAME...
...I FEEL SO PEACEFUL... AND SAFE?
AND AT THE SAME TIME... I FEEL SOMETHING WARM IN MY HEART...
STRANGE...
SINCE WHEN...
SINCE WHEN HAVE I FELT THIS WAY...?

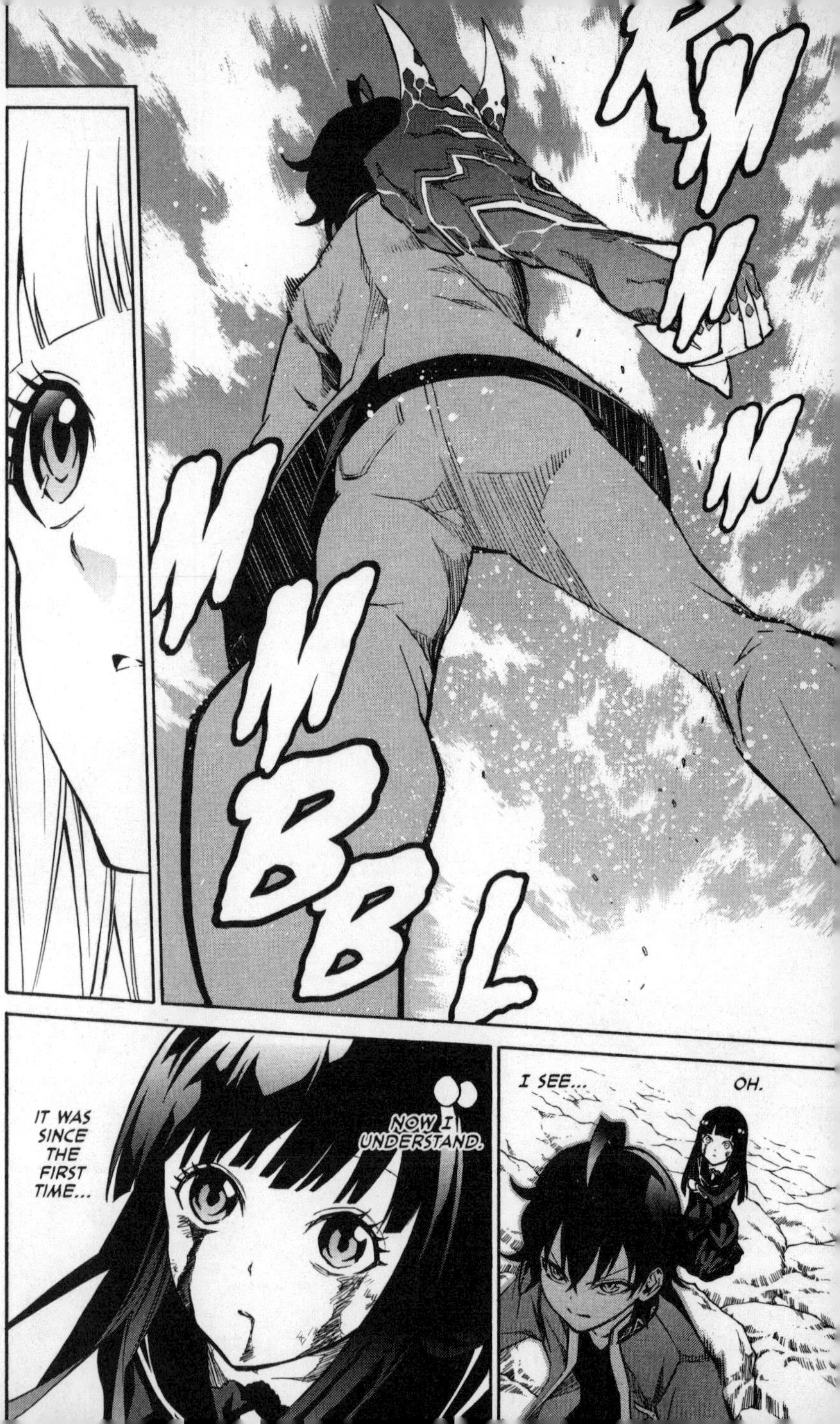
KMMM
MMMBBL
OH.
I SEE...
NOW I UNDERSTAND.
IT WAS SINCE THE FIRST TIME...

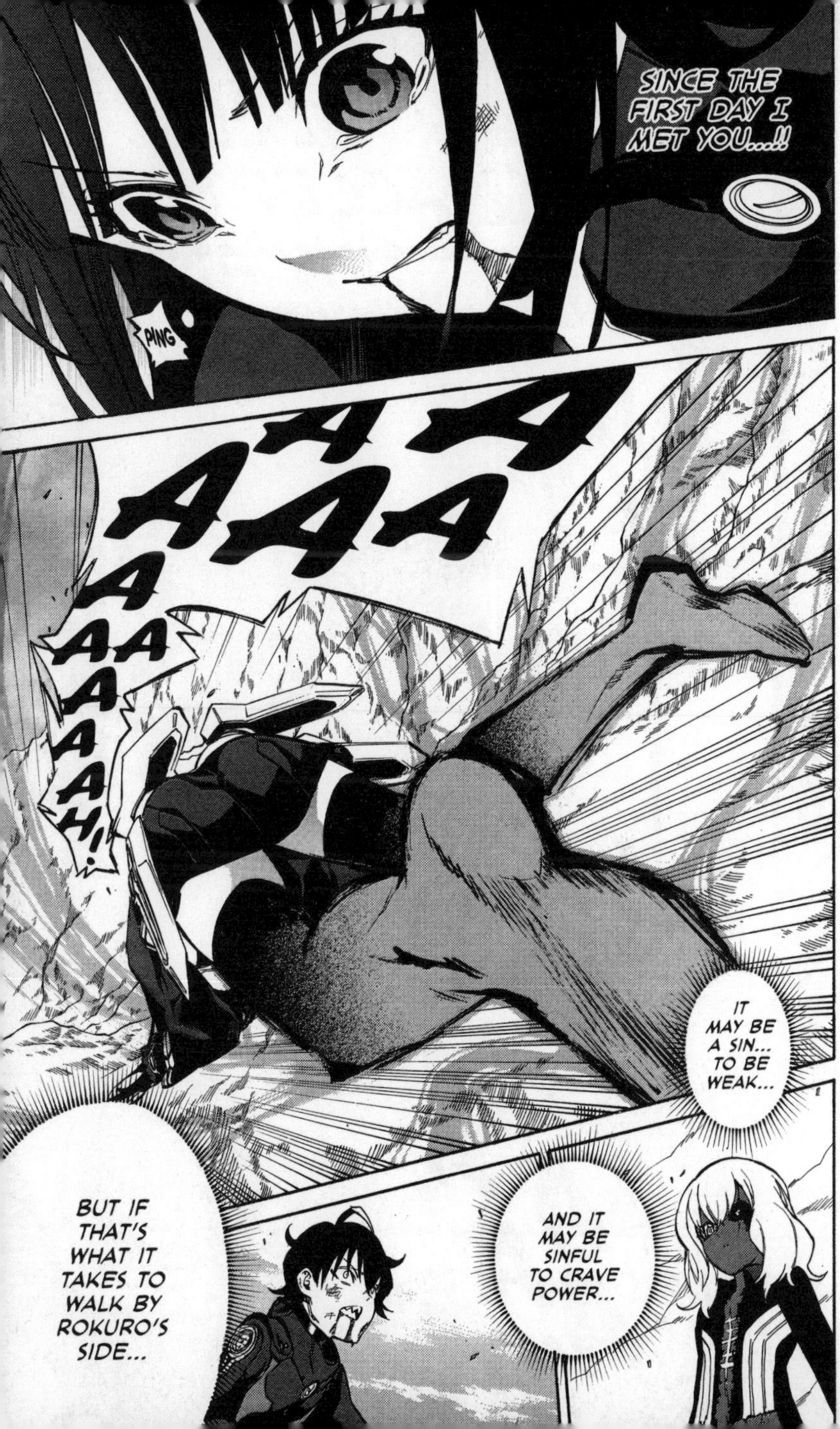
SINCE THE FIRST DAY I MET YOU...!!
PING
AAAAAAAAAAAH!
IT MAY BE A SIN... TO BE WEAK...
AND IT MAY BE SINFUL TO CRAVE POWER...
BUT IF THAT'S WHAT IT TAKES TO WALK BY ROKURO'S SIDE...

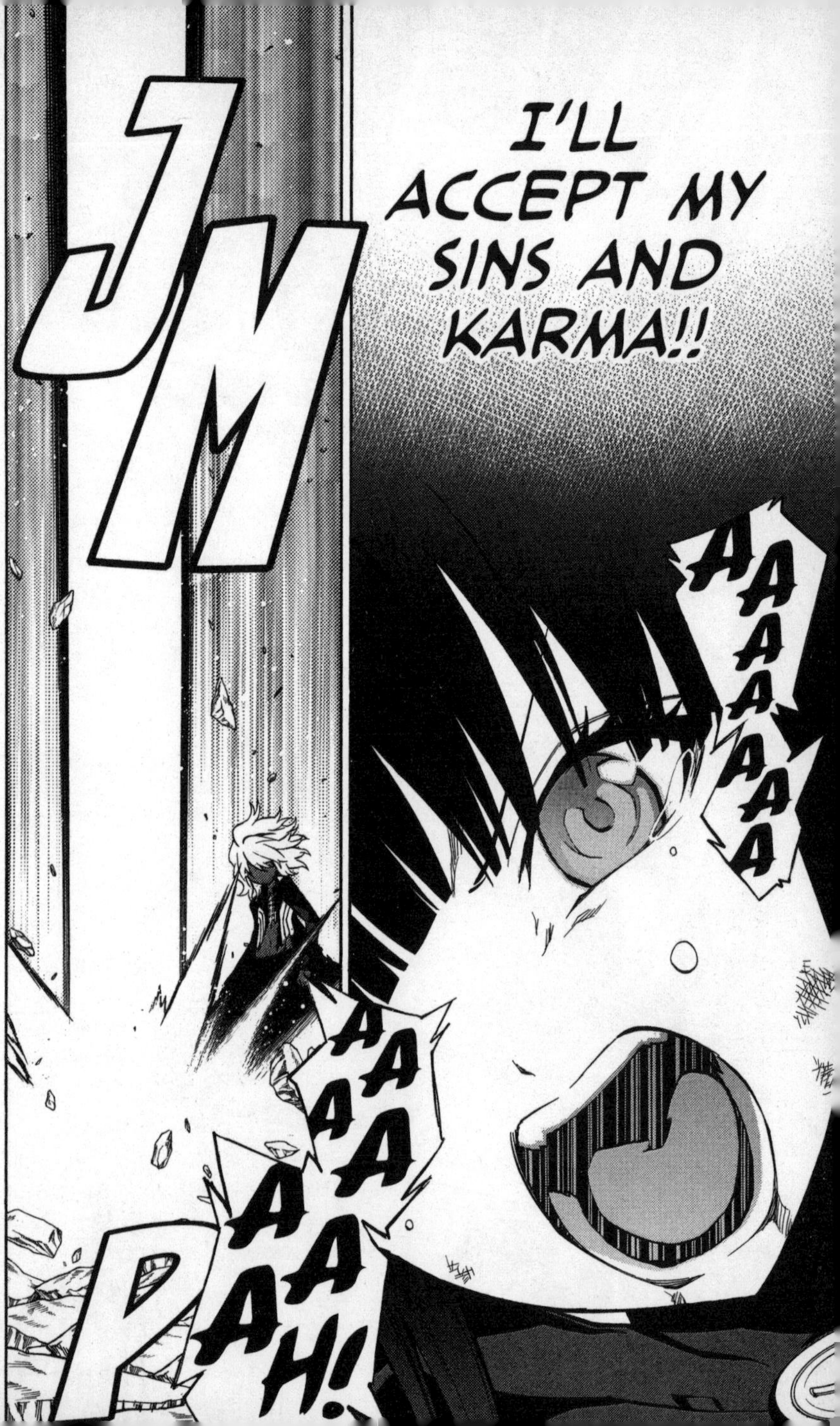
I'LL ACCEPT MY SINS AND KARMA!!
AAAAAAAA
JUN
AAAAAAAA
DAH!

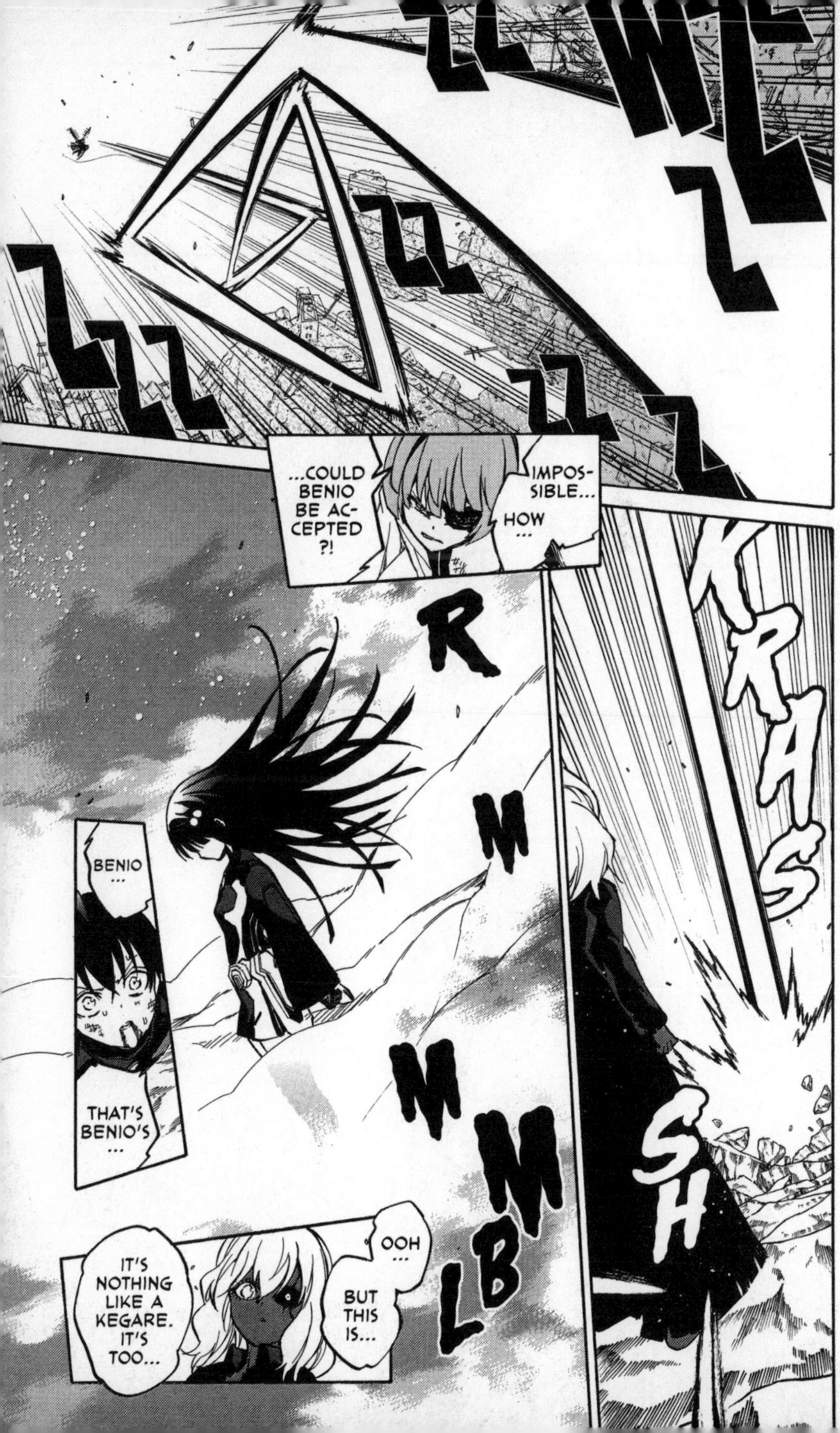

IMPOSSIBLE... HOW ...
...COULD BENIO BE ACCEPTED ?!
KRASH
BENIO ...
THAT'S BENIO'S ...
OOH ... BUT THIS IS...
IT'S NOTHING LIKE A KEGARE. IT'S TOO...

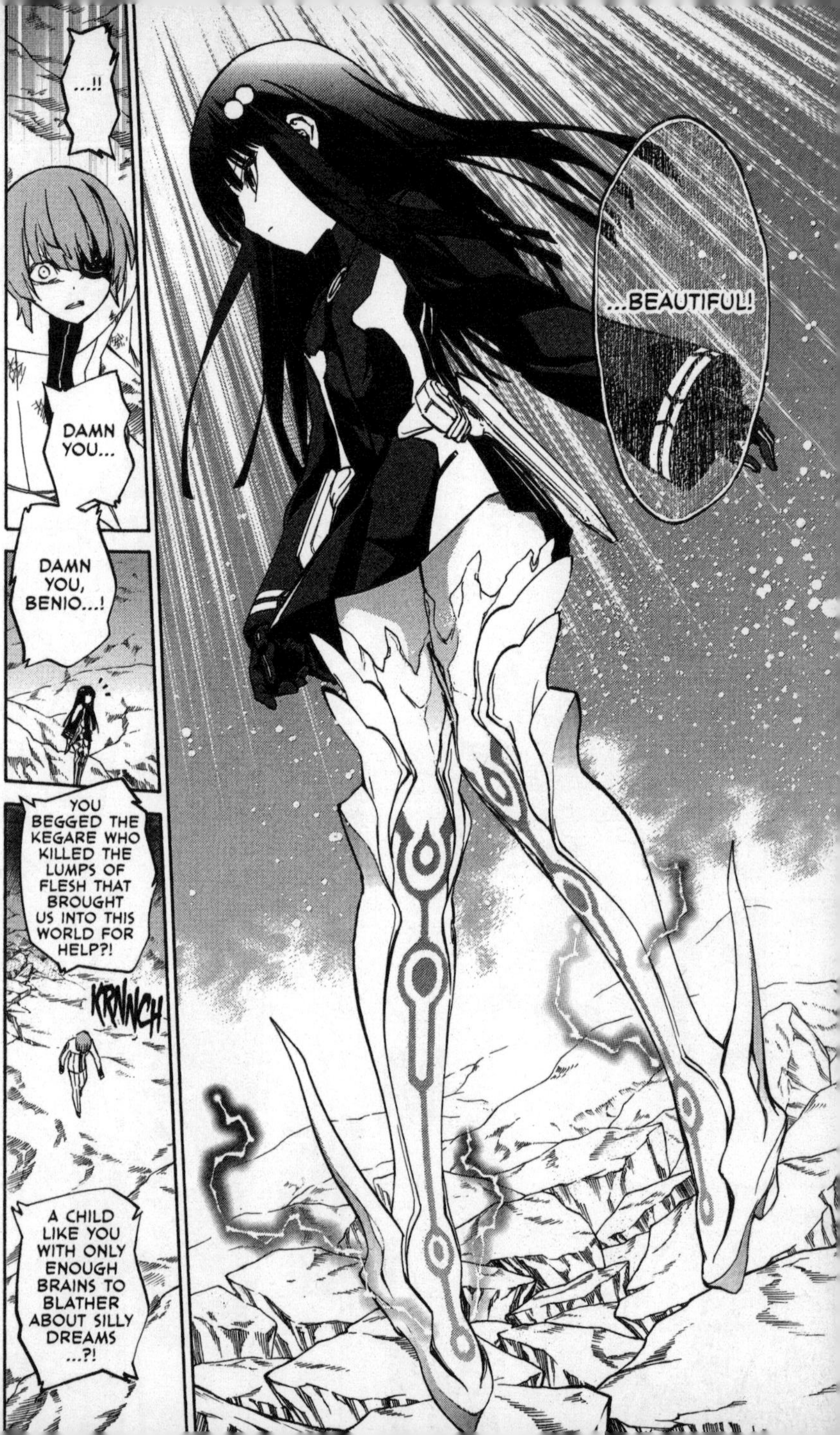
...BEAUTIFUL!
...!!
DAMN YOU...
DAMN YOU, BENIO...!
YOU BEGGED THE KEGARE WHO KILLED THE LUMPS OF FLESH THAT BROUGHT US INTO THIS WORLD FOR HELP?!
KRNNCH
A CHILD LIKE YOU WITH ONLY ENOUGH BRAINS TO BLATHER ABOUT SILLY DREAMS ...?!

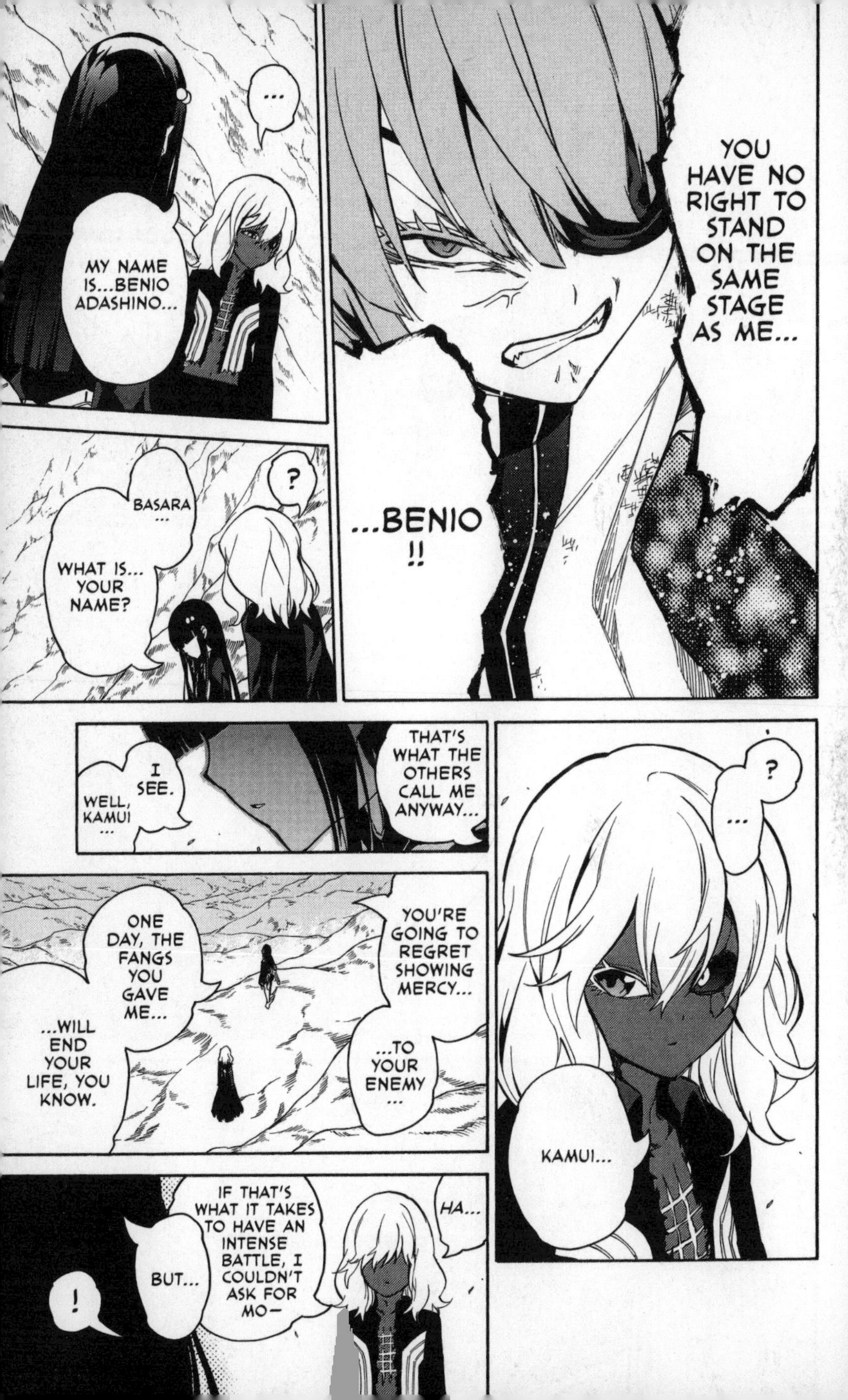
YOU HAVE NO RIGHT TO STAND ON THE SAME STAGE AS ME...
...BENIO !!
...
MY NAME IS...BENIO ADASHINO...
?
BASARA...
WHAT IS... YOUR NAME?
?
...
KAMUI...
THAT'S WHAT THE OTHERS CALL ME ANYWAY...
I SEE.
WELL, KAMUI...
YOU'RE GOING TO REGRET SHOWING MERCY...
...TO YOUR ENEMY...
ONE DAY, THE FANGS YOU GAVE ME...
...WILL END YOUR LIFE, YOU KNOW.
HA...
IF THAT'S WHAT IT TAKES TO HAVE AN INTENSE BATTLE, I COULDN'T ASK FOR MO—
BUT...
!

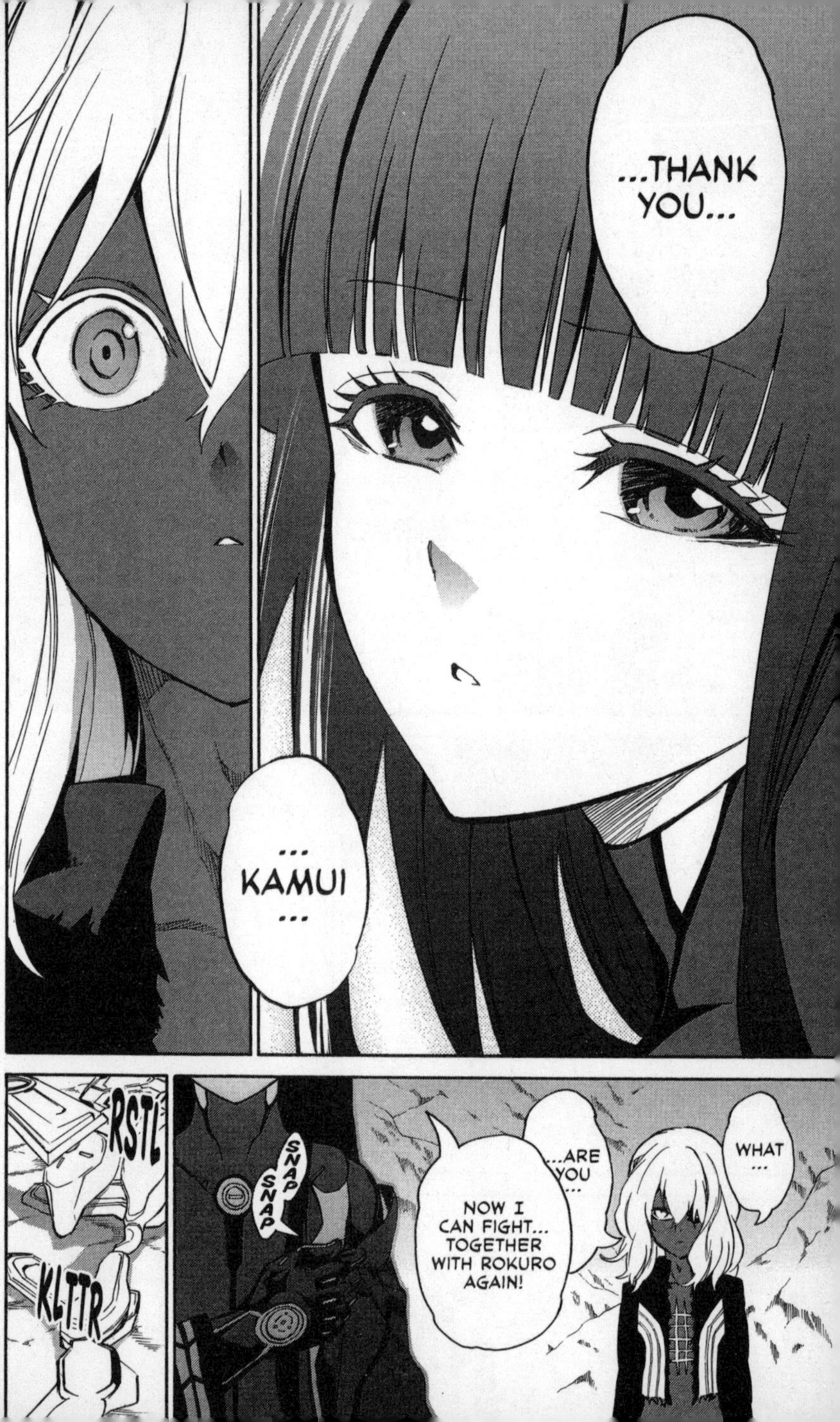
...THANK YOU...
...KAMUI...
WHAT...
...ARE YOU...
NOW I CAN FIGHT... TOGETHER WITH ROKURO AGAIN!
SNAP SNAP
RSTL
KLTTR

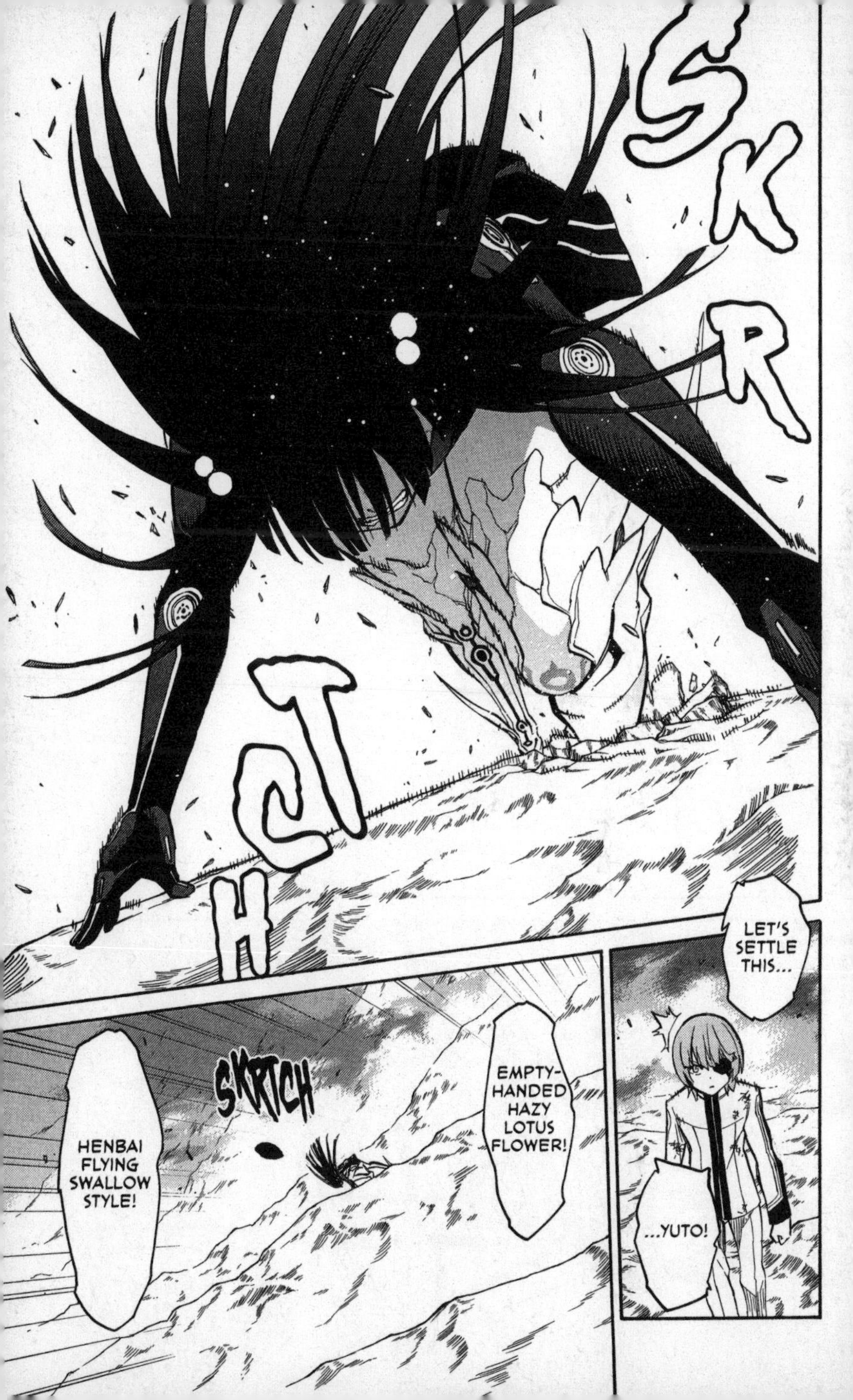
SKRTCH
LET'S SETTLE THIS...
...YUTO!
EMPTY-HANDED HAZY LOTUS FLOWER!
SKRTCH
HENBAI FLYING SWALLOW STYLE!

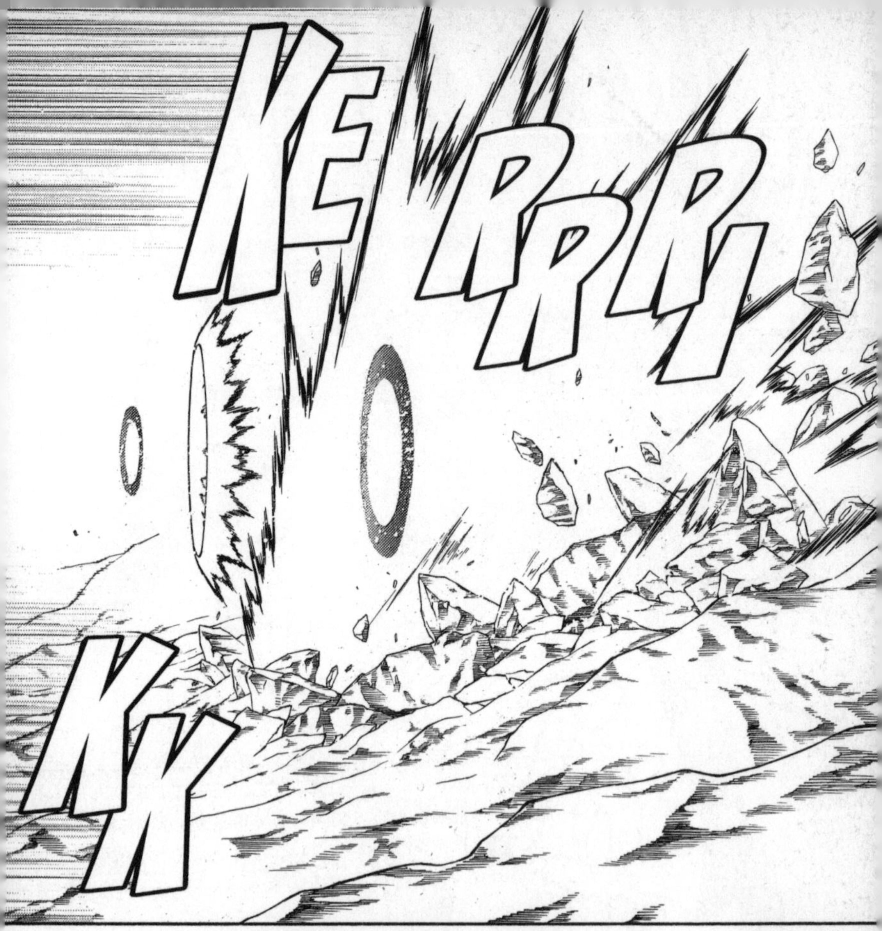
KERRRI
KK
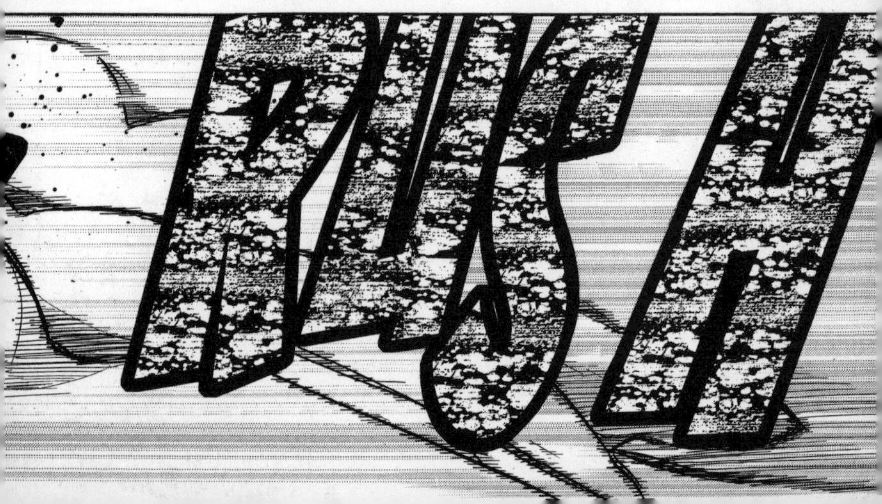
KRUSH

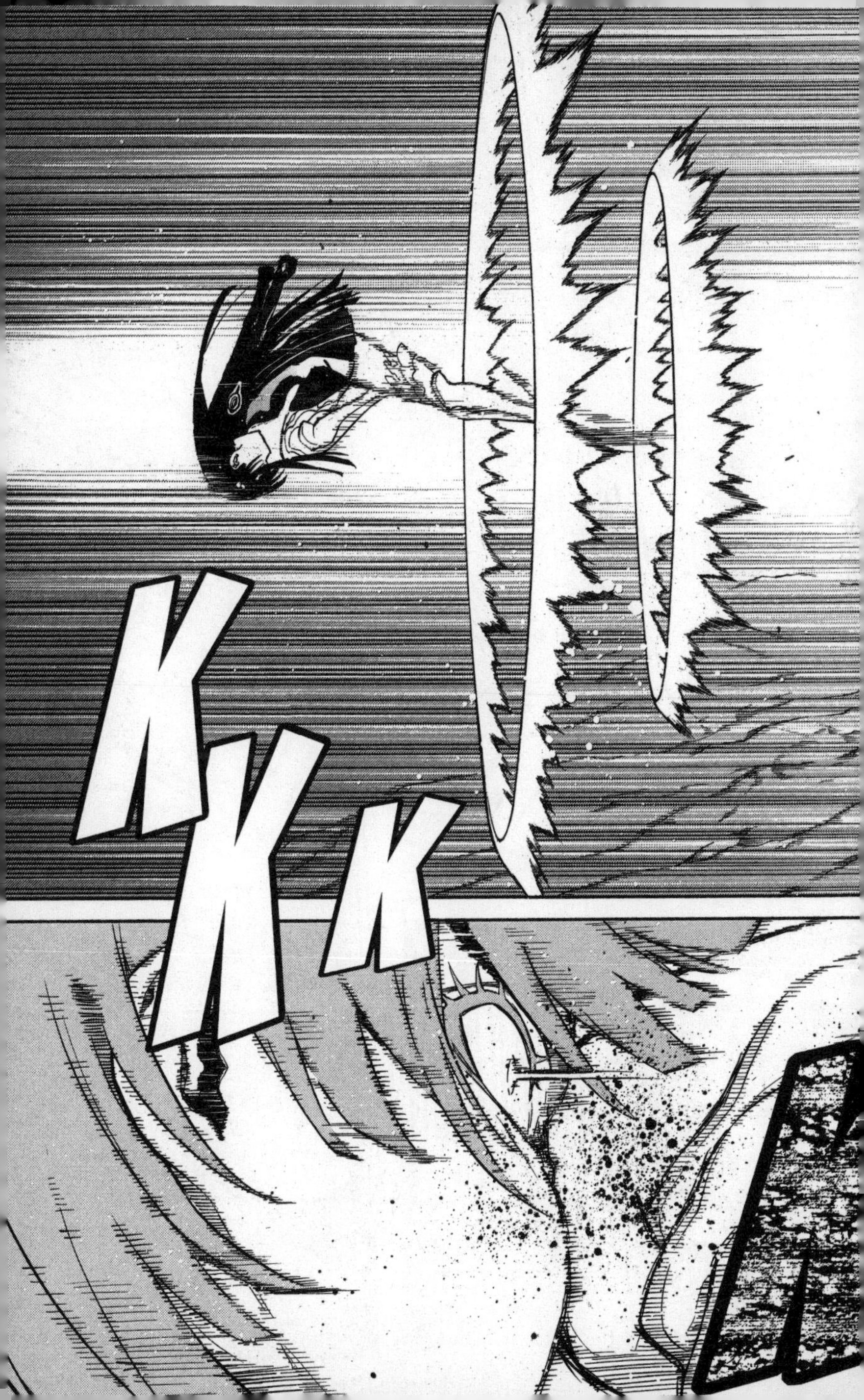
KKK

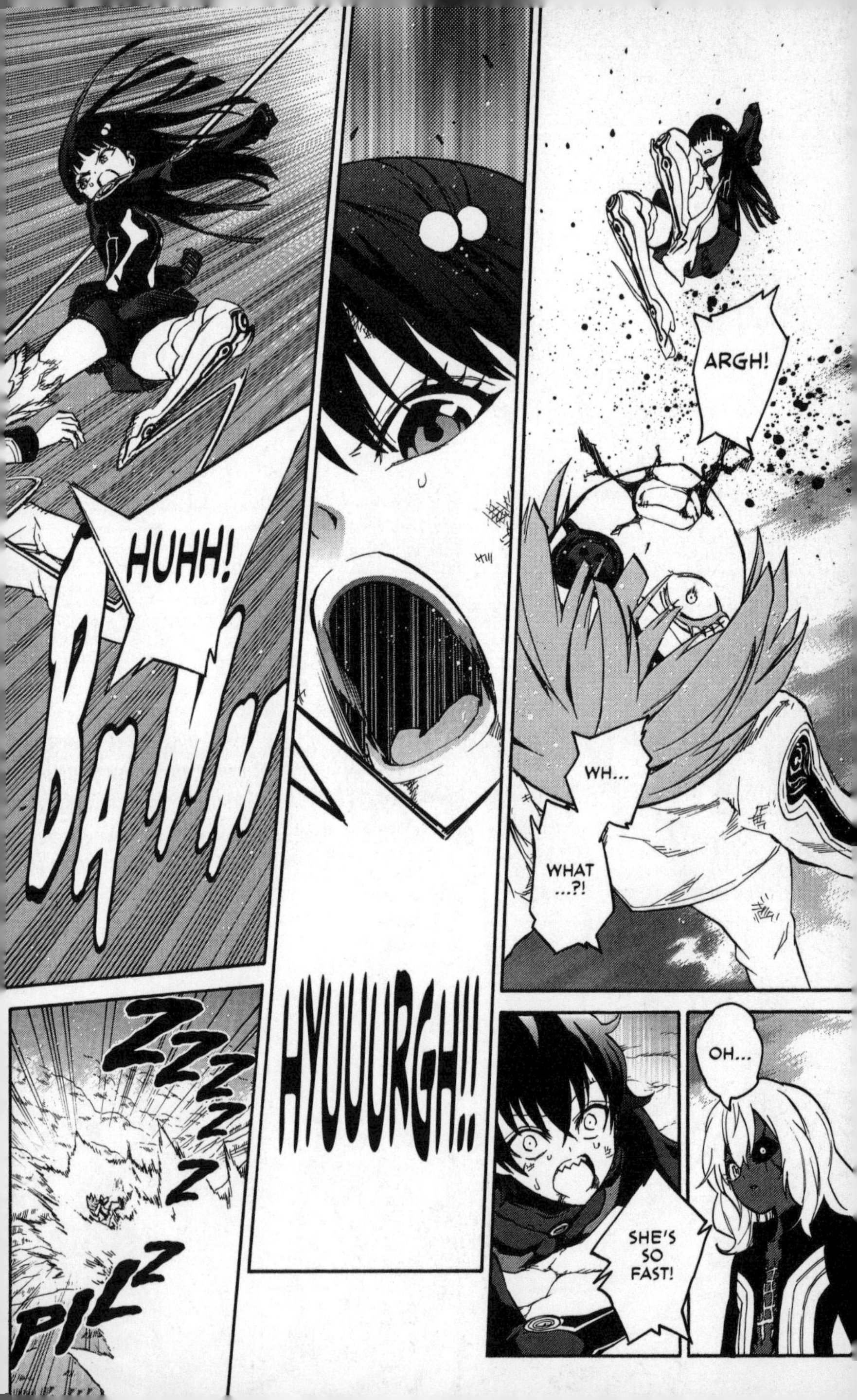
ARGH!
WH...
WHAT ...?!
OH...
SHE'S SO FAST!
HYUUURGH!!!
HUHH!

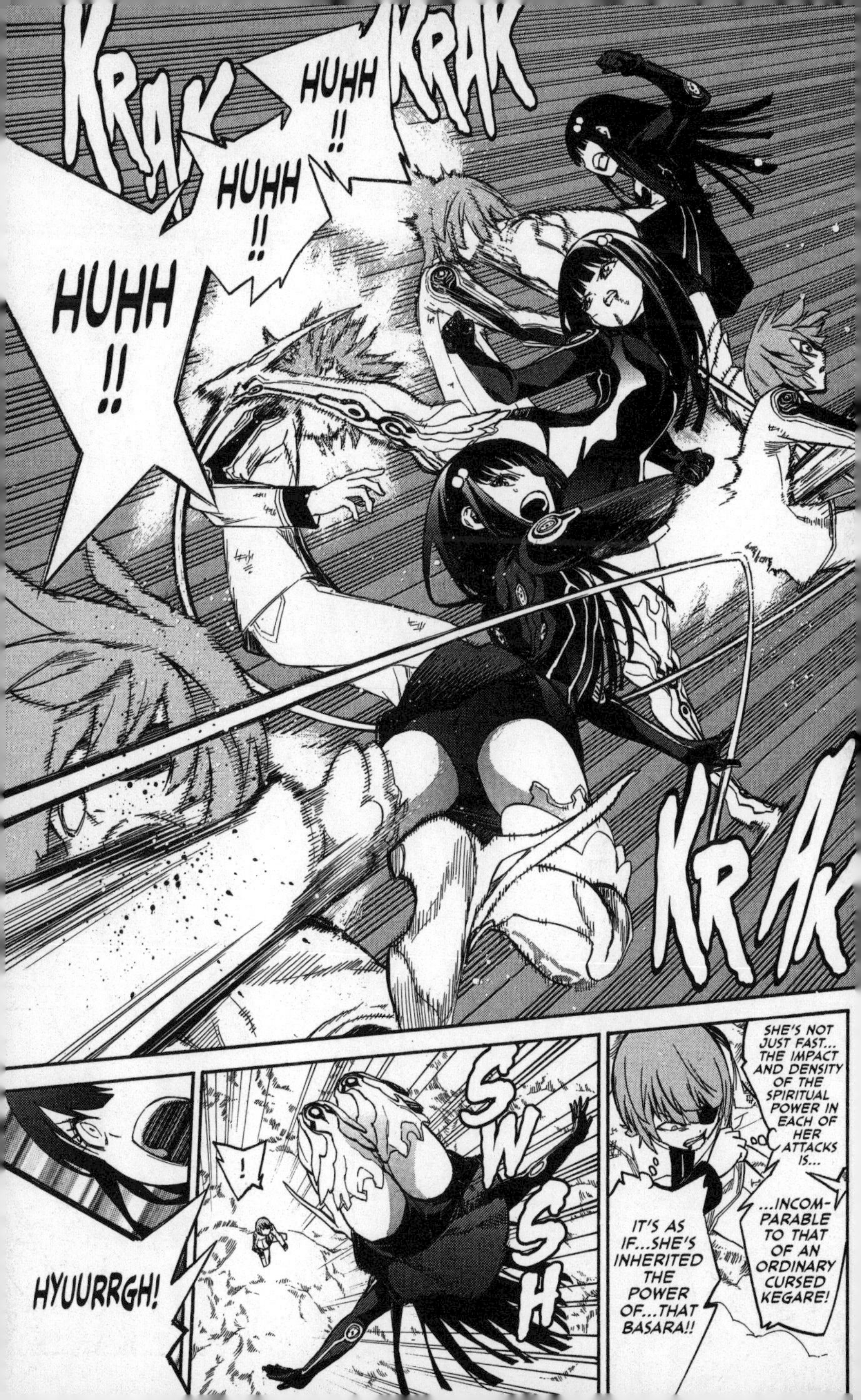
KRAK
HUHH!!
KRAK
HUHH!!
HUHH!!
KRAK
SHE'S NOT JUST FAST... THE IMPACT AND DENSITY OF THE SPIRITUAL POWER IN EACH OF HER ATTACKS IS...
...INCOMPARABLE TO THAT OF AN ORDINARY CURSED KEGARE!
IT'S AS IF...SHE'S INHERITED THE POWER OF...THAT BASARA!!
SWSH
!
HYUURRGH!

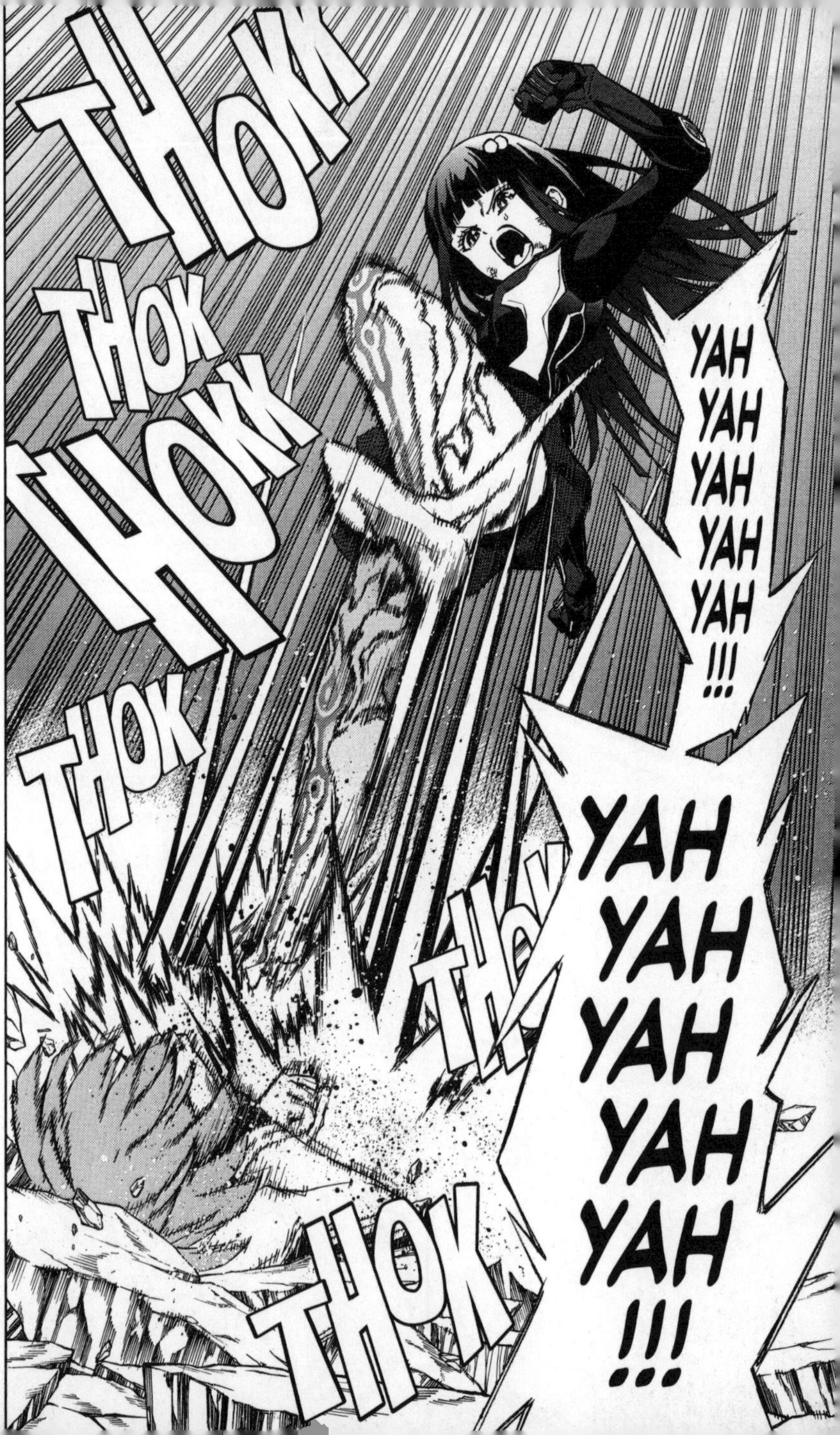
YAH YAH YAH YAH YAH !!!
THOKK
THOK
THOKK
THOK
YAH YAH YAH YAH YAH YAH !!!
THOK

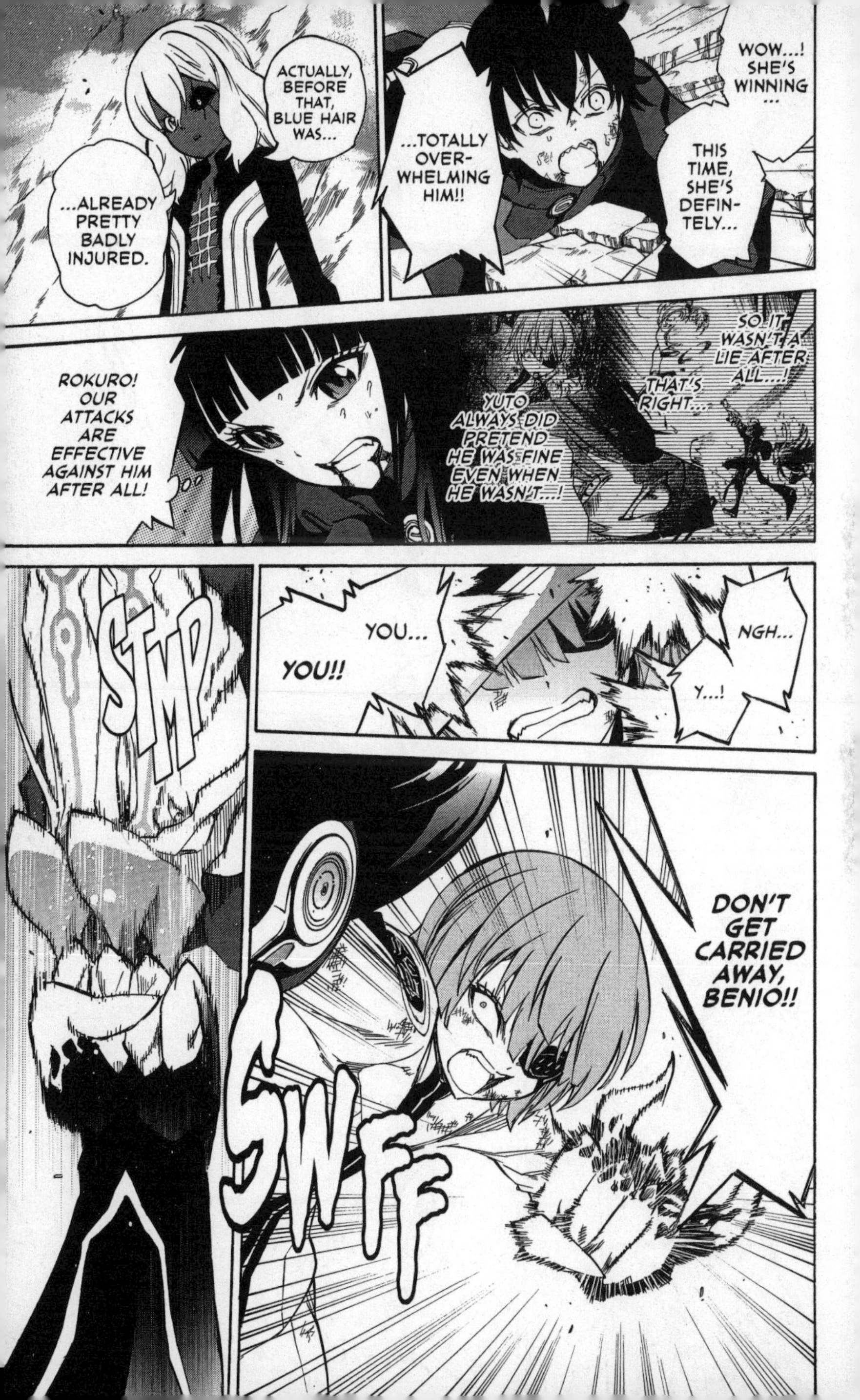
WOW...! SHE'S WINNING ...
THIS TIME, SHE'S DEFINTELY...
...TOTALLY OVER-WHELMING HIM!!
ACTUALLY, BEFORE THAT, BLUE HAIR WAS...
...ALREADY PRETTY BADLY INJURED.
SO IT WASN'T A LIE AFTER ALL...!
THAT'S RIGHT...
YUTO ALWAYS DID PRETEND HE WAS FINE EVEN WHEN HE WASN'T...!
ROKURO! OUR ATTACKS ARE EFFECTIVE AGAINST HIM AFTER ALL!
NGH...
Y...!
YOU...
YOU!!
DON'T GET CARRIED AWAY, BENIO!!
SWF
STMP

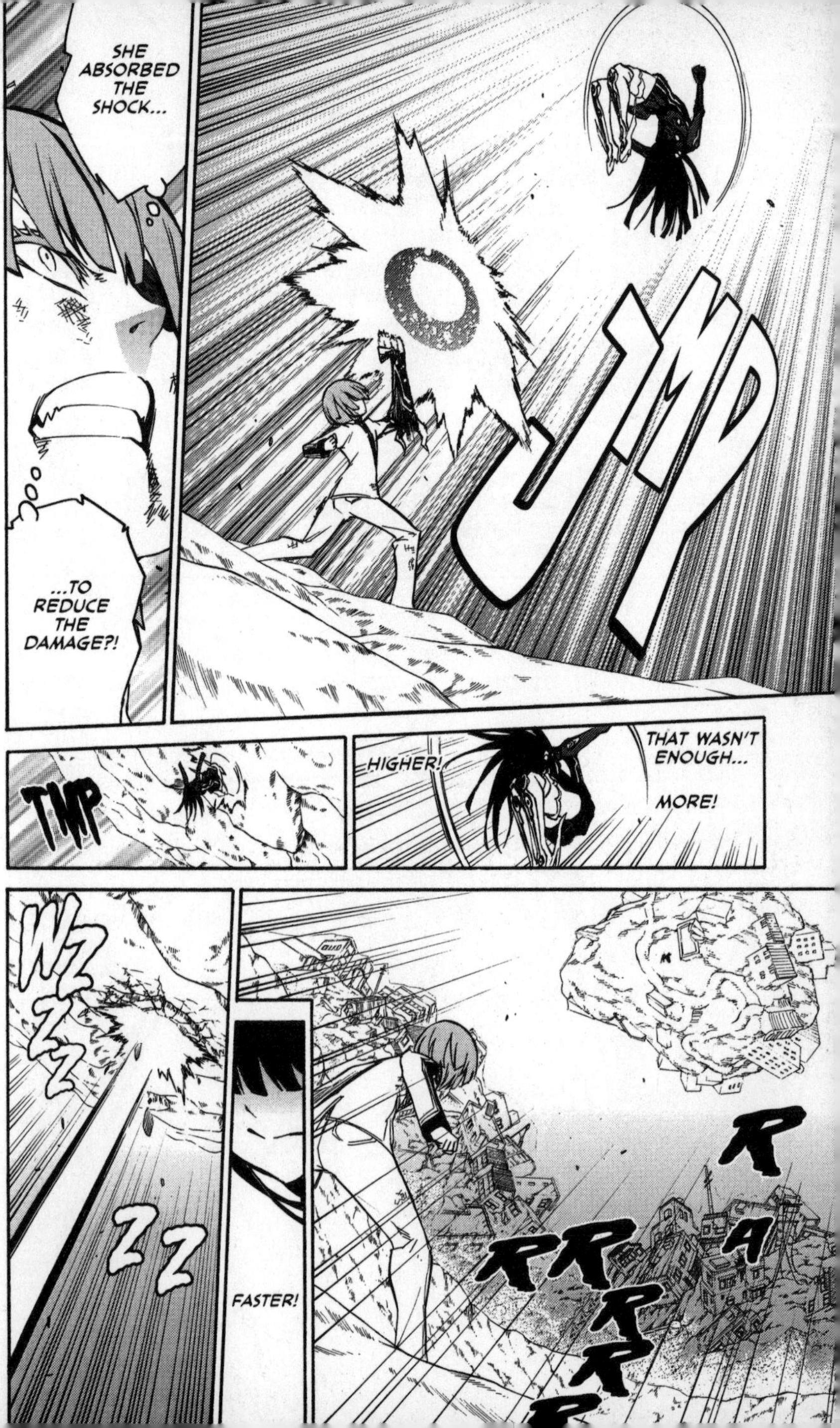
TMP
SHE ABSORBED THE SHOCK...
...TO REDUCE THE DAMAGE?!
THAT WASN'T ENOUGH...
MORE!
HIGHER!
TMP
R
A
RRRRRR
FASTER!
WZZZZ
ZZ

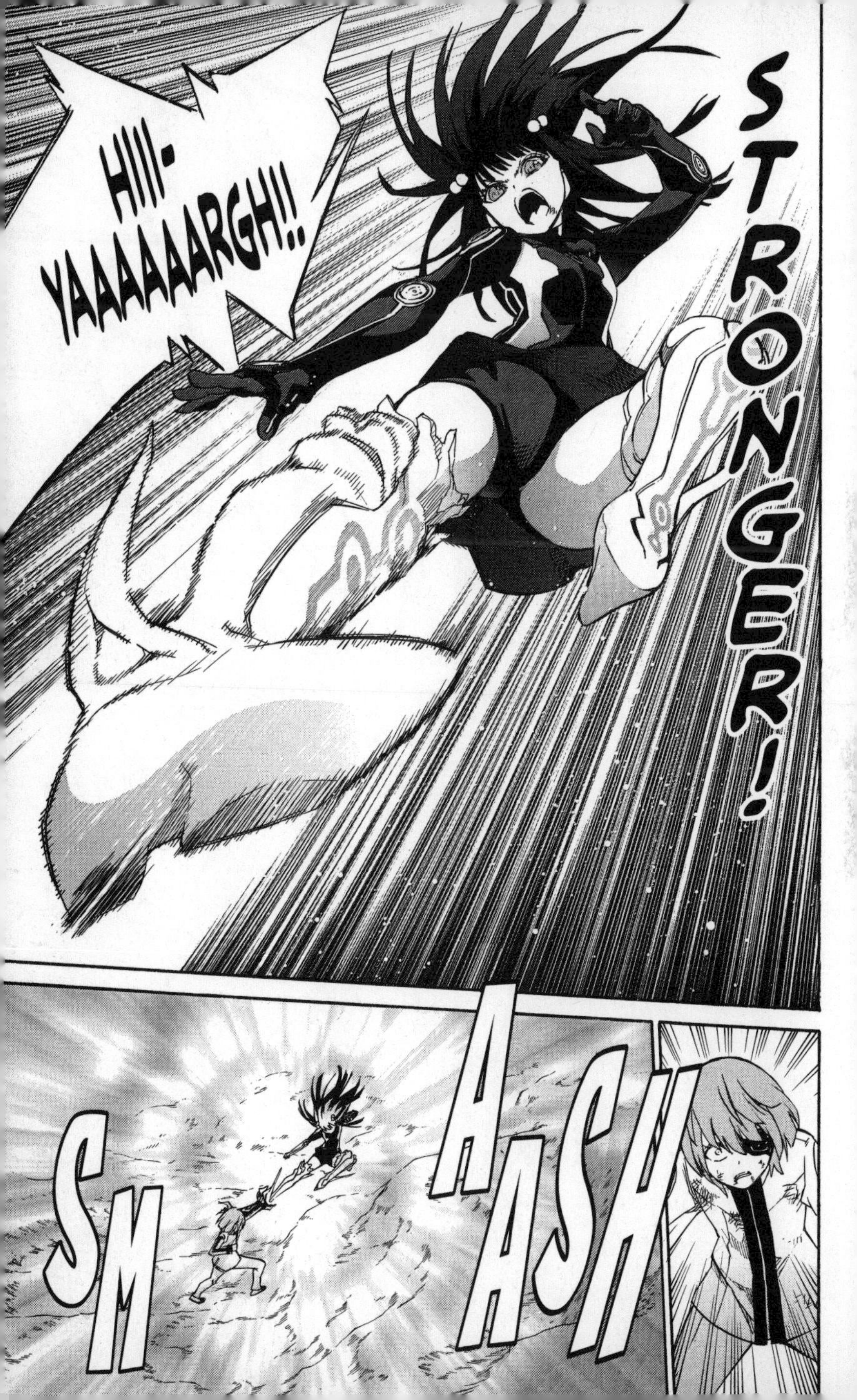
STRONGER!
HIII-YAAAAAARGH!!
SMAASH

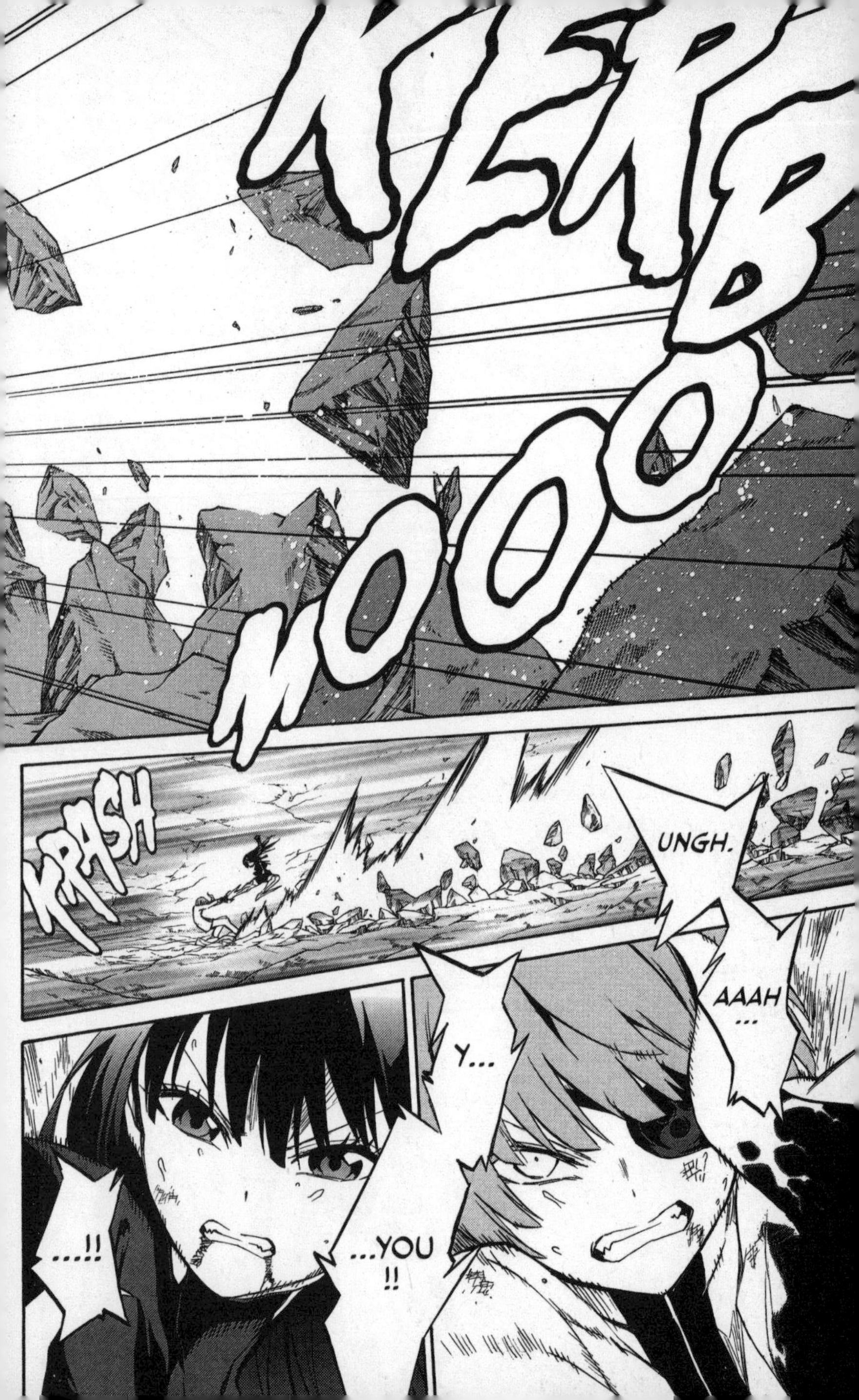
UNGH.
KRASH
AAAH...
Y...
...YOU!!
...!!

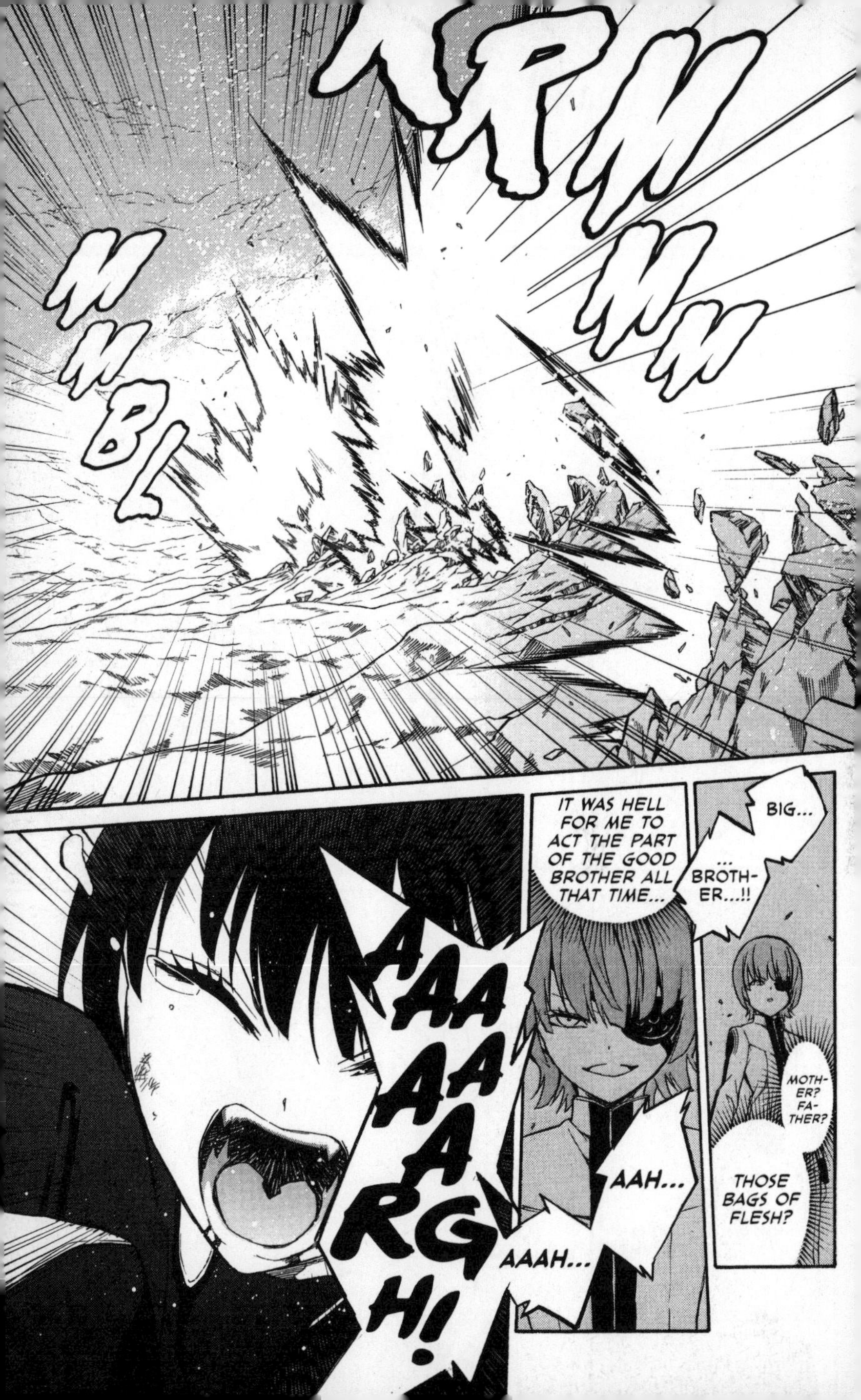
KRMMM
MMBL
BIG...
...BROTH-ER...!!
MOTH-ER? FA-THER?
THOSE BAGS OF FLESH?
IT WAS HELL FOR ME TO ACT THE PART OF THE GOOD BROTHER ALL THAT TIME...
AAH...
AAAH...
AAAAAAARGH!

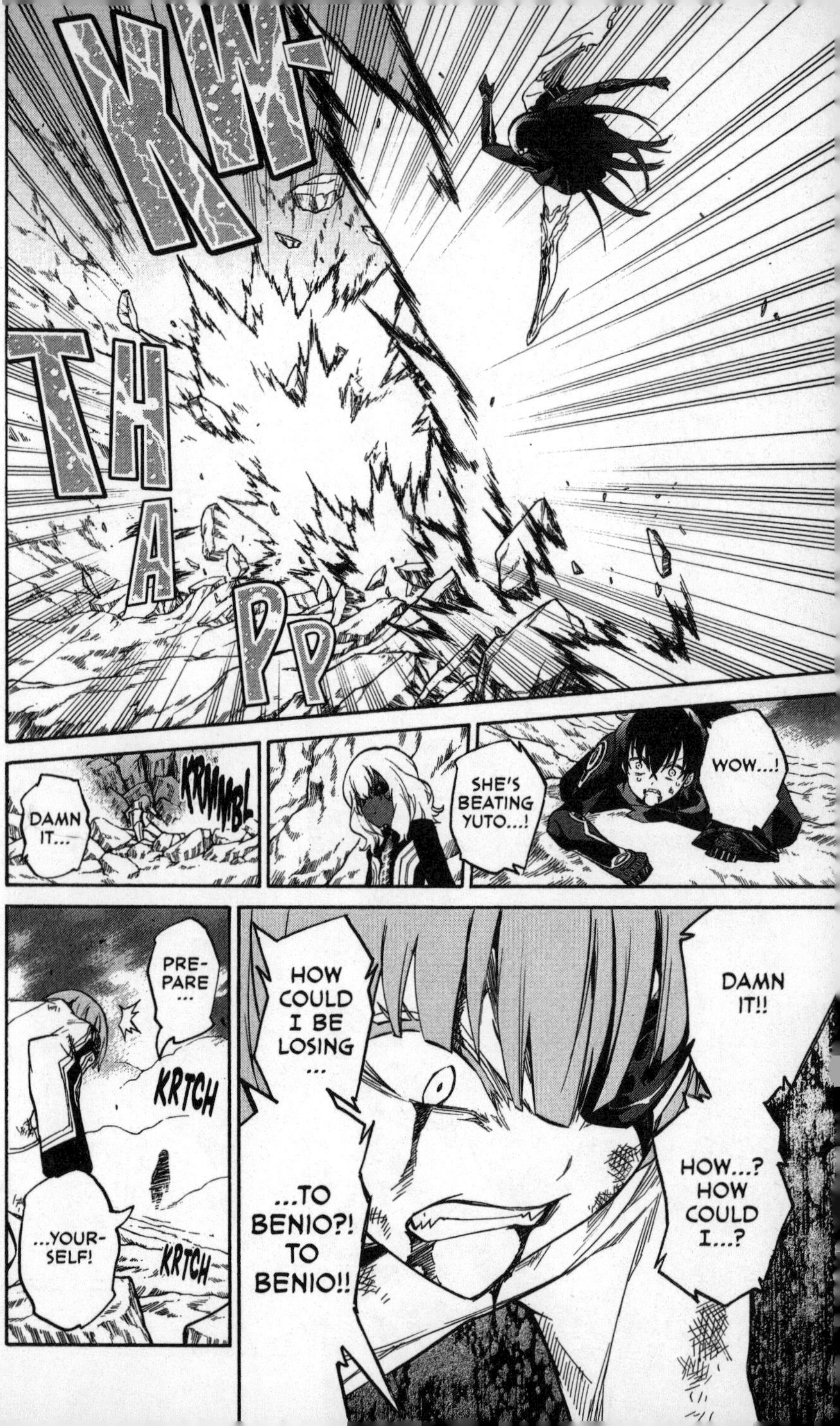

KW
THAPP
WOW...!
SHE'S BEATING YUTO...!
KRMMBL
DAMN IT...
DAMN IT!!
HOW COULD I BE LOSING...
HOW...? HOW COULD I...?
...TO BENIO?! TO BENIO!!
PRE-PARE...
KRTCH
...YOUR-SELF!
KRTCH

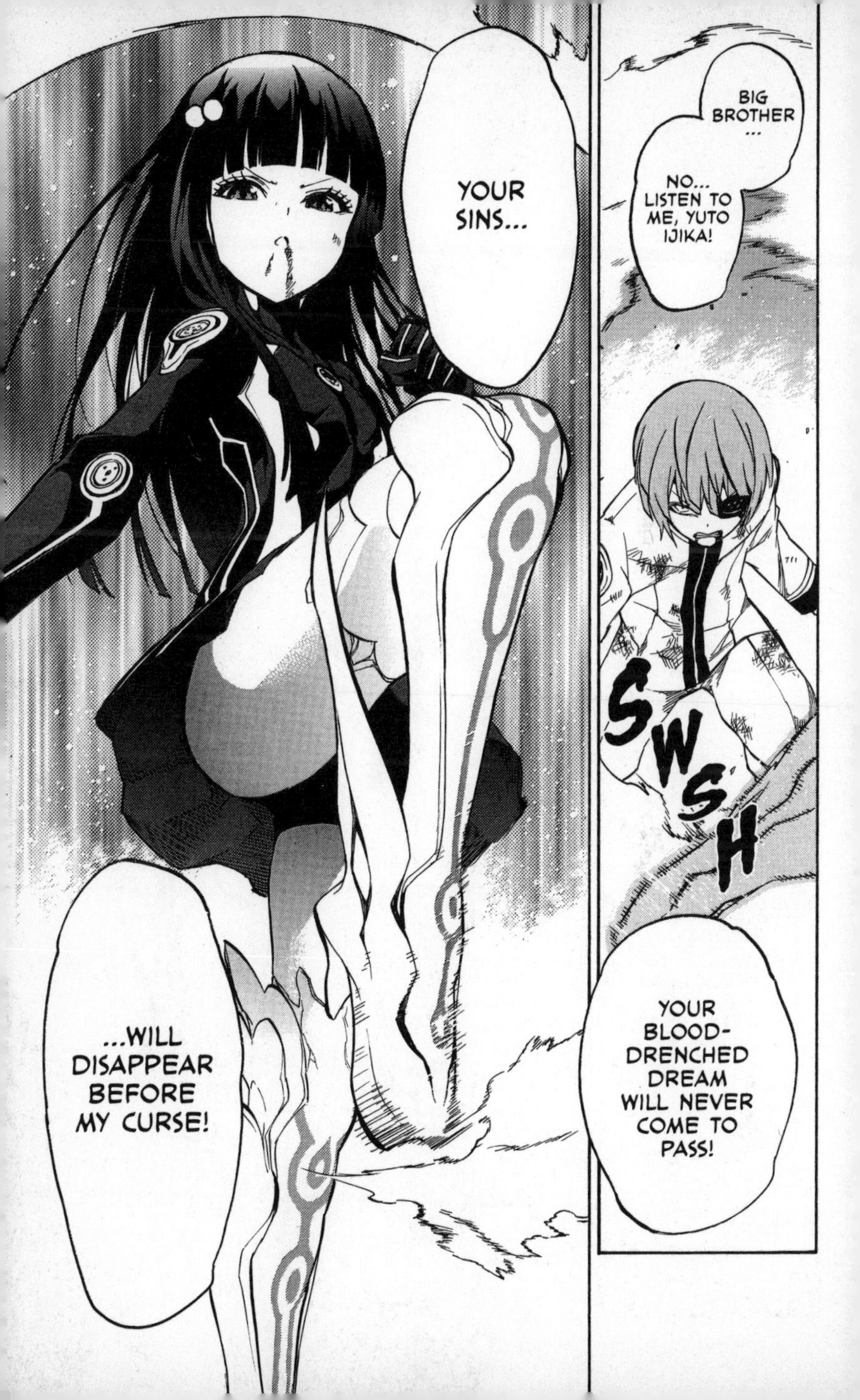
BIG BROTHER ...
NO... LISTEN TO ME, YUTO IJIKA!
SWSH
YOUR BLOOD-DRENCHED DREAM WILL NEVER COME TO PASS!
YOUR SINS...
...WILL DISAPPEAR BEFORE MY CURSE!

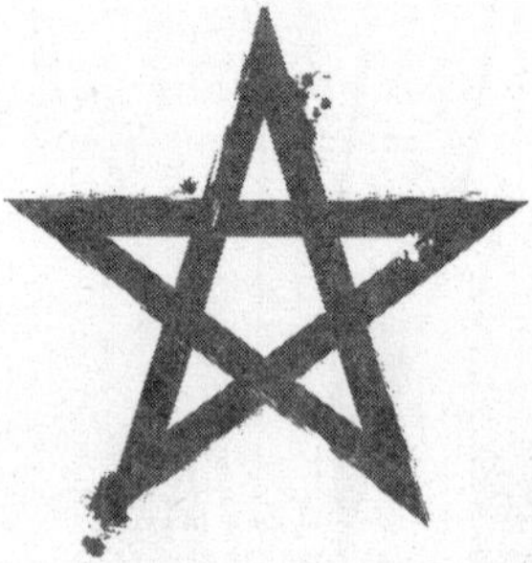

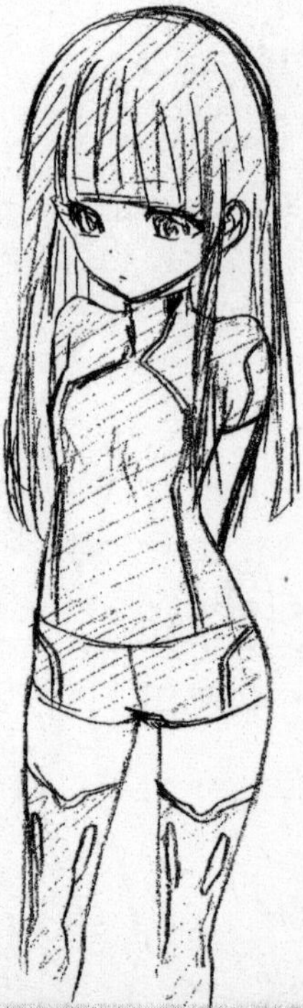

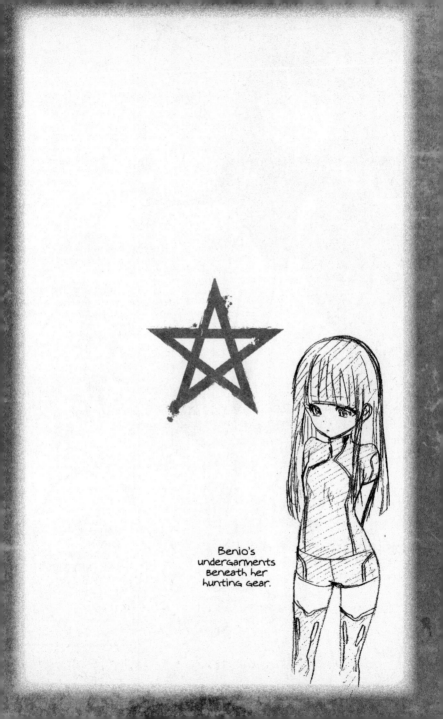

Benio's
undergarments
beneath her
hunting gear.

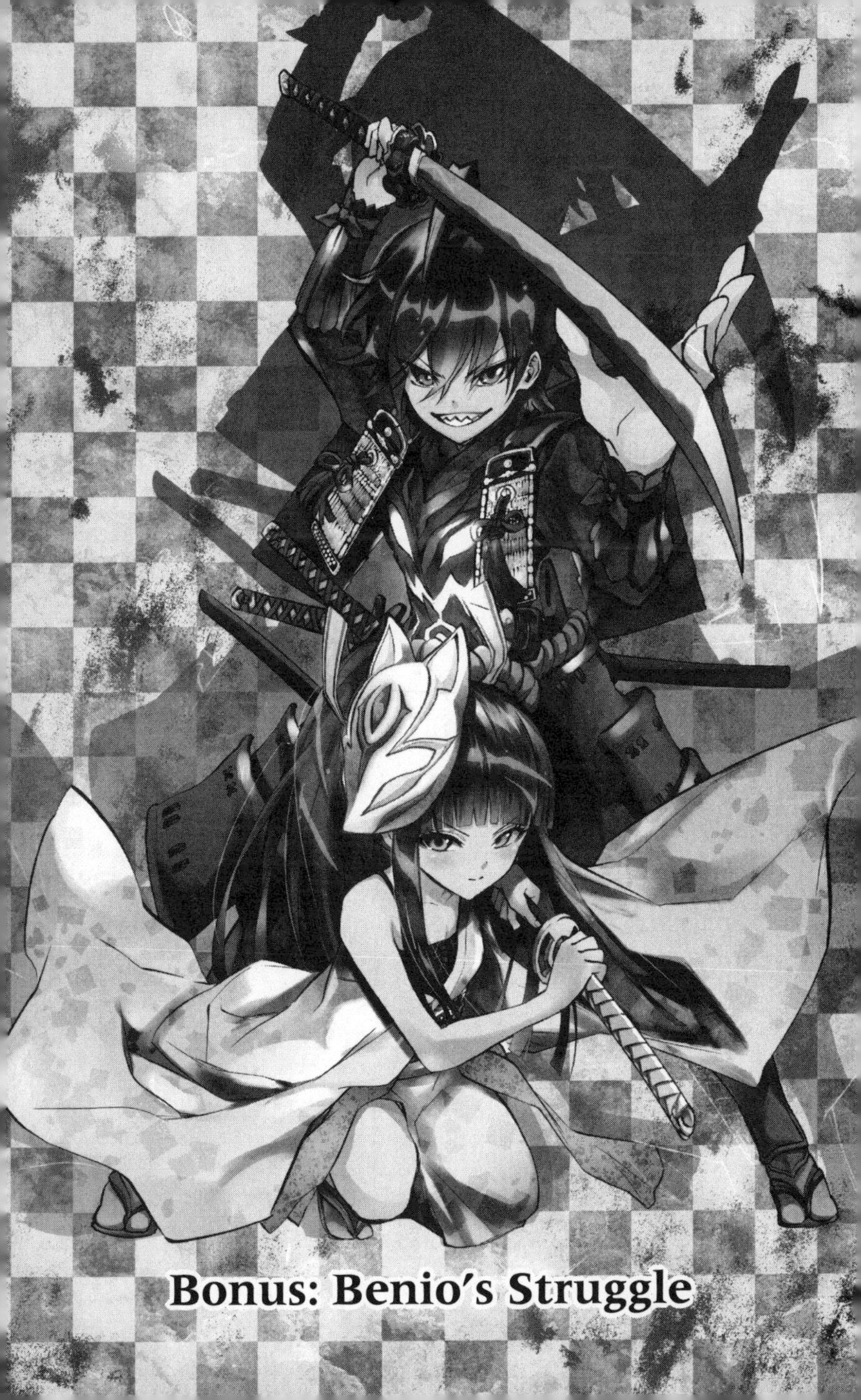

Bonus: Benio's Struggle

Twin Star Exorcists

ONMYOJI

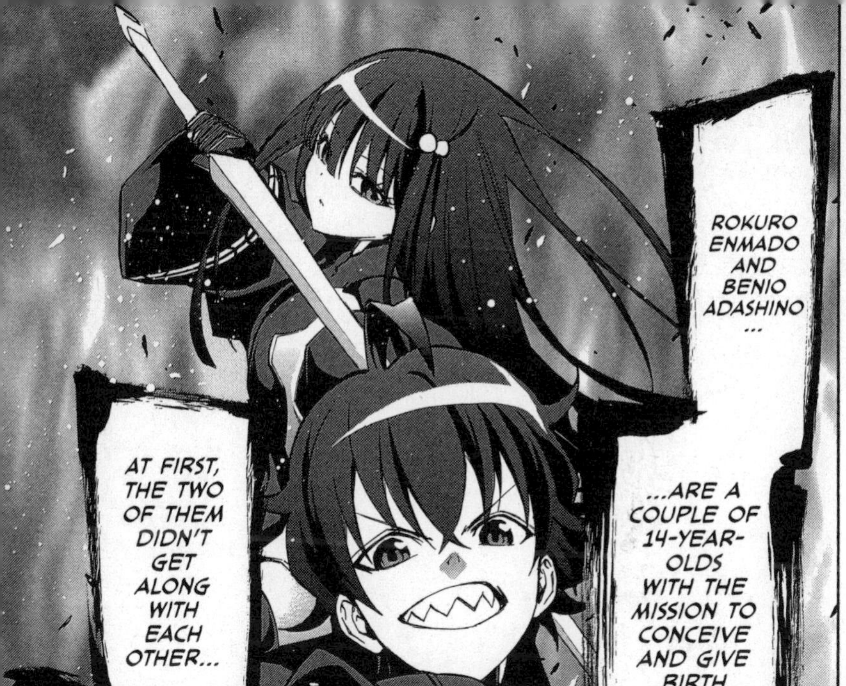
ROKURO ENMADO AND BENIO ADASHINO...
...ARE A COUPLE OF 14-YEAR-OLDS WITH THE MISSION TO CONCEIVE AND GIVE BIRTH TO THE PROPHESIED CHILD, THE GREATEST EXORCIST OF ALL.
AT FIRST, THE TWO OF THEM DIDN'T GET ALONG WITH EACH OTHER...
...BUT THEIR RELATIONSHIP BEGAN TO CHANGE AS THEY TRIUMPHED IN VARIOUS DEADLY BATTLES TOGETHER.

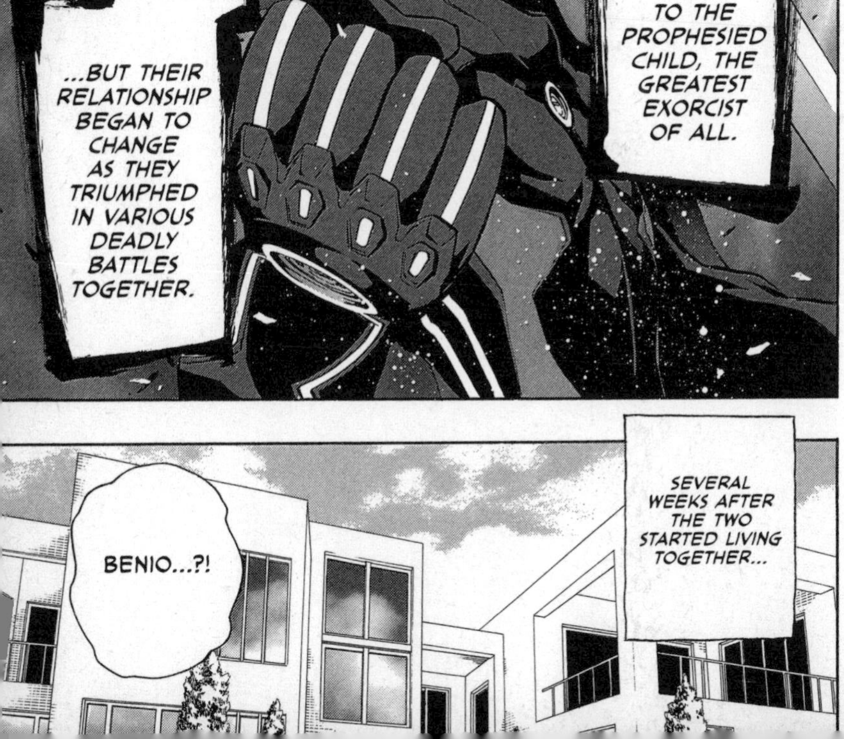
SEVERAL WEEKS AFTER THE TWO STARTED LIVING TOGETHER...
BENIO...?!

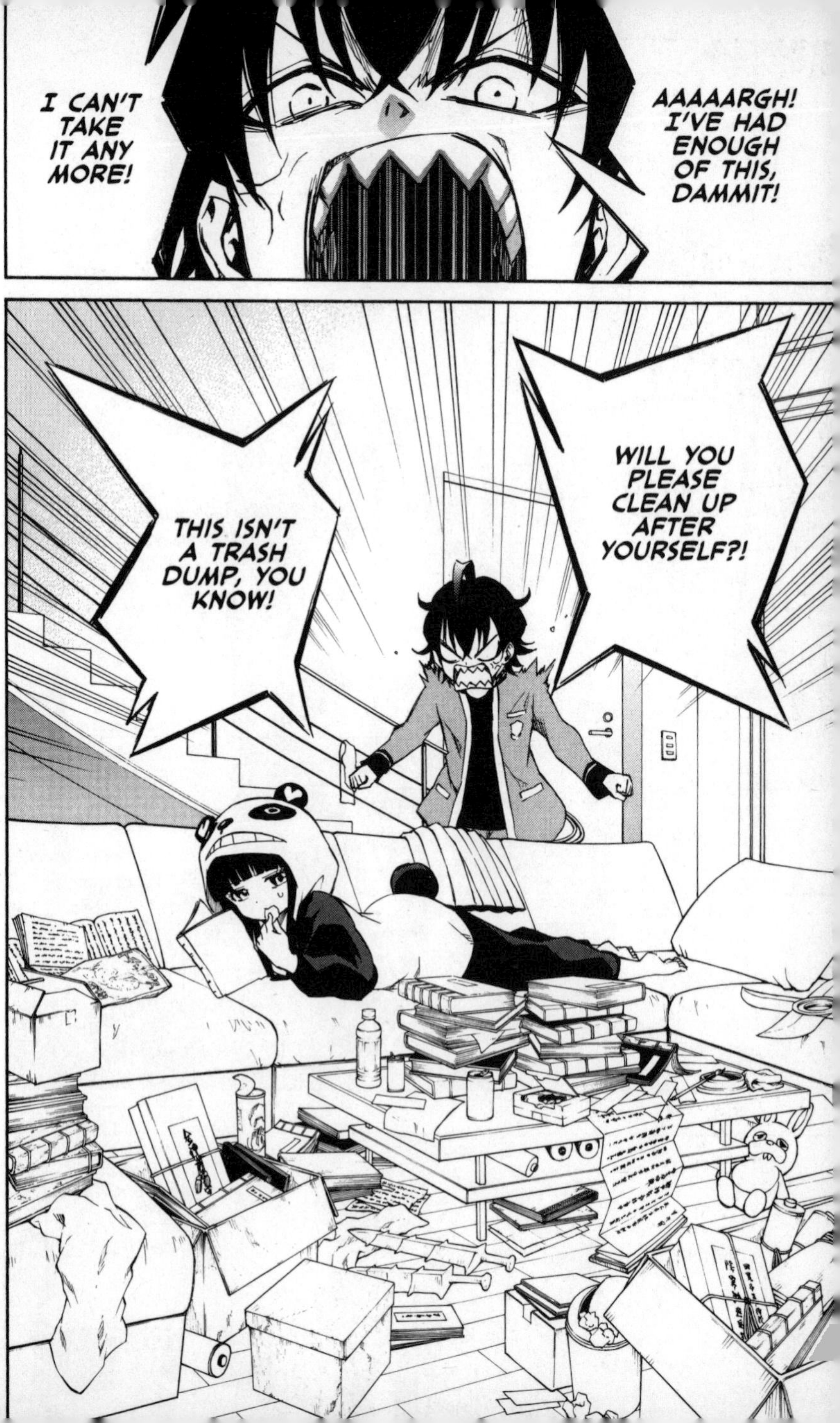
AAAAARGH! I'VE HAD ENOUGH OF THIS, DAMMIT!
I CAN'T TAKE IT ANY MORE!
WILL YOU PLEASE CLEAN UP AFTER YOURSELF?!
THIS ISN'T A TRASH DUMP, YOU KNOW!

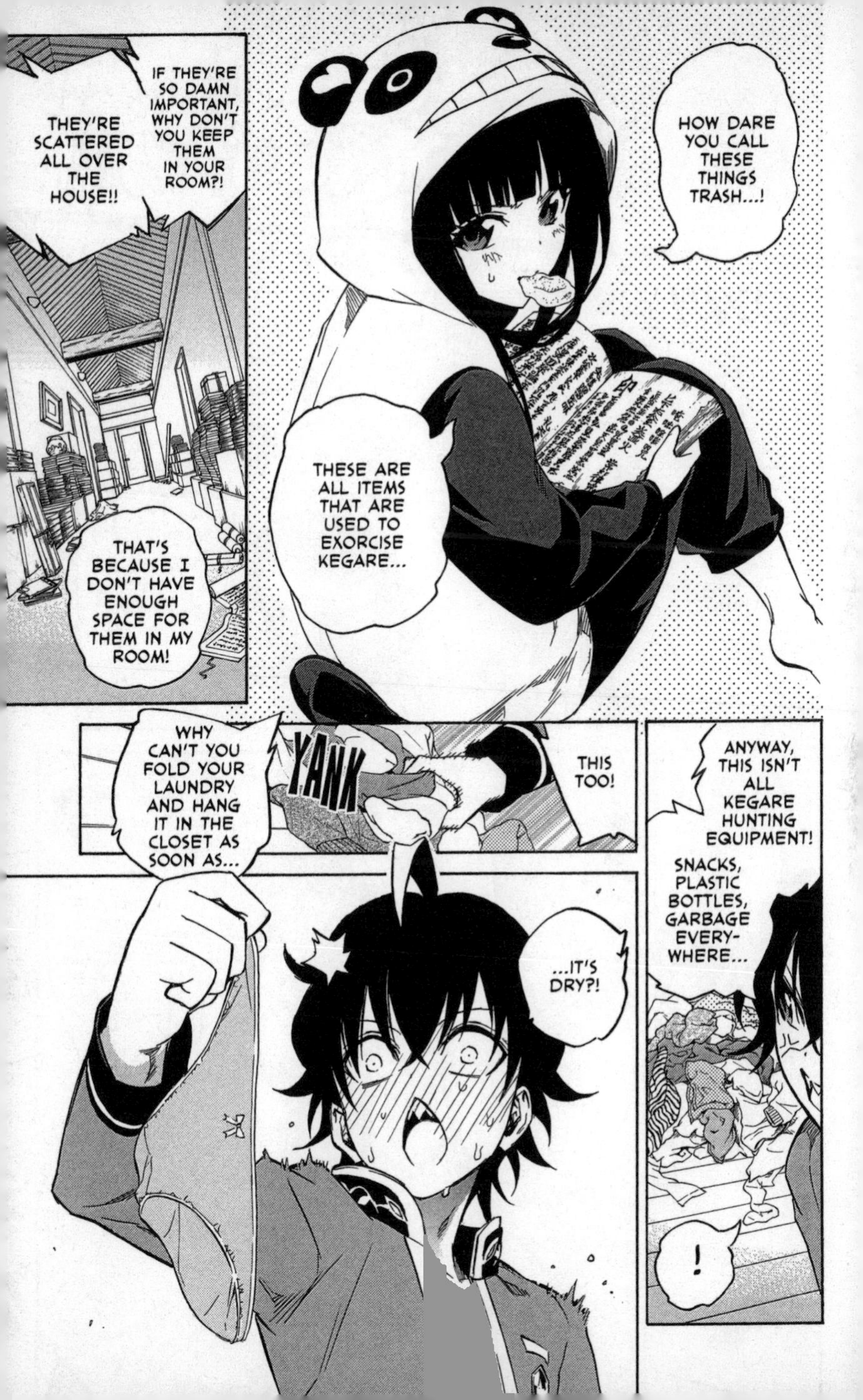
HOW DARE YOU CALL THESE THINGS TRASH...!
THESE ARE ALL ITEMS THAT ARE USED TO EXORCISE KEGARE...
IF THEY'RE SO DAMN IMPORTANT, WHY DON'T YOU KEEP THEM IN YOUR ROOM?!
THEY'RE SCATTERED ALL OVER THE HOUSE!!
THAT'S BECAUSE I DON'T HAVE ENOUGH SPACE FOR THEM IN MY ROOM!
ANYWAY, THIS ISN'T ALL KEGARE HUNTING EQUIPMENT!
SNACKS, PLASTIC BOTTLES, GARBAGE EVERY-WHERE...
!
THIS TOO!
YANK
WHY CAN'T YOU FOLD YOUR LAUNDRY AND HANG IT IN THE CLOSET AS SOON AS...
...IT'S DRY?!

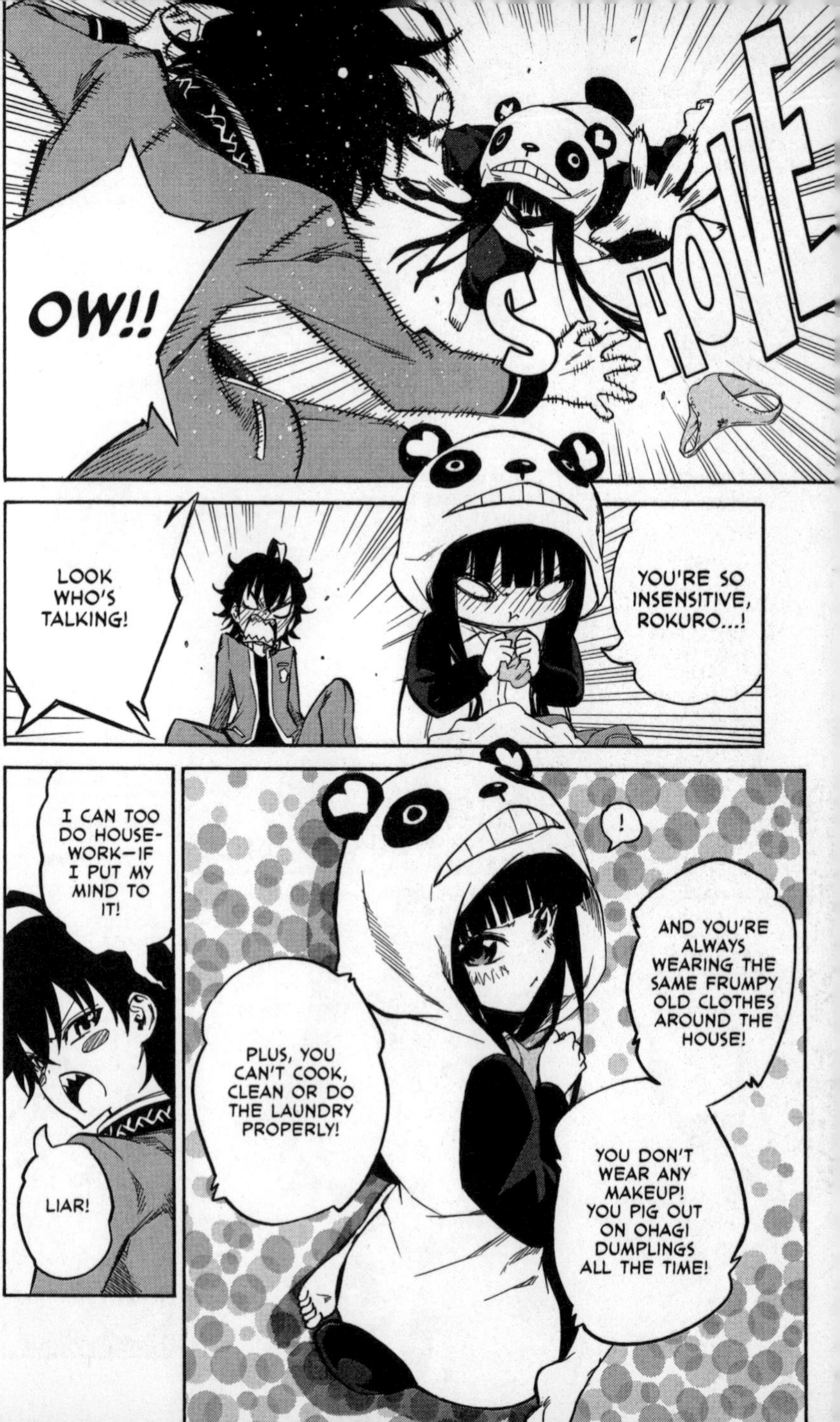
SHOVE
OW!!
YOU'RE SO INSENSITIVE, ROKURO...!
LOOK WHO'S TALKING!
!
AND YOU'RE ALWAYS WEARING THE SAME FRUMPY OLD CLOTHES AROUND THE HOUSE!
PLUS, YOU CAN'T COOK, CLEAN OR DO THE LAUNDRY PROPERLY!
YOU DON'T WEAR ANY MAKEUP! YOU PIG OUT ON OHAGI DUMPLINGS ALL THE TIME!
I CAN TOO DO HOUSE-WORK—IF I PUT MY MIND TO IT!
LIAR!

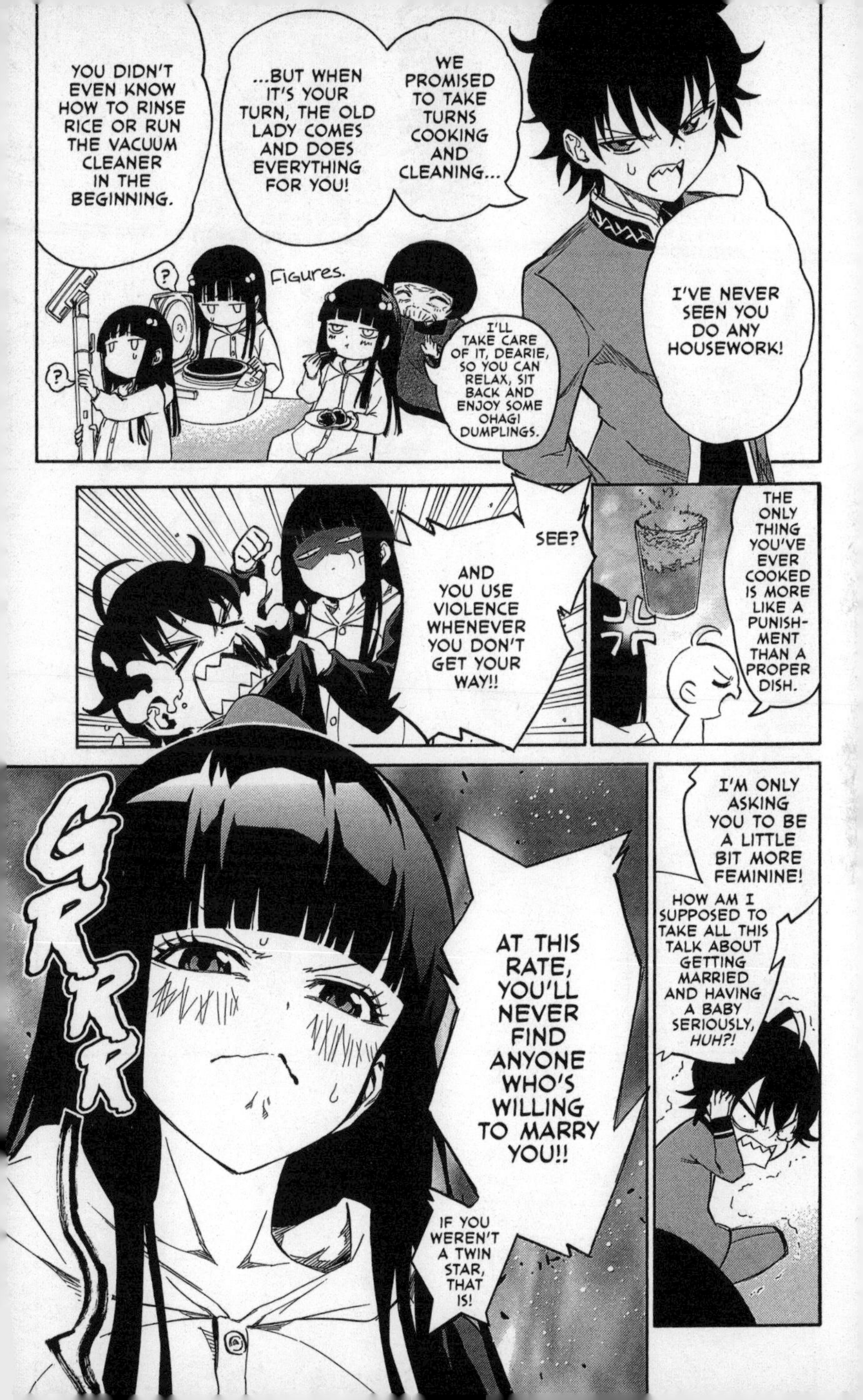
I'VE NEVER SEEN YOU DO ANY HOUSEWORK!
WE PROMISED TO TAKE TURNS COOKING AND CLEANING...
...BUT WHEN IT'S YOUR TURN, THE OLD LADY COMES AND DOES EVERYTHING FOR YOU!
YOU DIDN'T EVEN KNOW HOW TO RINSE RICE OR RUN THE VACUUM CLEANER IN THE BEGINNING.
I'LL TAKE CARE OF IT, DEARIE, SO YOU CAN RELAX, SIT BACK AND ENJOY SOME OHAGI DUMPLINGS.
Figures.
?
?
THE ONLY THING YOU'VE EVER COOKED IS MORE LIKE A PUNISHMENT THAN A PROPER DISH.
SEE?
AND YOU USE VIOLENCE WHENEVER YOU DON'T GET YOUR WAY!!
I'M ONLY ASKING YOU TO BE A LITTLE BIT MORE FEMININE!
HOW AM I SUPPOSED TO TAKE ALL THIS TALK ABOUT GETTING MARRIED AND HAVING A BABY SERIOUSLY, *HUH?!*
AT THIS RATE, YOU'LL NEVER FIND ANYONE WHO'S WILLING TO MARRY YOU!!
IF YOU WEREN'T A TWIN STAR, THAT IS!
GRRR

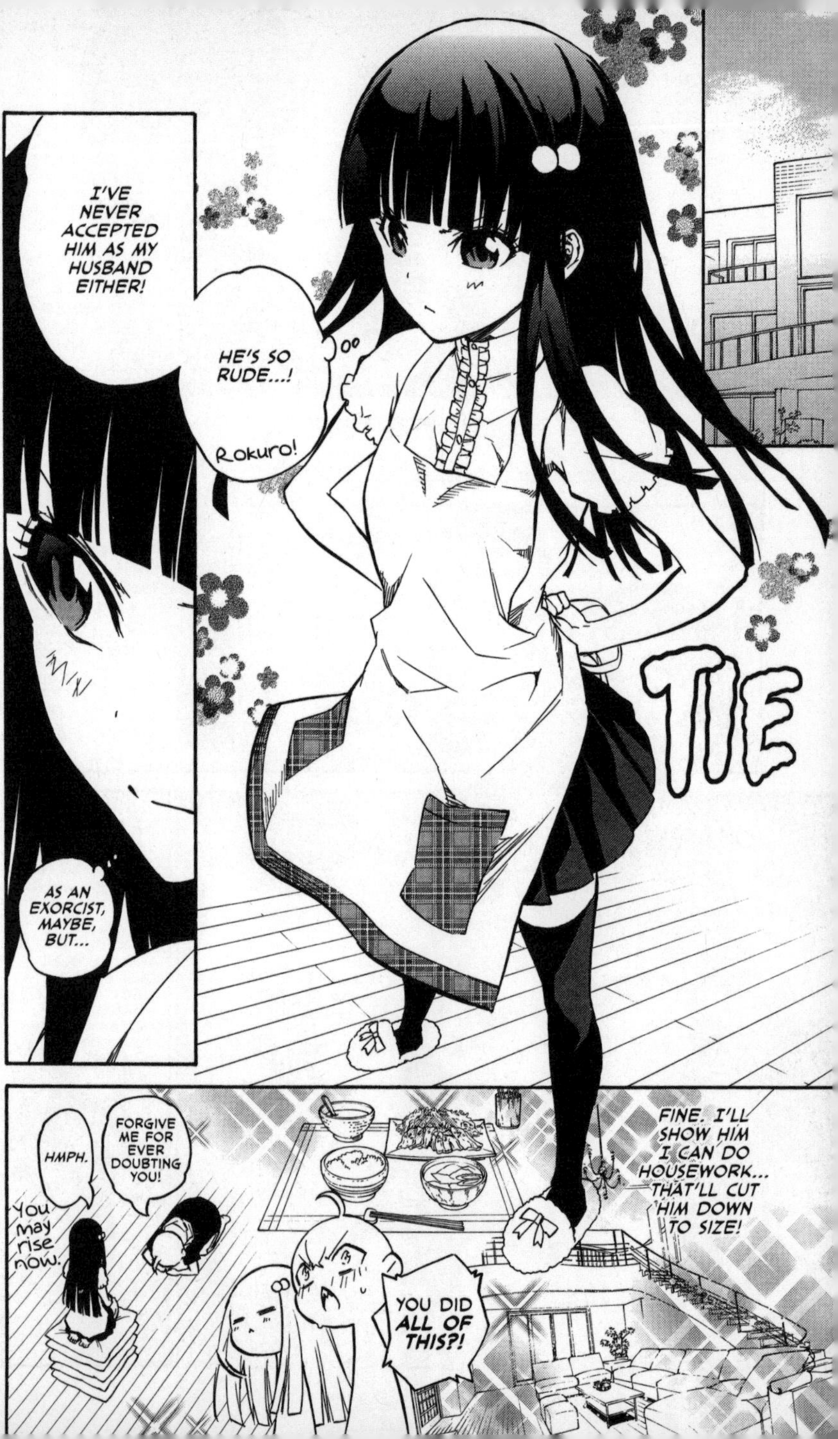
HE'S SO RUDE...!
Rokuro!
TIE
I'VE NEVER ACCEPTED HIM AS MY HUSBAND EITHER!
AS AN EXORCIST, MAYBE, BUT...
FINE. I'LL SHOW HIM I CAN DO HOUSEWORK... THAT'LL CUT HIM DOWN TO SIZE!
YOU DID ALL OF THIS?!
FORGIVE ME FOR EVER DOUBTING YOU!
HMPH.
You may rise now.

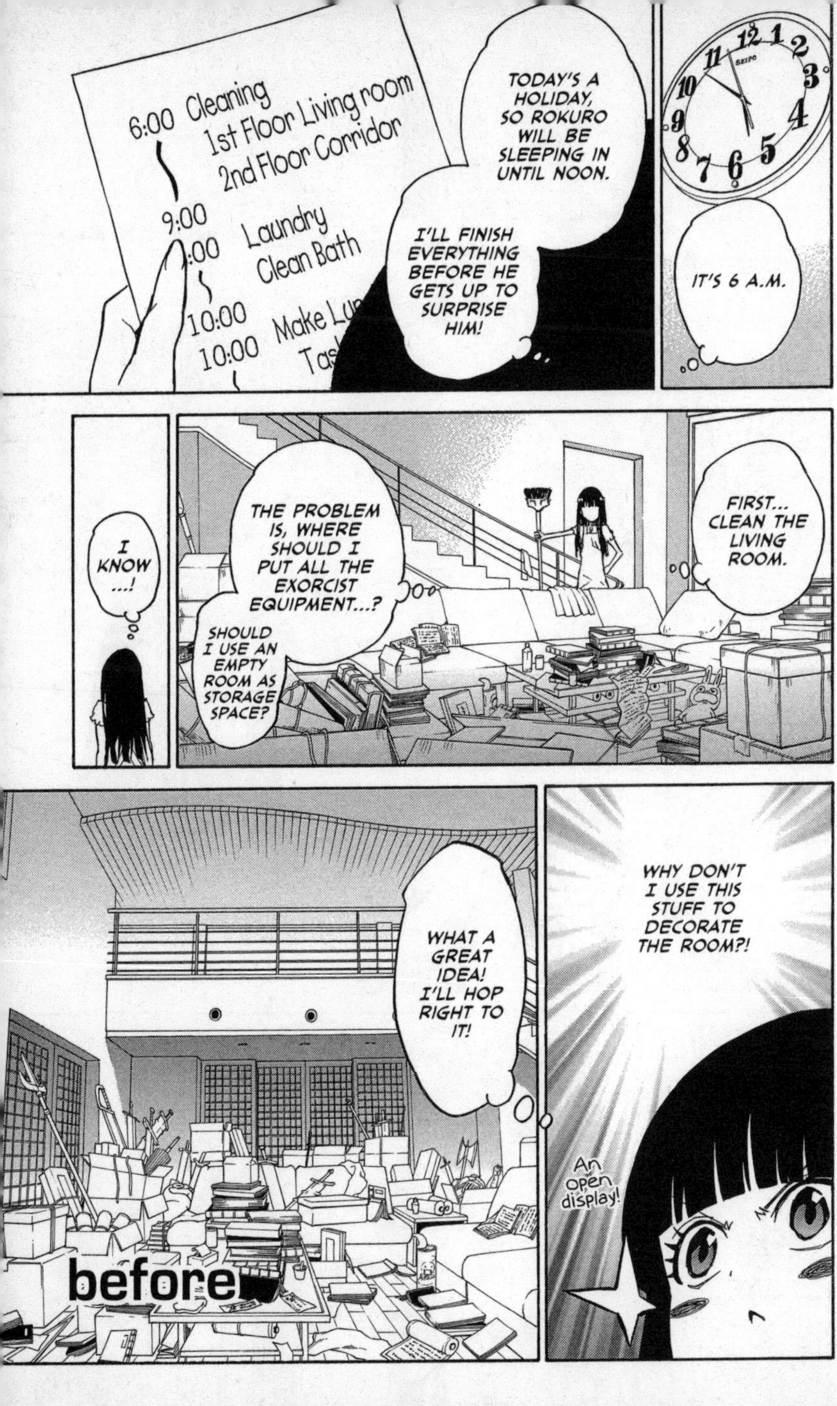

IT'S 6 A.M.
TODAY'S A HOLIDAY, SO ROKURO WILL BE SLEEPING IN UNTIL NOON.
I'LL FINISH EVERYTHING BEFORE HE GETS UP TO SURPRISE HIM!
6:00 Cleaning
1st Floor Living room
2nd Floor Corridor
9:00
:00 Laundry
Clean Bath
10:00
10:00 Make Lu
Tas
FIRST... CLEAN THE LIVING ROOM.
THE PROBLEM IS, WHERE SHOULD I PUT ALL THE EXORCIST EQUIPMENT...?
SHOULD I USE AN EMPTY ROOM AS STORAGE SPACE?
I KNOW ...!
WHY DON'T I USE THIS STUFF TO DECORATE THE ROOM?!
An open display!
WHAT A GREAT IDEA! I'LL HOP RIGHT TO IT!
before

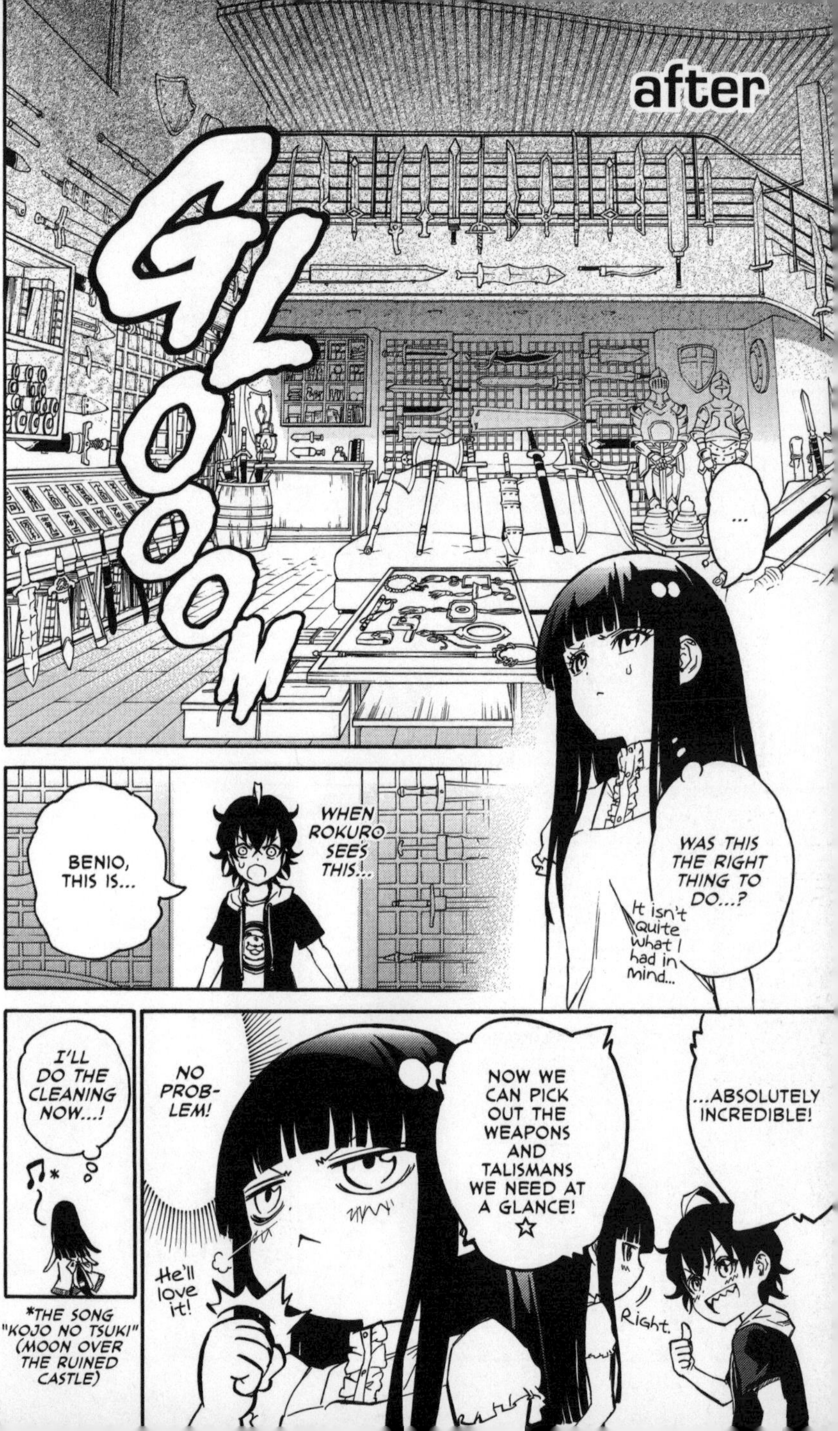
after
GLOOOOM
...
WAS THIS THE RIGHT THING TO DO...?
It isn't quite what I had in mind...
WHEN ROKURO SEES THIS...
BENIO, THIS IS...
...ABSOLUTELY INCREDIBLE!
NOW WE CAN PICK OUT THE WEAPONS AND TALISMANS WE NEED AT A GLANCE! ☆
Right.
NO PROBLEM!
He'll love it!
I'LL DO THE CLEANING NOW...!
♪*
*THE SONG "KOJO NO TSUKI" (MOON OVER THE RUINED CASTLE)

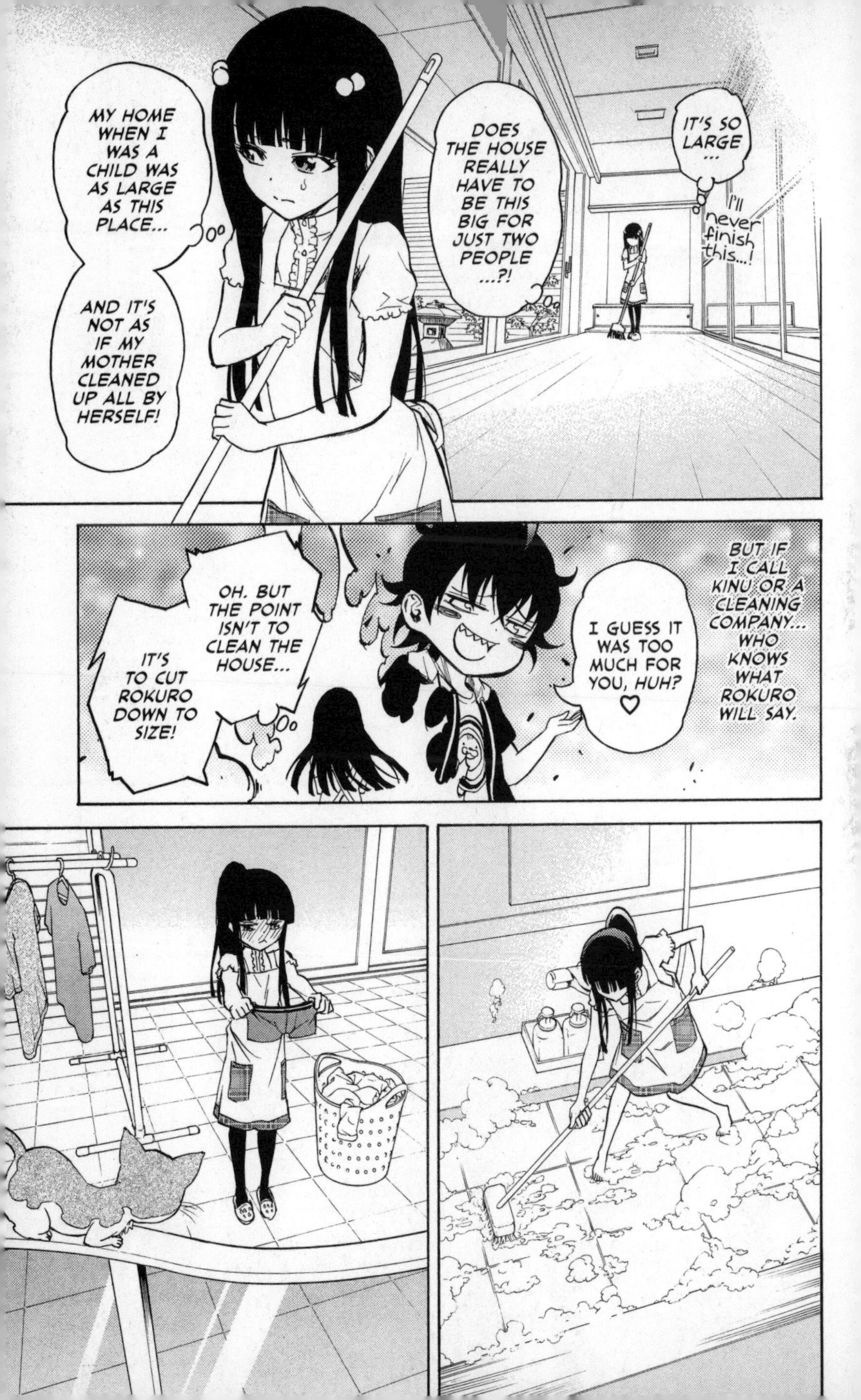
IT'S SO LARGE ...
I'll never finish this...!
DOES THE HOUSE REALLY HAVE TO BE THIS BIG FOR JUST TWO PEOPLE ...?!
MY HOME WHEN I WAS A CHILD WAS AS LARGE AS THIS PLACE...
AND IT'S NOT AS IF MY MOTHER CLEANED UP ALL BY HERSELF!
BUT IF I CALL KINU OR A CLEANING COMPANY... WHO KNOWS WHAT ROKURO WILL SAY.
I GUESS IT WAS TOO MUCH FOR YOU, HUH? ♡
OH. BUT THE POINT ISN'T TO CLEAN THE HOUSE...
IT'S TO CUT ROKURO DOWN TO SIZE!

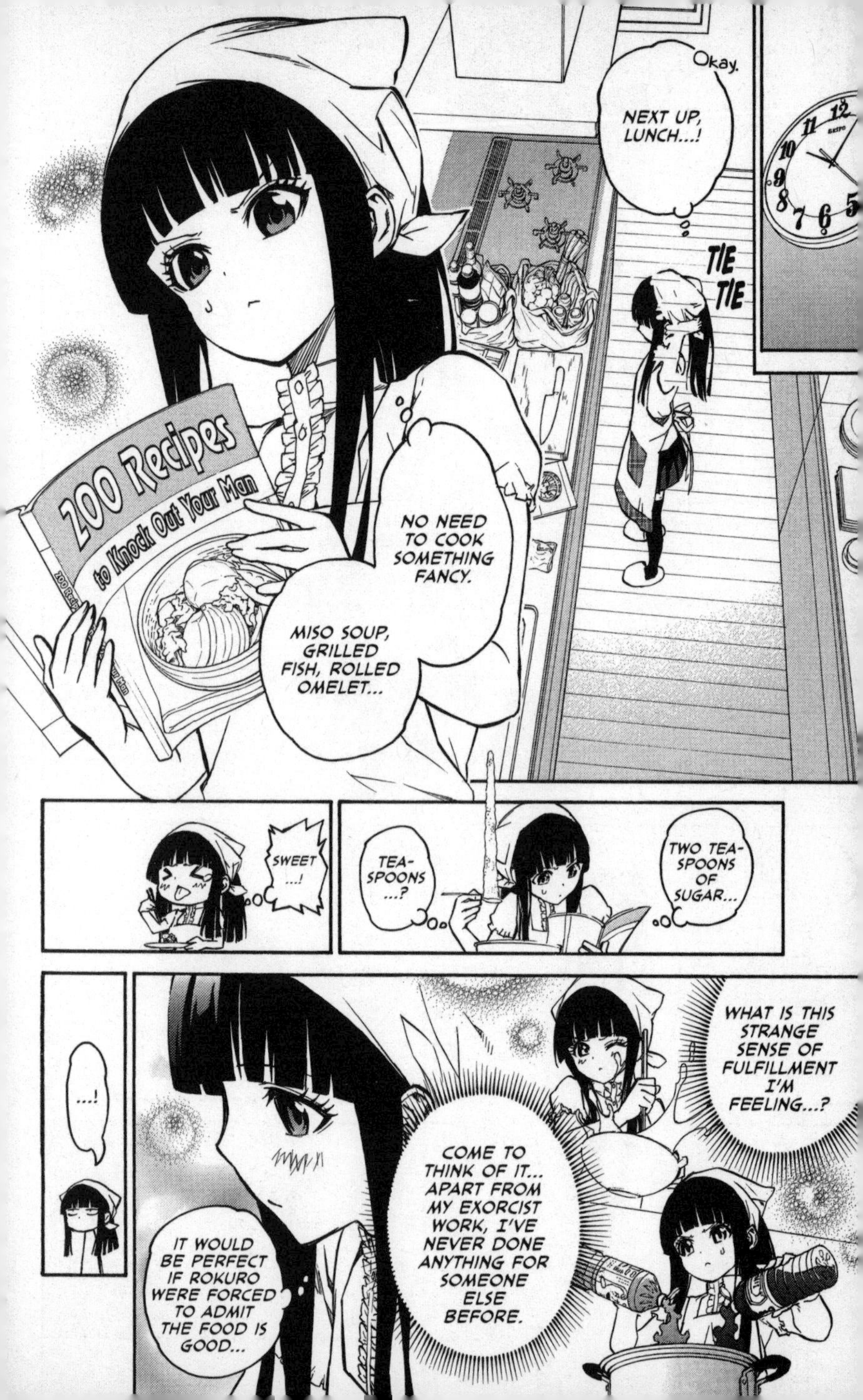
Okay.
NEXT UP, LUNCH...!
TIE TIE
200 Recipes to Knock Out Your Man
NO NEED TO COOK SOMETHING FANCY.
MISO SOUP, GRILLED FISH, ROLLED OMELET...
TWO TEA-SPOONS OF SUGAR...
TEA-SPOONS ...?
SWEET ...!
WHAT IS THIS STRANGE SENSE OF FULFILLMENT I'M FEELING...?
COME TO THINK OF IT... APART FROM MY EXORCIST WORK, I'VE NEVER DONE ANYTHING FOR SOMEONE ELSE BEFORE.
IT WOULD BE PERFECT IF ROKURO WERE FORCED TO ADMIT THE FOOD IS GOOD...
...!

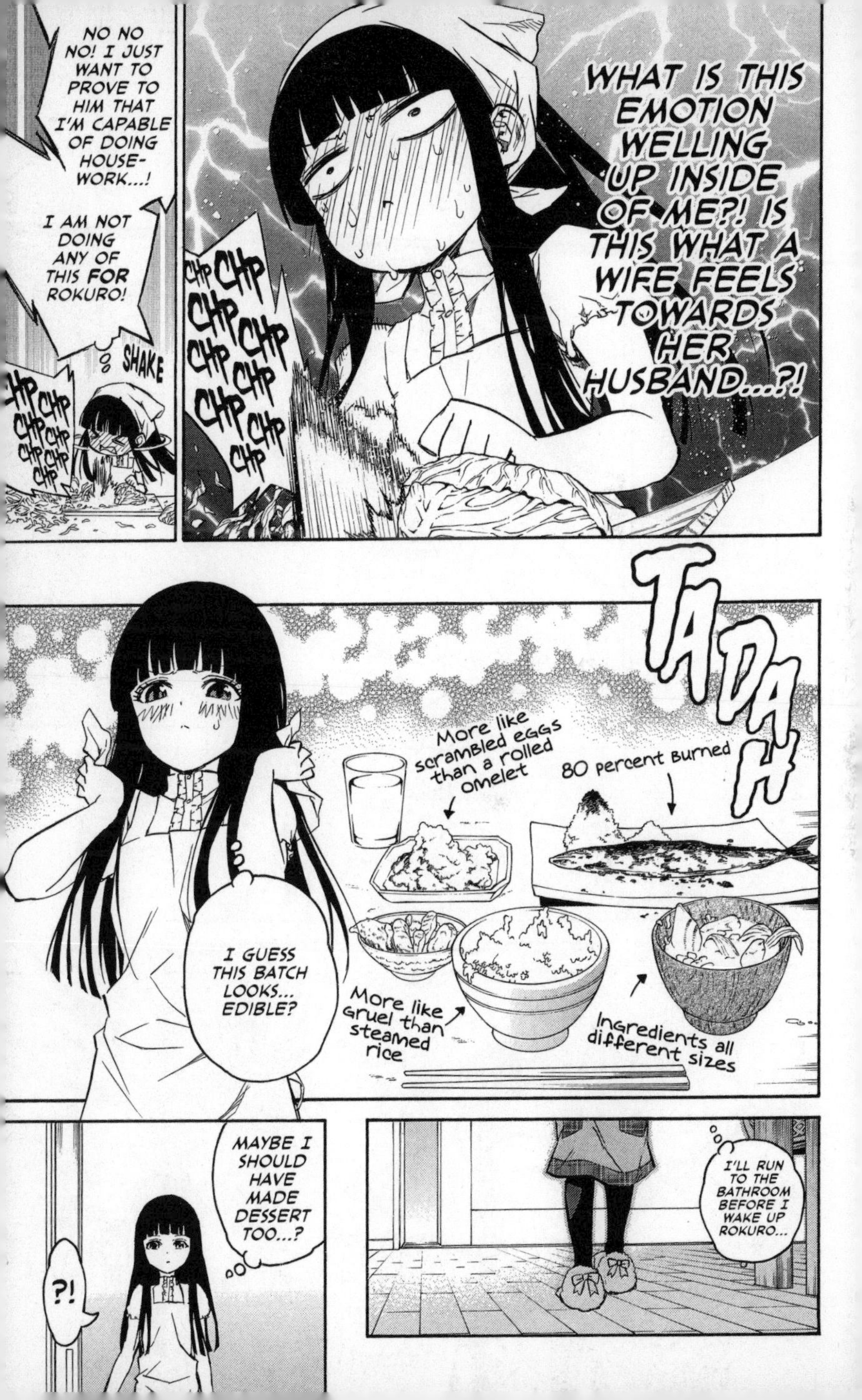
WHAT IS THIS EMOTION WELLING UP INSIDE OF ME?! IS THIS WHAT A WIFE FEELS TOWARDS HER HUSBAND...?!
CHP CHP CHP CHP CHP CHP CHP CHP CHP CHP
NO NO NO! I JUST WANT TO PROVE TO HIM THAT I'M CAPABLE OF DOING HOUSE-WORK...!
I AM NOT DOING ANY OF THIS FOR ROKURO!
SHAKE
CHP CHP CHP CHP CHP CHP CHP
TADAH
80 percent burned
More like scrambled eggs than a rolled omelet
Ingredients all different sizes
More like gruel than steamed rice
I GUESS THIS BATCH LOOKS... EDIBLE?
I'LL RUN TO THE BATHROOM BEFORE I WAKE UP ROKURO...
MAYBE I SHOULD HAVE MADE DESSERT TOO...?
?!

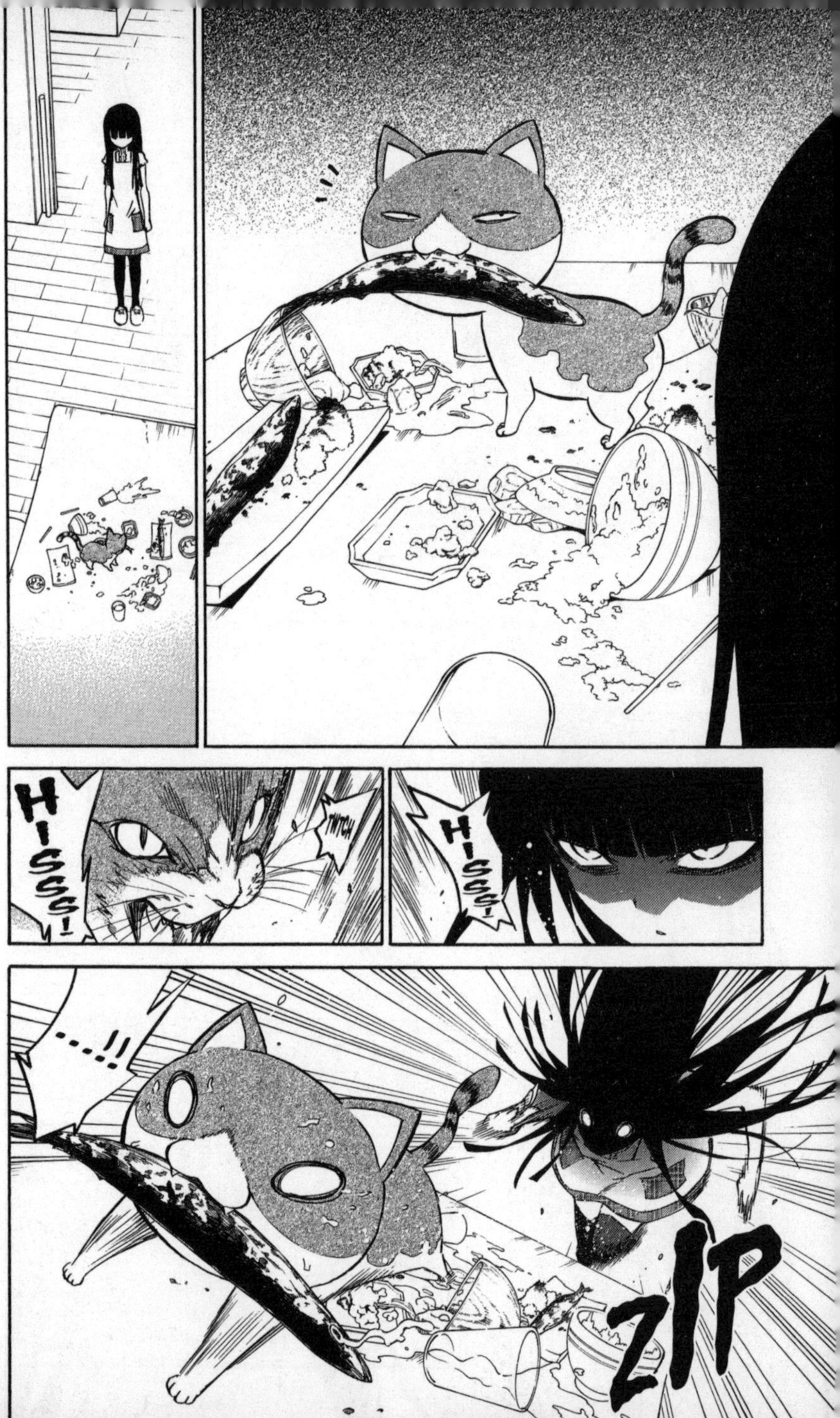
HISSS!
TWITCH
HISSS!
...!!
ZIP

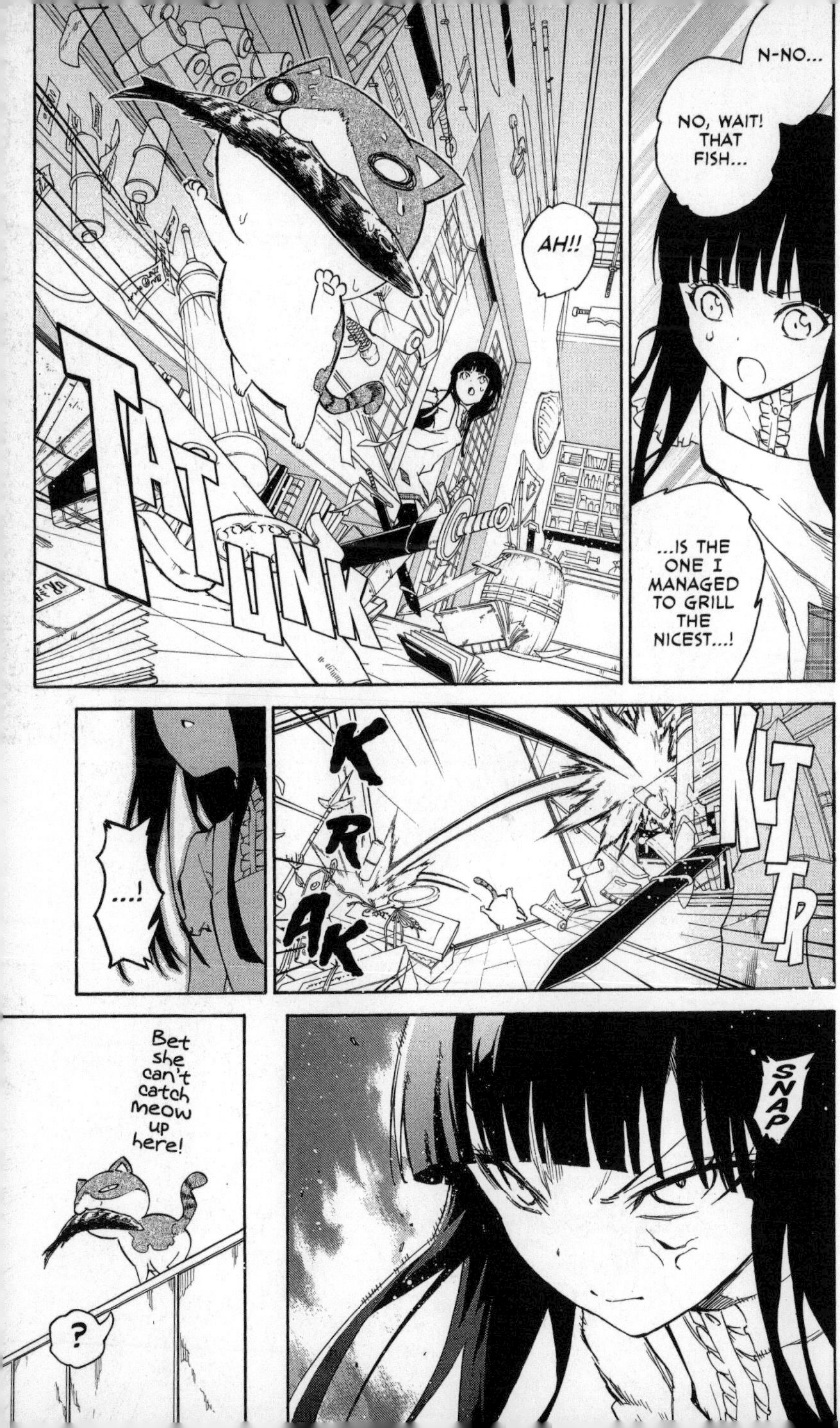
N-NO...
NO, WAIT! THAT FISH...
...IS THE ONE I MANAGED TO GRILL THE NICEST...!
AH!!
TATUNK
KLTTR
KRAK
...!
SNAP
Bet she can't catch meow up here!
?

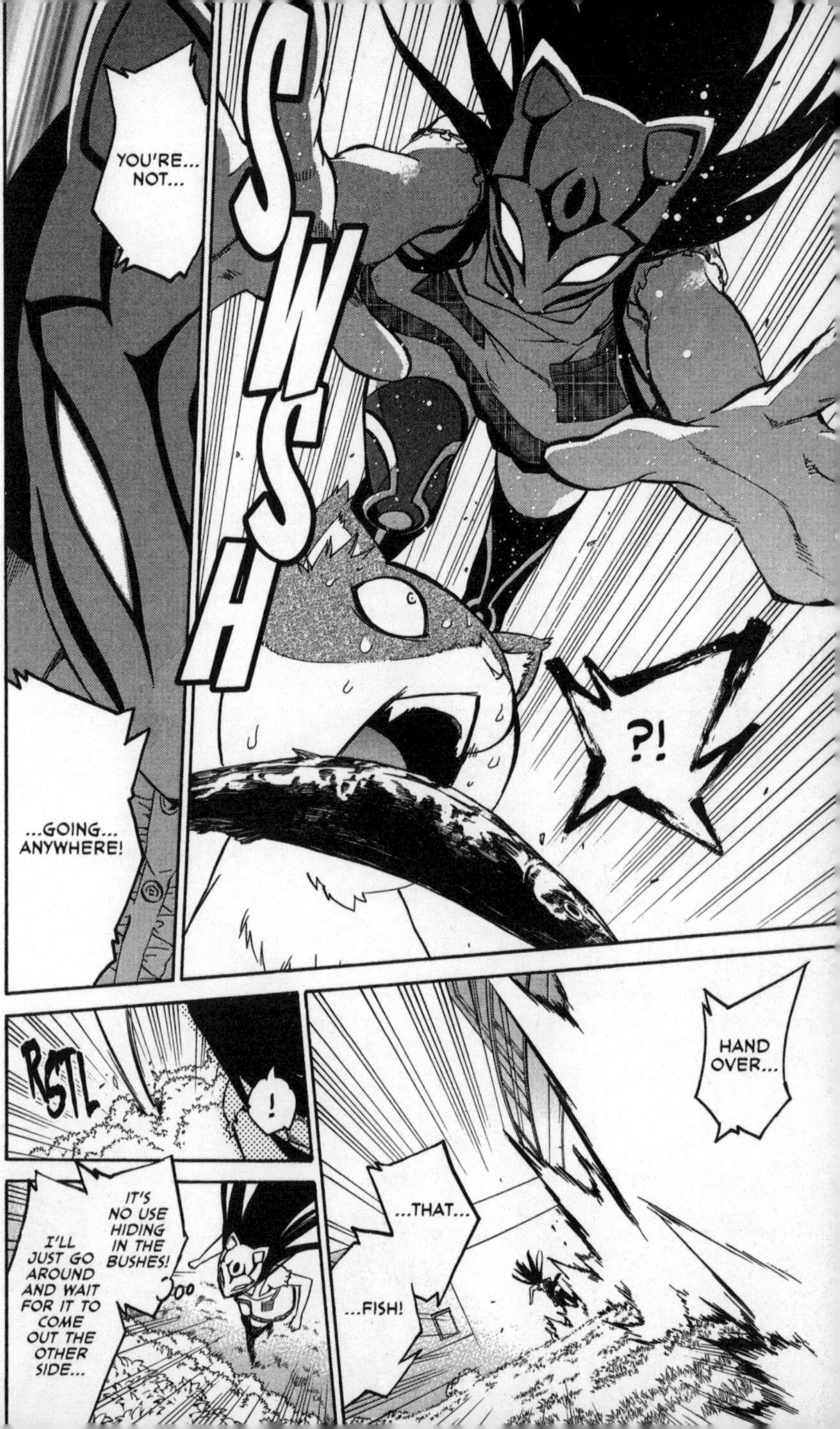
YOU'RE... NOT...
SWISH
?!
...GOING... ANYWHERE!
HAND OVER...
...THAT...
...FISH!
RSTL
!
IT'S NO USE HIDING IN THE BUSHES!
I'LL JUST GO AROUND AND WAIT FOR IT TO COME OUT THE OTHER SIDE...

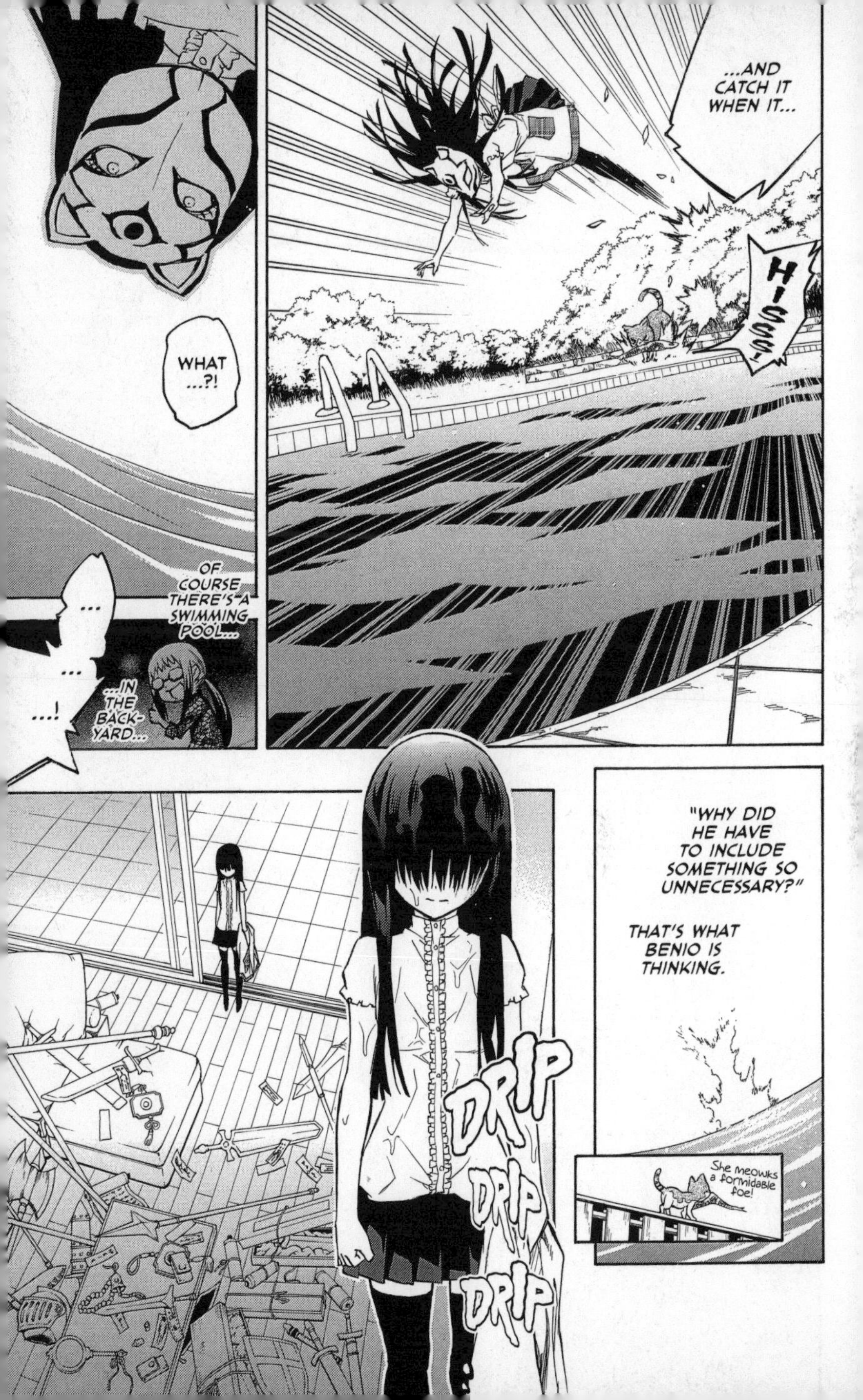
...AND CATCH IT WHEN IT...
HISSS!
WHAT ...?!
OF COURSE THERE'S A SWIMMING POOL...
...
...
...IN THE BACKYARD...
...!
"WHY DID HE HAVE TO INCLUDE SOMETHING SO UNNECESSARY?"
THAT'S WHAT BENIO IS THINKING.
She meowks a formidable foe!
DRIP
DRIP
DRIP

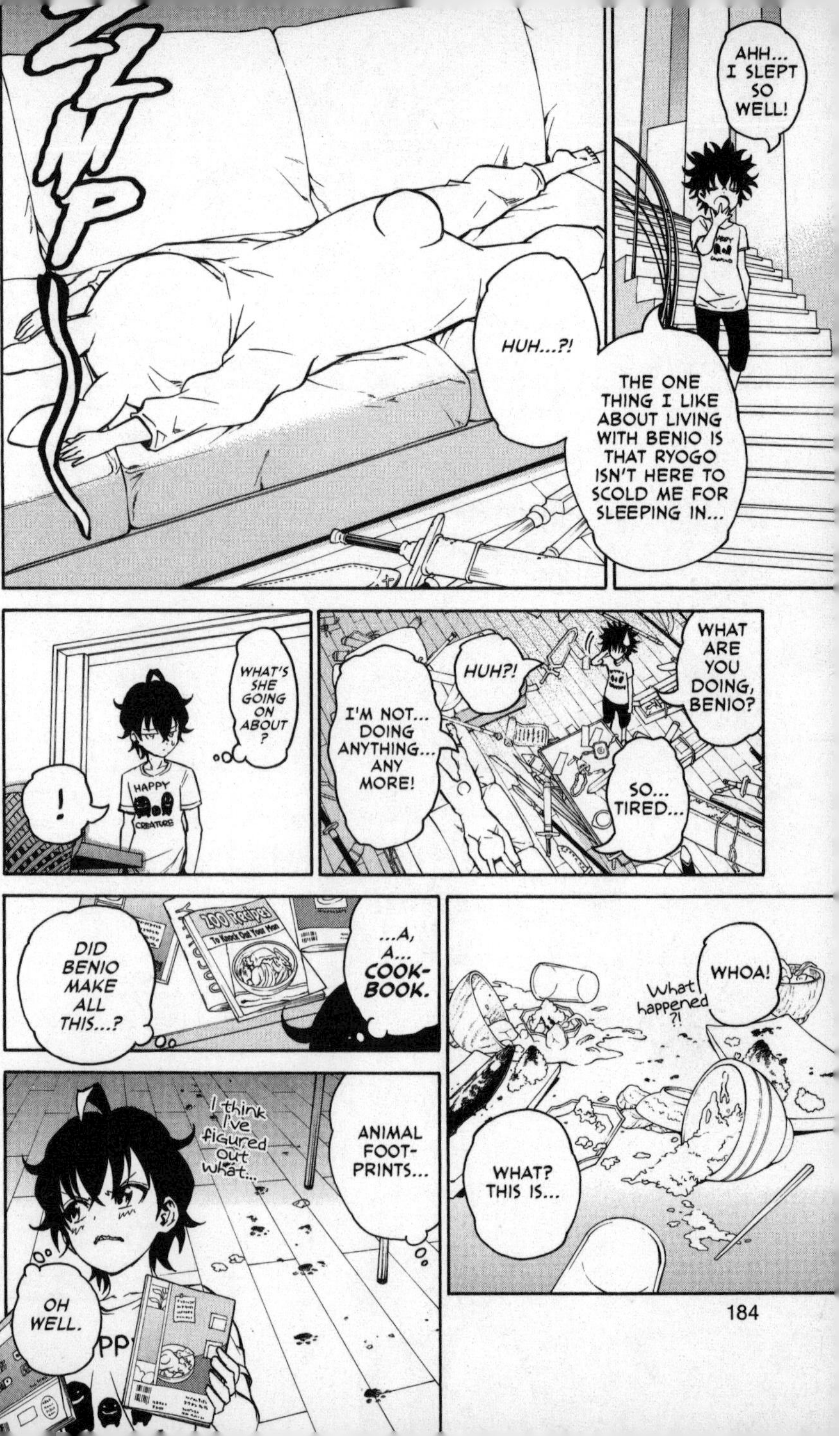
AHH... I SLEPT SO WELL!
THE ONE THING I LIKE ABOUT LIVING WITH BENIO IS THAT RYOGO ISN'T HERE TO SCOLD ME FOR SLEEPING IN...
HUH...?!
WHAT ARE YOU DOING, BENIO?
HUH?!
SO... TIRED...
I'M NOT... DOING ANYTHING... ANY MORE!
WHAT'S SHE GOING ON ABOUT?
!
WHOA!
What happened?!
WHAT? THIS IS...
...A, A... COOK-BOOK.
200 Recipes
To Knock Out Your Man
DID BENIO MAKE ALL THIS...?
ANIMAL FOOT-PRINTS...
I think I've figured out what...
OH WELL.

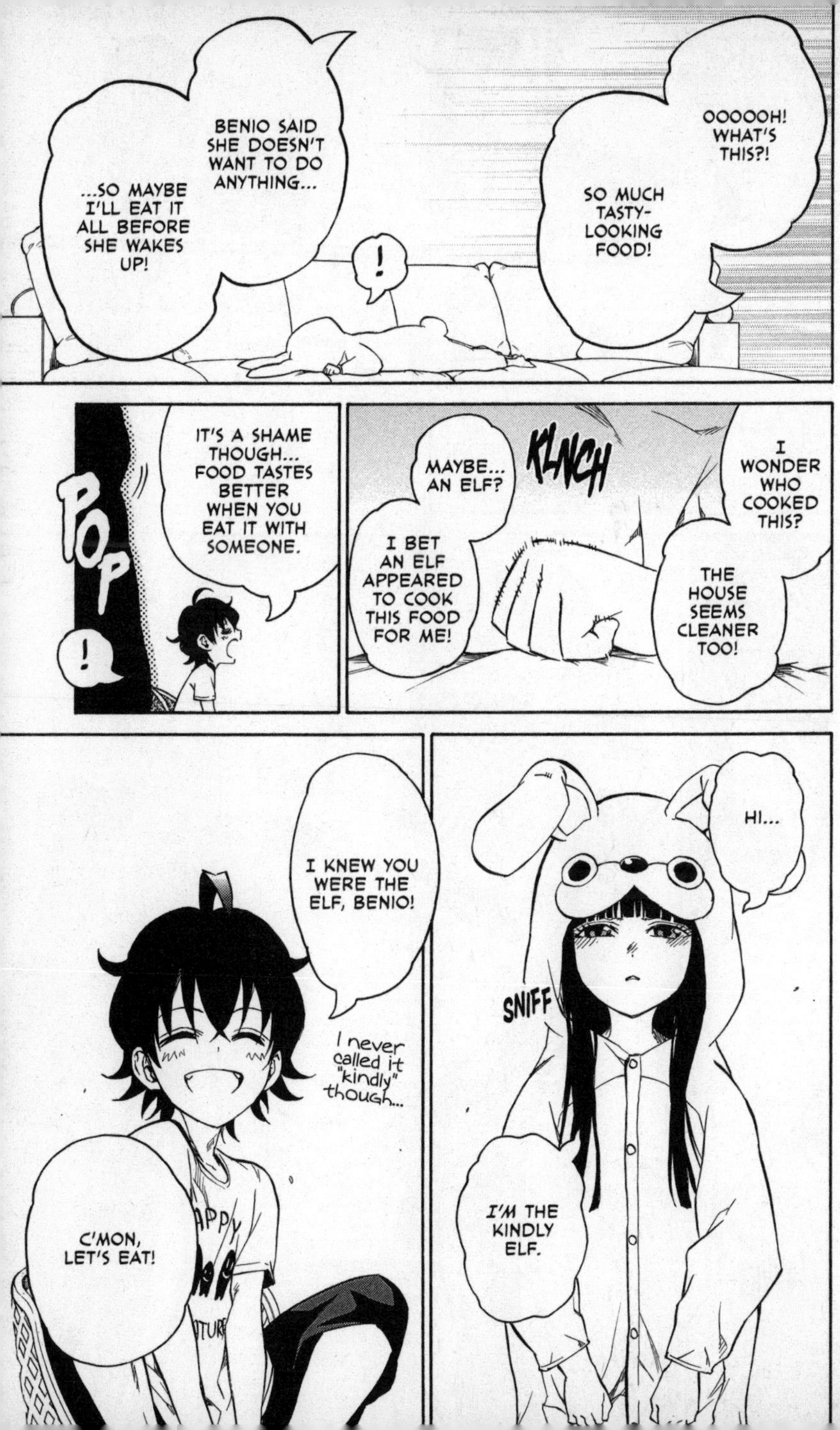
OOOOOH! WHAT'S THIS?!
SO MUCH TASTY-LOOKING FOOD!
!
BENIO SAID SHE DOESN'T WANT TO DO ANYTHING...
...SO MAYBE I'LL EAT IT ALL BEFORE SHE WAKES UP!
I WONDER WHO COOKED THIS?
THE HOUSE SEEMS CLEANER TOO!
KLNCH
MAYBE... AN ELF?
I BET AN ELF APPEARED TO COOK THIS FOOD FOR ME!
IT'S A SHAME THOUGH... FOOD TASTES BETTER WHEN YOU EAT IT WITH SOMEONE.
POP
!
HI...
SNIFF
I'M THE KINDLY ELF.
I KNEW YOU WERE THE ELF, BENIO!
I never called it "kindly" though...
C'MON, LET'S EAT!

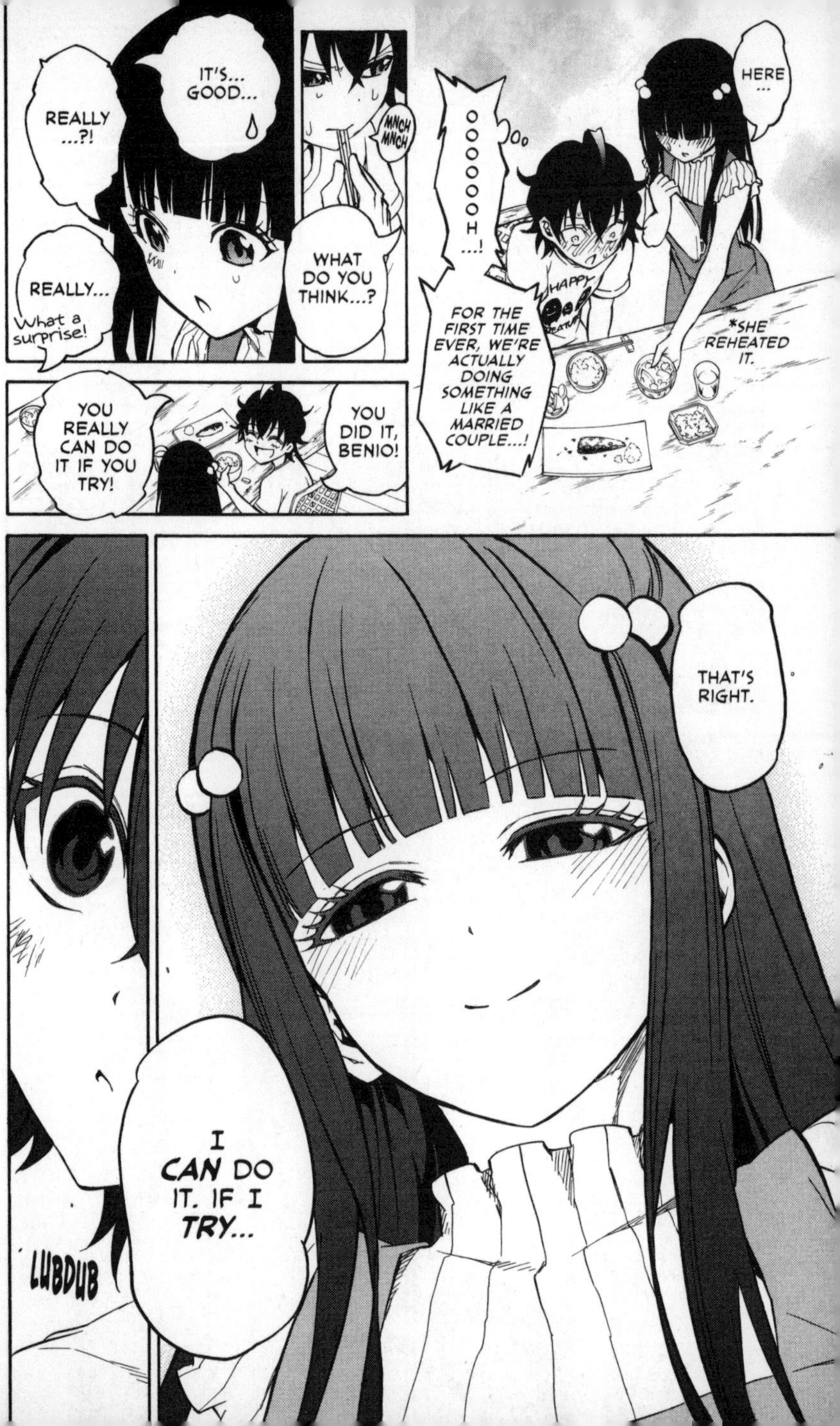
HERE ...
OOOOOOOOH ...!
Oo
FOR THE FIRST TIME EVER, WE'RE ACTUALLY DOING SOMETHING LIKE A MARRIED COUPLE...!
*SHE REHEATED IT.
HAPPY
MNCH MNCH
WHAT DO YOU THINK...?
IT'S... GOOD...
REALLY ...?!
REALLY...
What a surprise!
YOU DID IT, BENIO!
YOU REALLY CAN DO IT IF YOU TRY!
THAT'S RIGHT.
I CAN DO IT. IF I TRY...
LUBDUB

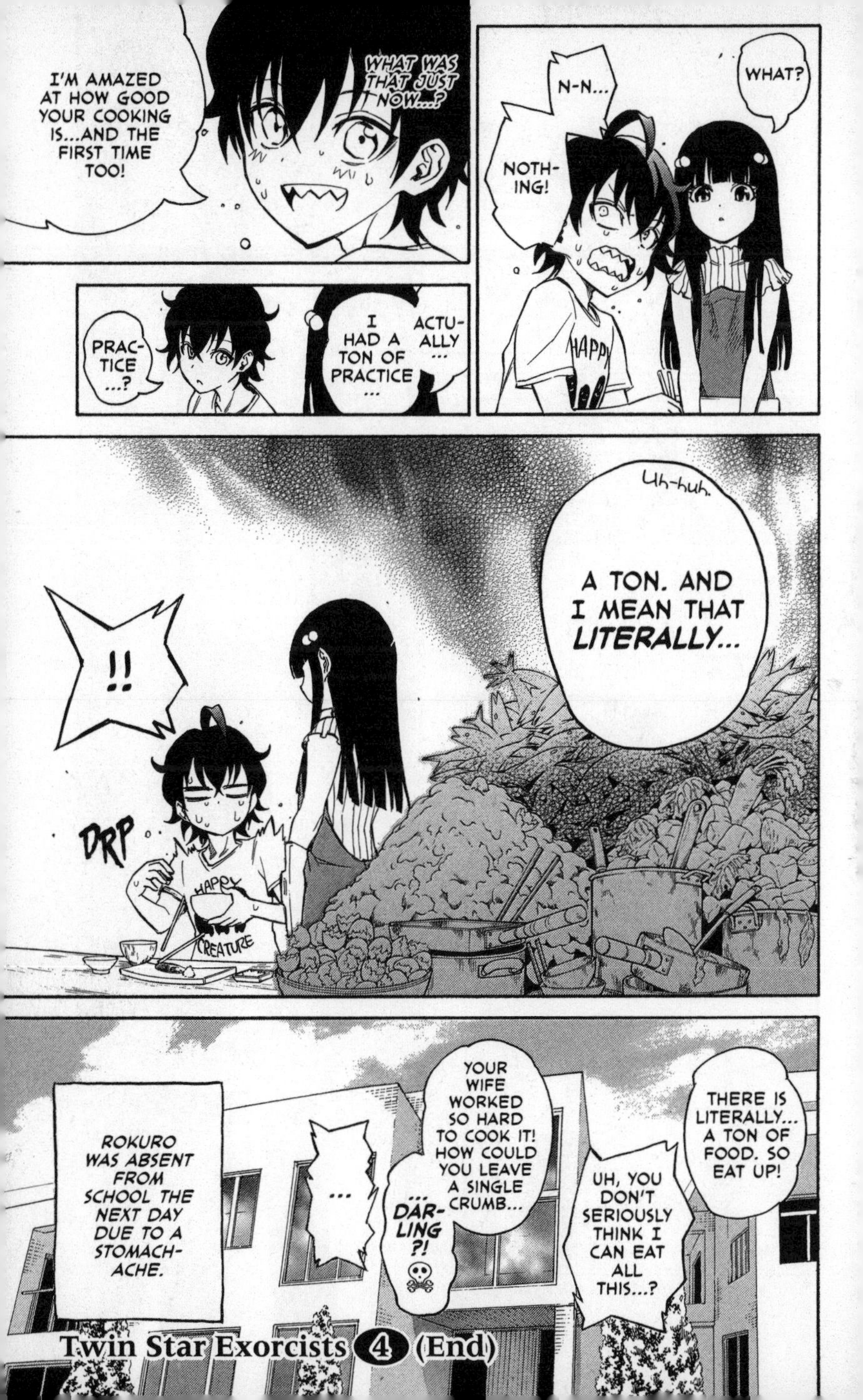
WHAT?
N-N...
NOTH-ING!
WHAT WAS THAT JUST NOW...?
I'M AMAZED AT HOW GOOD YOUR COOKING IS...AND THE FIRST TIME TOO!
ACTU-ALLY...
I HAD A TON OF PRACTICE...
PRAC-TICE...?
Uh-huh.
A TON. AND I MEAN THAT *LITERALLY...*
!!
DRP
THERE IS LITERALLY... A TON OF FOOD. SO EAT UP!
UH, YOU DON'T SERIOUSLY THINK I CAN EAT ALL THIS...?
YOUR WIFE WORKED SO HARD TO COOK IT! HOW COULD YOU LEAVE A SINGLE CRUMB...
...DARLING?!
...
ROKURO WAS ABSENT FROM SCHOOL THE NEXT DAY DUE TO A STOMACH-ACHE.

Twin Star Exorcists 4 (End)

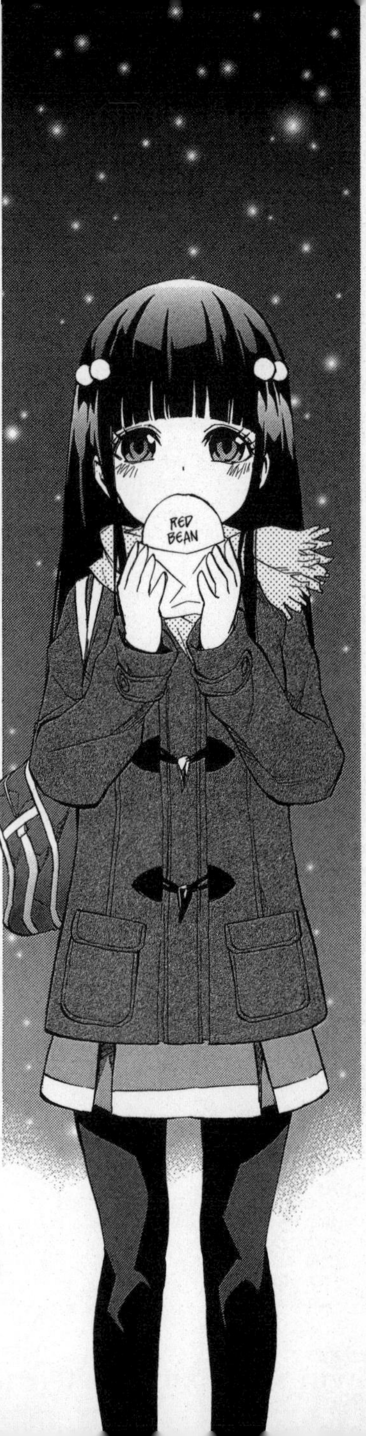
RED BEAN

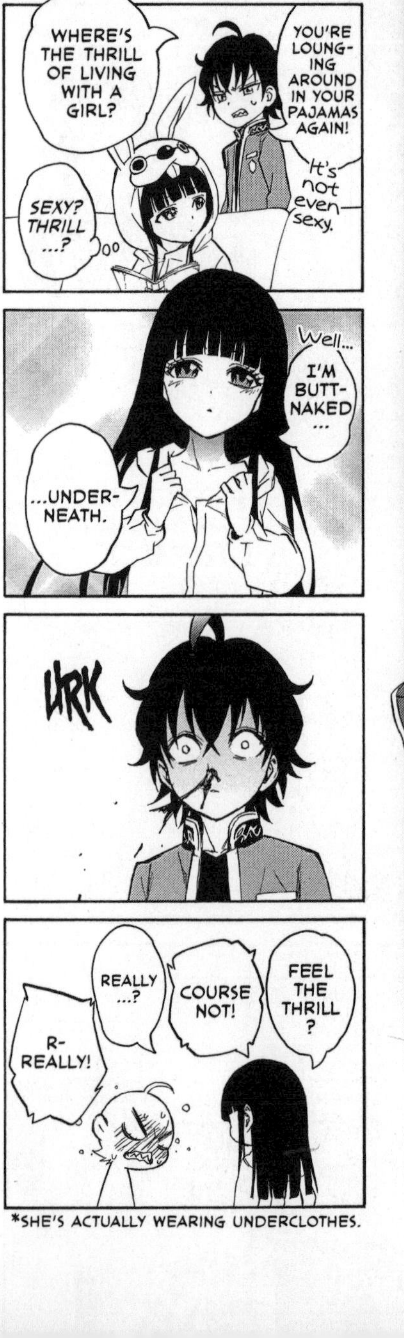
YOU'RE LOUNGING AROUND IN YOUR PAJAMAS AGAIN!
It's not even sexy.
WHERE'S THE THRILL OF LIVING WITH A GIRL?
SEXY? THRILL ...?
Well...
I'M BUTT-NAKED ...
...UNDERNEATH.
URK
FEEL THE THRILL?
COURSE NOT!
REALLY ...?
R-REALLY!

*SHE'S ACTUALLY WEARING UNDERCLOTHES.

RESONANCE TRAINING

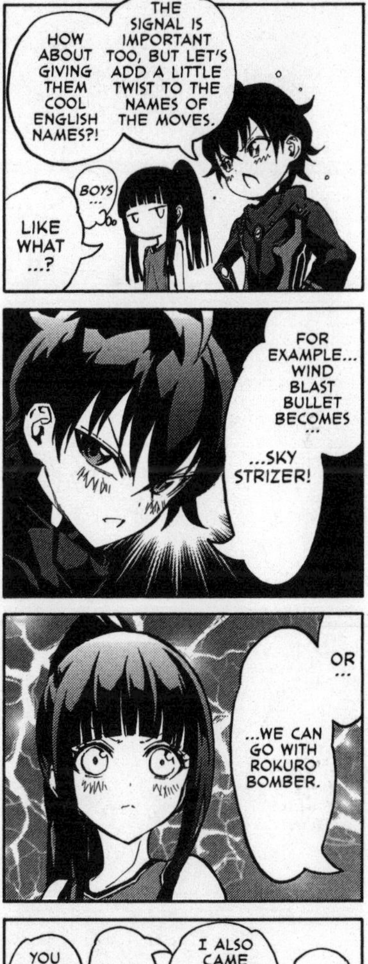
THE SIGNAL IS IMPORTANT TOO, BUT LET'S ADD A LITTLE TWIST TO THE NAMES OF THE MOVES.
HOW ABOUT GIVING THEM COOL ENGLISH NAMES?!
BOYS...
LIKE WHAT...?
FOR EXAMPLE... WIND BLAST BULLET BECOMES...
...SKY STRIZER!
OR...
...WE CAN GO WITH ROKURO BOMBER.
ROKURO BOMBER?!
I ALSO CAME UP WITH DOUBLE WIND BLAST BULLET!
ROKURO BOMBER?!
YOU LIKE THAT, DON'T YOU...?
OR WE CAN COMPROMISE AND GO WITH BENIO STRASH.
WHAT COMPROMISE?

BENIO DEVELOPS AN INTEREST IN COOKING

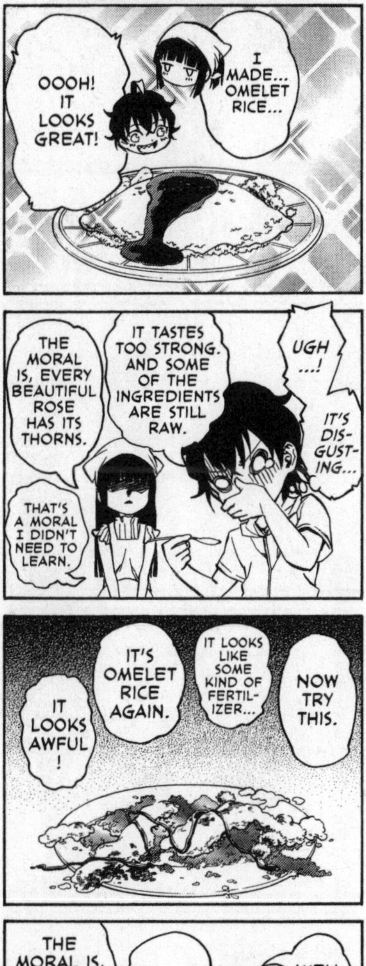
I MADE... OMELET RICE...
OOOH! IT LOOKS GREAT!
UGH...!
IT'S DISGUSTING...
IT TASTES TOO STRONG. AND SOME OF THE INGREDIENTS ARE STILL RAW.
THE MORAL IS, EVERY BEAUTIFUL ROSE HAS ITS THORNS.
THAT'S A MORAL I DIDN'T NEED TO LEARN.
NOW TRY THIS.
IT LOOKS LIKE SOME KIND OF FERTILIZER...
IT'S OMELET RICE AGAIN.
IT LOOKS AWFUL!
WELL?
OH, IT'S REALLY GOOD!
THE MORAL IS, YOU CAN'T JUDGE A BOOK BY ITS COVER.
I DON'T KNOW WHAT FOLK WISDOM TO TRUST ANYMORE...

LESSONS AT HINATSUKI

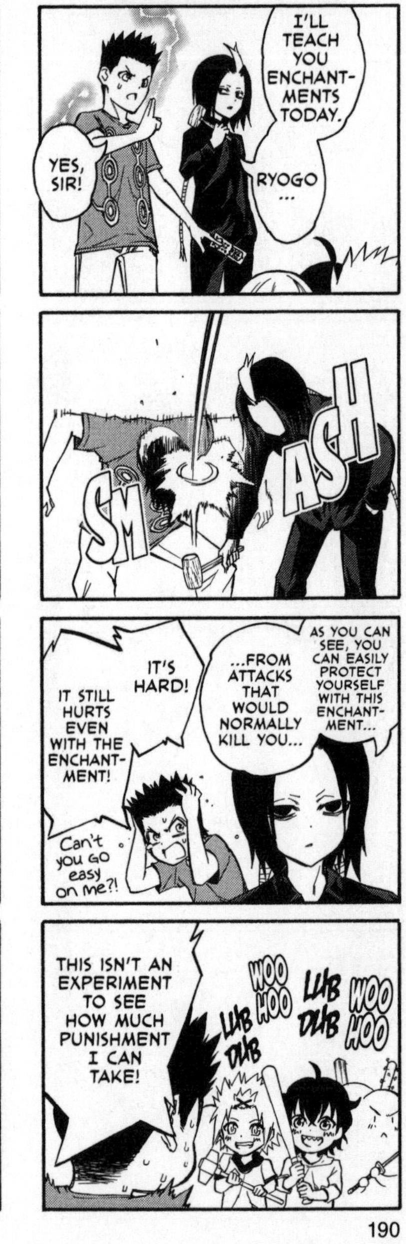
I'LL TEACH YOU ENCHANTMENTS TODAY.
RYOGO ...
YES, SIR!
SMASH
AS YOU CAN SEE, YOU CAN EASILY PROTECT YOURSELF WITH THIS ENCHANTMENT...
...FROM ATTACKS THAT WOULD NORMALLY KILL YOU...
IT'S HARD!
IT STILL HURTS EVEN WITH THE ENCHANTMENT!
Can't you GO easy on me?!
THIS ISN'T AN EXPERIMENT TO SEE HOW MUCH PUNISHMENT I CAN TAKE!
WOO HOO
LUB DUB
WOO HOO
LUB DUB

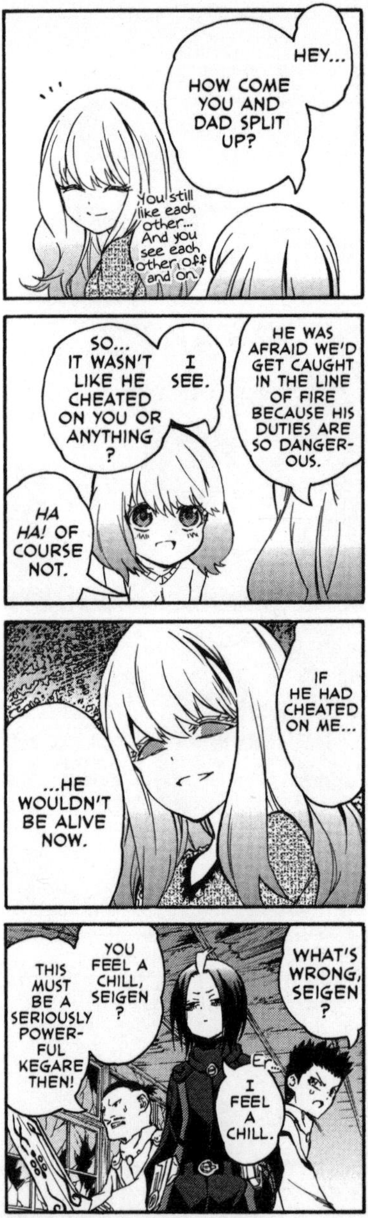
HEY...
HOW COME YOU AND DAD SPLIT UP?
...
You still like each other... And you see each other off and on.
HE WAS AFRAID WE'D GET CAUGHT IN THE LINE OF FIRE BECAUSE HIS DUTIES ARE SO DANGEROUS.
I SEE.
SO... IT WASN'T LIKE HE CHEATED ON YOU OR ANYTHING?
HA HA! OF COURSE NOT.
IF HE HAD CHEATED ON ME...
...HE WOULDN'T BE ALIVE NOW.
WHAT'S WRONG, SEIGEN?
YOU FEEL A CHILL, SEIGEN?
THIS MUST BE A SERIOUSLY POWERFUL KEGARE THEN!
Er...
I FEEL A CHILL.

★Artwork★

Kota Tokutsu

Tetsuro Kakiuchi

Kosuke Ono

Takumi Kikuta

Hidetoshi Nakashima

Artist:
Yoshiaki Sukeno

★Editor★
Junichi Tamada

★Graphic Novel Editor★
Hiroshi Ikishima

★Graphic Novel Design★
Tatsuo Ishino (Freiheit)

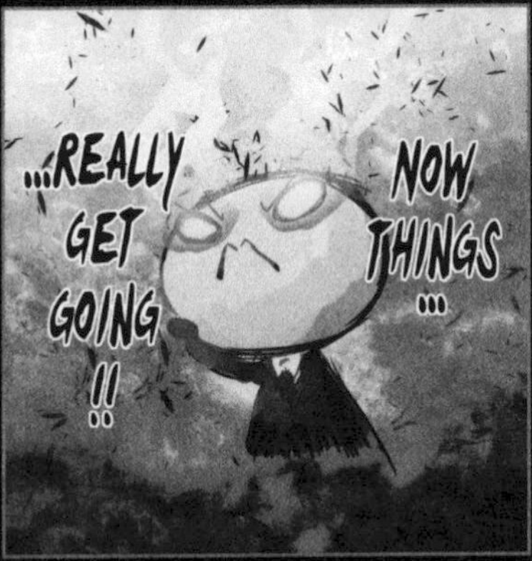
NOW THINGS...
...REALLY GET GOING!!

Okay! This is the volume where the hard-core fistfights come in!

Like I wrote in the bonus chapter in volume 1, I've always had a thing for hand-to-hand combat, so the battle against Yuto is filled with everything I've always wanted to draw from the beginning of the series.

And to top it off, chapters #13 and #13.5 originally ran in *Jump SQ* magazine as an extra-long sixty-page chapter. This was ~~because of~~ thanks to the editorial office deciding to back up my desire to draw a long-drawn-out battle.

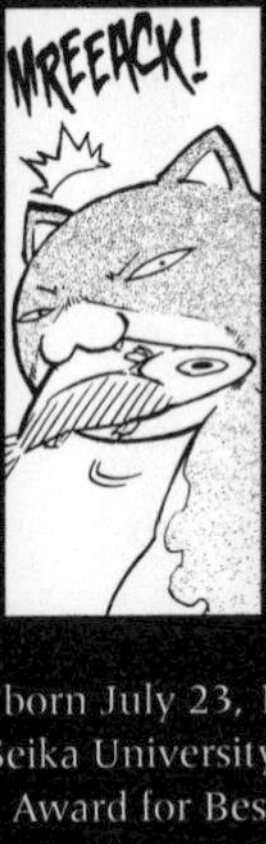
MREEACK!

YOSHIAKI SUKENO was born July 23, 1981, in Wakayama, Japan. He graduated from Kyoto Seika University, where he studied manga. In 2006, he won the Tezuka Award for Best Newcomer Shonen Manga Artist. In 2008, he began his previous work, the supernatural comedy *Binbougami ga!*, which was adapted into the anime *Good Luck Girl!* in 2012.

BENIO'S PAJAMAS

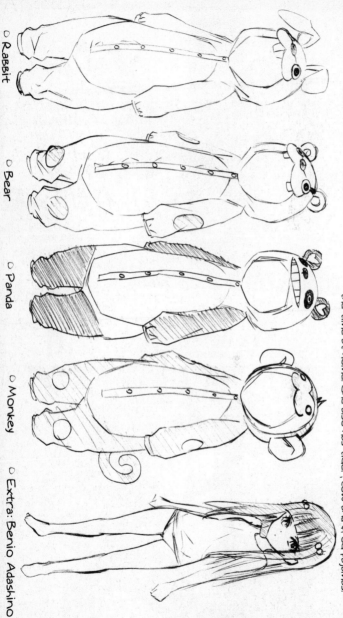

Not just for sleeping anymore! Benio wears them for lounging around the house too. When she and Rokuro first started living together, Benio was a little self-conscious about wearing them around him. But in less than three days, she figured, "Who cares? It's just Rokuro." So now she wears them all the time at home. She also has tiger, cow and frog pajamas.

○ Rabbit

○ Bear

○ Panda

○ Monkey

○ Extra: Benio Adashino

DR. ROKURO: SURGEON!!

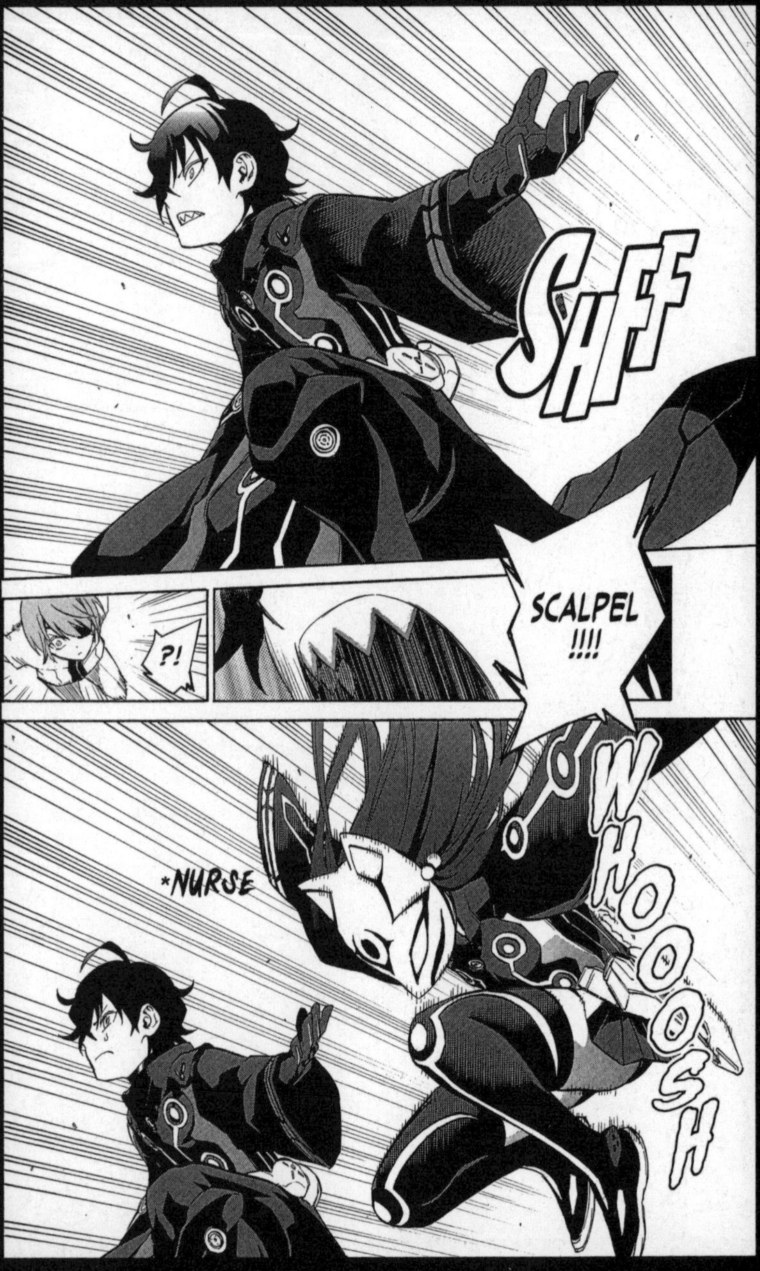
SHFF
SCALPEL !!!!
?!
WHOOOOOSH
*NURSE

—SHONEN JUMP Manga Edition—

STORY & ART Yoshiaki Sukeno

TRANSLATION **Tetsuichiro Miyaki**
ENGLISH ADAPTATION **Bryant Turnage**
TOUCH-UP ART & LETTERING **Stephen Dutro**
DESIGN **Shawn Carrico**
EDITOR **Annette Roman**

SOUSEI NO ONMYOJI © 2013 by Yoshiaki Sukeno
All rights reserved.
First published in Japan in 2013 by SHUEISHA Inc., Tokyo.
English translation rights arranged by SHUEISHA Inc.

Printed in the U.S.A.

Published by VIZ Media, LLC
P.O. Box 77010
San Francisco, CA 94107

10 9 8 7 6 5 4 3 2 1
First printing, April 2016

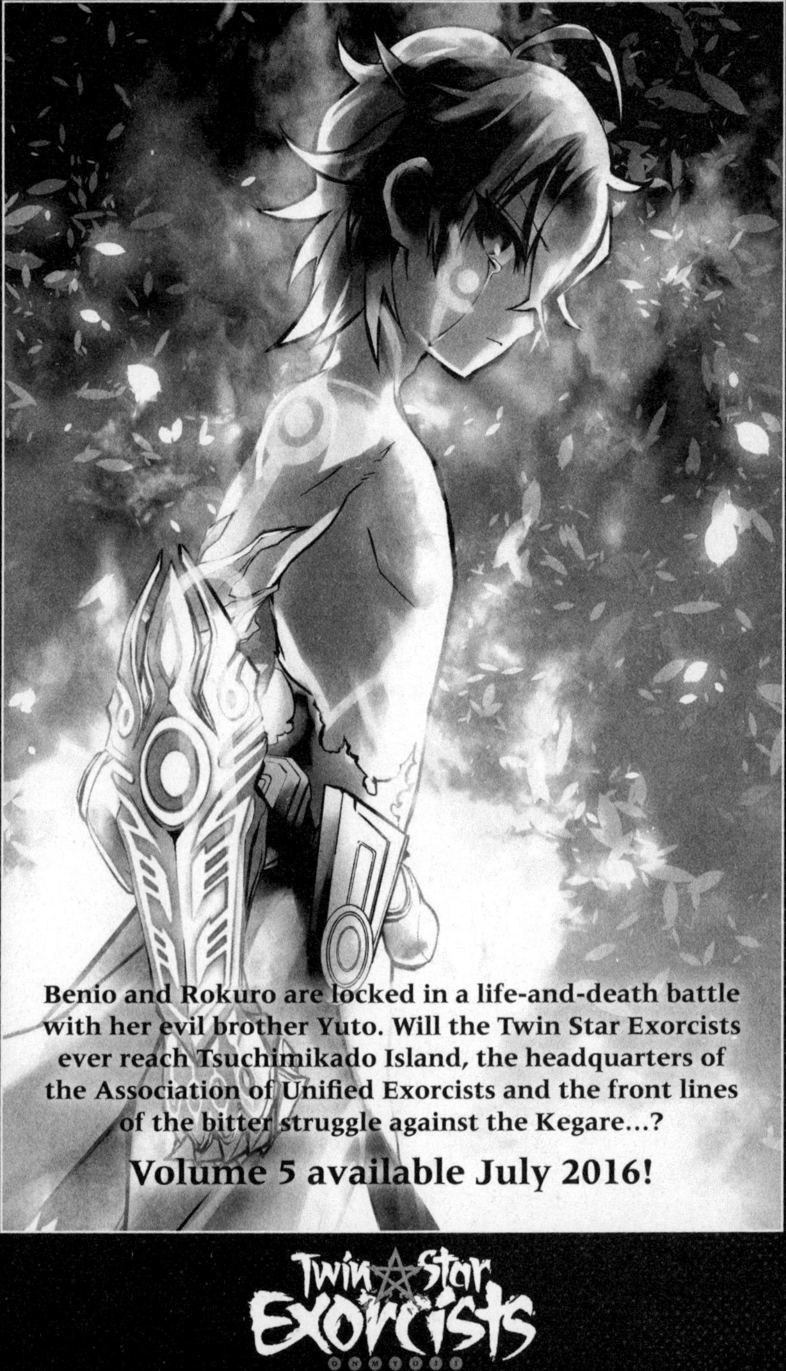
Benio and Rokuro are locked in a life-and-death battle with her evil brother Yuto. Will the Twin Star Exorcists ever reach Tsuchimikado Island, the headquarters of the Association of Unified Exorcists and the front lines of the bitter struggle against the Kegare...?
Volume 5 available July 2016!
Twin Star Exorcists

YOU'RE
READING
THE
WRONG
WAY!

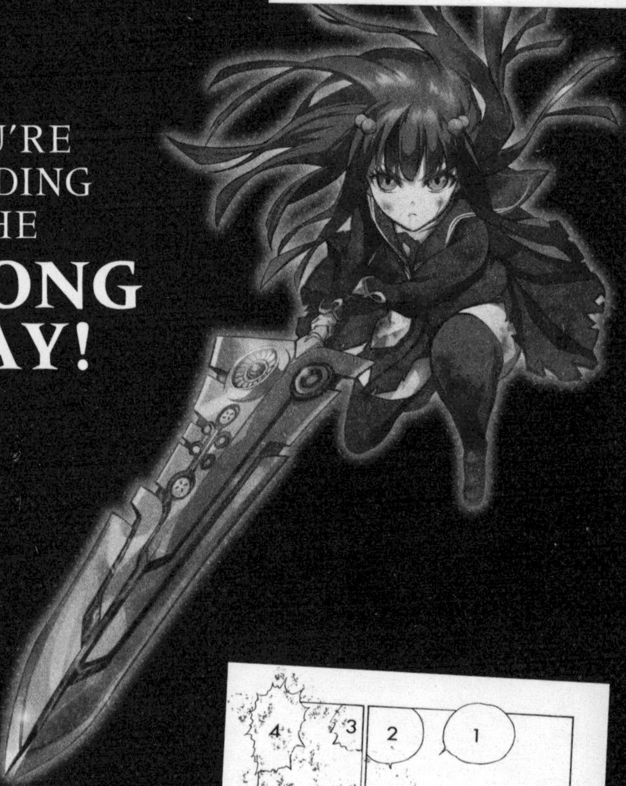

Twin Star Exorcists reads from right to left, starting in the upper-right corner. Japanese is read from right to left, meaning that action, sound effects and word-balloon order are completely reversed from English order.

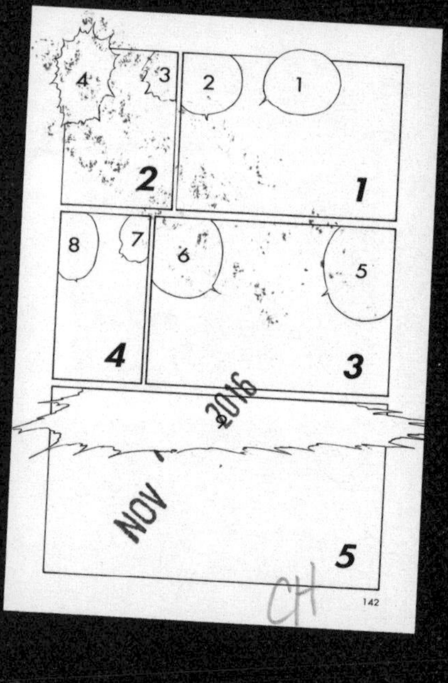
1
2
3
4
1
2
5
6
7
8
3
4
5
142